OUR ONE COMMON COUNTRY

OUR ONE COMMON COUNTRY

*Abraham Lincoln and the Hampton Roads
Peace Conference of 1865*

JAMES B. CONROY

LYONS PRESS
Guilford, Connecticut
An imprint of Globe Pequot Press

Lyons Press is an imprint of Globe Pequot Press.

Project editors: Meredith Dias and Lauren Brancato
Layout: Melissa Evarts

Library of Congress Cataloging-in-Publication Data

Conroy, James B.
Our one common country : Abraham Lincoln and the Hampton Roads peace conference of 1865 /
James B. Conroy.
    pages cm
ISBN 978-0-7627-7807-2 (hardback)
1. Hampton Roads Peace Conference (1865) 2. United States—History—Civil War, 1861-1865—
Peace. 3. Lincoln, Abraham, 1809-1865. I. Title.
E469.C66 2014
973.7'38—dc23

                                                                          2013016670

Printed in the United States of America

10 9 8 7 6 5 4 3 2 1

To my wife and children, with love and gratitude

In memory of my grandmother

CONTENTS

It is impossible to say precisely when the conviction became general in the South that we were beaten. I cannot even decide at what time I myself began to think the cause a hopeless one, and I have never yet found one of my fellow Confederates, though I have questioned many of them, who could tell me with any degree of certainty the history of his change from confidence to despondency. We schooled ourselves from the first to think that we should ultimately win, and the habit of thinking so was too strong to be easily broken by adverse happenings. Having undertaken to make good our declaration of independence, we refused to admit, even to ourselves, the possibility of failure.

GEORGE CARY EGGLESTON
VETERAN OF THE ARMY OF NORTHERN VIRGINIA
POSTWAR MANHATTAN NEWSPAPERMAN

These men are to be punished for their crimes; they are to be punished for their barbarities; they are to be punished as traitors and murderers, and not welcomed back into the social circle or legislative halls by any loyal man who now stands by this Government, in my estimation.

ZACHARIAH CHANDLER OF MICHIGAN
ON THE FLOOR OF THE UNITED STATES SENATE,
ADDRESSING THE CONFEDERATE LEADERS' FATE
ON THE EVE OF THE HAMPTON ROADS PEACE CONFERENCE

Cast of Principal Characters

Northerners

FRANCIS PRESTON BLAIR SR.

Longtime Washington powerbroker, cofounder of the Republican Party, Virginia-born and Kentucky-bred; a Lincoln loyalist and an ardent enemy of Secretary of State William Seward's.

MONTGOMERY BLAIR

Lincoln's postmaster general and conservative adviser before the Radical Republicans forced his resignation in September 1864; irascible eldest son of Francis Preston Blair.

ORVILLE HICKMAN BROWNING

A friend of Lincoln's, a partner in James Singleton's presidentially authorized business trips to the South, and a former senator from Illinois, defeated for reelection in 1862.

SAMUEL S. ("SUNSET") COX

An Ohio congressman and a moderate War Democrat.

CHARLES DANA

Assistant Secretary of War under Edwin Stanton; a former journalist at Horace Greeley's *New York Daily Tribune*.

THOMAS ECKERT

Union Army major in charge of the military telegraph; one of Secretary of War Edwin Stanton's closest aides.

JULIA DENT GRANT

The Missouri-born wife of Ulysses S. Grant.

ULYSSES S. GRANT

General in Chief of the United States Army.

HORACE GREELEY

Eccentric Republican editor of the *New York Daily Tribune,* a leading abolitionist, and one of the North's most influential opinion leaders.

JOHN HAY

Along with John Nicolay, one of Lincoln's two permanent live-in secretaries.

ELIZABETH BLAIR LEE

Daughter and aide of Francis Preston Blair, known as "Lizzie."

ABRAHAM LINCOLN

President and commander in chief of the United States.

GEORGE G. MEADE

Major general in command of the Army of the Potomac; defeated Lee at Gettysburg.

SAMUEL NELSON

A United States Supreme Court justice from New York; Judge Campbell's friend and former colleague.

JOHN NICOLAY

Along with John Hay, one of Lincoln's two permanent, live-in secretaries.

EDWARD ORD

Major general in command of the Army of the James; a close friend of Grant's.

DAVID DIXON PORTER

One of the US Navy's leading admirals.

HENRY J. RAYMOND

Founder, publisher, and editor of the *New York Times;* chairman of the Republican National Committee, a leader of its moderate wing, a loyal Lincoln supporter.

WILLIAM H. SEWARD

Lincoln's Secretary of State and closest adviser; former governor of New York, US senator, and presidential hopeful; a participant in the Hampton Roads Peace Conference.

WILLIAM TECUMSEH SHERMAN

Major general in command of the Union's western armies; pioneer in the art of scorched-earth warfare.

JAMES L. SINGLETON

Copperhead friend of Lincoln's, who endorsed his entrepreneurial buying trips to Richmond and exploited his ability to gain access to its leaders.

EDWIN M. STANTON

Lincoln's remorseless Secretary of War; an old-time Democrat and a native of Ohio.

THADDEUS STEVENS

Radical Republican congressman from Pennsylvania, the aging but powerful chairman of the House Ways and Means Committee; a longtime scourge of the South.

CHARLES SUMNER

Radical Republican senator from Massachusetts, a leading abolitionist, beaten with a cane on the Senate floor by a South Carolina congressman in 1856; Lincoln's frequent critic.

THURLOW WEED

Seward's political mastermind, an Albany-based editor and Republican Party boss.

GODFREY WEITZEL

Young major general in command of the occupation of Richmond after its fall.

GIDEON WELLES

Lincoln's avuncular Secretary of the Navy; a Blair ally and a Seward rival.

FERNANDO WOOD

A former mayor of New York, now a pro-Southern peace Democrat in Congress.

Southerners

JUDAH BENJAMIN

Jefferson Davis's Secretary of State and closest adviser.

JOHN C. BRECKINRIDGE

Former vice president of the United States, close to the Blairs, a Confederate major general, then Confederate Secretary of War.

JOHN A. CAMPBELL

The Confederacy's Assistant Secretary of War; a former justice of the United States Supreme Court; a member of the Confederate peace commission at Hampton Roads.

ARTHUR S. COLYAR

A Confederate congressman from Tennessee, a fierce Davis critic, a Unionist before the war; an early advocate of peace negotiations.

JEFFERSON DAVIS

President and commander in chief of the Confederate States of America.

VARINA DAVIS

The wife of Jefferson Davis.

HENRY S. FOOTE

A volatile Confederate congressman, former governor of Mississippi, and former US senator; Jefferson Davis's career-long nemesis; a leader of the Southern peace movement.

JOSIAH GORGAS

The Confederacy's Richmond-based, Pennsylvania-born Chief of Ordnance.

WILLIAM A. GRAHAM

Moderate Confederate senator; former governor of North Carolina and former US senator.

WILLIAM HATCH

A Confederate lieutenant colonel and Assistant Commissioner of Exchange; the peace commissioners' aide.

BENJAMIN H. HILL

Confederate senator from Georgia; a Davis supporter and a longtime enemy of Alexander Stephens.

JOHN BELL HOOD

In reckless command of the Army of Tennessee after Davis relieved Joseph Johnston.

ROBERT M. T. HUNTER

President pro tempore of the Confederate Senate; a former US senator and Speaker of the House; a member of the Confederate peace commission at Hampton Roads.

JOSEPH E. JOHNSTON

One of the South's most capable generals and one of Davis's longtime detractors, in command of the Army of Tennessee before and after Davis consigned it to Hood.

JOHN B. JONES

A clerk in the Confederate War Department, subordinate to Robert G. H. Kean.

ROBERT G. H. KEAN

Head of the Confederate Bureau of War, reporting to his friend, John Campbell.

ROBERT E. LEE

In command of the Army of Northern Virginia; later appointed General in Chief.

JAMES LONGSTREET

A prominent general in the Confederate Army, one of Lee's most senior subordinates.

GUSTAVUS ADOLPHUS MYERS

Richmond lawyer and city councilman; a leader of the city's Jewish community.

JAMES L. ORR

Confederate senator from South Carolina; a Davis critic and an advocate of peace talks; a former Speaker of the House in Washington.

JOHN A. ORR

Confederate congressman from Mississippi; a peace movement leader.

ROBERT OULD

The Confederate Commissioner of Exchange, in charge of exchanging prisoners of war.

EDWARD POLLARD

An editor of the *Richmond Enquirer;* a relentless critic of the Davis administration.

ROGER A. PRYOR

Former editor and US congressman from Virginia; now a prisoner of war.

SARAH RICE PRYOR

A Petersburg, Virginia, memoirist; Roger Pryor's wife.

WILLIAM CABELL RIVES

A Confederate congressman from Virginia; one of the South's elder statesmen.

JAMES A. SEDDON

Davis's Secretary of War until November 1864; a former US congressman.

ALEXANDER H. STEPHENS

Jefferson Davis's vice president and perennial critic; a member of the Confederate peace commission at Hampton Roads; a former US congressman from Georgia.

JOHN L. STEPHENS

Nephew of Alexander Stephens; a Confederate Army lieutenant and a prisoner of war.

PROLOGUE

Shortly after breakfast on a springlike day in the winter of 1865, Abraham Lincoln slipped out of the White House alone and into a waiting carriage. To deceive passersby, his Irish-born valet, carpetbag in hand, lagged a minute or two behind him. At the Washington City depot, a train with a single car had been summoned to take him to Annapolis, where the fastest ship on Chesapeake Bay would be ready to run him south to Hampton Roads, Virginia, for a peaceful talk with the enemy in the midst of a shooting war. It had never happened before. It has never happened since. Apart from his Secretary of State, who had quietly gone ahead of him, neither his Cabinet nor his staff had been told that he was going.

After nearly four years of war, Northern forces had taken much of the Confederacy's territory, cornered its battered armies, and all but broken the rebellion, but no one knew when it would end. Indeed, it might yet be revived. Over 600,000 young Americans were dead. A Northern push to victory would kill tens of thousands more, humiliate the South, and delay for generations what Lincoln wanted most and the beleaguered Rebel leader in his capital at Richmond even now refused to consider—a reconciled nation, healed of its painful wounds. Reasonable men of the North and South were coming to Hampton Roads in search of a way out.

Entrenched in a fortified arc on the edge of Petersburg, Virginia, one day's march from Richmond, General Robert E. Lee was praying for their success. The 50,000 men and boys of the Army of Northern Virginia were ragged, gaunt, and bleeding. The opposing Union forces—smartly uniformed, splendidly equipped, more than 100,000 strong—had failed to dislodge them in June and had dug in beside them instead, grinding them down night and day, taking their blows in return. Half a century later, fighting side by side in France, their grandsons would call it trench warfare. It was in its eighth month when Lincoln went south to the enemy. A seventeen-year-old Union infantryman would still be reliving its horrors in 1926, deep in old age. "Wish I could forget many, many dread sights that I saw around Petersburg." Even on dress parade, assembled for inspection with other frightened boys, he had seen arms and legs reaching out from shallow graves.

Interspersed with the trench-side tombs were dozens of primitive forts named for officers struck dead in the vicinity, an old American tradition. Out of place in the nineteenth century, they were throwbacks to the ninth, with walls of earth and timber impaled by sharpened stakes, ringed by pits and moats like some Dark Age warlord's stronghold. One such edifice on the Union side of the lines intersected the Jerusalem Plank Road. The War Department called it Fort Sedgwick. Its residents called it Fort Hell. On the opposite side of no-man's-land was the Rebel fortification known as Fort Mahone or Fort Damnation, depending on who was asking. Hell and Damnation were a few hundred yards apart, sporting range for sharpshooters who honed their country marksmanship taking aim at careless heads. Mortars and artillery wreaked indiscriminate mayhem and respected no safe havens. A South Carolinian was struck in the mouth while lying at the bottom of a trench, reading a letter from home. "The piece of shell broke his left jaw-bone, severed two arteries on that side of his face, tore out several teeth and lodged there. He was laid out dead. Providentially the blood clotted and prevented his bleeding to death" until someone caught him breathing.

Within Fort Hell was the warren of holes and hovels that its garrison called home. The most desirable Hellish residences were dug from the battered ground, covered with logs and branches, roofed with a yard of earth to absorb exploding shells. A former Yankee coach maker described the "undiscoverable, almost inconceivable nooks" where less fortunate men lived. The "upholsterer's art," he found, had not been "lavished upon our beds." Less agreeable still were the lodgings outside the walls, "little pits the size of a common grave, though not half so well furnished."

And then there were the pickets—the unfortunate souls pushed out in front of the trenches in parallel lines of holes to serve as human trip wires in the event of an attack and kill the other side's pickets. A veteran of the 48th Pennsylvania said a brick could be tossed with ease from one picket line to the other. Bullets traveled faster.

Closer to death than anyone, pickets behaved oddly when they found themselves within chatting distance. They chatted. An unwritten code of picket etiquette determined when its subscribers could socialize and when they could try to kill each other. After dark, the popping of picket fire could be as constant as "the dropping of hail," but pickets stopped firing at dawn and gave fair warning when ordered to do otherwise. One Rebel threw a rock with a note tied around it: "Tell the fellow with the spy-glass to clear out or we will have to shoot him." In the quiet of the day, pickets traded rumors, jokes, and whatever was edible, readable, or smokeable, negotiating with their lungs, making airborne deliveries with their pitching arms. Ever short of ammunition, Rebel pickets had been known to toss tobacco plugs to their trading partners in exchange for the lead they had fired at them the night before.

Pickets were not alone in the art of fraternization. A teenaged Midwesterner was proud to distinguish himself as "the boy that caused peace at times." Confronting a regiment of overactive Virginians, he shouted across the way that the 60th Ohio had moved in, and urged them to quit wasting good ammunition. They proposed to stop shooting if the Ohioans did. "A glad cry went up along the lines, and there was peace and quiet for some time after that. We exchanged coffee with them for some tobacco and papers."

Joining forces to fight the cold, axmen in blue and gray felled trees together for fuel and shared the proceeds equitably. On Christmas Day, pickets had stood up "in full sight of each other, shouting the compliments of the season, giving invitations to cross over and take a drink, to come to dinner, to come back into the Union." Well-provisioned Yankees could afford their generosity. More than a few Northern regiments opened gifts sent down by rail and enjoyed a festive dinner. The same could not be said for the Americans across the way. Six Southern men had about as much to eat as one of their Northern counterparts. "While our men were dressed in good warm pants, blouses, and overcoats and evidently well fed and taken care of," a New Englander said, hardly two of "the poor Johnnies" were dressed alike. Many of them were barefoot, their eclectic outfits "ragged and worn with long service, a blanket with a hole in the centre placed over their shoulders forming jacket and overcoat, and with hats of all shapes. But let them hear the word 'forward' and you would be surprised to see what a lively set of men they could be."

Their alacrity had limits. From his headquarters nine miles east of the front, Ulysses S. Grant was extending his trenches daily, filling them with fresh troops, killing Lee's stick figures one and two and three at a time, starving and bleeding and breaking them. Unaccustomed to the cold, Captain John Evans of the 23rd South Carolina wrote home in a heavy snow. "It makes me sorry to see so much suffering . . . we poor fellows are in the mud and water . . . the dissatisfaction is spreading fearfully, and especially in the North Carolina brigade it looks like a general stampede for home will take place before spring." Every night, a Yankee said, "half-frozen and repentant Rebels, in large numbers, made their appearance on our picket line, and were sent to the rear."

Their suffering was not entirely unrelieved. From time to time official truces were called to recover the dead and wounded in the wake of an attack, discuss a prisoner exchange, or adjust the rules of engagement. When the white flags flew, foul-smelling men crawled out of their holes, the colonels conducted their business, and the privates conducted theirs. Blue and gray laundry was washed side by side in the same refreshing streams. Memorable feats of marksmanship were acknowledged and admired. A consensus was reached on the ineptitude of officers. There had even been North–South wrestling matches, cheered on by partisan fans. A Rhode Island regiment's football games "never failed to interest the Johnnies," who would gather a stone's throw away, "taking as much pleasure therein as if no deadly feud existed between us."

When the truce flags came down, the combatants returned to their work. Some of them died every day. Others would still be suffering when FDR was president, getting dressed with one hand in Alabama, crying out in the night in New York, burdening their families in Mississippi, enduring their pity in Maine. The killing rarely stopped. As the North replenished its ranks, the South's diminished daily. "I think hardly any man in that army entertained a thought of coming out of the struggle alive," a Virginian would later say, but the most intrepid of them persisted "in vaguely hoping and trying to believe that success was still to be ours, and to that end we shut our eyes to the plainest facts, refusing to admit the truth which was everywhere evident, namely, that our efforts had failed, and that our cause was already in its death struggles."

On Sunday, January 29, 1865, a Rebel flag of truce appeared in front of Fort Damnation, and the neighborhood mood improved. A sergeant of the 8th Michigan reported the enemy overture to Captain Thomas Parker of the 51st Pennsylvania, a bright young man with a walrus mustache, commanding the local picket line. Parker climbed up on a parapet to take a look for himself.

On both sides of no-man's-land, hundreds of men and boys were doing the same, with a keener intensity than usual. For the past several weeks, Northern and Southern newspapers had been full of rumors of peace, deplored by most editorialists (none of them under fire) as a Yankee trick, or a Rebel play for time, or a craven substitute for victory. The pundits on the siege line were decidedly more bullish. Southern pickets had been shouting peaceful forecasts to their Yankee interlocutors. "This Rebellion is played out." "There will be glorious news within ten days."

Having reported the flag of truce, Captain Parker shed his sword, walked out to the middle of no-man's-land with his own white flag, and saluted Lieutenant Colonel William Hatch, a handsome young Kentuckian. After "passing the compliments of the day," Hatch requested an audience with no less a figure than General Grant's Chief of Staff. Three Southern dignitaries had just arrived from Richmond, he said, to meet with President Lincoln for the purpose of ending the war. The general was expecting them. They would wait for his pass in Petersburg, and hoped to reach his headquarters that night. Stunned, no doubt, to hear it, Parker promised a quick reply, the officers returned to their lines, and a Northern lieutenant colonel came out to speak with Hatch.

Rumor was on the wing on the overlooking parapets. From the moment the flag of truce appeared, Parker said, "the enemy and our men watched the whole proceeding in silence until its import was made manifest." In a triumph of military intelligence, its import was made manifest in both armies simultaneously, and both started shouting.

As the officers down in no-man's-land walked on and off the stage, applauded from the balconies, "the works were covered with men, yelling, cheering, and making every demonstration of joy at the prospect of having no more fighting to do." The news "spread like a contagion" as officers of every degree went "flying on horseback in all directions" to pass the jubilant word. A citizen of Fort Hell recalled how "very soon a bit of white cloth stuck on the end of a stick or ramrod could be seen floating from the top of each picket post on both sides." With the winter sun shining on a hundred daubs of white, some enterprising men ventured out into no-man's-land, scanning the lunar landscape in search of lead or fuel. Entertainment was provided while the scavengers plied their trades. "One of our boys invited a reb to come out on neutral ground and have a free fight," a Union man said. "The reb whipped the Yank, when each returned to their respective sides amid loud and prolonged cheers from the rebs."

Monday morning broke cold and sunny, and thousands of men and boys stood up in perfect safety to watch the doves fly through the lines, only to be disappointed. The disconcerting word was spread that the War Department was holding them up, but the truce stayed in place like a second day of Christmas. With the dignity characteristic of his publication, the *New York Times* correspondent on the siege line allowed that there was "considerable excitement" about the prospect of getting out of it alive, but the *Times* was skeptical of peace talks. "Our men know that peace is not to be gained by smooth words. 'Talk is cheap,' said one the other day."

On the following morning, a wire came through from Grant's headquarters, producing shouts of joy. The general's senior aide was on his way to the front to receive the Rebel peace commission. The word came none too soon. In the course of the past two days, so many men and boys had been crossing over to "confer with the enemy," a Northern soldier said, that both sides had posted guards. Otherwise, "the blue and the gray would have got so mixed up, that so far as regards these two armies, the war would have ended right *there* and *then*, in spite of all officers and orders to the contrary."

But officers and orders still reigned. At the eastern end of the siege line, two miles away from the momentous happenings, an artillery officer in blue peered out from Fort McGilvery at an enemy team at work on their fortifications, a faux pas during a truce, and decided to break it up. The Rebels scattered promptly, but their own artillery replied. The commotion remained local but continued until dark, rumbling down the siege line. To the sound of distant cannon, a Rebel general made a stirring address, or so said the *Petersburg Express*. The defenders of the South must not let down their guard "on account of the so-called peace commission," but "depend on their arms" for the peace that would come from their "manly exertions." The man from the *Express* did not hear the oration, but understood that it generated much enthusiasm.

There was surely much enthusiasm when the lightning word was flashed that the peacemakers were coming. Rebel troops lined the Petersburg road and spilled out into the fields as a coach passed by on a wave of jubilation. When it pulled up behind the Confederate lines, the celebrities stepped down, attended by the mayor and the gracious Colonel Hatch. Slaves unloaded their trunks and joy washed over their heads as they parted a cheering crowd of buoyant Southern men and beaming Southern women down from Petersburg to witness history in their hoop skirts and bonnets. One of the three commissioners looked plump and rosy, another stiff and formal. The third, a sickly little Georgian, had been Lincoln's friend and ally in the old Congress. Now he was leaning on the arm of a slave, feeble but excited.

Not everyone was. A former Buffalo newspaperman had lost 70 of the 135 companions who had started the war with him. As the bitter Yankee saw it, the Southern peace commission emerged to the sound of protesting cannon, as "the hazy mist, which is not unusual here at sunset, began to obscure the distant horizon and give the landscape a gloomy and somber aspect. At first as we watched, they seemed as shadows moving in the hazy light, but as they approached their forms became clear and distinct, and we soon stood face to face with the representatives of treason, tyranny and wrong."

Not as traitors but as dignitaries, the Southerners were saluted by a party of Northern officers and escorted to the Union lines. As a thousand troops on both sides chanted "Peace! Peace! Peace!" an excited Rebel soldier called for "three cheers and a tiger for the whole Yankee army," and got them. The Yanks returned the favor, and a loud Northern voice demanded the same for the ladies, who waved their "snowy handkerchiefs" in decorous reply. Behind the Union lines, a gleaming horse-drawn ambulance was waiting to take the Southerners to the train that would bring them to Grant. A team of matched horses drove them smartly away. By accident or design, all four of them were gray.

As darkness fell, the artillery duel up the line petered out. The federal officer in charge would soon recount his losses almost cheerfully. "I have no casualties to report among the artillery and but two killed and four wounded among the infantry." It is safe to assume that the brass took the news in stride and the dead boys' families took it harder.

General George G. Meade, the celebrated victor at Gettysburg, came to visit the Rebel ambassadors the next day and wrote to his wife that night. One of them had asked to be remembered to her family. Another had brought a letter addressed to their common kin. Skeptical though he was, Meade had his hopes for peace. "I do most earnestly pray that something may result from this movement."

Lincoln was prayerful too, old at fifty-five with the weight of 600,000 dead. A portrait painter named Carpenter had been living with him for weeks, absorbing "the saddest face I ever knew. There were days when I could scarcely look into it without crying."

In the previous spring, after three cautious years of indecisive battle, Grant had taken command of all the Union armies and designed a new kind of war with the help of a brash subordinate, General William Tecumseh Sherman. "Sanguinary war," Grant called it—bloody war— and Lincoln had given it his blessing. While Sherman attacked General Joseph Johnston's outnumbered Army of Tennessee and another Union force marched on Richmond, Grant and Meade would bludgeon Lee until he stopped struggling. In May and June alone, the North had sustained some 95,000 casualties. The South's horrific losses were unreliably counted. Lincoln had barely slept. Carpenter came across him in a corridor, "clad in a long morning wrapper, arching back and forth a narrow passage leading to one of the windows, his hands behind him, great black rings under his eyes, his head bent forward upon his breast."

Tens of thousands of young Americans had lost their lives since then, and the war was not yet won. On his way to Hampton Roads to see an old friend from Georgia, Lincoln had a chance to end it.

PART I

Friends in Power

Jefferson Davis before the war

CHAPTER ONE

A Self-Immolating Devotion to Duty

On a trip to the infant Confederacy in the spring of 1861, the *Times of London*'s American correspondent was presented to its president and found himself faintly surprised. The gaunt Mississippian was "a very different looking man from Mr. Lincoln," remarkably "like a gentleman," reserved, erect, and austere. Despite his noble bearing, he welcomed his foreign visitor in "a rustic suit of slate-colored stuff," a slight, "care-worn, pain-drawn" man of little more than middle height. Though William Howard Russell had expected a grander figure, the Rebel leader's cigar commended him to his guest. "Wonderful to relate, he does not chew, and is neat and clean-looking, with hair trimmed and boots brushed," distinctions worth mentioning on the Western side of the Atlantic, Jefferson Davis not excepted.

To Russell's keen ear, Jeff Davis's speaking style was laced with "Yankee peculiarities," attributable, no doubt, to four years at West Point, seven in the US Army, and a dozen in Washington City. He had taken the public stage as a promising young congressman in 1845, left in 1846 to serve in the Mexican War, fought as a wounded hero at the head of the Mississippi Rifles, accepted an appointment to replace a departed senator, served with great distinction as Franklin Pierce's Secretary of War, and returned to Capitol Hill as the South's charismatic champion in the Senate. The New Yorker William Seward had called his friend and adversary "a splendid embodiment of manhood." Their colleague Sam Houston had taken a different view. "Ambitious as Lucifer and cold as a lizard."

Now he told his British guest that the people he led were a military people who would earn support with their deeds. "As for our motives, we meet the eye of Heaven."

Always confident of Heaven's favor, Davis could not have earned it through consistency. In the antebellum years, he had wrestled with himself as much as his critics, professing in a single speech a "superstitious reverence for the union" and a willingness to serve as a standard bearer for secession. In 1858, he had led the Southern moderates in the Democratic Party, promoting national unity at Faneuil Hall in Boston, embracing the flag in Maine. Less than two years later he was leading the South to disunion. From his desk at the *Richmond Examiner*, an able young editorialist by the name of Edward Pollard saw a "record of insincerity which cannot be overlooked."

There was no risk of Pollard overlooking it. As one Rebel officer said, the *Examiner*'s very mission was to torture its country's president, and the *Examiner* was not alone. For much of the Southern press, everything Davis did was wrong. Though a passion for states' rights was the Confederacy's very reason for being, its president grasped the need for a strong central government while it fought the North for its life. Unprecedented taxes, an ever-expanding draft, public takings of private property to keep the war going, and arrests without trial for its dissidents (all of which Lincoln pursued more aggressively in the North) had subjected Jeff Davis to peals of public outrage almost from the start. His temperament did not help. A Virginian expressed the common view. The president at first had been thought to be a mule, but a good mule, and had turned out to be a jackass; honest and hardworking but a poor judge of men, blind to the flaws of his pets, unforgiving of his critics, irritable, unbending, and hair-splitting. Distracted by petty disputes with governors, senators, and generals, he had his loyal friends, but his enemies were as petulant as he. His devotion to General Braxton Bragg reminded a senator from South Carolina of "the blind and gloating love of a mother for a deformed and misshapen offspring." It was not a happy polity.

By the summer of 1864, Davis's confidence was undimmed, but three horrific years fighting Yankees in the field and schools of sharks in Richmond had not improved his looks or brightened his disposition. Regal in his youth, he was spectral at fifty-six, with a hollow-cheeked face and a clouded left eye that could see only darkness and light. His right hand and arm often shook from a painful nerve disease. More often than not, his armies had outfought the North and were still more than dangerous, but the war had bled them pale. One tubercular draftee was conscripted for ten days' service and died on the eleventh. Most of the Confederacy's wealth was spent. A naval blockade was strangling it. The loss of the Mississippi had cut it in two. Much of its territory was gone. Its people were demoralized. Demands for negotiations gained ground in its bickering Congress. In Georgia and North Carolina, there were rumblings in high places about a separate peace.

None of it moved Jeff Davis, who was heard to say unflinchingly that the people of the South would eat rats, and their twelve- and fourteen-year-old sons would "have their trial" before this war was over. With his faith in the divine protection of the cause he led intact, he spoke in public and private as one who owned the truth, dismissing his misinformed critics, as Edward Pollard said, with "the air of one born to command."

His birth, in fact, had been humble. He came into the world in a Kentucky log cabin scarcely grander than Lincoln's, eight months before him and less than a hundred miles away; but the Davises moved to Mississippi and prospered, and fortune dealt Jeff a sibling twenty-four years his senior who parlayed the practice of law into land and slaves, plucked his little brother from a one-room school, had him educated properly, polished the results himself, gave him his own plantation, and taught him how to run it. The product was the near equivalent of the planter aristocracy, lacking only the pedigree, but the pedigree could not be fixed, and it barred him from his culture's inner ring, accounting, perhaps, for the fragility beneath the hauteur. His devoted wife, Varina, knew how easy it was to wound him, "a nervous dyspeptic," she said, ill-served by a "repellent manner," so thin-skinned that even a child's disapproval discomposed him.

According to Varina, her husband was easily persuaded where a principle was not at stake, but principles were everywhere in the mind of Jefferson Davis. He "could not comprehend" how any informed observer might differ with him on a point of public policy, and suspected insincerity in anyone who did. Years before the war, he had chastised his fellow senators on the Compromise of 1850, "proud in the consciousness of my own rectitude," regarding "degraded letter writers" with "the indifference which belongs to the assurance that I am right, and the security with which the approval of my constituents invests me." Debating a Northern Democrat, he abhorred the very notion of compromise—that senators of the same party might construe the Constitution differently and cooperate politically. "I do not believe that this is the path of safety. I am sure it is not the way of honor." As commander in chief of the Confederacy, his Secretary of the Navy said, Davis never doubted his military genius. After the twin disasters at Gettysburg and Vicksburg in 1863, he confessed to Robert E. Lee that nothing required "a greater effort of patience than to bear the criticisms of the ignorant."

Varina helped him bear them. At the gracious Executive Mansion on Clay Street, she bantered with his guests on the novels they had read and the romances they were handicapping, and discussed the issues of the day with all of the president's brains, none of his knack for gratuitous provocation, and "admirable flashes of humor." Her husband emitted no such flashes. He would materialize at her soirees an hour after they started, endure in near silence the talk of lesser men, ignore the opinions of the ignorant, shake ten or twenty hands in his "not over cordial grasp," and excuse himself to his study. He was capable of grace and a winning smile, but the cruel whip of sarcasm was his only brand of humor. There was no frivolity in him. He took careful note of the wardrobes of Richmond's ladies and described one that displeased him as "very high-colored" and "full of tags, and you could see her afar off."

All of that said, he was far from cruel or insensitive. "I wish I could see my father," his little daughter Maggie once said when her mother disciplined her; "he would let me be bad." Desperate letters from desperate people broke his heart. "Poor creature, and my hands are tied!" He had truly loved the Union, treasured his Northern friends, watched their children grow from infancy to adolescence. Now their boys were of military age. Varina called their parting "death in life." In his final speech to the Senate, her husband's voice had cracked as he wished them farewell. Not so cold a lizard after all.

In his own time and place, his attitudes on race were progressive. He greeted his slaves with handshakes and bows, made one of them his overseer, submitted their transgressions to the judgment of other slaves, and strictly forbade the lash. He endorsed the conventional rationalization that their bondage had brought them from heathen darkness into Christian civilization but embraced the most progressive view that a Southerner could espouse and remain on the public stage: Over time, Christianity, education, and discipline would make the slave unfit for slavery.

Upright to a fault, he lashed himself to a code of honor so rigid as to allow for no exceptions, however disproportionate the consequences. Varina counted among his virtues "a self-immolating devotion to duty." When the war began in Charleston in 1861, he rejoiced at the news that the only blood spilled at Fort Sumter had been a mule's, and told Varina with some hope that a final separation was still avoidable; but once Southern men had died for independence, there was no place for reconciliation in his psyche. "This struggle must continue until the enemy is beaten out of his vain confidence in our subjugation. Then and not til then will it be possible to treat of peace."

In the summer of 1864, the chance for independence was very much alive. The South was in extremis, but the North was wearing down. A little over a year before, while surprising and routing a much larger Union army, Stonewall Jackson had been killed at Chancellorsville, shot in the dark by confused North Carolinians, but Jackson and Robert E. Lee had left 11,000 Northerners dead or writhing on the field, 6,000 captured or missing, and Lincoln crying out in despair, "My God, my God. What will the country say?"

In the wake of the disaster, Colonel James Jacques of the 73rd Illinois, an ordained Methodist minister, had asked the president's leave to undertake a peace mission to his coreligionists in Richmond. Lincoln let him go, anticipating neither good nor ill. Some Southern doves broke bread with the Reverend Colonel but Davis would not see him. Jacques rejoined his regiment in time for Chickamauga. Another Rebel victory. Another 16,000 Union casualties.

In the spring of 1864, over 55,000 of Grant's men and boys had been killed, wounded, or captured in the space of six weeks, exceeding the eight-year toll of the American Revolution. Lee had done better, taking something in the range of 40,000 casualties, but the South could not replace them, and Lincoln kept sending more men, not to mention more boys. Measured in blood alone, Grant was winning his sanguinary war, but the voters of the North were choking on it. Mary Todd Lincoln was "half wild" with letters from their mothers, wives, and sisters. Nearly every Northern village had lost a favorite son, and the end was not in sight. Davis's six-year term had two years to run, but Lincoln's was expiring, and the Democrats were the party of peace. Another four months of bleeding could not win the war for the South, but could lose it for the North if the Rebels held on until Election Day.

CHAPTER TWO

Lacking in the Quality of Leadership

On Tuesday, November 8, 1864, the election went off quietly in the Army of the Potomac, said the *New York Daily Tribune*. Some regiments voted in long blue lines, others in company roll calls, others "miscellaneously, as the spirit moved them." On the treacherous Petersburg siege line, they shuttled between the rifle pits and the polling stations one regiment at a time, "to make a sure thing of keeping the Rebs from disturbing the election." One hundred fifty Rebs, more or less, would disturb the electorate no more. Fresh in the minds of the voters' Third Division was the sight of their twisted corpses, left where they had fallen in Saturday's failed attack. Southern men and boys recovered the remains under white flags of truce as the Northerners cast their ballots in kettles and ammunition crates.

Early in the war, the Democratic challenger, General George B. McClellan, had trained and inspired these same Union men. They had loved him then for his reluctance to spend their lives. In 1862, Lincoln had relieved him for spending them too cautiously. Now the Democrats promised them peace while Lincoln promised them victory. They were voting for Lincoln by a margin of three to one, as the *Tribune* reported with no pretense of objectivity: "It is unnecessary to say that an overwhelming majority of the vote cast was for the present Administration and its no compromise with traitors and vigorous prosecution of the war policy."

Just a few weeks earlier, when the Democrats had convened on August 29, the *Tribune* was pleading for compromise, the administration's policy was in flapping disarray, and almost no one thought that Lincoln could win, least of all Lincoln. Editors, politicians, and preachers who were not demanding peace were demanding vengeance, and the president favored neither.

No one rejected peace without reunion more firmly than he. The very name of the Richmond government was unutterable to him. He would speak of "the Rebels" or "the other fellow," never of the Confederacy, but he spoke of the war in sadness, not in anger. He called it "this great trouble." For Jefferson Davis, the Yankees were "brutes in human form." True Southerners, he said, would prefer to combine with hyenas. For Lincoln, the people of the South were "lost sheep." He had issued a proclamation asking God not to crush them but to soften their hearts, enlighten their minds, and quicken their consciences, "that they may not be utterly destroyed." We are fighting for the Union, he would say, and reunion would entitle the Southern people to all of their rights and privileges as soon as they came home. Supported by fellow moderates in the fractious Republican Party, he had already offered amnesty to every returning Rebel who would take an oath of allegiance, excepting their senior leaders. In private he said he would look the other way if even the worst of them fled the country.

But the Radical Republican wing—the Jacobins, they were sometimes called, after the French Revolution's executioners—objected almost violently to Lincoln's magnanimity, looking forward as they were to cartloads of traitors being hauled to the scaffold on coffins. Fond of bloody rhetoric, they declared that the seceded states had committed suicide. Far from welcoming their leaders back to Congress, the Jacobins meant to hang them, subdue their beaten people like so many broken tribes, and govern their conquered territory "as England governs India."

They despised their Republican president, expected to consign him to a single term, and vetted potential successors in 1864 who would crush the beaten South in 1865. Descended from two presidents, Congressman Charles Francis Adams had been mentioned. Allowing in 1860 that Lincoln seemed "tolerably capable," Adams had lowered his grade after reading his rustic speeches as president-elect. "I am very much afraid in this lottery we have drawn a blank." When they met face-to-face, the rail splitter impressed the Bostonian as "a vulgar man, ill-fitted both by education and nature for the post of President." Lincoln's aide John Hay, a handsome young poet and a graduate of Brown, said the people understood Lincoln well, but the "patent leather kid glove set" knew "no more of him than an owl does of a comet. . . ."

Lincoln's brother moderates prevailed. Swallowing their misgivings and renaming themselves the National Union Party, the Republicans renominated him in June and endorsed his campaign for a Constitutional amendment banning slavery, which had already passed the Senate but was sure to fail in the House. His reconstruction policy was something else again. The platform demanded for traitors "the punishment due to their crimes."

On July 2, Congress passed a punitive reconstruction bill coauthored by Republican senator Benjamin Wade of Ohio and Republican congressman Henry Winter Davis of Maryland, both of whom held the Republican chief executive in low esteem. Senator Wade replied to a dinner invitation to the White House with the puritan streak emblematic of his kind: "Are the President and Mrs. Lincoln aware that there is a civil war? If they are not, Mr. and Mrs. Wade are, and for that reason decline to participate in feasting and dancing."

When Congress adjourned on the Fourth of July, Lincoln pocketvetoed the Wade-Davis bill, spinning its supporters into twirling fits of rage. A few weeks later, Wade and Davis released a reply that fell just short of calling the commander in chief a traitor on the eve of his reelection campaign. Henry Raymond, the moderate founder, editor, and publisher of the *New York Times* and the chairman of the Republican Party, lined up with the president, which might have carried more weight had he not been running his campaign. For the Radicals, said the *Times*, the war was not fought to restore the Union but to pillage the South and reduce its people to peonage. John Albion Andrew, the Radical Republican governor of Massachusetts, would not have put it much differently. In 1863, the Emancipation Proclamation had left him ecstatic, parading around the Governor's Council Chamber while a friend sang "Old John Brown," but Andrew had now discovered that Abraham Lincoln was "lacking in the quality of leadership. A man of a more prophetic nature would have led the party better."

If the Radicals were tough on Lincoln, the Democrats were tougher. Sympathetic to the South, they were strong in several states and, counterintuitively, in Manhattan, disgruntled as she was by her lost cotton trade. Softest on secession and hardest on the war were the Peace Democrats—Copperheads, the Republicans called them. Their cousins the War Democrats were a step or two nearer the center. Neither faction was upset by the Southern choice of labor systems. If the government fell to the Democrats, the odds were good that the Union would be dissolved or restored by negotiations preserving slavery, a contingency that did not disturb the sleep of most of the Northern electorate.

In the bloody month of July 1864, Lincoln flirted with peace talks, pushed by Horace Greeley, the most influential journalist in America, who had said he would "drive Lincoln into it." His advice to a restless youth epitomized his style: "Go west, young man, go west! There is health in the country and room away from our crowds of idlers and imbeciles!" Horace Greeley was a fearless crusader, a brilliant mind, and a very odd duck. Lincoln had known him since they served together in Congress in 1848. He admired him as others did, in a distasteful sort of way, with a wary respect for his power. Among the labeled pigeonholes on the president's upright desk, full of clippings, notes, and letters, was a slot for Ulysses S. Grant and another for Horace Greeley. Everybody knew his name. Everybody who was anybody read his newspaper. Shunning libidinous scandals and bottled cancer cures, the *New York Daily Tribune* was respected in the North, vilified in the South, and a ripping good read. Greeley made it ring with incisive editorials, intelligent book reviews, and more accurate news than was customary. Republican in its politics, abolitionist in its passions, the *Tribune* gave space to thinkers of every stripe. Karl Marx had been a correspondent. So had the Transcendentalists. Now it printed extracts from the pestilent Richmond press. Horace Greeley was unafraid of ideas.

Round-faced and paunchy, with wire-rimmed glasses, an egg-bald pate, and wild white hair on the back and sides of his head, he shaved his face clean with the exception of his neck, where a thick white ruff protruded from ear to ear like a rabbit fur collar, a tonsorial eccentricity in an age that perfected the genre. Unmistakable on sight, an amused admirer said, Greeley stormed the streets in a battered top hat pointed backward on his head, a trademark linen overcoat—once white, now less so—flying open to the breeze, a flamboyant silk kerchief knotted loosely at his neck, the buttons and buttonholes of a greasy brown vest mismatched in biblical fashion: "The last shall be first and the first last." To give his look some punch he would sport a pink umbrella. An atheist among evangelicals, a socialist when the word was new, he promoted free love in a sexually repressed culture; condemned capital punishment in a country that hanged thieves; was violently opposed to liquor, monopolies, and corsets; and passionately in favor of labor unions, women's suffrage, and human waste as fertilizer. A bully to his staff, he sat for the camera with an arrogant jaw, a pitiless mouth, and unforgiving eyes, proclaiming the simple truth that Horace Greeley's *Tribune* could make or break a cause, elect or unseat a politician.

Having helped Lincoln win the presidency, Greeley had berated him ever since, for wildly erratic reasons. In May of 1864, the *Tribune* had proclaimed that the war must be won without compromise. Swerving left in July, appalled by Grant's losses, flattered by Rebel agents in Canada who approached him as a go-between, Greeley wrote to Lincoln all but begging him to negotiate. The South was eager to end the war, he said, while "our bleeding, bankrupt, almost dying country also longs for peace." Lincoln replied sardonically that Greeley could bring to Washington any Rebel agents who were authorized to offer reunion and abolition, whatever else they might propose. To receive them in the White House without such a pledge, said the president's aide John Hay, would have raised false hopes and assured a Republican defeat. No such pledge materialized.

On July 13, Greeley urged Lincoln again to meet with Davis's Canadian-based envoys. Lincoln sent Hay to see them at Niagara Falls instead, just enough accommodation to deny the Democrats' claim that the president scorned peace. As Hay would soon record, the Rebel lead negotiator had false teeth, false hair, false eyes, and no authority at all, let alone the required pledge. It was clear in due course, as Davis would tacitly confess, that his agents in the frozen North had no more noble purpose than to damage the Republicans at the polls.

Boxed in by Greeley at one end and Davis at the other, Lincoln climbed out with a letter, addressed "To Whom It May Concern," which Hay delivered to the Rebels: Any Southern offer "which embraces the

restoration of peace, the integrity of the whole union, and the abandonment of slavery, and which comes by and with an authority that can control the armies now at war with the United States" (an avoidance of the
Rebel government's legitimacy, if not an invitation to a coup) would be
met by "liberal terms." Until now, Lincoln had not made abolition a condition of peace. Knowing that Davis would reject abolition *and* reunion,
he had thought it astute to demand both. In this he was mistaken.

Seeing the letter's value, the Rebels released it to the press. Overnight,
negotiation became anathema in the South, and Lincoln's stock plunged
in the North. Democrats who were willing to die for the Union refused to
die for the slaves. On the other side of the aisle, the Jacobins exploded, set
off by the very idea of negotiations, let alone by liberal terms.

On July 6, a writer friend of Greeley's named James Gilmore asked
Lincoln to let Colonel Jacques, the fighting Methodist minister, make
another peace overture to Davis, abetted by Gilmore and his Southern
friends. Purporting to be moved by the colonel's belief that God had
blessed his mission, Lincoln blessed it too. After Gilmore and Jacques
won an audience with Davis in the presidential office in Richmond's
Capitol Square, the colonel shed his linen duster, revealed his dress blue
uniform in the heart of the enemy camp, and admonished its commander
in chief, respectfully if not wisely, that slavery was dead and the South
must lose the war, but a generous amnesty might be had if the Rebels gave
up now. Having spoken as a military man, Jacques reverted to his ministry
and asked how a Christian peace might be obtained.

"In a very simple way," Davis said. "Withdraw your armies from our
territory and peace will come of itself." Mr. Lincoln's terms were "*very* generous," but the South had no need of his amnesty. "Amnesty, sir, applies to
criminals." Nor was it fighting for slavery. "We are fighting for independence, and that, or extermination, we *will* have." Showing Gilmore and
Jacques the door, Davis suggested they might "say to Mr. Lincoln that I
shall at any time be pleased to receive proposals for peace on the basis of
our independence. It will be useless to approach me with any other."

The popular *Atlantic Monthly* published Gilmore's account of Davis's
intransigence, relieving pressure on Lincoln. Davis had been outfoxed in
the public relations war. The shooting war would go on.

CHAPTER THREE

A Problematical Character,
Full of Contradictions

In December 1860, young Henry Adams, son of Charles Francis Adams, grandson of John Quincy Adams, great-grandson of John and Abigail Adams, was fresh from Harvard Yard and new to Washington City when he met William Seward, the bright Northern star of the United States Senate, the Secretary of State presumptive in the incoming Lincoln administration, the devil himself in the South's iconography. According to Horace Greeley, a former ally and longtime adversary who praised him for little else, Seward hated slavery "and all its belongings." As governor of New York in 1839, he had refused to extradite to Virginia three black seamen accused of hiding a slave. People were not property, the governor had said, and their rescue from human bondage was a crime not recognized in Albany. His demonization in the South began then and there, and his maiden speech in the Senate perfected it. Debating the Compromise of 1850, Southern senators relied on the Constitution to protect their slave property, as they always had. Seward invoked "a higher law" and incited them to apoplexy. A South Carolinian compared the gentleman from New York to "the condor that soars in the frozen regions of ethereal purity, yet lives on garbage and putrefaction." Speaking for the *Richmond Enquirer*, Edward Pollard dismissed him as "a wretch whom it would be a degradation to name." His name had been famous ever since.

Henry Adams was prepared to be unimpressed nonetheless when his father's old friend, "the governor," as everyone called him, came alone to the house for dinner and declared himself a disciple of Henry's grandfather. For Henry at twenty-two, awed celebrities breathing reverence for his ancestors had long since lost their novelty.

As they bantered across the dinner table, the education of Henry Adams had just begun. He watched the governor closely, a little gray man of sixty with a "slouching, slender figure; a head like a wise macaw; a beaked nose; shaggy eyebrows; unorderly hair and clothes; hoarse voice; off-hand manner; free talk, and perpetual cigar," not to mention a colorful vocabulary in the company of men. There was no awe in him, and no reverence either. In the coming war, Lincoln would ask a cursing mule driver if he belonged to the Episcopal Church. When the startled man replied that he was a Methodist, the president would say, "I thought you must be an Episcopalian, because you swear just like Governor Seward, who is a churchwarden."

Henry loved him before the soup was served, absorbing his charm and disingenuousness with an amused sort of fondness for both. As a sitting US senator, he had quietly made his home in the little town of Auburn a stop on the Underground Railroad, a felony under federal law, putting his "higher law" where his family was. There was no insincerity in that. But after thirty years in politics, no one could tell the governor from the mask, Henry said, not excepting the governor. Born and raised wealthy in upstate New York in its unpretentious style, well heeled if not well dressed (his suits were said to be twenty years old, and made by a poor tailor), he was everyone's favorite dinner guest, with a highly contagious fondness for provocative conversation, amusing children, expensive wine and brandy, knee-slapping stories, and the widespread expectation of his future presidency. Fire-breathing slaveholders who reviled him in the Senate entertained him in their homes, beguiled like everyone else.

Humility was not his strength. He had been known to raise his hat to tourists under the mistaken impression that they had recognized him. Self-righteous, humorless people thought him glib and insincere, both of which he was, but even his enemies never doubted the agility of his mind. The French ambassador called him *très sage*. "Hopelessly lawless," Henry Adams called him. At posh dinner parties, he would take off his shoes and warm his damp feet by the fire. In the midst of a weighty discussion, he was capable of stopping in mid-sentence to ask Lincoln's aide John

Hay if he knew Daniel Webster's recipe for poaching a codfish, which ended with a mandate to send for Daniel Webster. Having told his little story, the Secretary of State got up and guffawed around the room, then returned to the risk of war with France and England.

Thurlow Weed, Seward's mentor and political mastermind, was an Albany publisher and editor, a Republican Party boss, and a famously unscrupulous tactician, the very personification of what the common man thought a politician was and ought not to be. Seward shared him with Lincoln, who gladly accepted the gift. Attesting to Weed's notoriety, Lincoln told Seward and Hay about a crafty supporter in Illinois, one Long John Wentworth by name, who had doubted his ability to outwit a wily adversary. The president told the story deadpan, to the governor's vast amusement and his own: " 'I tell you what, Lincoln,' said John with a look of unutterable sagacity, 'You must do what Seward does—get a feller to run you.'"

To a generation of Southern statesmen obsessed with their honor to the point of killing at twenty paces any man who accused them of chicanery, Seward cheerfully confessed it. According to Montgomery Blair, a caustic Border State rival, "I could fill a volume with his narratives of the tricks he has played if I could recall the half part of what I have heard from him," though he was generous and kind in his personal life and opened his home and family to his critics as well as his friends. No less a pair of authorities than Jeff and Varina Davis echoed Blair's mixed review. In 1849, Seward had asked the Senate to honor Father Matthew, an immigrant Irish priest well known for his work against drunkenness and slavery. Only one of these sins offended the senator from Mississippi, who took offense at the priest's attacks on "his adopted country's institutions." Father Matthew "comes covertly as a wolf in sheep's clothing," Davis said, "and I hold the Senator from New York to be the very best authority on that subject." And yet, after war, defeat, and heartbreak had given her every reason to feel otherwise, Varina confessed to "heartily liking him."

"Mr. Seward was a problematical character, full of contradictions," she said. In 1858, when her husband lay blindfolded for weeks in a shuttered room at home with an eye in danger of bursting from infection, Seward spent an hour with him and Varina every day, easing their suffering with diverting reports from the Senate: "Your man out-talked ours.

You would have liked it. I didn't." His wit was often lost on his hosts. In a moment of intimate friendship as they sat by her husband's side, Varina asked Seward, in perfect sincerity, how he could rail against slavery as evil, having spent too much time in the South to believe it. Seeing his chance to shock and entertain, he replied that he meant not a word—that he spoke for political effect. Davis reacted incredulously. Did he never speak from conviction? "Nev-ur," Seward said, with the deepest mock solemnity. The Mississippian raised his bandaged head and whispered through his pain. "As God is my judge, I never spoke from any other motive." Varina would never forget how the governor put his arm around him and gently soothed him back to his pillow. "I know you do not. I am always sure of it." After he left with tears in his eyes, the Davises shook their heads and wondered if he had been joking. It had only dimly dawned on them.*

When the Republicans convened in 1860 to choose a presidential nominee, Seward was sure of victory. Even Davis showed him sympathy when Lincoln was chosen instead. Two weeks had passed before the governor told his wife that the last of the humiliation had been endured. It hadn't. He buried his disappointment in a mission to avert civil war. When the South Carolinians seceded and started the great catastrophe, he said they didn't mean it. If a foreign power attacked Manhattan, "the hills of South Carolina would pour forth their population to the rescue of New York." In January 1861, with four Southern states gone and his future as Secretary of State well known, he proposed a set of concessions to a fully assembled Senate. The very hallways were jammed. Mississippi had seceded, but Jefferson Davis had not yet resigned his seat. He was in it as Seward spoke, listening intently. Among other conciliations, the New Yorker proposed a Constitutional amendment barring interference with slavery in the states as opposed to in the territories. Almost every Republican disavowed it. It was not good enough for the South.

When the president-elect arrived in Washington for the first time in twelve years, the governor's plans for a de facto Seward presidency ran aground on his realization that Lincoln would be his own man and a better writer and thinker than his Secretary of State. After making

---

* Soon after Davis recovered, Seward's cooler head averted a duel between the Mississippian and a future Jacobin, Senator Zachariah Chandler of Michigan.

the required adjustments, the worldly Eastern aristocrat and the gangly Western yarn spinner discovered how much they liked each other. Seward grew closer to Lincoln than any other man. He often arrived at Cabinet meetings before the others did, was asked to stay when they left, dominated their discussions, meddled in their portfolios, never troubled them with his own. Jealousy ensued.

Secretary of the Navy Gideon Welles was an old Connecticut Democrat with a long, white beard, an unconvincing wig, and a wise, incisive diary—a "man of no decorations," a contemporary said. Lincoln, who especially liked him, sometimes called him Uncle Gideon. "The Rebel leaders understand Seward very well," Uncle Gideon told his diary. "He is fond of intrigue, of mystery, of sly, cunning management. Detectives, secret agents, fortune-tellers are his delight." Lincoln's Cabinet was a candid fraternity, Welles said, "with the exception of Mr. Seward, who had, or affected, a certain mysterious knowledge which he was not prepared to impart." The Kentucky-born Mary Todd Lincoln despised him. "That hypocrite Seward," she called him, "that dirty abolition sneak." So deeply did she loathe him that she instructed her coachman to avoid the street on which he lived. She was heard to tell her husband, "He draws you around his little finger like a skein of thread."

Her husband was the only judge who mattered, and he valued Seward highly. On many a troubled evening, he took a walk with John Hay to the governor's rented townhouse, a few steps away on the eastern edge of Lafayette Square, for an hour or two of diversion. On one of their nights out, they brought for Seward's edification a Portuguese guide to English conversation, which the president read aloud. The three of them hurt from laughing. Apart from a depth of friendship that permitted public ribbing ("Mr. Seward," the president explained to a soldier, "is limited to a couple of stories which, from repeating, he believes are true"), Lincoln valued Seward's knowledge of foreign affairs, his longtime relationships with the men of the day, North and South, and his inbred savoir faire, all of which the president lacked. Seward taught him how to present himself, sent him memos on the subject, schooled him on the statesmen he had plotted, dined, and fought with since the 1830s, when Lincoln was defending hog thieves in the unwashed regions of Illinois.

The learning ran both ways. As Hay understood and said, Seward was astute enough to see and generous enough to admit that Lincoln's goodness of heart, well known to everyone in the city, was the least of his claims to respect. As the governor had done at first, many distinguished men would go to the White House expecting to pat him on the head and come away "confused and dissatisfied at finding he stood six feet four in his slippers. Seward was the first man who recognized this."

Ironically enough, apart from Lincoln himself, whose election had caused them to secede, no Republican leader was more committed to reconciliation with the gentlemen of the South than their antebellum nemesis William Seward, whom the Radicals roundly despised and had tried to force the president to depose. In a downcast evening at the governor's in the summer of 1864, with the Jacobins and the Democrats at either side of his throat, Lincoln told Seward he was ready to hand the nomination to him, to save what they had built together and cure the disappointment of 1860.

Seward said no, "that is all past and settled." The South had refused to accept the last election, hoping to reverse it in battle, he said. Now "they hope you will lose the next one," and vindicate them. "When that election is held and they find the people reaffirming their decision to have you President, I think the Rebellion will collapse."

They were far from reaffirming it now.

CHAPTER FOUR

Good and True Friends

The sainted Andrew Jackson had been dead for nineteen years, but Francis Preston Blair, his famous friend and collaborator, was alive and well in the thick of things, enjoying his golden years as Jackson's voice from the grave—a spitfire for the Union with deep Southern roots and strong Southern ties. When he wasn't charming senators at his country estate in Maryland (Silver Spring he called it, after the mica-flecked stream that ran through it), he was plotting war and peace at the buff-colored limestone townhouse on Pennsylvania Avenue known as Blair House, a three-minute stroll from the Executive Mansion. The path was well worn in both directions. Through ten administrations, Francis Preston Blair— "Preston" to family and friends, "the Old Gentleman" to Abraham Lincoln—had built a potent brand.

Born in Virginia in 1791, he had made his name in Kentucky as a banker, editor, and kingmaker with a slippery sort of cunning. Jackson brought him north in 1830 to sit in his Kitchen Cabinet and run his *Washington Globe*. Filling several Jacksonian needs, Blair supplied the president with speeches and ideas, helped him win his battles with John C. Calhoun and avoid war with South Carolina in the nullification crisis of 1832, and left a pail of milk on the White House steps at the start of every day, contributed by the cow kept in residence behind Blair House.

Three decades later, in 1861, he sent to President Lincoln a plan to free the slaves and send them as colonists to Central America, which the president endorsed. Toward the end of 1864, he turned his nimble mind to a still more ambitious scheme, a plan to restore the Union, emancipate the slaves, and save his native South from defeat and occupation, all at the same time. If anyone could work such a miracle it was Francis Preston Blair, a counselor to Abraham Lincoln and a father figure to Jefferson Davis.

He had been a leading Democrat for a quarter of a century when he helped give birth to the Republican Party in 1855, fed up with the old fixation on slavery and states' rights. Committing political treason in the eyes of Southern friends, he put air under the Republicans' wings by calling them Jackson's true successors and chairing their first national convention, where every mention of his name drew applause. A newspaperman saw how hard he worked the room, with a head too big for his body, a hat too big for his head, and a "badly-fitting set of false teeth." Having erred in one particular, the newspaperman dispatched a correction. The teeth were not false but real.

Preston Blair was a strikingly homely man, with the bald, boney look of a gaunt Dickensian undertaker, but his charm and his wit made his looks disappear. Eliza, his wife, was proof. A heart-stopping beauty in her day and a striking woman still, she had chosen to limit her marital role to raising the Blair children, brandying Silver Spring's peaches, presiding over capital society, co-editing the *Washington Globe,* schooling congressmen on politics and senators on war, and abetting her husband's intrigues. Eight presidents ago, Martin Van Buren had called her the best politician in the city. Not for nothing was she known as the lioness.

Their children were absurdly accomplished.

Montgomery, the eldest, was a scholarly lawyer and a West Point veteran of the Seminole War who had set out for Missouri as a young man, ascended to the bench, represented Dred Scott in the Supreme Court, served as Lincoln's postmaster general, modernized the mail, turned a deficit into a surplus, and advised the president on military affairs more wisely than most of his generals. Montgomery was no charmer (awkward, homely, and repellent, a friend of Lincoln's said), but the president enjoyed his children, who played a nascent form of baseball with the Lincoln boys on the lawn behind the White House. Lured from his office window, the commander in chief had been known to join in, his elbows and coattails flying comically around the bases.

After graduating from Princeton, Montgomery's younger brother, Francis Preston Blair Jr., had followed Montgomery to St. Louis, risen high in politics, saved Missouri for the Union, won a seat in the House of Representatives, chaired its Committee on Military Affairs in the midst of the Civil War, and resigned to raise his own army. He was now a major general leading one of Sherman's divisions, having first helped Grant take Vicksburg. People spoke of Frank as a future president, not exclusively people named Blair.

Their articulate sister, Lizzie, the social register's Elizabeth Blair Lee, was a favorite of Jackson's in her girlhood and had lived from time to time in his White House, outrunning boys in races despite her fragile health. Now she was her father's astute collaborator and the heart, head, and soul of the Washington Orphanage Society. Mary Lincoln was a friend. So was Varina Davis. Happily for Lizzie, her looks had come from her mother, her humor from her father.

Lizzie's husband, Phillips Lee, was a hard-fighting admiral in the US Navy, the architect of the blockade, and a cousin of Robert E. Lee's, to whom the Old Gentleman had offered the command of all the Union armies at Blair House in 1861 at Lincoln's behest. Preston had caused a new house to be built for Lizzie and Phil next to Blair House, where Montgomery and his family now lived. While Phil was away at sea, Preston and Eliza came down from Silver Spring to live with Lizzie and her little boy, a future US senator.

The Blairs had "the spirit of clan," Lincoln said, and "a way of going with a rush" for whatever they undertook. Their politics were much like his—fiercely pro-Union and moderately antislavery—which seemed a touch hypocritical in view of their household slaves, until one learned that their "servants" had a standing offer of freedom that only one of them had ever accepted. Preston put them on wages in 1862.

The Blairs' influence with Lincoln had slipped by the summer of 1864, positioned as they were more heretically than he—more cautious on abolition, more sympathetic to the South—but he valued their dogged loyalty and their willingness to draw some Radical fire away from him to them. He loved his trips to their country home, enjoyed their scrappy patriarch, profited from his wisdom and his multigenerational contacts. As several of his predecessors had done, the president revealed himself freely to the Sage of Silver Spring on difficult, sensitive issues, testing new ideas in the crucible of his mind. Their affection remained mutual even after Lincoln sacrificed Montgomery to the Jacobins and asked him to leave the Cabinet.

Others were not so enamored of the old schemer. Despite a former friendship (they had once joined a group of outdoorsmen on a long Canadian fishing trip), Seward was an old enemy. Preston Blair had worked hard to keep the governor out of the Cabinet, and Seward had worked harder to keep Montgomery out. Some thought the old man would rather have Seward out than Montgomery in. He was known to allude to the Secretary of State as Billy Bowlegs.

They had locked horns early on, when the South Carolinians threatened war in 1861, as they had in 1833. Alone in the Cabinet, Montgomery dissented from Seward's plan to let them take Fort Sumter and lure them back with concessions. When Lincoln invited the Old Gentleman's opinion, he ranted against Seward's advice with such red-faced passion that he asked Montgomery to "contrive some apology for me" after he had composed himself at home. Those traitors in the South were not threatening disunion to win concessions, he had shouted. Disunion was their goal. If Lincoln gave in, he would give up the country he had just been elected to save. Gideon Welles said Blair's rant "electrified" the president, out of character as it was for the cagey old man, and deflected him from Seward's accommodationism.

When Lincoln's aide John Hay drew the president's attention to a prudent letter from the Old Gentleman and compared it to Montgomery's bile, Lincoln told a story. He had once heard a man remark in a tavern that a local old-timer had been tricked in a trade. "That's a lie," said one of his sons. "The old man ain't so easily tricked. Ye can fool the boys but ye can't the old man."

——◆——

Hot for a fight though the old man had been, by the summer of 1864 he had set his mind on ending it, before it destroyed his beloved South and killed his cherished son. Its outcome he thought inevitable if Lincoln survived Election Day—it was only a matter of time—but time was destroying the South, and the Jacobins would see it crushed, Lincoln's kindness notwithstanding, unless he could find a path to reconciliation. So Blair went to see Horace Greeley.

No friend of the Blairs, Greeley would soon describe them as "a dangerous family," and the *Tribune*'s observation that Lincoln was under their thumbs complimented neither party. Quite apart from their divergence on fundamentals—capitalism, for instance—Greeley would soon tell Preston Blair that the latter had moved for forty years "in the inner circle of public affairs, while I have been on the outside, where I doubtless belong." But they shared a common interest in pursuing a common agenda—reelecting Lincoln, ending the war with the Union preserved, rescuing the South from the Jacobins—and their strengths were symbiotic. Blair had the president's confidence. Greeley had the *Tribune*. They proceeded to pretend to admire one another.

In the middle of July 1864, Blair took a train to Manhattan and climbed the wooden stairs to Greeley's disheveled office. Wary though it was, their meeting was conveniently cordial. Greeley made his case that the time to seek peace was now, before Lincoln lost the election. The South was ready to talk. If the president healed the nation, his reelection would be a formality. Blair begged to differ. Lincoln must be reelected first and shatter the Rebels' last hope: that a Democrat in the White House would let them have their country, or at least restore the Union with a brokered peace, saving slavery for their grandchildren and abolition for the twentieth century. With Lincoln reelected, they would have to face up to defeat. Any terms would be better than subjugation, and the president could be generous with reelection won. Greeley disagreed, but Blair had built a bridge.

On the same trip to New York, Blair sat down with other prominent men, including General McClellan, and tried to talk him out of a White House run. Surely, Blair said (probably with Lincoln's blessing), the president would give him an important new command if he deferred his political ambitions. But the general was looking to his future, not his past. In 1862 (when he spoke of the president among friends as "the original gorilla"), he had been sure he could take Richmond. Now he was sure he could take Washington.

The Rebels had nearly taken it just a week before. With the North on the offensive in Georgia and Virginia, Washington was lightly defended. On July 9, General Jubal Early rolled up out of the Shenandoah Valley at the head of Stonewall Jackson's old corps and led it within sight of the capitol dome, having first brushed aside a small defending force on Maryland's Monocacy River that included Seward's son and namesake. General Early had too few men to take and hold the city, but men enough to torch it, as the British had done in 1814, leaving Lincoln unelectable. On July 10, the president stood up in his stovepipe hat on an embattled Union parapet as Rebel sharpshooters peppered it, the first and only time an American commander in chief had sent himself into battle. A lieutenant by the name of Oliver Wendell Holmes shouted at him to get down. In the heat of the moment, the fate of a damned fool was mentioned. When Lincoln returned the next day, an officer was mortally wounded mere feet from his side. Reinforcements saved the day.

As Lincoln watched the enemy withdraw, smoke was rising from Silver Spring. Before the war, Jeff and Varina Davis had enjoyed a pleasant summer at Montgomery's cottage there. Falklands, it was called. Now the Rebels had burned it to the ground. The Blairs were not there to see it. Montgomery and his boys were hunting in Pennsylvania with Preston, the women vacationing on the Jersey shore with Lizzie's seven-year-old son.

Preston and Eliza's mansion was spared the flames but not the attentions of the Rebels, who liberated its wine cellar. The fun got started in the morning and continued until five, when General Early and his second in command rode up in a spitting rage. Early descended on the officers while General John C. Breckinridge laid into the troops, some of them with loot in their hands and lingerie around their necks. Breckinridge put men in irons and summoned a different regiment to guard the house. Early was enraged by the diversion of his attack on the enemy capital but not very much by the looting of one rich Yankee's house. Breckinridge thought otherwise. Before the war, he said, Silver Spring was "a home to me on this side of the mountains."

The dashing John Breckinridge had a good sense of humor, good political skills, and a good Kentucky family. Eliza Blair was his cousin. She had nursed his dying father. In 1850, the Blairs had welcomed Breckinridge to Silver Spring as a newly elected congressman. With no little help from them, he had risen in his thirties to become James Buchanan's vice president, the youngest in American history. As the Southern Democrats' presidential nominee in 1860 at the age of thirty-nine, Breckinridge took Maryland and Delaware from Lincoln, as well as the Deep South. He loved Silver Spring and the Blairs. He was crushed by what his men had done to them.

When Lizzie got home a few days later, shaken servants told her what had happened. She wrote her husband, Phil, that the house had been the scene of "a perfect saturnalia." One drunken Rebel had danced in her father's red velvet wrapper, another in the butler's uniform, a third in a lady's riding habit. The vandals had drained a barrel of bourbon, cleaned out the larder, absconded with the poultry. "All the kitchen utensils have gone to Dixie." Oddly, the horses and crops were untouched. Gone were the mules, a pony, a donkey with its cart, all of Preston's clothes, and "the presents of a lifetime," as the Old Gentleman would later say. The lawn was strewn with rags left behind in poor exchange. Books and papers were torn and scattered. The pommels had been cut from the ladies' saddles for the sheer enjoyment of the thing. The maids' humble finery was in tatters. A servant named Olivia had fled in terror, permanently, she said. Lizzie hoped Olivia's husband, Harry, would not choose to follow her. Preston had just sold Lizzie and Phil a lot adjoining Blair House for a thousand dollars, declining to take the money unless he needed it someday. He took it now.

A note had been left on the library mantel: A Confederate officer, "for himself & all his comrades," apologized for the pilfering, though federal officers had permitted "darker crimes" in the South. Another note was leaning on a photograph of Emma Mason, a Virginian who had married General Frank Wheaton, the Rhode Islander whose troops had repelled Early's raid. "A confederate officer has remained here until after eleven to prevent pillage & burning of the house because of his love of Mrs. Wheaton who found in this home good & true friends."

A neighbor informed the Old Gentleman that Rebel officers who dined at her table told her Breckinridge had saved Silver Spring. He had called it his place of refuge, and "made more fuss about things there than if they had belonged to Jeff Davis."

Jubal Early had barely left Silver Spring when a procession of blue-ribbon committees and blue-blooded Republicans descended on Lincoln and urged him to yield the presidency to a better man. Horace Greeley was one of the instigators. Lincoln told his Cabinet that "Greeley is an old shoe," valuable in his day but lately grown "so rotten that nothing can be done with him. He is not truthful; the stitches all tear out."

In the summer of 1862, a series of enemy victories had nearly broken the president's spirit. "I have been driven many times upon my knees by the overwhelming conviction that I had nowhere else to go." In the summer of 1864, it was his friends who were driving him to despair, less than four months before the election, with the fate of the Union in the balance.

CHAPTER FIVE

The Only Way to Make Spaniels Civil Is to Whip Them

In August of 1864, Seward's alter ego, Thurlow Weed, pronounced Lincoln's political death sentence. The people were "wild for peace," he told Seward, and their leader would not give it to them. His reelection was "an impossibility." Lincoln thought Weed was right.

On August 17, the president composed an answer to a letter from a Wisconsin editor who supported the war on secession but not a war on slavery. To abandon abolition, Lincoln wrote, would ruin the Union cause. "All recruiting of colored men would instantly cease, and all colored men in our service would instantly desert us. And rightfully too. Why should they give their lives for us, with full notice of our purpose to betray them?" Besides, the Rebels refused to abandon their cause on *any* conditions. If Davis would accept reunion, "saying nothing about slavery, let him try me." If Lincoln was considering such an overture, he could not bring himself to say so. He drafted the letter twice and filed it away unsent.

On August 22, the *New York Times*'s publisher Henry Raymond told the president that his friends in every state said the tide was setting against him. He had no stauncher friend than his home state congressman Elihu B. Washburne, who told him the stunning truth. If the election were held today, Lincoln would lose Illinois.

Attributing the disaster to the military stalemate—with Grant bogged down at Petersburg and Sherman unable to punch his way through to Atlanta—and a public misimpression that reunion could be had were it not for abolition, Raymond urged the president to offer the Rebels peace on the sole condition of accepting the Constitution, every other issue to be solved at a convention. If they agreed, the war would be over, the Union restored, and Lincoln reelected. If they refused, as they surely would do, the people of the North would salute the flag and return their commander in chief to his post. The next day, Lincoln drafted instructions to Raymond to go down to Richmond and inquire of Jefferson Davis whether he would like to accept reunion, all other issues to be adjusted peacefully. His aide John Hay would later say that he was stating the proposition to make Raymond "a witness of its absurdity." Perhaps so. Perhaps not.

If Lincoln had been wavering, he called Raymond and the rest of the Republican National Committee to the White House and stopped. They were panicky. Lincoln steadied them. Sending envoys to Richmond to yield on slavery would be worse than losing the election, he said. It would give it up cravenly in advance. The Radicals would abandon him. The platform on which he had been nominated would be scrapped. His promises to the blacks would be broken. At about the same time, he told two White House guests that he would never let Negro troops be reenslaved as the price of reunion. If he did, "I should deserve to be damned in time and eternity. Come what will, I will keep my faith with friend and foe."

More than worth fighting for, abolition was worth losing for. The election would run its course. If the Rebels came to the table while Lincoln was president, peace with honor would be considered. Peace with slavery would not.

———

Everything changed on September 2 when Sherman took Atlanta, two days after the Democrats nominated McClellan on a peace platform. "All Yankeedoodledom is clapping hands and flinging up caps as though there were no longer a 'live rebel' in all America," a Northern paper raved. Sherman was said to have kicked in the South's back door with Grant hunkered down on its porch.

In a brilliant war of maneuver at the head of the Army of Tennessee, the badly outnumbered General Joseph E. Johnston had been making Sherman pay for every step toward Atlanta. At loggerheads with Johnston since West Point, Davis had replaced him in July with John Bell

Hood, an old friend of Sherman's whose useless left arm and missing right leg were badges of reckless bravery. Hood wasted lives in suicidal charges, then destroyed ammunition and supplies, abandoned Atlanta, and withdrew his broken army, shedding deserters along the way. Davis shrugged it off. His people knew better. Mary Chesnut was the wife of a former US senator from South Carolina. "No hope," she told her diary, "we will try to have no fear."

On September 20, Davis left Richmond on a whistle-stop tour in an effort to rally his people. His rhetoric was delusional and stunningly indiscreet. The *Philadelphia Inquirer* called it "so damaging to the Rebel cause that attempts are being made to raise doubts as to its authenticity."

He spoke in Macon, Georgia, on September 23, openly appealing to deserters to return. "To the women, no appeal is necessary. They are like the Spartan mothers of old. I know of one who had lost all her sons, except one of eight years. She wrote me that she wanted me to reserve a place for him in the ranks." On September 26, he proceeded from self-parody to self-destruction, revealing Hood's plans to recapture Tennessee, giving Sherman time to thwart them. Three days later, Davis replied to the First Tennessee Infantry's serenade in Palmetto, Georgia, with the mind-boggling admission that "there are on the books of the war department at Richmond the names of a quarter of a million deserters, yet you, my brave soldiers, captains all, have remained true and steadfast." When he visited Hood the next day, a chipper officer urged his men to give the president three cheers and a Rebel yell. "Give us Johnston," they shouted. "Give us back our leader!"

Davis addressed the Alabama legislature on September 29. He would have preferred a military role, he said. He had made some mistakes in the role thrust upon him. His earnestness made him rigid when he thought he was right. But if half of Hood's deserters returned, they would drive Sherman back to his masters in a month. The more he thought about the war, the more confident he became. Victory was "the surest element of strength to a peace party."

Then he met with General Richard Taylor, President Zachary Taylor's son, a Skull and Bones man at Yale. Hood's army was in great spirits, Davis said. Taylor advised him that a leader should beware of being told what he wanted to hear. Hood was incapable of reaching Tennessee, Taylor said. He could only hope to survive the winter. A letter from a captain of the 38th Alabama arrived at the Executive Mansion in Davis's absence. Hood's men had "a fixed, ineradicable distrust" of him, the captain said. Their morale could not be lower. Davis's home state senator James Phelan wrote two days later. Mississippi was awash with deserters, some in armed bodies, intimidating politicians, defying arrest. The "infernal Hydra of Reconstruction is again stirring its envenomed head in our State."

At the Columbus, Georgia, depot, Davis belittled critics who cried for peace and kept their distance from the front. He assured an Augusta crowd that the South was stronger than when the war began. He would welcome negotiation, but there was no alternative to independence. An invincible ally gave him confidence. "I believe that a just God looks upon our cause as holy, and that of the enemy as iniquitous." When he spoke in Columbia, South Carolina, schoolchildren were let out for the occasion. The South would prevail, he told them, and "every man who does not live to see his country free will see a freeman's grave." Some were misinformed that "we are not stronger today than when we began this struggle." Others were willing to reconstruct the Union. He was glad they were scorned in South Carolina. He had sought an honorable peace, but every overture had been met with insolence. Did anyone imagine that the Yankees could be conquered in retreat, "or do you not all know that the only way to make spaniels civil is to whip them?" He brought good cheer from Hood's army, he said, which had grown since Atlanta had fallen. Sherman would be limping back north in a month. It was only natural that Hood's retreat had produced some despondency, "but as I approached the region occupied by our troops, the hope increased, until at last I found in the army the *acme* of confidence itself."

Poorly fed, clothed, and led, the South Carolinians cheered.

On November 7, the day before the Yankee election, Davis told his Congress that independence was not negotiable. No one was surprised. Then he spoke the unspeakable. If the South must accept subjugation or make soldiers of its slaves, he saw "no reason to doubt what should then be our decision." Shock waves rolled out from the capital. The South had declared its independence to preserve its slaves. Now Davis would free its slaves to preserve its independence. The war of secession that had ruined his country and killed six hundred thousand of her sons had become an end in itself.

The once-handsome city of Richmond was rusty and unkempt. In the winter months to come, the coldest in recent memory, the city would be rife with beggars, many of them women and children. To the shame of a young Rebel officer, the poorer classes would be "scantily clad in every kind of makeshift garment." Hungry men and women lacking overcoats, subsisting on bacon and peas, would talk of peace "with their teeth chattering." Rats, mice, and pigeons would disappear from the streets.

One hundred twenty-five miles to the north in Washington City, Seward wrote his wife: The Rebels were exhausted and did not know it. Lincoln's reelection would make them conscious of it.

CHAPTER SIX

Who Will He Treat With,
or How Commence the Work?

The crowd began to gather on the moonlit White House lawn an hour before the parade. "Every face was visible in the bright moonlight," said the *Daily National Republican*, "and a more joyous and enthusiastic throng was never seen." By the appointed hour of nine, when the sound of distant drums could be heard marching west down Pennsylvania Avenue from the foot of Capitol Hill, a sea of eager celebrants, well fed, well dressed, flush with the glow of victory, had overflowed the Executive Mansion's grounds and spilled into Lafayette Square, come to cheer the reelection of Abraham Lincoln.

Lincoln's friend Noah Brooks, a newspaperman who had covered him in Illinois, was watching from a White House window when the parade curled into view, "gemmed with colored lights," bright with "illuminations." A regimental band lent a military air to a cavalcade "gay with banners and resplendent with lanterns and transparencies." The Sixth Ward contributed a band of its own. Hock's Drum Corps brought up the rear. As the marchers started down the White House carriageway, artillerymen in blue discharged a pair of cannon, blasting the crowd with excitement and the reek of half-burned powder. Assembled around the portico, the bands played "Hail, Columbia" and "The Star-Spangled Banner," punctuated by artillery. The president's eleven-year-old son, Tad, "the pet of the house," a doting bodyguard called him, a lovable boy with a speech impediment, ran laughing from window to window, igniting illuminations of his own proud design, thrilled beyond words when the cannon concussed the windowpanes.

Having read his own obituaries, the president was grateful for his resurrection, but Noah Brooks thought that few who had known him in Illinois would recognize him now. He looked like a sick man. On the day before the parade, he confided in Brooks that he would have been "a little mortified" had the people turned him out, but the lifting of his burdens would have been worth the sting. He had said more than once that "nothing touches the tired spot," and his triumphant reelection was no exception. Twenty-five states had voted. McClellan had carried three: New Jersey and the loyal slave states of Delaware and Kentucky. Lower down the ballot, many Copperheads had been smoked. Though the incoming Congress would be more Republican than ever, the Radicals had gained strength to overpower their temperate president.

But now his people were calling for him. When the moment seemed right, he showed himself at the open center window beneath the pillared portico where Jefferson and Jackson had spoken. According to the *National Republican* (a partisan source to be sure), the crowd cheered for minutes before they let him speak. Then their hero positioned his spectacles on the end of his nose and read a little speech in his high-pitched Western twang, his practiced voice carrying over the crowd.

A national election had been held in the midst of a civil war, he said. The world had not known that such a thing was possible. The voters had shown that "he who is most devoted to the Union and most opposed to treason" could win the most votes. But their president wished no man ill, and the war was not yet won. Would the voters now unite "to save the common country"? Buoyed by their cheers, he said a few more words of thanks and reconciliation, delighting the upturned faces in the bright November moonlight, then stepped away from the window and turned to his aide John Hay. "Not very graceful," he said, "but I am growing old enough not to care much for the manner of doing things."

Then the crowd rolled on to Seward's with torches, sparklers, and bands until the governor appeared at his own upper window. From Lincoln they looked for eloquence. From Seward they wanted a laugh. He gave them half a dozen, compared himself to Saint Paul, predicted that within a short time "you will have to look mighty hard" to find anyone in the South who admitted he had been a secessionist, thanked God for bringing the end of the rebellion near, wished them luck the rest of the way. Basking in cheers and applause, his favorite kind of music, he exhorted the crowd to enjoy themselves, to visit his fellow Cabinet members and keep their spirits high. For hours to come, the revelers happily complied, keeping Washington City awake with bugles, drums, and torchlight.

Some five hundred miles to the southwest, Rome, Georgia, was lit by arson. Earlier that day, out of touch with the high command, having cut his own telegraph wires, General Sherman had marched his legions out of Rome, leaving a smaller force behind with orders to take whatever it might need and destroy that night all workshops, warehouses, depots, factories, bridges, and public property before moving on to join him, fulfilling his pledge to make Georgia howl. The exercise would be repeated for a month and a half to come, as sixty thousand men burned an ugly path to Savannah, sustaining themselves on the way, taking cattle, crops, and silver, crushing the heart of the South, bringing the war to her people, punishing them for starting it, pressuring them to stop. "Sherman's bummers," they called themselves. Jefferson Davis and his generals had moved their warriors elsewhere, leaving nothing more formidable than isolated cavalry and ornery old men for the bummers to push aside. Their commander told a colleague, "I am going into the very bowels of the Confederacy, and propose to leave a trail that will be recognized fifty years hence." William Tecumseh Sherman had begun his march to the sea.

Uniquely distinguished as a friend of Abraham Lincoln's and an unapologetic Copperhead with a brother in the Rebel Congress, James W. Singleton had been born into an old Virginia family and moved to Illinois. He had made himself wealthy in business and influential in Whig politics, forged ties to Lincoln, and kept them in good repair after he defected to the Democrats. In 1861, John Hay had called him the idol of his friends. Four months later, when Hay told the president that his friend was behaving badly, Lincoln called Singleton "a miracle of meanness."

Railing against the war in the 1864 campaign, he had crossed a forbidden line. When Lincoln called him to task for it and told him that some were calling for his arrest, he said it was nothing personal.

On Thanksgiving Day, Singleton told Orville Hickman Browning, a former senator from Illinois and another old Lincoln man, that he had just come from Clay and Tucker, the Rebel agents in Canada who had charmed Horace Greeley but not John Hay. Now he was in Washington to see Lincoln about peace, Clay and Tucker having told him that the South would accept reunion if amnesty were given and slavery let alone. Lincoln had confided in him before the election, Singleton said, that after it was won he would not insist on abolition if the South rejoined the Union. He would leave it to the courts. His letter in the Niagara Falls fiasco, making the abandonment of slavery a condition of peace, had been a mistake, he said. Slavery would not prevent a settlement. Now that the election was over, Singleton was going to see him again.

Two days later, Singleton told Browning that he had not yet seen the president but had received a message from him, repeating that slavery would not stand in the way of an adjustment. After Congress reconvened in December, Singleton said, Lincoln would decide whether to send an envoy to Richmond. If anyone could influence "those people," the president had told Singleton, "you are the man."

━━━◦━━━

Lincoln was struggling with his annual message to Congress. None of the others had troubled him so. To Gideon Welles it "seemed to dwell heavy on his mind." With the election safely behind them, the victors were warring among themselves on whether to coax the Rebels home or simply to club them down, pitting Jacobins like Wade and Davis against moderates like Lincoln and Seward, and Democrats against both. It was plain to the Secretary of the Interior, John Usher, a potbellied man with heavy-lidded eyes who had ridden the judicial circuit with Lincoln in the 1840s, that his friend was weighted down by the disconcerting thought that many Republicans who had helped him win the war despised his plans to win the peace. On the issue of reconstruction, Usher said, there were "as many minds as there were men," every one sure he was right, and passionate about it, "without regard to the opinions of Mr. Lincoln or any one else; yet he felt that the responsibility all rested upon him."

On Friday, November 25, Lincoln read his Cabinet an unimpressive draft of his message to Congress. Uncle Gideon heard "nothing very striking" in it, "and he evidently labors in getting it up." With the war all but won, what seemed to try him most was how to end it quickly, how to stop the waste of lives and reconcile the people. The question of whom to deal with seemed to worry him most of all. "He says he cannot treat with Jeff Davis and the Jeff Davis government, which is all very well, but who will he treat with, or how commence the work?" If the war were to end short of abject conquest, if Southern voices were to be heard on the shape of the postwar future, someone must speak for the South. If not Jeff Davis, who?

Welles was pleased that the president refused to negotiate with the Rebel government, and the rest of the Cabinet agreed, but Uncle Gideon thought the states were different. "We are one country," he said. Davis's government was illegitimate, "but the States are entities and may be recognized and treated with."

On Saturday, Lincoln reconvened the Cabinet and read them another draft. Welles thought it much improved, and said so, but was not entirely satisfied. The president should invite the rebellious states to come home under their own powers, he said, appeal more earnestly to their people, assure them that they would not be outlaws—that their persons and property would be respected.

The humorless Edwin Stanton, the Jacobins' favorite Cabinet member, had decided to show up for the first time in a month and a half, with his nerve-chilling stare and his perfumed beard. Another former Democrat, he had served as James Buchanan's Attorney General. In three grim years as Lincoln's Secretary of War, he had done a formidable job. Lincoln sometimes called him Mars. Jefferson Davis called him venomous.

Every other Cabinet member had spoken, and the subject had been changed when the war god thundered on peace. The president should include no new offers or sentiments on the subject, Stanton said. He should merely say that the door was open, invite the ordinary people to return to their duties, ask them if they would not be better off if they had taken his offer a year ago and come back to the Union with their lives, their liberty, and their property.

Lincoln did not disagree. But how was he to know what those ordinary people were thinking? There was no mail service between the North and South. What impressions the occasional traveler brought back were anecdotal. The Southern journalism that made its way above the Mason-Dixon Line was little more than fiction, belching fire about the people's will, but with almost no objective reporting. Many thousands of Southern soldiers were in Northern prisons. (In an effort to reach them, Southern papers ran notices of weddings, deaths, and missing men, accompanied by the legend, "New York papers, please copy," which the New York papers did.) Still, no one knew much about the man in the Southern street, let alone the woman. Governor Francis Pierpont of "The Restored Government of Virginia" led a rump administration in a Washington suburb as if it were the real thing. Lincoln would soon tell Pierpont that he had no idea what the ordinary Southerner was thinking, implying inadvertently that Pierpont didn't either.

⸺～⸺

The president brought forth his message on the state of the Union on December 6, and had it sent to Capitol Hill.* The election had confirmed that the loyal people's purpose was never firmer, it said. Despite much debate over ways and means, not a single congressional *candidate* had proposed to give up the Union. The men and resources required to save it were "unexhausted, and, as we believe, inexhaustible." The public will to reestablish federal authority in the South was unchanged, "and as we believe, unchangeable. The manner of continuing the effort remains to choose." It was here on the matter of choice that Lincoln said something new.

"On careful consideration of all the evidence accessible, it seems to me that no attempt at negotiation *with the insurgent leader* could result in any good. He would accept nothing short of severance of the Union, precisely what we will not and cannot give. His declarations to this effect are explicit and oft-repeated. He does not attempt to deceive us. He affords

---

* Not since Jefferson called the practice reminiscent of the crown had any president read it in person.

us no excuse to deceive ourselves. He cannot voluntarily re-accept the Union; we cannot voluntarily yield it. Between him and us the issue is distinct, simple and inflexible. It is an issue which can only be tried by war, and decided by victory. If we yield, we are beaten; if the Southern people fail him, he is beaten. Either way, it would be victory and defeat following war." [Emphasis added]

And then came the salient point: "What is true, however, of him who heads the insurgent cause is not necessarily true of those who follow. Although he cannot re-accept the Union, they can." It was a call to the Southern people to ignore their elected leader. "They can, at any moment, have peace simply by laying down their arms, and submitting to the National authority under the Constitution." If they did, Washington could not keep warring on them even if it wanted to. The loyal people would not allow it. Any issues that remained would be adjusted by lawful means. Some were beyond the executive's power, which the end of the war would diminish. But pardons and remissions of forfeited property were within his control, and the people of the South could expect their liberal use. He had offered pardons a year ago to all but a few Rebel leaders. Even they had been told that they could earn one, and many already had. The door was still open. "But the time may come—probably will come—when public duty shall demand that it be closed" and "more rigorous measures" taken. The rigors were left unnamed.

The president set only one other condition for peace. "I retract nothing heretofore said as to slavery." He would never revoke the Emancipation Proclamation, nor return to slavery any person freed by its terms, or by any act of Congress. "If the people should, by whatever mode or means, make it an Executive duty to reenslave such persons, another, and not I, must be their instrument to perform it. In stating a single condition of peace, I mean simply to say that the war will cease on the part of the Government whenever it shall have ceased on the part of those who began it."

Lincoln called on the lame-duck House to vote once again on the Constitutional amendment banning slavery, before the new Congress convened. The Republicans had run on an abolition platform. The people had been heard. Prompt, united action abolishing slavery forever would help win the war by erasing the evil that had caused it.

The Radicals loved it. Thaddeus Stevens was thrilled. Jacobin in chief in the House, the grim Pennsylvanian chaired the Ways and Means Committee, feeble at seventy-two, with a miraculous mop of dense brown hair that did his wig-maker no credit, but sharp of wit and tongue. He would soon attack Andrew Johnson, whom a colleague would defend as a self-made man. "Glad to hear it," Stevens would say, "for it relieves God Almighty of a heavy responsibility." Stevens had been skewering Lincoln for years. Now he rushed to his side. The president had "never made much pretension to a polished education," Stevens said, but no fault could be found in his message "that the war must go on without seeking negotiation," and be waged until slavery was gone.

The president had said neither of these things. There were reasons why his message had been difficult to compose. It did not invite negotiations but nor did it preclude them, so long as they included reunion and no *backward* steps on abolition. It said not a word about fighting the South to the death, or warring until slavery was gone. In practical effect, the Emancipation Proclamation had only freed the slaves in the conquered parts of the Confederacy, and the Constitutional amendment banning slavery had not yet passed the Congress, let alone been ratified by the states. If peace came now, there was room for negotiation on the timing, particulars, and rewards of moving *forward* with abolition, a priority that Lincoln embraced but had always ranked second to the restoration of the Union.

In the end, Lincoln had invited Southern peacemakers to proceed where "the insurgent leader" would not go.

CHAPTER SEVEN

The Wise Men Are Those
Who Would End It

A week before Lincoln sent his message to Congress, Horace Greeley resumed his peace initiative in a letter to Preston Blair. "You have Mr. Lincoln's ear, as I have not, and can exert influence on every side where it is needed. Do urge and inspire him to make peace among our friends any how, and with our foes so soon as may be."

On the same day, unbeknownst to Greeley, the brilliant Alabamian John A. Campbell, a former justice of the United States Supreme Court, now Assistant Secretary of War in Richmond, sent a letter to a friend, Justice Samuel Nelson of New York, a friend of Seward's as well, a good-hearted man with a judge's scowl. In 1861, Campbell and Nelson had worked with Seward to try to avert the war. Now Campbell would try to stop it, and no one was better qualified to achieve the unachievable.

John Campbell may have been the smartest man in America. He was surely the most diligent. The grandson of a Revolutionary War officer, he enrolled in the future University of Georgia at the tender age of eleven, graduated first in his class in three years, won a place at West Point at fourteen, and resigned to support his family when his father died. After he learned the law at the knee of a former judge, a special act of the legislature was required to admit him to the bar at the unlawful age of eighteen. Georgia was too sleepy to hold him. On his way to legal eminence before he was old enough to vote, he devoted himself to his practice in the thriving port city of Mobile, Alabama. A friend recalled him in his *twenties* as "absorbed in thought, with heavy brow," holding "all elegance and imagination in utter contempt, as unworthy of a practical man."

His New Hampshire–born wife and thoughtful Alabamians were fond of him nonetheless, and comfortable with his quiet mien. They sent him to the legislature at the age of twenty-five. But a political career was not John Campbell's calling. The best that could be said of his most companionable moments was not especially engaging. "At times he is pleasant, and always respectful when it becomes necessary for him to converse."

He was one of the South's leading lawyers before he was middle-aged. Induced by Jefferson Davis, Franklin Pierce appointed him to the Supreme Court in 1853. He was not yet forty-two. The Senate confirmed him unanimously, with the approval of the *New York Times*. He had argued controversially for the education of slaves and for banning the separation of their families. A year later, sitting as a trial judge in Mobile, he excoriated the illegal African slave trade and the "depraved" public sentiment that condoned it. In his native South, all of this brushed the edge of respectability. That said, he owned house slaves and laborers until 1858 and concurred in the infamous *Dred Scott v. Sandford* decision of 1857—a slave was not made free when taken into free territory. Slavery should be reformed and eliminated gradually, Campbell thought, but the federal government's "enormous pretensions" to take the issue from the states and territories were unconstitutional.

When Alabama seceded, against his stern advice, Campbell stayed on the Court and tried to heal the breach, for which he was pilloried in the South. A man without a country, his heart was with the Union but his state no longer was. When Davis sent envoys to Washington to discuss a peaceful parting, Campbell and Justice Nelson urged Seward to receive them. He wished he could, Seward said, but Lincoln would not permit it, for fear of implying recognition. Nevertheless, the president would relinquish Fort Sumter in Charleston Harbor, as the Southerners demanded, gaining time to negotiate reunion. Seward asked Campbell to speak with Davis's men and tell them so: "You might stop a civil war."

Campbell called on one of the Rebel emissaries and vouched for Seward's pledge. His reputation suffered further when Lincoln decided otherwise. Convinced that Seward had betrayed him (an opinion he would later change), Campbell resigned and went home to Alabama, "to follow the fortunes of my people."

He met a cold reception. In July of 1861, the South Carolinian Mary Chesnut visited friends in Warrenton, Virginia, not far from Washington City. "We saw across the lawn, but not to speak to them, some of Judge Campbell's family. There they wander disconsolate, just outside the gates of their paradise. A resigned judge of the Supreme Court of the United States! Resigned and for a cause that he is hardly more than half in sympathy with. His is one of the hardest cases." Later that month, shunned in Mobile and Montgomery as a Yankee collaborator, he moved his family to New Orleans and eventually to Richmond.

He did nothing to support the Confederacy until 1862, when he agreed to serve as Assistant Secretary of War, processing paper, advising the Secretary on minor legal issues, hoping to be useful in finding a peaceful settlement if the opportunity arose. He would later refuse a Cabinet seat. He would do what he could in a subordinate role, he said, but he was not among the men who had ruined his country, and he would take no leading role in their government. The best legal mind of his generation had become little more than a clerk with an overwrought title. The war that had split his country had wrecked his brilliant career.

In December of 1864, now fifty-three years old, Judge Campbell, as everyone called him, had not grown frivolous with age. The letter he wrote to his old friend Justice Nelson was neither impulsive nor unauthorized. Their mutual friend, the Confederate Senator Robert M. T. Hunter of Virginia, had suggested it. Campbell shared a draft with Robert Kean, his War Department protégé, an articulate young lawyer and a Rebel Army veteran with shining eyes and a full mustache. Kean thought the letter too formal, which cannot have been a surprise. Campbell showed a revision to Hunter, then presented it to his superior, Secretary of War James Seddon, a courtly Virginia aristocrat and a former US congressman who had owned in the 1850s what was now Jefferson Davis's Executive Mansion. To the Blairs' dismay, the Yankees had burned Seddon's rural Virginia home in reprisal for the vandalism at Silver Spring.

Dark-eyed and drawn at the age of forty-nine, with long, salt-and-pepper hair, Sedden wore a skull cap that lent him the look of a Talmudic scholar. Like the mission he had led since 1862, he was reeling toward collapse. A diary-keeping War Department clerk named John B. Jones could see it. "His eyes are shrunken and his features have the hue of a man who has been in his grave a full month. He is an orator and a man of fine education, but in bad health, being much afflicted with neuralgia," a debilitating disease of the nerves. Davis had the same affliction.

Willing to grasp at straws, Sedden showed Campbell's letter to Justice Nelson to Davis, who let the attempt be made. As peace overtures go, Campbell's began pessimistically. It had more than once occurred to him, he wrote, to approach his old friend to try to end the war. He had feared it would do no good, and expose them both to "misconstruction." But a door had now been opened to "an intelligent reverend friend" who had just passed the lines of two Northern armies. An unnamed Union general had told this friend that he favored a candid exchange "between citizens of the different sections" (sections, as opposed to countries, must have slipped past Davis's eye) and had offered to try to facilitate a meeting. Campbell's own wish to settle things had not changed since he and Nelson had parted. He continued rather cryptically: "I can say to you now what I expressed then, that the consequences of such a peace I was ready to accept." In the time appointed by Providence, "all that a good or wise man ought to desire" must result. Campbell offered to see Nelson and other mutual friends "in the U.S." Justice Benjamin Curtis of Massachusetts had come to mind, along with Senator Ewing of Ohio and Secretary of War Stanton. If Nelson preferred to come to Richmond, Campbell would let him know if it could be arranged. Campbell would bring no authorized proposition. A simple exchange of views was all he had in mind. It might do some good; it could scarcely do harm. He authorized his friend to show the letter to whomever he saw fit, though he did not wish to give it unnecessary publicity.

Campbell had no illusions about its prospects, despite the support of Ulysses S. Grant, the general who had inspired it. While passing him through the lines, Grant had told Campbell's reverend friend, the Episcopal Bishop of Arkansas, that Lincoln would give the South much better terms than its leaders might think, and Grant would like to talk with General Lee himself.

The Confederate secret signal service sent Campbell's letter to Washington. He never got an answer. "In lieu of this," he said, "there came Francis P. Blair."

<hr />

On December 15, a letter from Horace Greeley flattered Blair once again. "You are an older, and doubtless an abler publicist than I," closer to "our great ones." Lincoln should have responded to the peace overtures that some North Carolinians had made in the Rebel Congress, perhaps by offering to buy the freedom of North Carolina's slaves in exchange for her return to the Union. "I believe you, if at Raleigh with large powers, could pull North Carolina out of the rebellion in a month." The Confederacy could not last three months without her.

But Blair had a bolder idea. He was pondering a plan not merely to deplete the Rebels but to end the rebellion. Outright. No one had heard it yet—no one, at least, beyond the house of Blair.

That day and the next, the Rebel Army of Tennessee was all but destroyed near Nashville, recklessly led by John Bell Hood, who fought as his critics said he did, with a lion's heart and a wooden head. It was the war's only battle of annihilation, and it brought the end in sight. With Lee's army pinned and a fragment of Hood's on the run, the South's offensive weapons were gone. The news fell on Richmond like a safe. Congressman Lafayette McMullen of Virginia, a teamster in his youth and a respected former member of the US House, introduced a resolution demanding a peace commission. Reunion was not on the table but was under it.

On December 19, Lincoln kept up the pressure with a call for another 300,000 volunteers. Grant wired Sherman that day: "Jefferson Davis is said to be very sick; in fact, deserters report his death. The people had a rumor that he took poison in a fit of despondency over the military situation. I credit no part of this except that Davis is very sick, and do not suppose his reflections on military matters soothe him any."

Blair answered Greeley's letter the next day: "To me it seems that the madmen are those who made this war. The wise men are those who would end it." In the ranks of the wise Blair included Horace Greeley. He was still under the influence of their meeting in New York, he said, and now felt emboldened to bring the president a plan. "I think I will hint it to Mr. Lincoln on Thursday, so far at least as to test his confidence in me, without which my project must be still born." Completing the natal analogy, the old man signed off with a wink. "In the meantime, you will keep my suggestions as secret as illicit embryos ought to be and generally are."

The embryo had its origins in forty-three years of intimacy between Preston Blair and Jefferson Davis. At the age of thirteen, young Jeff had been sent to Preston's alma mater, Transylvania University in Kentucky, where Preston and Eliza Blair, who lived not far away, took a liking to the boy and tucked him into their nest. In 1845, when he came to Washington City as a newly wedded congressman, the Blairs were there to greet him. Eliza introduced Varina to society as Frank introduced Jeff to their fellow Democrats and mentored his career. The two families rented summer cottages together in the mountains at Oakland, Maryland, where Montgomery's daughter had saved Varina's life when she fell into convulsions, or at least Jeff thought she had. Preston's daughter Lizzie's wartime letters to her husband, Admiral Phillips Lee, made discreet, sympathetic allusions to "our Oakland cronies." In the crisis of 1860, with their men on opposite sides, Lizzie had gone to visit Varina and heard her call to a servant. "That's the Blairs' carriage. Don't let any of them in but Mrs. Lee."

Now Lizzie lamented for the South. "I cannot for an instant divest myself of feeling that they are my people, my countrymen; mad men as they are, my heart aches for them." Two months into the war, Mary Chesnut whispered a scandal to her diary. "A Richmond lady told me under her breath that Mrs. Davis had sent a baby's dress to her friend Mrs. Montgomery Blair," whose thank-you note promised friendship to the grave, though the men might kill each other. Mrs. Chesnut did not know whether to believe it.[*]

[*] Before he died in 1942, Lizzie's son, Senator Francis Preston Blair Lee, recalled family lore that Mrs. Davis had sent him baby clothes too.

Jeff Davis was no friend of Montgomery's (neither man was flush with friends), but their wives were close. In 1859, when Montgomery all but gave the Davises his Silver Spring house for the summer, Jeff wrote his mother about Montgomery's generosity. "What guarantee he offered for keeping the peace with me I did not learn." Montgomery's own mother, Preston Blair's wife, thought better of Jeff than Montgomery did. Two years *after* the war, she would call Jefferson Davis one of the greatest men she ever knew. One of the greatest who ever lived.

From its floor-to-ceiling windows, President Lincoln's commodious office on the second floor of the White House overlooked the stable and out-buildings that cluttered its back lawn, the unfinished stub of the Washington Monument, and the enemy state of Virginia, subdued as far as the eye could see. His friend Noah Brooks says the room was "furnished with green stuff, hung around with maps and plans with a bad portrait of Jackson" presiding over the mantle. It comfortably accommodated the table where the president seated his Cabinet; his pigeonhole desk, pushed up against a door; and assorted Victorian furniture, oversized and overstuffed. An American eagle hearth rug lay before the elaborate fireplace.

Crudely rendered or not, Andy Jackson's craggy face glaring down on Abraham Lincoln's must have warmed the scheming heart of Francis Preston Blair. They met beneath Old Hickory's gaze on Thursday, December 22, as Blair had told Greeley they would. By way of introduction to his embryonic plan, the Old Gentleman reminded Lincoln of his friendship with Jefferson Davis. "At the proper time, I might do something towards peace." Lincoln stopped him before he got started. "Come to me after Savannah falls." Blair surely grasped the point. When Sherman took Savannah and was ready to march on Richmond, peace and a pledge of amnesty might look better than war and the noose to most of the men who ruled there, and the men who ran the US Congress might see less weakness in it.

That very day, Sherman sent Lincoln a message that took two days to reach him. "I beg to present you, as a Christmas gift, the city of Savannah, with 150 heavy guns and plenty of ammunition, and also about 25,000 bales of cotton."

In a captured Savannah mansion, Sherman made his plans to burn his way up through the state that had started it all. He sent a wire to the War Department on December 24. His army was bent on "vengeance upon South Carolina," he said. "I almost tremble at her fate, but feel that she deserves all that seems in store for her." With Charleston's rail lines cut, the city was "dead and unimportant." Sherman would leave the Charlestonians to their misery and keep moving north, the Rebels having shifted half of their available forces to her defense and the other half to Augusta's, leaving Sherman an open path between them.

After dark that Christmas Eve, the unseated Senator Orville Hickman Browning came to Lincoln about getting their friend James Singleton through to Richmond to buy cotton. Browning had invested in the venture. Knowing that Singleton would be seeing influential men in the Rebel capital, Lincoln described to Browning his letter "To Whom It May Concern" in the Niagara Falls fiasco just as Singleton had. Its meaning had been misconstrued, he said. He had never intended to demand abolition as a condition of peace.

"The despondent Christmas of 1864" was a trial for the people of Richmond. Worried parents sang carols with their children and listened for the rumble of cannon borne in on the southern wind. When Varina Davis was told that the Episcopalian orphanage for girls had been promised a festive Christmas and "one pretty prize for the most orderly girl," she marshaled thin resources. A confectioner pledged "the simpler kinds of candy." With less than lavish charity, the Davis children contributed eyeless dolls, three-legged horses, "monkeys with all the squeak gone." To reward the model orphan, one of the household slaves suggested a dollhouse, and built one. Varina and her mother and friends made furniture of pasteboard and twigs.

The Army of Northern Virginia was making do as well. On Lee's orders, the War Department clerks drew lots to determine which half of them would go to the front. Secretary Seddon told one sickly loser to stay.

Another was sent to a medical board to be judged for his fitness to man a trench for a few days. "Great commotion" ensued, said their colleague John Jones, "and it is whispered that General Lee was governed in the matter by the family of the President, fearing a Christmas visit from the negro troops on this side of the river."

On a bleak Christmas Day, Richmond's finest families sat down to humble dinners and counted vacant chairs. The *Examiner*'s Edward Pollard observed how low they had fallen. Socialites "in old finery, in which the fashions of many years were mingled, were satisfied to make a display at Saint Paul's about equal to the holiday wardrobes of the Negroes at the African Church." On Christmas Day, Judge Campbell's friend and subordinate Robert Kean bemoaned the disasters that had "filled the land with gloom." Lee's army had no meat; "not a pound remained in Richmond." The War Department was "totally broken down," and Congress seemed alarmed. "The truth is we are prostrated in all our energies and resources." Lee left word for the president that a barrel of precious sweet potatoes, a Christmas gift for the Davises, had been sent to him instead. The error had gone undetected until the general took a few for himself and sent the rest to his hungry men.

On a festive Christmas morning, the people of Washington City woke up to the squeals of their children and the boom of celebratory cannon. The news had arrived that Sherman had emerged from the ruined heart of Georgia and finished his march to the sea. Lincoln sent him a wire. "Many, many thanks for your Christmas gift, the capture of Savannah." The president confessed he had been "anxious, if not fearful" about the wisdom of Sherman's march through Georgia, supplied by whatever he could rip from her people, out of contact for over a month, and now the general had proved himself right. "But what next? I suppose it will be safer if I leave Gen. Grant and yourself to decide."

Sherman moved north the next day. His bummers' rape of Georgia had been a mere rehearsal for what they would do to South Carolina. "We marched with thousands of columns of smoke marking the line of each corps," a division commander said. "The sights, at times, as seen from elevated grounds, were often terribly sublime," despite painful thoughts of "the distressed and frightened condition of the old men and women and children left behind" in midwinter. Many years after the war, Sherman would concede that the Georgians in his path "bore their afflictions with some manliness," but in South Carolina, "the people whined like curs."

⸻

Congressman Samuel S. Cox, also known as Sunset Cox, was a dapper Ohio War Democrat and a scourge of the Lincoln administration. His lush Victorian rhetoric was excessive even for its day. A florid ode on a setting sun had earned him his sardonic nickname. To mix zoological metaphors, Sunset Cox was no Copperhead but had lately become a lame duck. He had lost his seat in November after accusing the Republicans of a "miscegenation plot" to solve the race issue through "interbreeding." It was too much even for southern Ohio.

Before he left office, Cox hoped to do his country a final service by accomplishing nothing less than ending the Civil War. Sometime during the holidays, having forgotten or forgiven the miscegenation plot, he enlisted a fellow Democrat, Congressman John T. Stuart, to go with him to see Lincoln and urge him to ask Richmond what terms it might accept. Cox did not pick his companion at random. Stuart represented Springfield, Illinois, and had been the president's law partner.

Lincoln listened courteously and began to work a deal. He was willing to consider reaching out for a peaceful reunion, he said, but he wanted some Democrats on his side on the Constitutional amendment banning slavery. Cox had been listening too. The election had made it clear that human bondage was out of favor. More than a few defeated Democrats who had voted against abolition in June were thinking again in December. A few had decided to leave the public stage on the right side of history. Others hoped to return in 1867 and could read the political winds. Cox promised to help garner votes for the abolition amendment if Lincoln made a sincere attempt at peace. If it failed, he said, many mainstream Democrats would turn their backs on the South. Slavery would be banned with Cox's vote and theirs, and the war would be pursued with bipartisan vigor. Lincoln took it in.

In a separate meeting with Seward, the governor told Cox he was putting the horse before the cart. A Constitutional amendment was needed *before* peace talks were broached. Nothing could help bring peace like abolition. With slavery gone, the cause of disunion would be gone as well. Cox came away convinced that Seward and the president "considered this amendment worth an army. Whether they were right or not, the amendment was not pressed until just before the negotiations at Hampton Roads."

—————

On December 27, the Confederate State Department sent a letter to John Slidell, Richmond's man in Paris. When it surfaced after the war, Lincoln's aides John Nicolay and John Hay called it a cry of despair. The South was fighting France's battles against the United States, it said, and England's too. Their failure to pitch in made it only fair for the South to seek terms. If London and Paris would recognize the Richmond government "under any conditions" (an allusion to emancipation, if not some form of subordination of the Confederacy's very sovereignty), let them say so now. Slidell quickly learned that Europe was not interested.

That afternoon, "some black-hearted artillery man" on the Petersburg siege line dropped a pair of spherical case shells on some blue-coated pickets heading back to the lines of the 35th Massachusetts Infantry. Dozens of lethal balls burst over their Yankee heads. Corporal Charles W. Gilman, "an excellent man," was killed on the spot. Henry Lenkorf died in a field hospital. Gilman was the luckier of the two. In fairness, their regimental historian would later say, the sportsmanship was arguable. The incident was reviewed on the picket line and "loudly condemned on both sides as a breach of the tacit agreement not to fire during the day," but these were pickets talking, and "the author of the deed would probably reply that the understanding had reference only to the pickets, and not to the artillery and mortars, which opened whenever they saw game worth the powder."

CHAPTER EIGHT

I Do Not Think I Would Get Back

On December 28, Savannah having fallen, Preston Blair came back to Lincoln and told him he had an idea that he thought could lead to peace, and he wanted to take it to Richmond. Lincoln cut him off, as he had the first time. "If you choose to go, I will not stop you," his collaborator said, but the President of the United States did not want to know what he would say or do when he got there. "You will have no authority to speak for me in any way whatsoever." The president went to his pigeonhole desk, scribbled on a card no bigger than a laundry ticket, and handed it to his guest: "Allow the bearer, F. P. Blair, Sr., to pass our lines, go South, and return. December 28, 1864. A. Lincoln." It was the bearer's only credential. Whatever F. P. Blair Sr. might say or do in the South would not be attributable to A. Lincoln. The president expected little if any result from the old man's trip, but the Sage of Silver Spring would surely bring to Richmond a thicker Kentucky accent than he left with, and return with what Lincoln coveted: a canny expert's read on the mood in the Rebel capital.

In the meantime, Lincoln kept it to himself. He may have informed Seward, but the rest of the Cabinet was not told. If Blair confided in anyone but his fellow Blairs, no record of it survives; but he claimed a few months later that the object of his trip, though conceived and undertaken on his own, was not without some "indefinite understanding with friends in power in Washington," an allusion that surely included the most powerful friend of all.

Whoever may have been in on it, it was too late for Private George Deutzer of the 48th Pennsylvania Volunteers. He lost his life that night to a shell lobbed into Fort Hell.

In his element on a mission of intrigue, the Old Gentleman must have crossed back over Pennsylvania Avenue with a spring in his step. He had been suffering from a toothache and a general sort of weakness, but the pass in his pocket revived him and dulled his pain. The house was full of holiday guests as his fretting wife and daughter packed cold Christmas leftovers for the two-day trip to Richmond, no easy thing in winter for a feeble old man with a bad tooth. He would steam down Chesapeake Bay to Fort Monroe—the massive stone-built citadel at Hampton Roads, Virginia, that had never left federal control—then on to Grant's headquarters at City Point, then up the James River on the Union flag-of-truce boat, then overland by coach three miles north to Richmond through the enemy fortifications. The Blairs had struck a bargain. Their patriarch would go to the enemy capital, but he would not go alone. His black servant Henry would go with him. Montgomery would come along as far as City Point.

They embarked the next morning on the paddle wheeler *Baltimore*, Preston and Montgomery in comfortable quarters, Henry and the baggage elsewhere. The trip down Chesapeake Bay took a day. Overnighting at Fort Monroe, they steamed past Jamestown in the morning. Several hours up the twisting river, nine miles east of the siege line, high on a steep plateau, City Point came into view. Next to nothing had been here six months ago. Now it was a military metropolis, its waterfront choked with vessels of every description, including a steam-driven fleet of paddle wheelers hauling generals, politicians, and war profiteers to Washington City and back. Steep wooden stairs ran up the bluffs to the army's nerve center, where tens of thousands of men assembled the tools of war in some three hundred buildings of every size and utility, all of it under the wing of Ulysses S. Grant.

It was hard not to like Grant, impossible not to respect him. Stanton's Assistant Secretary of War Charles Dana, a sharp-eyed newspaperman fresh from Horace Greeley's *Tribune*, thought Grant was the most modest, honest, fearless man he ever knew. "Not a great man, except morally; not an original or brilliant man, but sincere, thoughtful, deep," fond of a good joke, "ready to sit up with you all night, talking in the cool breeze in front of his tent." Possessed of a certain wit, Grant had once said that he only knew two songs. One was "Yankee Doodle" and the other wasn't. A superb horseman, he was fit and athletic but smaller than most of his men, with sloping shoulders, brown hair and beard, and "a foxy tinge to his moustache." Bereft of a warrior lineage, the general was a tanner's son, born in a two-room house, raised in rural Ohio. The most powerful man in the army at the age of forty-two, he was unselfconsciously plain. "He talks bad grammar," an admirer said, "but talks it naturally, as much as to say, 'I was so brought up, and if I try fine phrases I shall only appear silly.'"

For all of his simplicity, Grant was a presence close up. His square-cut features seemed "carved from mahogany," set off with blue-gray eyes, lion's eyes, Dana called them, that could stare down the devil or shine with pure benevolence. An aide said no coarse language was uttered in his presence and none "passed his lips, and if by some rare chance a story a little broad was told before him, he blushed like a girl." Unfailingly courteous to men of all ranks and women of all stations, there was "no noise or clash or clangor in the man." There was no need for any. When Ulysses S. Grant talked, people listened.

Now he welcomed the Blairs to City Point. Preston's younger son, Frank, serving further south with Sherman, was one of Grant's favorite generals. The Blairs who stood before him needed no introduction. They were awed by the might laid before them, impressed by Grant and his officers and their talk of catching Hood. The odds are more than good that Preston charmed the general as he charmed almost everyone else; Montgomery, not so much. Like the Blairs, Grant was a former Democrat, and had lived in St. Louis, Montgomery's home ground, quite enough for Preston to work with. When the pleasantries were done, the Old Gentleman handed Grant two sealed letters addressed to Jefferson Davis. The general had them sent up the James immediately on the Union flag-of-truce boat, *City of New York*. Both letters asked for leave to come to Richmond, and both gave a reason, one true, one false.

The first letter said that Blair was in search of documents taken by "some persons who had access to my House" when General Early's army were in possession of it (a polite way to put it), and he wished to come to Richmond to look for them. The second letter said that the first would answer any bureaucrats' questions about his visit. The truth he would share with Davis alone. He had come to explain his views on the state of "our country," to help repair the ruin that the war had brought on "the nation" and, rather cryptically, to "promote the welfare of other nations that have suffered from it." He would bring no official message, merely his government's leave to make his own suggestions. Nor would he divulge them to anyone in Washington unless Davis thought something might come of them. Their conversation would be unbalanced. "I will confidentially unbosom my heart frankly and without reserve. You will on your part, of course, hold in reserve all that is not proper to be said to one coming as I do merely as a private citizen, and addressing one clothed with the highest responsibilities." Both letters reached Davis that day.*

On the following day, a blustery New Year's Eve, Davis had his cheerless Secretary of War James Seddon send Blair a pass through the lines with a cover note restricting him "to the purposes indicated in his letter of application." Whether Davis showed Seddon both letters or only the pretext is unclear, but word got around the War Department that Blair was coming, on his honor to confine himself to a search for missing papers.

Late on New Year's Day, Seddon's letter came to Union forces "below Chaffin's Bluff," to which it had mistakenly been sent. The letter reached Grant on January 2, but Preston had left for home with Montgomery and Henry, thinking himself rebuffed. Despite his disappointment, Preston had enjoyed a "very pleasant trip," his daughter Lizzie said, "seeing and hearing much that was of great interest to him," and returned "in the finest spirits possible," hoping Davis might yet see him. The same could not be said of Davis's Secretary of War. When the War Department clerk

---

* Davis's memoirs would later mischaracterize them. He had let Blair come to Richmond to retrieve "personal objects," he said, leaving the dishonorable circumstances of their loss unmentioned, as well as his knowledge that Blair was on a peace mission when he came. An impression was left that the old man had sprung it on him.

John Jones came to work that day, Seddon "had his head between his knees before the fire." It was not an inspiring sight. "Affairs are gloomy enough," Jones thought. "The question is how Richmond and Virginia shall be saved. General Lee is despondent."

—◆—

Inevitably, rumors of Blair's journey were afoot in Washington City, but most of Lincoln's circle pleaded innocence with a clear conscience. The *Times* reported that if Blair had gone to Richmond, "he has done so without the knowledge of high officials here." The highest official was preserving his ignorance. As a Cabinet meeting broke up, Gideon Welles noticed "Old Mr. Blair" sitting in an adjoining room. His appointment with the president was canceled.

Blair had already briefed Horace Greeley, who came down from Manhattan for the occasion. Not without reason, the old man shared a suspicion that Stanton, the fiercest of all hawks, had sabotaged his mission, out of enmity for the Blairs, for peace negotiations, or both. In 1862, when Secretary of War Stanton was being vetted for the Cabinet, Montgomery had described him to Lincoln as an able lawyer, faint praise for a prospective Secretary of War, especially with the addendum that Stanton was corrupt. Whether Stanton got wind of this particular slander or not, others had come to his attention.

On Wednesday, January 4, Greeley's *Tribune* ran a special dispatch from Washington, the accuracy of which "we have no doubt." Blair's mission had died at City Point, it said, because the Secretary of War had told General Grant he did not approve of it, which the *Tribune* much regretted. "We do not know, and at no time have felt confident, that the rebels are yet prepared to agree to any terms of pacification that our Government either would or should deem acceptable; but we can imagine no possible harm that could result from ascertaining precisely what they are ready to do." The "recognized object of war, at least among civilized and Christian nations, is an honorable and satisfactory peace."

By the time the story ran, Grant had forwarded Seddon's letter to Blair, predicting to a colleague that "Mr. B may be looked for back again by Friday next." Greeley duly ate crow in the *Tribune*.

Embarassed though he may have been by the manner in which it reached him, Blair had his pass to Richmond and was eager to put it to use. He made another appointment with Lincoln. The White House canceled it too. The Old Gentleman inferred that the president wanted to hear no more about his amateur diplomacy but merely to see him launch it, a perfectly fair deduction. Lizzie wrote to her husband, Phil. "Father sets out tomorrow. If he had been more patient & [in] less of a hurry to get back home he would have been spared this double trip."

The next day, Gustavus Vasa Fox, Gideon Welles's Assistant Secretary of the Navy, married to a sister of Montgomery's wife, sent a wire to Grant. Mr. Blair would sail for Richmond on Saturday morning, expected off City Point around noon. "As he goes by consent of the President, at the request of Mr. Davis, I ask for Mr. Blair that you will make arrangements to get him through comfortably as early as practicable, and as secretly." Fox had arranged to send the old man to Grant on a naval vessel to avoid the public exposure that a passenger ship would bring. With the navy at his service, there was no need for Montgomery to come.

Other arrangements were made that day for a passage through the Rebel lines. A Union brevet major took a flag of truce to the enemy and delivered the remains of a captain of the 40th Virginia to General Lee's designee. Approached by the young man's mother, Lee had sent a personal request to Grant to return him to his family. On Grant's particular orders, "a diligent search" had found him.

Blair's preparations for his second trip to Richmond were unknown to the world at large, but the first had inspired talk of peace, and the weight of opinion was negative. On January 5, Henry Raymond's *New York Times* misinformed its readers that Grant had put a stop to Blair's "irresponsible errand." Ready as Raymond had been to sacrifice abolition last summer, he now declared—with Atlanta in ashes, Lee under siege, and Lincoln reelected—that the North would not barter away the "glorious results" of the sacrifices it had made to win them. No mission to the Southern people could dispel their delusion that the North would subject and degrade them if they gave up their cause. The Rebel leaders to whom the missionaries would be sent knew otherwise, and would not let their people be evangelized. "Our armies are the only effective propagators of the truth."

On the subject of truth and its propagators, the Jacobin Thaddeus Stevens and the Democrat Sunset Cox went head to head in the House that day as a month of debate began on the Constitutional amendment banning slavery. The galleries were filled with abolitionists, but the talk on the street was of peace, and peace trumped abolition in the minds of many Democrats. There was nothing but unconditional surrender in the mind of Thaddeus Stevens. Understating the case, a contemporary said the look of the man was "not sympathetic," peering maliciously at the world over a cruel mouth and chin as he limped across the floor with a foot deformed at birth, belittling overmatched Democrats in a voice "devoid of music." Richard III in a Prince Albert suit. Noah Brooks called him "the ablest man in congressional life." A Southern counterpart called him "this wicked man, whose terrible wretchedness gapes frighteningly at him from the hopeless grave upon whose brink he stands . . . this demon who will soon leave an immortality of hate and infirmity for an eternity of unutterable woe . . . this malicious, pitiless, pauseless enemy of an entire nation . . . this viperous, heartless, adulterous beast. . . . This living sepulcher of all hideous things, upon whose body in his mother's womb was fixed hell's seal of deformity." Things of that nature.

For the historic first day of debate on the Thirteenth Amendment, Horace Greeley and Montgomery Blair were admitted to the floor as guests. If Thaddeus Stevens spoke in his usual style, he linked his hands loosely before him, dropping sentences "as though each one weighed a ton." He praised Lincoln's annual message as the best in sixty years. It was "easy to see what perplexities surrounded him" in crafting it (perplexities in which Stevens did not include himself). The president's refusal to beg "parricides and rebels" for peace and reconciliation embraced the public will. So "hateful to the people was the cowardly suggestion that we should lay down our arms" to traitors that even patriotic Democrats (i.e., Sunset Cox) had been beaten in November, poisoned by their Copperhead infestation. The president had rebuffed some of "his own leading friends" (i.e., Greeley and the Blairs), who beseeched him to "humble the nation before defiant traitors and ask a compromise." Instead he "took counsel of his own wiser judgment, stood firmly erect, and saved the nation from disgrace."

Taking none of this lying down, Sunset Cox stood up, drawing laughter as he spoke. Horace Greeley would soon vote for President Lincoln in the Electoral College, the Ohioan told the House, and here he was among them "in reference to a *projet* of peace." Cox had the clerk read the *Tribune*'s praise for Blair's mission. Would the gentleman from Pennsylvania "reproach the leading editor of his own party for holding precisely the same opinions entertained by members upon this side?" Why did the gentleman not "denounce that editor who is now conferring with his brother Republicans about peace?" Why did he not have the rules of the House read, "and drive him as an interloper from this Chamber?" Why did the gentleman confer with Mr. Blair, "the suppositious ambassador, who even now as I speak, is also present in the Chamber?"

Before the House acted on the gentleman's wish, Cox said, turning somber now, "before he asks us to change the organic law of this land for seventy years, I beseech him that he will at least try to ascertain, formally or informally," whether the insurgents might agree to rejoin the Union. Jefferson Davis might demand independence, "but I say, in the language of this able, distinguished, and patriotic editor, let us at least 'take some means to ascertain that fact.' " If Davis proved intransigent, it would "inspire a more healthful and united sentiment among the people"; but he might accept reunion. And what if he asked for something in return? The South would never rejoin a country in which slavery was a crime. So many sacrifices had been made in this war, would the gentleman from Pennsylvania not make one now? "Give up his doctrine of negro equality? Give up his idea of breaking down State institutions by Federal law?"

Stevens replied indignantly. "The gentleman will allow me to say that I never held to that doctrine of negro equality."

"Then I understand the gentleman from Pennsylvania not to hold that all men are created equal?"

"Yes, sir, but not equality in all things, simply before the laws, nothing else."

"I ask the gentleman to give up his idea of equality of the black and white races before the law."

"I won't do it," Stevens said, drawing laughter of his own.

A few minutes later, Sunset Cox had another idea. An alternative might be found to sending Montgomery Blair "and his venerable father to Richmond. Perhaps it would be best to send the distinguished gentleman from Pennsylvania."

"Oh, no," Stevens said, rocking the House with hilarity. "I do not think I would get back."

CHAPTER NINE

As Once a Friend and Still, I Hope, Not an Enemy

In the winter of 1848, seventeen years before the House of Representatives held its roll call vote on slavery, Daniel Webster, Henry Clay, John C. Calhoun, and other great men whose celebrity would fade with time were holding the nation in thrall in the Senate. With the notable exception of John Quincy Adams, less illustrious names were encountered in the House, names like Asa W. H. Clapp, John H. Lumpkin, and Abraham Lincoln. On February 2, 1848, the lightly regarded newcomer from Illinois wrote home to his law partner from his desk on the House floor. "I just take up my pen to say that Mr. Stephens of Georgia, a little slim, pale-faced, consumptive man with a voice like Logan's, has just concluded the best speech of an hour's length I ever heard. My old, withered, dry eyes are full of tears yet." Lincoln's eyes were thirty-eight years old, and Alexander Hamilton Stephens, three years his junior, had just condemned the Mexican War as a naked bid for conquest unworthy of the American people. It was Lincoln's view precisely. Standing together literally and figuratively in the unpopular antiwar movement, the feisty little Georgian and the six-foot-four-inch rail-splitter made a memorable pair.

When the war ended gloriously if not nobly, with several new states in the bag, Lincoln and Stephens cofounded the Young Indians, a club of congressional Whigs promoting the presidential candidacy of General Zachary Taylor, whose limited qualifications consisted of a knack for killing Mexicans, an ignorant silence on the issues of the day, and a consequent ability to unite Whigs. Lincoln and Stephens liked Mexican War heroes better than Democrats. Their friendship was cut short in 1849, when Lincoln's congressional career ended after a single undistinguished term, and revived in 1865 when they tried once again to end a war, this time with Lincoln in the White House and Stephens as Vice President of the Confederate States of America.

Alec Stephens's early life was much like Lincoln's. Born poor in rural Georgia, he was put behind a plow as soon as he could handle one, lost his mother as a child, and was left with a father "never much given to mirth." When Alec was fourteen, his father and stepmother died of fever in the same week. Like a scene from a Victorian novel, his luck took a near-miraculous turn when a wealthy benefactor got him admitted to Franklin College, Judge Campbell's alma mater, and paid for it. Like Campbell, Stephens graduated first in his class and learned the law by reading it.

In physique he was less fortunate. To put the matter plainly, Alec Stephens was an odd-looking man. He was five-foot-seven, just a little under average for the day, but never weighed as much as a hundred pounds. Fondly or otherwise, many Georgians called him Little Alec. To one appalled observer he resembled "a boyish invalid escaped from some hospital." Another was put in mind of "a refugee from a grave-yard," and his health was as poor as it looked. His chronic disabilities alone included rheumatoid arthritis, a pinched nerve, colitis, hives, migraine headaches, aching teeth, bladder stones, and cervical disk disease. Together they afflicted his head, neck, back, hands, arms, legs, and innards almost constantly, compelled him to walk with a cane, and often left him bedridden for days. An abscessed liver and several bouts of pneumonia nearly killed him one by one. A friend said he "never looked as if he had two weeks' purchase on life." The tortures he endured to treat his ailments rivaled them: drawing fluids with suction cups from incisions cut in his side, blistering his chest, imbibing extract of liverwort. Unremarkably, he dosed himself with whiskey. He took it by the spoonful but may have been an alcoholic, though he never would have known it, let alone admitted it.

His voice matched his childlike frame. An admirer called it "shrill but musical" and "singularly pleasing." A crueler reviewer called it a squeak, but insisted that his listeners would "cease to be annoyed when energized by his ideas." Horace Greeley, who rarely shared his views, remarked before the war that "you forget you are listening to the most eloquent man in Washington, and only feel that he is right." The Senate's great men found time to cross the Rotunda to hear him speak. His memoir's declaration that he was friendly with Lincoln "anterior to the war" is a typical ornamentation, but such was the style of the day. Still and all, Little Alec's elocution was more decorative than most, even in everyday speech.

Though his feeble, even freakish appearance could hardly be called an advantage ("Oh what I have suffered from a look!"), it gave him the curious power of an animated corpse, an image often invoked. The *Charleston Courier's* correspondent watched him speak on the floor of the House, "a shrunken and spectral figure" with a quality that the camera could not see. If Rembrandt could only paint him, the "pallor of the grave should sit upon his face," conveying "an expression of ghostly power," with flashing black eyes and parchment skin. A Northerner was impressed by a speech he gave in Pennsylvania and astonished to see it delivered by a well-preserved mummy.

Despite his afflictions, he appreciated humor. "Coffee is one of three things of which I have long considered myself a judge," he said. "The other two are lizards and watches." Books and ideas were his passion, the weightier the better. The flesh held little interest. He enjoyed a good cigar and a generous slice of pie but professed a rank disgust for the very existence of sexuality. He never married or had a requited love, and probably died a virgin.

Not surprisingly, he was a lonely, self-pitying man. "Weak and sickly I was sent into the world with a constitution barely able to sustain the vital functions. The torture of body is severe. I have my share of that; most of the maladies that flesh is heir to. But all these are slight when compared with the pangs of an offended and wounded spirit. The heart alone knoweth its own sorrow. I have borne it these many years. I have borne it all my life." A student of Shakespeare, he was bitter enough to describe himself as "a malformed, ill-shaped, half-finished thing," taking comfort in his rectitude. As a newly minted congressman, he regarded his colleagues as the "grandest set of blockheads" who ever failed to grasp an idea. Returning to Washington City in 1844, he wrote to his beloved half brother, Linton, with something less than uncontained joy. "I am once more in this great sewer of political filth."

A "proud, independent, unyielding spirit" was his model of a man, and for this Alec Stephens was a paradigm, ready to sacrifice everything to the unshakable conviction that he was right. To step back on a matter of principle for the sake of eventual progress, as Seward would crisply do, was unthinkable for him.

In 1848 he was told that a judge named Cone had called him a traitor to the South for killing a popular bill, abetted by Northern votes. When they met at a political barbecue, Cone denied that he had said it. Stephens let him know that he would have slapped him if he had. Cone chose to take it as a joke, but the story spread, and the judge grew tired of being asked if he would need help if Little Alec slapped him. They ran into each other in Atlanta on the piazza of Thompson's Hotel. Judge Cone was as big as two Little Alecs. His Honor had a knife; Stephens had his cane. Cone called him "a miserable little traitor" or "a damned puppy." Perhaps both. Stephens struck him with his walking stick. Cone counterattacked with his knife, severed a spurting artery, and threw his tiny victim on his back. With one hand on Stephens's forehead and his knife in the other, the judge demanded a retraction, "or I'll cut your damned throat!"

"No! Never! Cut!"

When the blade came down, Stephens caught it in his hand. Cone twisted the knife until bystanders pulled him away. Apart from the mangled hand, Stephens suffered six different wounds. The severed artery alone would have bled him out had an army surgeon not happened by. Cone was charged with attempted murder. Stephens refused to prosecute. His embarrassed assailant paid a fine. Stephens pronounced forgiveness. The whole thing burnished his résumé.

He never fought a duel, but not for lack of trying. He challenged three men, and none of them took him up on it. Little Alec was not to be trifled with.

The antebellum House in which he served eight terms held no more devoted believer than Alexander Stephens in the supremacy of states' rights, a small federal government, and a moral foundation for "African slavery." Resisting these things in every particular, Congressman John Quincy Adams, the irascible former president, admired the little Georgian, took an avuncular interest in him, and wrote him a sweet poem about their intersectional friendship as a model for their peers. It was found among Stephens's papers when he died.

Little Alec made his name in Congress as a North-South peacemaker, rose to national prominence helping Henry Clay save the Union with the Compromise of 1850, and retired in 1859, fed up with the swelling bile. As Stephens would later recall, his prediction of civil war was greeted with concern that "the weakness of my body was extending to my head." When Lincoln was elected president, his old friend Alec Stephens addressed the Georgia legislature and decried the result as "a great public calamity," but reminded his compatriots that Congress and the Supreme Court were still under Southern control, leaving Lincoln and those fanatics in New England equipped to do little harm. To abandon "our common country" for the loss of a fair election "would put us in the wrong." He sat down "to great applause," and Georgia soon left the Union.

Lincoln read his speech, wrote him from Illinois "as once a friend, and still, I hope, not an enemy," and asked for his help in averting civil war. Stephens replied that he was surely no enemy, but nothing on earth could "save us from the madness," or so, he feared, it seemed.

After his fellow Georgians chose him to help pick an interim Confederate government, he was urged to seek the presidency and respectfully declined. He had not been part of "the movement," he said, but agreed to accept a unanimous draft. The burden passed when Davis was chosen instead. His selection as vice president, a sop to his fellow moderates, was a distinction he neither sought nor relished. Mary Chesnut attended a reception where he spread no cheer on the subject of the Confederacy's prospects. "I called him half-hearted and accused him of looking back." On New Year's Day, 1864, Mrs. Chesnut contributed to her diary a list of leading Southerners who "never believed in this thing. Stephens, the Vice-President, is Number One."

As Little Alec saw it, his acceptance of secession was a tragic necessity but not a struggle of conscience. He opposed it "with all my power," but came out of the Union unreservedly with Georgia, for his loyalty was to her. For him, *any* union of the states, federal, Confederate, or otherwise, was a union of "separate Political Societies," dependent on consent. Indeed, the Southern people owed no allegiance to the Confederacy at all, its vice president said; only to their states. To maintain a legitimate union by force was preposterous. "Superior power may compel a union of some sort; but it would not be the Union of the old Constitution nor of our new; it would be that sort of union that results from despotism."

As early as the capture of New Orleans, a year into the war, Stephens told a friend that the South was ruined irreparably, and he should never have taken his office. "I don't know how I came to make the mistake, but I hoped it would do good in the way of preserving harmony." Harmony was not its result. If anything was a match for Alec Stephens's rigidity it was Jefferson Davis's own, and their differences could hardly have been sharper. Before the war, Davis called Stephens "the little pale star from Georgia," mocking his moderation. Stephens would insist that he never bore Davis ill will, but was pleased to adjudge him an imbecile, and soon started calling him a despot. By April of 1864, Stephens would tell a friend that Davis was bent on absolute power, impeded by a defective character—"weak and vacillating, timid, petulant, peevish, obstinate, but not firm . . ." In contrast to Stephens's obsession with states' rights and small government, Davis was a nationalist, by habit and necessity. After a honeymoon ruined by Stephens's resistance to his leadership, he ignored his vice president in the time-honored American tradition, gave him nothing to do, told him little more, and ignored his views except to mock them in private and not infrequently in public. Their relationship declined from chilly to nonexistent. They did not speak at all in 1862.

Stephens addressed the Georgia legislature in 1864, attacking the draft and arrests of war resistors without trial, deploring the abdication of legislative powers to the Davis administration, of which he was second in command. Neither war nor the fight for independence could justify tyranny, he said. Like its readers, the Confederate press was split on these things, and on Stephens's insubordinate handling of them. The *Southern Recorder* inquired whether the Northern war effort would not be impaired if the Vice President of the United States attacked the Lincoln administration in his home state of Maine.

Members of Congress, Stephens said, were "children in politics and statesmanship," whom he schooled against Davis unabashedly. At one point, Davis offered to resign if Stephens would, but refused to hand the Confederacy to a man who would surrender it at once to Grant. Giving up on it all, Stephens spent most of the war sulking in Georgia, urging its legislature to pressure Davis and Congress alike, visiting Richmond only briefly to harass them at close quarters.

Despite his ferocity when crossed, a friend called Little Alec "as simple and genial in his manners as a child." Made rich by investments in land, he paid for the educations of scores of poor young men. "As I had been assisted when in need," he said, "so I ever afterward assisted those in like circumstances, as far as I could." His Crawfordville, Georgia, estate—called Liberty Hall—was graced with a house of the second or third tier. Eliza, his housekeeper, had instructions to feed all uninvited visitors who came to its door, which suffered no shortage of invitees. Liberty Hall's mealtimes were synchronized with the train schedule. Eliza's husband, Harry, oversaw the plantation in Stephens's absence. A newspaperman interviewed him about its owner, "Mars Alec," Harry called him ("Master Alec" in Harry's dialect). "He is kind to folks that nobody else will be kind to," Harry said. "Mars Alec is kinder to dogs than mos' folks is to folks." The folks to whom Mars Alec was said to be kind included Harry, Eliza, their five little children, and the other human beings enslaved at Liberty Hall.

"God knows my views on slavery never rose from any disposition to lord it over any human being," Stephens said, "or to see anybody else so lord it. In my whole intercourse with the black race, those by our laws recognized as my slaves [an uncomfortable circumlocution] and all others, I sought to be governed by the Golden Rule. I never owned one that I would have held a day without his or her free will and consent." By 1845 he owned ten. He eventually accumulated about 5,000 acres and the slaves who worked them.

Harry nursed him through his illnesses and managed the other slaves, the only overseer Stephens had. The field hands Stephens treated like laboring wards. He housed, fed, and clothed them comfortably; had them taught to read and write, defying the laws against it; never punished them physically; never sold them; bought relatives he didn't need; cared for them in sickness and old age. Harry and Eliza's children, Ellen, Fanny, Dora, Tim, and Quinn, did odd jobs and played more often than they worked. After one of his slaves "got in trouble with a white woman," another slave said, Stephens gave him money and told him to go away.

When Harry had asked his leave to marry Eliza, Stephens had written from Washington to his brother, mixing kindness with condescension. "Say to him I have no objection. And tell Eliza to go to Solomon & Henry's and get a wedding dress, including a fine pair of shoes, etc., and to have a decent wedding of it. Let them cook a supper and have such of their friends as they wish. Tell them to get some 'parson man' and be married like Christian folks. Let the wedding come off when you are at home so that you can keep good order among them. Buy a pig, and let them have a good supper." Like other gentle racists uneasy with the word, Stephens referred to his society's forced-labor system as "so-called" slavery, "which was with us, or should be, nothing but the proper subordination of the inferior African race to the superior white."

What came to be known as "The Cornerstone Speech" was the blunder of his career. He delivered it in Savannah a month after his inauguration as vice president. It alienated Europe, motivated the North, and energized the abolitionists. Jefferson and many of his elite contemporaries had thought that slavery was wrong, Stephens said, an evil to be eliminated, a premise based on equality of the races. "This was an error." The Confederacy's "cornerstone rests upon the great truth that the negro is not equal to the white man; that slavery, subordination to the superior race, is his natural and normal condition." Stephens cared nothing for the thought that a nation built on slavery would repel the civilized world, certain as he was that "if we are true to ourselves and the principles for which we contend, we are obliged to, and must triumph."

No less than he had before the war, Vice President Stephens aspired to the role of peacemaker. In June of 1863, with Lee's army full of hubris on its way to Pennsylvania, he sought Davis's permission to go to Hampton Roads and discuss a prisoner exchange at Fort Monroe. Treading on eggshells in a letter to his president, he mentioned a grander goal. "I am not without hope that <u>indirectly</u> I could now turn attention to a general adjustment upon such basis as might ultimately be acceptable to both parties and stop the further effusion of blood in a contest so irrational, unchristian, and so inconsistent with all recognized American principles." Davis let him go, and Stephens took a steamer to Fort Monroe. Lincoln wanted to see him. His Cabinet talked him out of it. Lee had been beaten at Gettysburg, Grant had taken Vicksburg, and the Yankees turned Stephens away, leaving him humiliated and Davis gloating.

In 1864 he was talking peace again. If the North would simply recognize the sovereignty of the states, Stephens believed, the war would stop immediately and "the great law of nature" would determine their proper union, in the old one or a new. "But you might as well sing psalms to a dead horse, I fear, as to preach such doctrines to Mr. Lincoln, and those who control that government, at this time."

In September 1864, Sherman sent a message inviting Stephens to captured Atlanta to negotiate a peace plan. Stephens replied that peace commended itself "to every well-wisher of his country." He would sacrifice anything short of honor to achieve it, but he had no power to negotiate it, and nor, it seemed to him, did Sherman. If the general would say there was any chance for terms to which their respective governments might agree, he would devote himself "cheerfully and willingly" to restoring a just and honorable peace to "the country." He closed optimistically. "This does not seem to me to be at all impossible, if truth and reason should be permitted to have their full sway."

Sherman had no such authority.

PART II

We Are But One People

THE PEACE COMMISSION.
Flying to ABRAHAM's Bosom.

Harper's Weekly, February 18, 1865
REPRINTED COURTESY OF APPLEWOOD BOOKS, CARLISLE, MA

CHAPTER TEN

A Treachery Unworthy of Men of Honor

General Josiah Gorgas presided over the Southern armaments industry, having built it almost from scratch. A balding, bearded West Point graduate from Pennsylvania, one of a handful of Northern-born generals in gray, he had sided with his wife, an Alabama governor's daughter, when the officer corps broke up. On January 4, 1865, after passing a pleasant wedding anniversary over supper and cards at home, he confided to his diary how depressed Richmond was. "Still, gaiety continues among the young people, and there is much marriage and giving in marriage. We were last night at a ball at Judge Campbell's, where dancing was kept up until 4 thirty in the morning." The gaiety was surely enhanced by the judge's lovely daughter, whom a smitten young officer had admired at a recent wedding as "the striking girl in pink."

But her father was in no dancing mood. The hapless commissary general had confessed that day that he could no longer feed the army. It was plain to Judge Campbell that the adjutant and the inspector general were incompetent too, though everyone, in fairness, had been dealt a barren hand. Campbell shared his dismay with General Gorgas as the young people flirted and danced. Gorgas was shaken too. "Is the cause really hopeless? Is it to be abandoned and lost in this way?"

As Assistant Secretary of War, Campbell was preparing a report to Secretary Seddon on eight urgent needs that must be met immediately if the war could go on at all. Seddon told the judge that Davis had been advised to consult now and then with the leading men in Congress, his critics as well as his friends, and received the idea with a frigid stare. Campbell asked what plans the president had to meet the current emergency. Seddon said he had none.

In the Confederate House of Representatives, a motion was made to pay a courtesy call on the president. A roll call vote was required after dissidents shouted it down.

On December 3, Alec Stephens had returned to Richmond with a terrible cold and a bladder attack. He had been gone a year and a half, long enough to notice the city's decay. The *Examiner's* Edward Pollard called it "a time when all thoughtful persons walked with bent heads." On January 6, the vice president addressed the Senate in secret session. Independence could still be had, he said, but the government must reverse almost all of its policies. Stop drafting proud men, and deserters will return; keep an army in the field for a year or two more, anywhere at all (an implied exhortation to abandon Richmond), avoiding battle whenever possible, and the North will wear down, broken by expense and its people's pleas for peace, despite its overpowering strength. Congress should demand negotiations now, conditioned only on the sovereignty of the states and their right to choose their own alignments.

On January 7, the worried War Department clerk John Jones saw Judge Campbell gravely beckon his friend Senator Hunter into his office. There was talk of Davis and Stephens both resigning. With the cautious Hunter next in line as president pro tempore of the Senate, Lee would be in charge as a practical matter. In a letter from Georgia, Davis was told that Savannah was submitting meekly—that the spirit of resistance in the rest of the state was dissolving. The shock of Sherman's cruelty had paralyzed it. There is "every indication that many people are almost prepared to abandon the struggle and submit to the Yankee yoke, with the hope of saving their property." Some despondent Rebels thought Grant would be spared the trouble of taking Richmond. The Confederacy was melting from within.

On January 5, former senator Orville Hickman Browning went to the White House again, looking for a pass to Richmond for James Singleton, Lincoln's friendly enemy. Singleton's Southern trading expedition was about to be launched in partnership with Browning. A retired federal judge was a partner too, and a sitting senator from New York, all of them friends of Lincoln's. Grant was hotly opposed to *any* Southern trade, but Lincoln believed that its benefits, including the satisfaction of the army's need for cotton—for uniforms, tents, and bandages—outweighed its risks. He gave Singleton a pass to cross the lines "with ordinary baggage" and return "with Southern products." While he was down there, Lincoln said, he might find six hundred bales of cotton that Mrs. Lincoln's half sister had mislaid, ardent Rebel though she was.

Singleton, like Blair, had friends in high Southern places. He would later say that Lincoln authorized him to tell them that, if they accepted reunion, the Emancipation Proclamation would be left to the courts, and he had no power to push abolition further.

———

Preston Blair had committed his peace proposal to writing, "which was done & tied up nicely," his daughter Lizzie wrote her husband, Phil. He was full of his plans for a happy result, Lizzie said, though discretion prevented her from disclosing the particulars. Neither father nor daughter was sanguine about his chances, but Lizzie told Phil that he felt very well. She had never seen him work so hard or so happily.

On Friday, January 6, even before he left, the Richmond press had gotten wind of his plans. SOMETHING WICKED THIS WAY COMES was the *Examiner*'s delicious headline. "We would not be superstitious, but we seem to perceive in the air a taint of sulphitic odors of Washington." It would soon be plain "what particular piece of Yankee villainy and treachery lurks under the unofficial visit of Blair, Sr. and Blair, Jr. within our lines." Presumably they were spies. A pair of "Hebrew blockade-runners would be more welcome." In the light most favorable to him, old Blair was "an officious busybody in a state of second childhood." President Davis should be pleased to welcome peace commissioners to Richmond if they came to acknowledge its independence, but not to "entertain spies as the honored guests of the Confederacy." The *Whig* was of the same mind. To supplement their spying, the Blairs were sure to add the "cool impudence" of a proposition that the North would not subjugate the Southern people if they only pled contrition. It was "absolutely delightful." They "richly deserve hanging."

The *Examiner* and the *Whig* were always hard on Davis, but the *Sentinel* was his voice, and the *Sentinel* would reserve judgment until the Blairs had disclosed their errand. If they came on behalf of the Lincoln administration, to abandon its unjust war, nothing could be more welcome. If they came to spy and sow discord, they would "add fresh insult, and attempt a treachery unworthy of men of honor. We will stand on our guard and await developments."

In Washington, the debate continued in the House of Representatives on the amendment banning slavery, its critics positioning abolition as a threat to peace and reunion. As mayor of New York in 1861, Fernando Wood had proposed to lead her out of the Union and take her cotton trade with her. Now he was a Copperhead congressman, though Thaddeus Stevens considered him no statesman. "Nay, sir, he will not even rise to the dignity of a respectable demagogue." In a passionate speech to the House, Wood said abolition would make it impossible to restore the Union on the old order of things.

Sunset Cox was inclined to agree. "So long as there is a faint hope of a returning Union, I will not place obstacles in the path." If abolition could bring reunion, Cox would vote to embrace it. "But as it stands today, I believe that this amendment is an obstacle to the rehabilitation of the States." The key phrase here was *as it stands today*. In the wake of their recent meeting, Cox would wait and see whether Lincoln offered peace to Richmond.

On January 6, a hard rain fell on Blair House as its patriarch huddled past midnight with Horace Greeley and other unpaid consultants, their papers and persons splayed across the heirloom furniture, driving the women of the house upstairs. The old man left the next morning on the naval steamer *Don*, the Potomac flotilla's flagship, on a fifteen-hour trip to Hampton Roads and Fort Monroe, accompanied by his freed black servant Henry and the *Don*'s attentive officers, conscious of his status as a president's friend and an admiral's father-in-law.

Blair and Henry spent three days at City Point as arrangements were made to convey them to the Confederacy. If Blair had not confided his mission to Grant when he'd first come to City Point a week earlier, he did so now, leaving the general better informed than the president, and considerably more enthused. The old man shared with Grant what Lincoln had chosen not to hear—a startling secret plan to end the war, involving Mexico.

Mexico had been graced with seventy-five presidents in the forty-four years since the Spanish had been expelled in 1821, and Europe was not alone in casting greedy eyes on her silver, gold, and land and her apparent inability to defend them. The spoils of the Mexican War had only fed American ambitions, especially in the South, where planters looked to Mexico and saw warm, fertile ground for slavery. Northerners were looking too. Seward had a dream of absorbing and democratizing the whole continent, not excepting Alaska.

The emperor of France had more-aggressive dreams. After the populist Benito Juarez had installed a democratic government in Mexico City, Napoleon III defied the Monroe Doctrine while its proponents were at war with each other. In 1864, a French expeditionary force of 35,000 troops in red caps and trousers helped Juarez's enemies eject him from the capital to the northern part of the country, enthroning the Austrian archduke Maximillian as emperor of Mexico, Napoleon's obedient surrogate, supported by a few thousand Austrians. It was unwelcome news in the Army of the Potomac, where talk was often heard of attacking foreigners in Mexico after the war against Americans was won.

Like many of its veterans, Grant had always thought that the Mexican War was wrong, an aggression against a weaker country that had done his own no harm. It weighed on his conscience, and he spoke of making amends. When he mentioned to Lincoln and Stanton the thought of ousting the French, they seemed sympathetic but unwilling to act. When he brought it up with Seward, "One war at a time" was the governor's unexceptionable reply. Seward had not been working for years to deter a European intervention in America's civil war only to intervene in Mexico's. Grant did not disagree, but after the Rebels were beaten, he said, a veteran American army might present itself on the Rio Grande "with a view to enforcing respect for our opinions concerning the Monroe Doctrine." Seward wanted the French out too, he said, "but we don't want any war over it. We have certainly had enough of war."

——————

Word of Blair's peace mission was out in the North as well as in the South, and most of the press was bad. On January 10, induced by a driving rain that flooded their lairs with ice water, the pickets on the Petersburg siege line agreed to stack their arms and pace their miserable beats in open view of one another. Safe and warm in Manhattan, the editor of the *New York Post* was "sorry to see that so sensible a man" as Blair was making a trip to Richmond more likely to cause mischief than good. The North's best peacemakers were its warriors, and "the black-mouthed bulldogs by which they enforce their persuasions . . ."

On January 11, Blair and his servant Henry left City Point on the Union flag-of-truce boat and steamed eight miles up the James in clear and pleasant weather. In the heart of old Virginia, the *City of New York* passed Bermuda Hundred on the left, one of the earliest English settlements, and Shirley Plantation on the right. From the dock at Boulwares Landing, an escort in blue drove them up to Fort Harrison, lately captured from the Rebels, four miles short of Richmond. Darkness had fallen when they got there. For four chilly hours they waited to be cleared through the Rebel lines, attended by Captain Edward Parker Deacon of the 1st Massachusetts Cavalry, a wealthy Bostonian's son. Knowing who was coming and why, blue and gray pickets bantered in the dark with a warm joviality that lifted Blair's hopes. We can only guess what Henry was thinking, a freed black slave on his way to the Southern capital in the service of a Yankee.

Late that night, word came across from the Rebels that a pass had arrived. Captain Deacon entrusted the Old Gentleman to a captain from South Carolina. They all gave each other their hands, the Bostonian produced a bottle, and they drank to the South Carolinian's health. As Blair would soon recall, goodwill was exhibited all around.

In the view of Alec Stephens, the sagacious Mr. Blair was the Republican "master spirit," whose arrival in Richmond put his name on every tongue. "What could have brought him there? And what was his business? These were the inquiries of almost every one." Desperation fed the rumors, as General Lee made a public plea to Richmond's hard-pressed citizens to send his hungry army some part of their meager supplies.

While Richmond's threadbare people heard their hero plead for food, Blair "fared sumptuously every day," so Lizzie would soon tell Phil, as a guest of Robert Ould, the Confederate Commissioner of Exchange. Sotto voce, it was said by some in Richmond that Ould brought Yankee delicacies back from Hampton Roads, where he traded prisoners of war at Fort Monroe. A soft-eyed Virginian with a well-trimmed beard, a friend of Blair's son Frank, Ould had been raised in Washington and had served as its district attorney. Blair chatted amiably with him, never deriding the Southern cause or its people. The old man spoke of Davis with affection and high regard, and insisted that peace was in the South's best interest. Richmond could not resist the federal armies, he said. Now was the time to accept good terms, for he feared, as a friend, that the South would be ground to powder.

On the day Blair arrived in Richmond, Congressman Henry S. Foote resigned from the Confederate House and took himself north toward Washington City, accompanied by Mrs. Foote on a freelance mission of peace, intending to tell Lincoln that the South would abolish slavery in return for readmission to the Union and a general amnesty. Foote was one of Davis's fiercest enemies and a fellow Mississippian. He planned to publish to the Southern people and their troops whatever terms Lincoln offered, whether "the personage now known as President of the Confederate States" liked it or not. Rebel cavalry overtook him on the banks of the lower Potomac and put him under arrest. It must have been at gunpoint.

As a sharp-tongued provocateur in the antebellum Congress, Foote had bucked the secessionist tide, provoking several duels, literally wrestling with one disapproving colleague, and leveling a pistol at another, all on the Senate floor. In 1852, as the head of the Unionist Party, he had beaten Jeff Davis in a race for the office of governor, having beaten him with his fists in the parlor of their Washington boardinghouse in 1847. In the Rebel Congress, a contemporary said, Foote blew "clouds of vituperative gas" at the Davis administration. Now he wanted to see Lincoln, and Lincoln wanted to see him.

When a wire reached Washington reporting on his mission and its interrupted end, Lincoln inquired whether his captors could be overtaken, but Foote already resided in a Fredericksburg jail. The Confederate authorities let his wife proceed to the Yankee capital, where Seward, an old Senate friend, escorted her in a carriage to Willard's Hotel.

It was at or about this time that Judge Nelson received Judge Campbell's letter, proposing to sit down with mutual friends and see what might be done about peace. It had not gone ignored, as Campbell thought it had. Nelson had shown it to their mutual friend, Lincoln's Secretary of War, Edwin Stanton, who called it the most promising idea he had yet heard. He surely made Lincoln aware of it. But the president had "initiated a scheme," Stanton said (a pointed choice of words), and Mr. Blair was executing it. Mr. Blair was in Richmond, and nothing could be done until the scheme was tried.

CHAPTER ELEVEN

A New Channel for the Bitter Waters

What some people called the White House was a stately shade of gray. It had stood since 1818 at the corner of Twelfth and Clay, built for a Richmond merchant in the straight-front neoclassical style. Though Lincoln's White House dwarfed it, it was three stories high, with elegantly furnished rooms over forty feet square. The Davises' little boys liked to kiss "the pretty ladies" in the parlor, the goddesses of youth and the hunt carved in the marble mantle.

On Blair's first morning in Richmond, a bright and frosty day, the Davises greeted him fondly at their door. Varina threw her arms around him. "Oh you rascal. I am overjoyed to see you." He had known her since her youth, and it struck him that she had never looked better. Stout, he thought, but fairer and more gregarious than ever. Life at the top had been kind to her. The same could not be said for her husband. In the fresh eyes of Preston Blair, Jefferson Davis was so "emaciated and altered as not to be recognized." Preston surely fussed over the children and brought them a gift or two. Refreshments were served, happy memories recalled, until the men were left alone.

Varina knew her husband "noticed every shade of expression" on the face of every man. Suspicious in all things, he would have seen no duplicity in Francis Preston Blair. The old man said he had told Mr. Lincoln about their friendship and his hope to do something in the direction of peace, but the president had let him go to Richmond not wanting to hear what he would say there. He had come with no credentials, no instructions. His views were entirely his own. He repeated it several times. He had no other power than to build communications between men disadvantaged by having none, he said, no way of knowing what the other side was thinking, nothing to help them end their quarrel. His private status entitled him to no reply. Davis bore great responsibilities and could speak or not, as he chose. Blair's denials notwithstanding, his host was convinced that the old man spoke for Lincoln. Davis's Secretary of State Judah Benjamin would soon suggest that had Blair denied it once, he should have been taken at his word. Having done so repeatedly, he was not to be believed.

Blair asked Davis if he had made any commitments to a European power that would bar an agreement with the United States. Davis said no. Emphatically. Had it been otherwise, Blair replied, he would not have had another word to say. As it was, he produced what he called a rough draft of his thoughts and proposed to read it aloud, adding with a grin that it was more like an editorial than a diplomatic paper. He could not change his ways, he said. A shoemaker sticks to his last. He had become an old man, and what he would read might be nothing but an old man's dreams. He depended on Davis's good sense to tell him whether they could be realized. He knew that his host would speak candidly, expecting candor in return. "I love my whole country," he said, "but my affections attach me to the South." Every drop of his blood and his children's blood was Southern. He wanted to see this war end. The South could not win it; slavery could not be saved, but Southern honor could be.

Davis assured his mentor that he knew him to be honest. The personal attachment was mutual, he said. He owed a great deal to the Blair family for kindnesses done to his. He would never forget them. That said, Blair's private role did differ from his, and he would let him present his proposal without interruption.

Blair started reading his shoemaker's editorial. Its opening was inauspicious. "The Amnesty Proclamation of President Lincoln" (more repugnant to Davis than a death sentence) would surely be enlarged to forgive every Southern man who swore allegiance to the federal government and abandoned slavery, the "cause of all our woes." Slavery was doomed, and "all the world condemns it." From the Southern point of view, the document rolled downhill from there: All but a few seceded states had already been subdued, it said. They had started the war for slavery. They were now prepared to abandon it as the price of foreign protection.

The room had acquired a chill, and the old man stopped in midstream. What had seemed so convincing when he had read it to the Blairs in Blair House had a different ring when he read it to Davis in Davis's house, perhaps at the point where the Southern states' cry for independence was said to have degenerated into "an appeal for succor to European potentates, to whom they offer, in return, homage as dependencies!" Blair would later say he decided to skip the parts that bore rather hard on the South. Turning the page theatrically, he drew a rare laugh from his friend. "I will pass this over," he said. "It smacks too much of the editorial."

And then he came to the point—the common need to end the Napoleonic threat in Mexico, a threat to "make the Latin race supreme in the Southern section of the North American continent." He surely read in comfort the effusive words that followed: "Jefferson Davis is the fortunate man who now holds the commanding position to encounter this formidable scheme of conquest, and whose fiat can at the same time deliver his country from the bloody agony now covering it in mourning. He can drive Maximilian from his American throne, and baffle the designs of Napoleon to subject our Southern people to the 'Latin race.'" President Lincoln had made this possible when he issued his amnesty proclamation "and the message which looks to an armistice." (Davis must have wondered which message this was. Lincoln's had looked to no armistice but surrender.) Secret preliminaries would let Davis march "a veteran army of invincibles" into Mexico where the democrat Juarez would rally his men to Davis's. And if more troops were needed, would not the Northern army enlist in an enterprise so vital to "our whole Republic"? If Davis added Mexico to a restored American Union, "rounding off our possession" to the Isthmus of Panama, he would finish the work of Jefferson and add new states to the South, "if indeed such sectional distinctions could be recognized after the peculiar institution which created them had ceased to exist."

It took several minutes for Blair to read the rest. Then he put his paper down and looked at his old friend. "There is my problem, Mr. Davis. Do you think it possible to be solved?"

Davis paused for a moment. "I think so," he said, and started Blair's heart racing. But how would such a plan be implemented?

The old man replied that every Northern political party supported the Monroe Doctrine and wished to apply it in Mexico. A secret treaty might be made. Then he told Davis the rest, too much to write down even in a document that he had no intention of relinquishing, insisting yet again that Lincoln knew nothing about it. He did not mention Grant.

Lee would abandon Richmond and retreat southwest, "to more defensible positions." Grant would follow in hot pursuit, but not so hot as to catch him, until he had driven him into Mexico, where Lee would provoke the French. With one American army attacked by a foreign foe, the other would leap to its side. Together they would decimate Napoleon's legions, embrace once again on the old familiar battlefields, reenact the triumphal march into Mexico City. After fighting in Mexico twice in twenty years, "our people" could not be made to leave. Once they joined hands to win a second Mexican War, no elaborate political devices would be needed to forge a reunion. It would follow as night the day.

Davis seemed intrigued, and shared what Lee had lately told him—that 25,000 men could conquer Mexico. Ever jealous of his stature, he said he would have liked the plan better if Mr. Lincoln and Mr. Seward had brought it to him in person. The implication was plain: He was sure it had come from them. As he typically did when negotiations were mentioned, he recalled the peace envoys he had sent to Washington in 1861, Mr. Stephens's mission to Fort Monroe in 1863, the message he had sent through Colonel Jacques in 1864. Mr. Lincoln had rebuffed them all. He could not see how the first step might be taken unless Mr. Lincoln changed course.

Blair said he thought Mr. Lincoln would send or receive a peace commission, remembering to add later that he could give no assurances; he could only return to Washington, explain his plan to Mr. Lincoln, who had yet to hear a word of it, and see what he would say. Mr. Lincoln did not sympathize with the extremists in his party who wanted to devastate the South, but they had great power in this Congress, and would have more in the next. Even the Cabinet was divided. Blair said he believed in state sovereignty. He hoped that the war would end and the Union be restored in such a way that Southern pride, power, and honor would suffer no shock and Southern territory would be extended.

Then he made it plain, as respectfully as the circumstances allowed, that if the war went on, Southern territory would cease to exist. Davis did not deny it, and came rather close to admitting it, recalling the war for independence that "our colonial fathers" fought. Had they lost that glorious war (a tacit admission that the South might lose its own), Britain would have borne the expense of holding in subjugation a people who deserved to be free, instead of enjoying the commerce between two countries that now enhanced her wealth.

Blair pursued the subjugation theme. If the Union stayed divided, both sides must keep standing armies, which always led to monarchy. As Davis was hearing it, Blair was implying for a second time some Confederate entanglement with a European crown. Davis denied it again, hotly this time. He was absolutely free, he said, and would "die a free man in all respects." Democracy was born and bred in him. He would not permit the French or any other foreigners to dominate the Confederacy. Napoleon was trying to flank it, but would not be allowed to do so. Left in control of Mexico, the French would attack Virginia for its coal, iron, and timber, to build a navy on Chesapeake Bay. The great difficulty of bringing "the sections" together, Davis said, had nothing to do with "Eu-rope," as he pronounced it. The "insurmountable obstacle to restoring fraternal relations" was the scar of the "fiendish cruelty" that the Northern armies had inflicted on the invaded states.

Blair conceded the need to build "a new channel for the bitter waters," a stronger bond than memories. A common effort to enforce the Monroe Doctrine would provide it.

If Davis acted according to habit, he nodded unconsciously as he spoke. Reconciliation must depend on time and events, he said, which he hoped would restore good feelings, but nothing could be better than to see the arms of "our countrymen" united against a foreign power that threatened the principle of self-government, which "both sections" treasured. The potentates of Eu-rope must be pleased to see "our people" destroying each other, hoping to see our form of government die, vindicating their monarchical principles, weakening us as prey.

Blair was encouraged to hear it, he said. If "our country" were encouraged too, as he thought it would be, happy unity would soon resume.

"You should know with what reluctance I was drawn out of the Union," Davis said. He had tried until the last to avoid it. He had followed "the old flag" with more devotion than anything else on earth. On the field at Bull Run, he had glimpsed it hanging loose on its staff and thought it was his own. When the wind unfurled the flag of the United States, he had seen it with a sigh as an enemy banner. Since then he had thought it was put away for good. But a foreign war might change things. If "the people" came together in Mexico to bear common sacrifices, face common dangers, gather shared renown in defense of shared principles, new memories would take the place of the ones the war had made. In time, they might restore the old feelings. If France were driven from Mexico, that country might be connected with this. No one could foresee how things would shape themselves. "It is for us to deal with the problems before us, and leave to posterity questions which they might solve, though we cannot."

Blair said Davis mistook the war's effects on the minds of the people. He had just spent four hours on the lines and had seen the kind feelings of the pickets who were sent there to kill each other. His Northern and Southern escorts had shared a drink and goodwill. "It is only the politicians," he said—forgetting, perhaps, that he sat with one—"and those who profit or hope to profit by the disasters of war who indulge in acrimony."

What Blair said was "very just, in the main," the politician replied. It was mostly the people at home who brooded over the war and indulged themselves in bitterness, not the men who led and fought it. On slavery Davis said nothing. The inequality of Blair's responsibility and his own, he thought, made the subject inappropriate. As for the Mexican idea, everything depended on "a well founded confidence."

Then Davis turned the subject to the men who led the North. He looked at his guest with what Blair perceived as a "very significant expression."

"Mr. Blair," he said, "what do you think of Mr. Seward?"

The old man knew what Davis thought; it was something they had in common. "Mr. Seward is a very pleasant companion," he said. "But I have no doubt that where his ambition is concerned his selfish feelings prevail over all principle. I have no doubt he would betray any man, no matter what his obligations to him, if he stood in the way of his selfish and ambitious schemes. But this matter, if entered upon at all, must be with Mr. Lincoln himself," a military matter, led by the commander in chief. "Mr. Lincoln is capable of great personal sacrifices, of sacrificing the strongest feelings of his heart, of sacrificing a friend, when he thinks it necessary for the good of the country." (He was thinking, no doubt, of a friend named Montgomery Blair.) But if he "plights his faith to any man, he will maintain his word inviolably."

Davis was glad to hear it. He said he did not know Mr. Lincoln, but Blair's endorsement was good enough for him. In Mr. Seward he had no confidence, and he knew of no Southern man who did. (A few days later, he would tell a Southern man that Mr. Seward was wily and treacherous, forgetting what he had told a Confederate general: For the kindnesses that Mr. Seward had shown his family, he had promised himself "never to say aught against him.")

An understanding should be reached on the Mexican proposal, Davis said. He was willing to appoint commissioners to pursue it, without regard to forms. "There must be some medium of communication." Mr. Lincoln could rely implicitly on whomever Davis would send. He had recently considered Judge Campbell (a reference to Campbell's overture to Judge Nelson). Blair expressed "unbounded confidence" in Campbell.

Now Davis authorized Blair to go back and tell Mr. Lincoln that he was ready to discuss the plan and knew of no insurmountable obstacle to "a treaty of peace." We may suppose that Blair could hardly keep still. He spoke of the fame that Davis would win for "relieving the country from all its disasters, restoring its harmony, and extending its dominion to the Isthmus." He did not bring up the fame that the author of the plan would win.

"What my name might be in history," Davis said, "I care not, if I can restore the prosperity and happiness of my country. That is the end and aim of my being. For myself, death will end my cares, and that is very easy to be accomplished."

Later that day, the War Department clerk John Jones saw Blair with his host, Colonel Ould, riding down Main Street in an open carriage. "He looks no older than he did twenty years ago," Jones thought, and "seemed struck by the great number of able-bodied men in the streets," which says more about what was on Jones's mind than Blair's.

—◦—

Though Blair spoke to few if any men in the Richmond street, he spoke with men of influence who looked at the world very differently than Jeff Davis, and wanted it known up north. Alec Stephens thought everyone in Richmond knew that Blair had met with Davis, but nothing "escaped from the Executive closet, or got to the public in any way." Blair kept the secret too. He sought out and met with influential men and women but did not disclose his mission. The rumors can be imagined. People spoke of little else. On Friday, the *Dispatch* said Blair had kept or *been* kept out of the public eye, but had met old acquaintances accidentally, with "the utmost cordiality on both sides." Some chance encounters there may have been, but Blair's meetings with Southern friends were no accident. They opened their homes to him.

Mrs. Stanard's, on the corner of Eighth and Franklin, was the nearest thing to Richmond's salon. A fellow socialite knew its hostess as a "handsome, dark-eyed" widow, "wonderfully persuasive with the other sex, who came when she called and left promptly when she gave some token of a change of mood." Blair was a family friend. To him, Mrs. Stanard was a good Union woman stranded on hostile ground. When he drew a crowd to her home, she entertained them in a style she could ill afford. Blair breakfasted there with Alec Stephens and other prominent men. "Mr. Blair did not talk much," the hard-line Virginian James Lyons thought. "He struck me as a man talking to conceal his opinions and draw out the opinions of others. In other words, like a *spy*, as I believed he was." He had no authority from Mr. Lincoln, Blair said, but knew his sentiments. The South could get better terms now than later. Stephens replied that he too wanted peace and, in Blair's attentive presence, denounced the Davis administration's conduct of the war so enthusiastically that Lyons asked him what *his* war-winning plan might be. Little Alec confided nothing in the presence of the spy.

Emily Mason, a friend of the Blairs and the Davises, implored the old man to let her in on his mission. He told her he was searching for General

Jackson's "long-sighted spectacles." She promised to help him find them if they were anywhere in the South to be found. The *Enquirer* sneered that "Francis P. Blair, Esq., of Lincolndom" had met at the Spottswood Hotel with some members of Congress and the Virginia legislature, who "waited on him" there and "resolved themselves into a Committee of the Whole on the state of the Union."

Virginia's senator Robert M. T. Hunter was not sneering. He knew that Blair spoke with particular effect to Southern Democrats, "who for so long had been in the habit of taking counsel with him on public affairs." Blair told them "what seemed to many of us to have much truth." In view of the North's almost boundless resources, resistance made no sense. Apart from their own huge manpower, the United States "could empty the population of Europe upon the southern coasts," enticing immigrant soldiers with a promise of confiscated lands. Like others, Hunter said, "my own attention was now more seriously directed to peace than heretofore."

Judge Campbell's friend Robert Kean took note that the public notoriety of Blair's visit to Davis put pressure on him just when the treasury's "hopeless bankruptcy" was becoming widely known, making Congress "more and more weak in the knees." Davis would later condemn the "cabal in Congress" who "held secret conversation" with Blair; "how low their spirit had sunk I do not know," but it made some soldiers angry. Davis was angry too. Blair's secret conversations with the cabal were no secret.

———

On the day Blair arrived in Richmond, General Grant sent his subordinate, General Lew Wallace, the future author of the novel, *Ben-Hur,* on an odd little mission of his own. Wallace had told Grant that a school friend in Mexico was convinced that Rebel forces in West Texas would "gladly unite with us" to cross the Rio Grande and drive Maximilian from his throne. Independently of Blair, and ignorant of his plan, Wallace told Grant that a joint invasion of Mexico would "stagger the rebellion." At Wallace's request, Grant sent him down to the southern tip of Texas for a surreptitious chat with the local Confederate commander. Wallace would soon report that the Rebel general endorsed the idea "heartily."

Davis sent Blair a note on his second day in Richmond, remarking that he might want something in writing about their meeting. Blair came over to get it. Davis had been as careful to document his thoughts as Blair had been, and as careful to omit details. He had written a synopsis of their conversation in his own hand. He showed it to Blair, invited corrections, and accepted them on the spot. The document made it clear that Davis had committed to nothing. Indeed, it said nothing about Mexico at all—for secrecy's sake, Blair thought.

Blair and Davis discussed the ins and outs of a Mexican invasion and a new American empire. Blair made his case more specifically, that the Confederacy could not survive with the Mississippi and the Atlantic seaboard gone. Davis did not reply, but, as Blair perceived it, "his manner indicated assent." His pen did not. He handed Blair a letter, written and dated the day before, after their first meeting. He addressed it to Blair but intended it for Lincoln, avoiding direct communication between the two heads of state just as Lincoln had done.

Richmond, Va., January 12, 1865

Sir: I have deemed it proper and probably desirable to give you in this form the substance of remarks made by me, to be repeated by you to President Lincoln, etc. I have no disposition to find obstacles in forms, and am willing, now as heretofore, to enter into negotiations for the restoration of peace; and am ready to send a commission, whenever I have reason to suppose it will be received, or to receive a commission, if the United States Government should choose to send one. That notwithstanding the rejection of our former offers, I would, if you could promise that a commissioner, minister, or other agent would be received, appoint one immediately, and renew the effort to enter into conference, with a view to secure peace to the two countries.

As Davis well knew, the last two words were fatal. He had told Blair face-to-face that there was no insurmountable obstacle to peace. Now he had imposed one, knowing as well as Blair did that Lincoln would scoff at two countries. But the old man's quixotic optimism would not be denied. He left for home the next day with a piece of paper in his hand and jubilation on his face, convincing himself that Lincoln would let two countries become one on the battlefields of Mexico.

On Saturday morning, January 14, Blair left Richmond on the *William Allison*, the Confederate flag-of-truce boat, to meet its federal counterpart at Boulware's Landing and steam back down the James to City Point for a voyage home on the *Don*. Before he boarded the *Allison*, Blair chatted with an old friend, whose twenty-four-year-old daughter stood by, thinking youthful thoughts. "Poor old Mr. Blair," she would later tell her diary. "I could feel almost kindly toward him. It must be difficult for the old to realize the possibilities of their youth are now but the dreams of the dotard."

James Singleton arrived in Richmond on the same flag-of-truce boat that took Blair away. All of Richmond knew of his coming, as it had of Preston Blair's. He spent the next few weeks talking money with Richmond's merchants and peace with its leading Rebels, not the least of whom were his brother, Jefferson Davis, and Robert E. Lee.

"Men feel peace in their bones," Horace Greeley's *Tribune* told its readers, "as they say many shrewd men today felt it in their pockets." More than one member of Congress sold their stocks, for "they dreaded a speedy fall."

On Sunday, January 15, Davis received a dispatch from the governor of South Carolina. Sherman was moving north, seemingly headed toward Charleston. There was practically no infantry to impede him. "Conceive the worst, and it is that."The worst was yet to come. On the next day, Davis read a wire from General Braxton Bragg, "mortified" to report the capture of Fort Fisher, the guardian of Wilmington, North Carolina, the Confederacy's last seaport. From Wilmington, as Alec Stephens would later say, the South had been breathing through a quill, shipping cotton to Europe in return for arms and supplies while otherwise choked by "a cordon of armed ships drawn around its neck."The quill had just been plugged.

On the day the news hit Richmond, Congressman John A. Orr of Davis's home state of Mississippi demanded on the floor of the House "an honest effort of statesmanship to end this carnival of death." On the same clear day, the Virginia legislature called on Davis to appoint General Lee to head *all* of the Confederate armies, a slap in the face of their beleaguered commander in chief. On the day after that, Davis received a letter from a leading Mississippian. "Unwelcome is the bearer of ill tidings." What was left of Hood's army was "a mere *mob* without spirit, but that of mutinous anger," its men "melting away daily." A letter from Georgia came too. Wealthy families were sending their sons out of the country as they approached draft age, "generally through the blockade, sometimes through the lines."

Sherman and his vengeful army marched north out of Georgia into South Carolina that morning. On the day after that, the Rebel War Department clerk John Jones made an entry in his diary: "It is published in the papers that Mrs. Davis threw her arms around Mr. Blair and embraced him. This, too, is injurious to the President."

CHAPTER TWELVE

We Are on the Eve of an Internal Revolution

As Blair made his way up Chesapeake Bay, reportedly in "a remarkably good humor," Sunset Cox asked the House of Representatives in Washington to resolve that "now, in this hour of victory, which is the hour of magnanimity," President Lincoln was duty-bound to send a peace commission south, or receive one from Jefferson Davis. Elihu B. Washburne, Lincoln's friend and Grant's patron, disagreed. Davis and his Congress had "again and again peremptorily and insultingly refused to entertain any overtures for peace." Washburne thought it disgraceful to beg them to receive one now. Cox replied that this was the Republican Horace Greeley's proposition. It was laid on the table and died.

Blair's daughter, Lizzie, wrote joyfully to Phil that night. Her aged traveler had come home, "very tired and silent," but pleased to have been "most cordially received by our old friends." He was perfectly well but overwhelmed with excitement and fatigue. He had given his happy daughter just a "glimpse" of what was said in Dixie, and a message from Jefferson Davis. He would remember her in his prayers, "even when dying." With her father safely home, Lizzie confessed to "no small sense of joy to know that he is in his own bed and sleeping with Mother by his side, happier than I have known her to be for some time past."

Before he came to bed, the old man crossed the street and reported to Abraham Lincoln. To his pleasure, he would later tell a friend, Seward was not there. They "did not draw well together," and he doubted that the Secretary of State would support negotiations conducted over his head. After stopping Blair cold a few days ago when he started to say what he meant to tell the Rebels, Lincoln was eager to hear what the Rebels had told *him.* Blair handed him Davis's letter and the memorandum he had read to his friend—"Suggestions to Jefferson Davis," he had titled it. Lincoln read the letter and scrawled a disclaimer on the Suggestions. "This paper first seen by me on this 16th day of January 1865. . . . I having had no intimation as to what Mr. Blair would say or do while beyond our military lines." After he read it, Lincoln asked if Davis intended to send a copy to Napoleon III. It was not a good start. Blair said he had left Davis nothing to send.

Lincoln surely wanted Napoleon out of Mexico but had no intention of evicting him, least of all in league with Jeff Davis. "There has been war enough," he would soon tell a French marquis. "I know what the American people want, but, thank God, I count for something, and during my second term there will be no more fighting." Blair had opened a door, but "peace to the two countries" and a war against a third did not tempt Lincoln through it. What the president said to Blair about the Mexican plan is unknown, but given what Blair said and did thereafter, Lincoln must have told him he would consider it, or at least implied that he would, if only to humor the old man.

Blair's report on his meeting with Davis told Lincoln not much new, but his chats with Davis's enemies were intriguing. Davis would later surmise that the defeatists who had "gathered themselves unto him" had exposed the cabal to Blair, who in turn had revealed it to Lincoln, giving the enemy aid and comfort. Davis had it right. The old Jacksonian told Lincoln that nearly everyone he had spoken to was convinced that the cause was hopeless, and eager to find a way out. Lincoln surely thanked him and duly consulted Seward.

Arrangements were made that night to send Blair back to Richmond immediately.

— ⁘ —

The "glorious news of the capture of Fort Fisher" arrived the next morning, to the joy of Gideon Welles. The Cabinet was assembled, aglow with the Rebels' loss of their access to the sea. By omission, Uncle Gideon's diary suggests that Blair's mission went unmentioned.

The *New York Times* was jubilant about Fort Fisher but no keener on peace talks than the Richmond press. "Unless the most explicit assurances in the highest quarters are utterly unreliable," said the *Times* (which often spoke for Seward), neither Mr. Blair nor Mr. Singleton had gone to Richmond to negotiate with the Rebels. That Mr. Blair had grand ideas was likely, but he had gone on private business, with "no shadow of authority, direct or indirect, to say one syllable on behalf of the Government concerning terms of peace." In fear, perhaps, that its president might go wobbly, the *Times* thought it wise to add that the people had just rejected the party seeking peace through negotiation, the "opposite plan" of the Lincoln administration, which "seeks peace and freedom *through war* more resolutely and more exclusively than before."

As the *Times* was proclaiming that Blair's trip to Richmond had nothing to do with the president, Blair was preparing to return at his behest. On the following morning, Lincoln handed him a letter. He addressed it to Blair, as Davis had done in reverse, "with the view that it should be shown to Mr. Davis." In response to the insurgent leader's invitation to bring peace to two countries, Lincoln poked a stick in his eye.

> *Sir: Your having shown me Mr. Davis's letter to you of the 12th instant, you may say to him that I have constantly been, am now, and shall continue ready to receive any agent whom he, or any other influential person now resisting the national authority, may informally send to me with the view of securing peace to the people of our one common country. Yours, etc., A. Lincoln*

With no other legitimate title, "Mr. Davis" was only one "influential person" resisting the national authority. There were many of them in Richmond. If Mr. Davis would not send an agent to bring peace to our one common country ("informally" was penciled in as an afterthought, underscoring Davis's illegitimacy), some other influential person might. Lincoln was inciting a Gray Revolution, expecting if not instructing Preston Blair to make his letter known to the cabal that kept Davis awake at night.

Blair caught Greeley up on things. He would have written sooner, he said, but until he had been to Richmond he could not weigh his chances. "And now I have to content myself & you with the saying of the old sage that 'all that is known is that nothing is known.' Still I can say to you my faith is strong that we shall have a happy deliverance, and that soon." There was goodwill for it on both sides, but "formidable obstructions" too, which "selfish bad men will abuse to thwart peace." (The miscreants' names and sections were left unspoken.) "I think your envoy has done much good," but his work must be secret, and "if your head full of sagacity should penetrate it or should grasp it, I beg you not to divulge even your conjectures. I have great hopes, and would not hesitate to indicate something of their foundation to you but that I have pledged to be tongue tied."

On the following day, as the Confederacy fought for its life, its Secretary of War left his post. The Virginia congressional delegation had demanded that Davis replace his entire Cabinet or face a vote of no confidence. Their fellow Virginian James Seddon, sickly, insulted, overwhelmed, took advantage of the chance to resign.

The congressional petition to make Lee general in chief kicked sand in Davis's face, though he had no choice but to endorse it. Lee's subordination to his president never wavered, despite his low opinion of Davis's military instincts, but the president's thin skin was pierced. When an ally who had voted for the petition called at the Executive Mansion, Varina confronted him hotly. "So you too, Mr. Henry, have turned against my husband?" The senator protested that the people required it, and the president should take comfort in knowing he did not deserve it. "I think I am the person to advise Mr. Davis," Varina said, "and if I were he, I would die or be hung before I would submit to the humiliation that Congress intended him."

Mr. Davis neither died nor was hanged, but the consequences for the Confederacy were worse. For the rest of its short life, its president and its Congress waged war against each other, to the conspicuous disadvantage of their war against the United States and any chance to negotiate a palatable end to the contest.

On Friday morning, January 20, just back from Savannah, Lincoln's Secretary of War told the Cabinet that, despite Sherman's lenient occupation and reports of the city's pacification, there were few loyal men there.
The women were "frenzied, senseless partisans," Stanton said. Gideon
Welles suspected that "the Rebels are not yet prepared to return to duty
and become good citizens. They have not, it would seem, been humbled
enough, but must be reduced to further submission." When would they
come to their senses? If the fall of Savannah and Wilmington had not
made them see reason, neither, perhaps, would the loss of Charleston and
Richmond. "They may submit to what they cannot help, but their enmity
will remain. A few weeks will enlighten us."

The Richmond press fed Welles's fears. The *Whig* told its readers that
no one in Georgia had any idea of abandoning the struggle "but a pack
of sneaks in Savannah." Their submission was surely encouraged by Sherman's surprising leniency and a committee of wealthy Philadelphians,
who contributed to their relief.

As Lincoln and his Cabinet discussed war and peace, the *Don* was gathering steam at the Navy Yard under secret orders. At 11:00 a.m., Blair and
his servant Henry rolled up in a closed carriage and came aboard quickly.
Fifteen minutes later the *Don* was under way. A trusted Southern officer
would be waiting for Blair on Saturday on the Rebel flag-of-truce boat,
William Allison. Barring a particular need, no one else in Richmond was
to know that he was coming.

Within hours it was front-page news in both cities. Lizzie wrote
Admiral Lee that the leak had been traced to some officers of the *Don*.
History does not record their fate. Government sources on both sides
had dismissed Blair's first visit as a personal trip. Hardly anyone believed
it then; no one could believe it now. Even moderate Republicans were
alarmed by the prospect of peace talks, and the Jacobins tore their hair.
Lincoln was moved to say that some of his friends in Congress "were
afraid to trust me with a dinner," let alone the Union cause. As hope-filled

rumors took hold in the South, the *Richmond Sentinel* told its readers what a peaceful return to the North would entail. "All the dark and malignant passions of a vindictive people, drunk with blood and vomiting crime, will be unloosed upon us like bloodhounds upon their prey."

The *New York Times* took its own dark view. There was no point in sending agents to "Davis and the Sanhedrim he has called around him." They would never give in, for "their names will be the curse and scorn of mankind; and they will either hang on gallows, or spend the remainder of their days among the dingy boarding-houses of Leicester Square, or the seedy tenement houses of the Latin quarters, or in some other miserable portion of a European capital."

On a page filled with advertising, the *Times* ran an item with the arresting headline: ALARMING REPORT FROM RICHMOND. "Old Mr. Blair" had reportedly been received "by some distinguished rebel ladies there with the most affectionate demonstrations, and it is surmised that this is the secret of his return to the rebel Capital." Whatever his designs on the ladies might be, "when our bodies are naturally feeble, or debilitated from excess of exertion, or from insidious disease, the lack of strength and vital-ity, in most cases, may be restored by those means of recuperation which nature and science have placed at our disposal. Of all these advertised restoratives," the reader should consider Hostetter's Celebrated Stomach Bitters.

As the *Don* headed south, Jefferson Davis's mail gave him reason to try Mr. Hostetter's wares. Congress was on the verge of a vote of no con-fidence. There was a letter from General Howell Cobb, a former governor of Georgia, Speaker of the House, and Secretary of the Treasury in the old concern, more lately General Sherman's absent host. After sleeping uninvited at Cobb's plantation, Sherman had punished the sin of treason. Instructing his bummers to "spare nothing," he had watched them warm themselves with bonfires fueled by the governor's fence rails and no doubt by dearer combustibles. The next day they had carried off an "immense quantity" of goods and provisions. Now Cobb told Davis that public sen-timent "becomes worse and more disloyal every day." General Johnston should be restored to his command, for Hood's reputation "is weakening your strength and destroying your powers of usefulness." Many people supported state conventions, some because "they believe it will lead to peace," others "to take control of affairs out of your hands." Another note from Georgia came from General William Browne, an alumnus of Davis's staff. "Submission is openly advocated and is gaining strength."

Topping off the day's post, Judge Campbell submitted his resignation as Assistant Secretary of War. Mr. Seddon having resigned as secretary, the president should reshape the War Department. The judge did not add that he disapproved of Davis's appointment of Seddon's successor, John Breckinridge, the savior of Silver Spring, but he told his friend Robert Kean that Breckinridge was "not a man of small *details*," and Campbell did not want to serve under him. The truth, Kean thought, was that Campbell was "glad of an opportunity to escape from the place." Davis would not give him one. He rejected his resignation.

———

Grant was away when Blair passed through City Point on his way back to Richmond. On January 22 the Rebel flag-of-truce boat took him back up the James with five hundred returning prisoners. According to the *Richmond Dispatch*, he lodged this time at the corner of Fourth and Leigh at the home of Lieutenant Colonel William Hatch, the Assistant Commissioner of Exchange under Blair's first host, Colonel Ould. The prisoners were welcomed too, though not so well housed.

Blair dined at the Executive Mansion that night, full of good cheer from Blair House. After Varina left them, Blair handed Lincoln's letter to Davis, who read it through carefully, then read it a second time. When he finally looked up, Blair, pointed out, as if Davis might have missed it, that Lincoln's reference to "our one common country" was a response to Davis's two. Davis said he understood it as such, and said no more about it. The inference that he had accepted reunion as a premise for negotiations was not an unreasonable one for an eager peacemaker to draw, especially in view of Davis's circumstances. Blair drew it.

As for a Mexican invasion as a means to restore our one common country, Blair gave Davis to understand, at the very least, that Lincoln had not rejected it. It was fortunate, he said, that Davis had agreed to negotiate at all, which gave Lincoln confidence in Blair's utility as a go-between.

"Further reflection," Blair said, had nonetheless altered his views on seeking peace. Mr. Lincoln was embarrassed by the extremists of his party who sought to drive him to harsher measures than he favored. It was not politically feasible to treat with the Confederate government. If anything could be done, it could only be through Grant and Lee, who might make a truce through a military convention, presaging a permanent peace.

Davis said he would willingly entrust a negotiation to Lee. The unsinkable Preston Blair was convinced that the host had accepted the premise of reunion and was willing to work out the details. They would never meet again.

Before he re-boarded the *William Allison,* Blair reflected and reconsidered yet again and sent a message to Davis. He was sure that Lincoln would not let Grant negotiate with Lee, leaving Davis no recourse but to send civilian envoys or abandon the whole thing.

North Carolina's governor Zebulon Vance, always at odds with Davis over Vance's fundamentalism on states' rights and Davis's faith in a central government, had written to him a year ago. North Carolina's disillusionment with the war could only be dispelled by an effort to negotiate peace. Not that it would go anywhere. A Yankee rejection of fair terms would rally support to the cause and convince the humblest citizens "that the government is tender of their lives and happiness, and would not prolong their sufferings unnecessarily for one moment."

Davis had let it sink in. Now he would put it in play.

———

Blair stayed in Richmond and went calling again, testing the political winds in a cold winter rain. A few dissident congressmen whispered reunion. With no more authority than half-remembered bits of presidential conversation, Blair delivered assurances that Lincoln would go along with thirty years of gradualism on the abolition issue and give the South whatever else it wanted, except independence; but the rabid Richmond press was no more enamored of his second visit than his first. "The mystic Blair," the *Enquirer* said, was "as mystical as before." The *Whig* was reasonably sure that he had not returned for his toothbrush, but "all this talk about negotiation and peace, while one party is still bent on conquest and the other on independence, is idle and meaningless." President Davis was wasting his time.

In a letter to his wife dispatched from City Point, General Meade took heart from the signs of dissent in Rebeldom. "The Richmond papers are very severe on Davis, and there is every indication of discord among them. I hope to heaven this will incline them to peace, and that there may be some truth in the many reports that something is going on!"

In the dark as much as Meade, Davis's vice president Alec Stephens only knew that "Blair is back again. What he is doing I do not know, but presume the President is endeavoring to <u>negotiate</u> with him for <u>negotiation</u> that same thing which on 17 Nov. seemed to him to be so absurd." This was unfair. On November 17, Davis had answered some Georgia legislators who had written him about the prospect of a peace convention initiated by the states, independently of Richmond. Mindful of the sacred dogma of state sovereignty, Davis had answered gingerly that separate state action would be objectionable and divisive. The president of the Confederate States of America could hardly say less.

❦

With Blair still in Richmond, Judge Campbell told his friend Robert Kean that he thought the peace men in Congress were about to demand reunion. On the following day, Kean got stark corroboration when Colonel Alfred L. Rives, a thirty-four-year-old godson of Lafayette, came to see him at his boardinghouse. A Washington City engineer before the war, Rives had designed its Cabin John Bridge, the longest, single-span masonry arch on earth. Now he was the Confederacy's Chief of Engineers.

Rives asked Kean if they could speak privately. The parlor was occupied, so Kean led the colonel to his room. When the door was closed, Rives said his father had just had a talk with Davis. Seventy-one years old and a Davis family friend, Congressman William Cabell Rives had been Jackson's minister to France. A pro-Union voice in the antebellum Senate, he was deeply respected now, and Davis had thoroughly shocked him. Everything was in jeopardy, Davis said. "Despondency and distrust" were everywhere. "We are on the eve of an internal revolution." He would do almost anything to stop it, including sending men to treat with Mr. Lincoln.

Colonel Rives told Kean what Davis had told his father. Lincoln was inviting a negotiation, with reunion as its sole condition. Davis had inferred that the South could come back with its Constitutional rights, including the right to slavery. It was plain to the elder Rives that Davis was in despair—that he had come to believe independence was unattainable, and was willing to accept reunion "to spare the people the effects of subjugation." To Kean's even greater astonishment, the younger Rives showed him a copy of a letter from General Lee to a Virginia legislator, supporting the enlistment of slaves as soldiers, promising freedom for them and their families. No deeper desperation was imaginable.

Colonel Rives went on. He had come to see Kean to discuss his views on the issue of whom to appoint to a three-man peace commission. Kean must have wondered why his opinion was being solicited. He suggested that one commissioner should come from Virginia or North Carolina, another from a cotton state, the third from across the Mississippi. Perhaps Rives's father would agree to go. If not, General Lee should be asked, or Senator William Graham of North Carolina. They had all been Union men before the war.

Then Rives gave away his mission. He wanted to know whether Kean thought Judge Campbell would be willing to negotiate on the basis of reunion. Kean endorsed the judge "as one of the ablest and best negotiators we could have, if it really be necessary to go into that subject." Kean hoped it would not be. Rives knew it would.

―――――

Before the day was out, General Lee issued a public plea for weapons and saddles. General Gorgas told his diary that "Old Blair has returned to this city from Washington and is again gone. What does it all mean? Are we really to make terms with the enemy before we are half beaten? Mr. Singleton has, I believe, gone off. His mission was more I think to see what could be made out of cotton, than one of peace. Would that these birds of evil omen could be kept outside our limits. They do us no good."

Nor did they do Mr. Singleton good. He returned to Washington City a happy man, bearing contracts for a staggering seven million dollars' worth of cotton, rosin, turpentine, and tobacco. His partner, Senator

Browning, made the glad observation that the loot would "make us rich if we can only get it out." In due course, Confederate troops burned it, making no one rich.

—⁓—

On January 25, the Rebel flag-of-truce boat appeared at the Union lines with Preston Blair aboard and asked for leave to disgorge him. On his way back north to Eliza, he met with Grant again at City Point, where Rebel gunboats had launched a sneak attack the night before. Had they not run aground, the consequences could have been ugly. The cagy old insider did not miss his chance to tell Grant how his son-in-law, Admiral Lee, had pressed for more ships to protect City Point.

Julia Grant had just arrived to spend the winter with her husband. A former Democrat like Blair, and a longtime resident of St. Louis, she had met the old man, not long ago, at a White House reception. He had walked her in on his arm. They surely chatted now. She loved to be in on a secret, and her husband had been known to indulge her.

—⁓—

Blair docked in Annapolis on the cold afternoon of January 26 and reached Washington City by train, looking weary, Lizzie thought. But he wrote Horace Greeley energetically the next day in a clearer hand than before. "My dear sir: I have only time to say that 'our plot thickens' & will I think come to a consistency to secure all our objects as well as peace." He had encountered "a very favorable feeling" among "all who have commanding influence in Richmond," and was confident that "nothing can defeat an early peace unless technicalities or points of honor be employed by the selfish & unpatriotic in the South" who profit from the war and are "nothing without it & who therefore will exert all their arts to continue it."

"Great was the excitement" when Blair got home and "it was noised abroad" that peace talks were in the offing, said Lincoln's friend Noah Brooks. The *Times* wished it all away. "The peace bubble that has for ten days past floated so brilliantly before the gaze of men has today come to a sudden collapse. Late last evening Francis P. Blair returned from Richmond, and brought with him precisely what sensible men expected—that is, just nothing. He brought neither olive branch in his hand, Peace Commissioners under his cloak, nor a treaty in his pocket. His mission, so far as practical results are concerned, is in fact as Mr. Blair expressed himself today, 'a total failure.'"

If Mr. Blair said that, he was lying for his country. His hopeful belief that peace was at hand was not among the news that the *Times* saw fit to print.

On Saturday, January 28, Blair returned to the White House and reported to the president. Davis had read his letter twice, he said, acknowledged Lincoln's rejection of "two countries," and understood that the North would only negotiate for one. Lincoln recorded these things on the back of his copy of his "one common country" letter. Should anything come of it all, the Jacobins could not fault him for agreeing to meet the enemy.

Attesting to his contacts in Richmond, Blair conveyed to the president an assortment of requests for favors from influential Southerners, including Davis himself, who pled for the lives of two Rebel prisoners condemned as spies—falsely, Davis said. Among other pleas, Blair sought leave to send to Mrs. Stanard "a pair of shoes, a box of tea, half a dozen shirts for her son & some coarse cotton to cover the nakedness of her Negro house servant."

The levelheaded Blair was so enthused about the chance for a peaceful reunion that it must have given Lincoln some encouragement. Noah Brooks did not claim to know what the president was thinking, but "strengthened by one or two conversations with Mr. Lincoln," he thought he had "no faith whatever" in peace feelers from Dixie.

Gideon Welles thought otherwise. The president, he told his diary, despite "much shrewdness and much good sense, has often strange and incomprehensible whims. Takes sometimes singular and unaccountable freaks. It would hardly surprise me were he to undertake to arrange terms of peace without consulting any one." Dismissing the public denials, Uncle Gideon had "no doubt that the senior Blair has made his visits in concert with the President."

Jefferson Davis could not be blamed for thinking so too.

CHAPTER THIRTEEN

A Determined Stand Ought to
Be Made for Peace

Two months before Abraham Lincoln came into the world in his proverbial log cabin, Robert Mercer Taliaferro Hunter was born into wealth and prominence in Essex County, Virginia, in a house that had a name. When Robert was two, his mother died giving birth to his brother. His father's second wife died in childbirth too, leaving him "twice motherless." A thoughtful boy he was, said the slave woman who raised him, "lonesome in his ways."

Educated at the new University of Virginia with Edgar Allan Poe, Robert went on to a rustic school of law and made good in politics despite his quiet mien. Advancing in short order from the legislature to the House of Representatives, he became at thirty-two the youngest Speaker in history, admired for his intellect, liked for his self-effacing style, chosen for his moderation. A portly, long-haired, smooth-shaven man, in the manner of the day, he advanced to the Senate in 1847 as Lincoln entered the House. When his friends grew beards and muttonchops, Hunter made no change, indifferent to fashion, indifferently groomed, "neither addicted nor adapted" to light conversation or "gossiping intercourse," a loving daughter said. The Mississippi firebrand Henry Foote, unforgiving of his fellow men, called his colleague from Virginia "tardy and sluggish in his movements," crafty and full of grand ambitions but lacking the boldness to achieve them. An admirer called him modest almost to diffidence, with a lifestyle as simple as any plain Virginia farmer's, a term that bears defining. In 1860, the senator owned more than three thousand acres, a flour mill, and about a hundred slaves, though an ever-growing family, bad investments, and a preference for politics over business caused financial strain.

No Virginian since the founding fathers had been more influential. A protégé of Calhoun's, Hunter, along with Jefferson Davis and the bombastic Robert Toombs of Georgia, made up what was known in the old Senate as the Southern Triumvirate. Looking down from the gallery, a spectator saw them huddled in a tableau vivant of temperaments, Toombs leaning forward aggressively, Davis imperiously erect, Hunter listening quietly with his cheek in his hand.

In 1860, Hunter made a bid for the Democratic presidential nomination with respectable Northern support. He condemned the Know Nothings' religious bigotry with no little courage and defended the right to own people. After Lincoln's election, he proposed a bizarre scheme to redesign the Union in an ill-considered effort to save it, including two presidents, one Northern, one Southern, with rotating portfolios. Wounded by the ridicule, he swung his support to secession and resigned from the Senate before Virginia left the Union, but his heart was not in it. He spoke of reconstruction when the Confederacy was barely born, damaging himself in the South while the North was condemning him for treason.

When excited Confederate officials crowded around a telegraph, cheering the news from Bull Run, Hunter only listened. Even friends read his caution as timidity. Davis thought it diminished him, but condescended "to take him as God made him, esteeming him for his good qualities, despite his defects," and made him Secretary of State in 1861 after Toombs left the job to fight Yankees instead of Davis. It lasted seven months. Knowing the president as he did, Hunter told a friend he would *be* Secretary of State, not Mr. Davis's clerk. The last straw fell when he commented on a military matter at a Cabinet meeting. "Mr. Hunter, you are Secretary of State," Davis said, "and when information is wished of that department it will be time for you to speak." Hunter resigned the next day and became once again a senator from Virginia, on the edge of Davis's world, no part of his inner circle but generally supportive.

Hunter's mood, rarely sunny, deteriorated with the war. His eldest boy came home from college with tuberculosis a month after the fighting began and died at the age of twenty-two. Hunter later said his ambition died with his son. In 1863, a Union general sent gunboats up the Rappahannock specifically to burn his mill and take his horses and cattle. Now "ruin stared him in the face." Though the Senate made him its president pro tempore, he faded into the wallpaper, until talk of peace emerged in the winter of 1865, cautiously backed by Hunter, who found himself nudging toward the cabal.

With Blair gone from Richmond, Rebel deserters reported "great exposure and suffering" on the Petersburg siege line. Dozens of shivering Southerners went over to the enemy every night, enticed by Yankee pickets hawking hot food and safety. Some Virginians simply walked home. In their frigid capital city, firewood was selling at five dollars a stick. Desperate women and children burgled their neighbors' coal bins.

On Friday, January 27, an exceptionally bitter day, the corpulent Senator Hunter hastened to the War Department almost at a run, expelling clouds of vapor. It was not the cold that animated him. Davis had dispatched him to ask his vice president to come to the Executive Mansion on special, important business. Hunter found Stephens and told him what the business was, then hurried to the War Department to share it with his friend Judge Campbell.

Davis was at home with the recurring nerve disease that crippled his right arm with pain and cannot have improved his mood. Stephens had been in Richmond for a month and a half, but had not spoken to Davis since 1863. His malignant speeches and letters had built no bridges between them. Now Davis thanked him for coming and told him he would speak in strict confidence about a matter he had discussed with no one but Mr. Hunter. Not even his Cabinet knew. He had asked them to assemble at 4:00 p.m., and wished to have the benefit of Mr. Stephens's judgment before they met. Having neither sought nor respected Mr. Stephens's judgment for years, his unexplained interest in collecting it now must have struck his vice president as odd.

Then Davis let Stephens in on what everyone wanted to know—why Blair had come to Richmond. Even Stephens may have been speechless as Davis recounted the old man's message: that the South could either be subjugated for a generation, or have a victory parade in Mexico City and a new Southern empire. Mr. Blair had said that the Radicals in Mr. Lincoln's party were pressing him hard for a punitive postwar policy, including "the most extreme measures" against the rebellion's leaders (Davis and Stephens being leaders one and two). Davis showed Stephens the letters that had passed between him and Mr. Lincoln. They were only a "cover," he said, for the "undisclosed object" of a joint invasion of Mexico in a reconciling brotherhood of arms.

Far from laughing it off, Davis told Stephens that the ejection of the French from Mexico could lead to reunion. Stephens understood him to be posing "a grave question for mature consideration." Davis wanted to know what Stephens thought. Stephens asked him if he believed that Mr. Blair really spoke for the Lincoln administration. Mr. Blair had denied it, Davis said, but with confidence that Mr. Lincoln would back him. Davis said he was sure that Mr. Lincoln understood what Mr. Blair proposed, despite Mr. Blair's disclaimers.

Stephens endorsed it on the spot. If nothing else, it would open a channel to Mr. Lincoln. Perhaps a truce could be had while the *North* invaded Mexico, "without committing us to an active participation." The chance to regroup would be precious. Whether reunion would result was uncertain. If it did, the seceded states would be returning voluntarily, securing the self-determination for which they had been struggling. It occurred to Stephens immediately that the Jacobins would quash any favorable terms for the South if they knew that peace talks were coming, while a public negotiation that failed would dishearten the Southern people. He stressed the need for "the utmost discretion and the most perfect secrecy" if a meeting were to accomplish anything. Davis said Mr. Blair had been "very particular in stating the same thing."

"Well then," Stephens said, "Mr. President, looking to the question in all its bearings, in my judgment, you and Mr. Lincoln yourselves are the persons who should hold the conference." They could meet near City Point without anyone knowing but Grant and Lee. Davis said no. Decisively. The Confederacy should send at least three commissioners, not its president.* Davis wanted to know whom Stephens would recommend. Stephens thought it over. Secrecy was vital, he said again. Able, discreet men were needed, men whose absence would not be noticed. Judge Campbell was circumspection itself, and respected North and South. General Henry Benning (a former Georgia Supreme Court justice who commanded a brigade near City Point) could slip away unmissed. The able Virginian Thomas Flournoy was visiting Richmond and would leave in a day or two. His departure would cause no comment. He and Mr. Lincoln had been friends in the old Congress.

For the first time in a long time, Davis agreed with his vice president, on the mission and its missionaries. Stephens considered it done, "for I did not think the Cabinet would object to what Mr. Davis so cordially approved." The ice had been broken between them, and they chatted until the Cabinet began to arrive for their meeting. The vice president was not invited.

~ ⌣ ~

Saturday, January 28, dealt the suffering people of Richmond another cold blow, but the War Department clerk John Jones thought Blair's visitation had warmed them. "Can't find a thermometer in the city," he wrote, but there were "many smiling faces in the streets, betokening a profound desire for peace." Early that morning, Jones saw Senator Hunter almost running down the street for a second day in a row, unaccustomed as he was to exertion. He was headed for the stone-built edifice at the foot of Capitol Square, the old US Customs House, the Confederacy's executive office building. Jones guessed the senator was eager for news about Breckinridge, the new Secretary of War, a rival in the old Senate, but Hunter was the one bearing news. Davis had asked him to summon Mr. Stephens again.

Stephens was not surprised when Davis let him know that the Cabinet had agreed to send envoys to Mr. Lincoln, but was taken aback when

---

* Thirty years later, Davis would say he would have met Lincoln in "the neutral border" between Grant's army and Lee's (not the most secret of all locations), but he understood from Blair that the conference would be in Washington, "whither, of course, it was not proper for me to go, however protected by a safe conduct." Why it would not be proper he did not say. Mr. Lincoln could come to him. He would not come to Mr. Lincoln.

he was told that he would lead them. Judge Campbell had been appointed, as Stephens had proposed, but General Benning and Mr. Flournoy had been dropped. Stephens and Mr. Hunter would go instead.

Stephens protested as forcefully as his childlike squeak allowed. He presided over the Senate, he said, and Mr. Hunter presided in his absence. They had never gone missing together. Explanations would be demanded. The Senate's very rules would have to be changed. Two more visible men could not have been named to a secret peace commission "if anything was expected to be accomplished by it." Davis said his Cabinet had made up their minds. Stephens thought again. If he refused to join the mission, Davis and his circle would blame him for its failure, and a crippled negotiation was better than none. Little Alec gave up the fight.

Neither man knew it, but the fight had been fixed, and their friends had fixed it.

Congressman Arthur S. Colyar of Tennessee was a charter member of the cabal, an antebellum Union man who supported Henry Foote in his renegade mission to Washington. A few weeks before the coming of Preston Blair, Congressman John B. Baldwin of Virginia, a friend of Robert E. Lee's and a veteran of his army, had asked Colyar to take a walk with him in the dark after an evening session. A crisis had come, Baldwin said, and "for the first time in my life I feel that I lack the moral courage to do my duty." He had seen General Lee, who had given him to understand that "the cause had to fail." Baldwin knew what had to be done. "A determined stand ought to be made for peace." But knowing Mr. Davis, he feared that "nothing could be done with him."

Shortly thereafter, Baldwin engineered the appointment of a fact-finding committee to which he and Colyar were named. Lee was examined in secret. His testimony was chilling. It was only a question of time before he must abandon Richmond, he said. Deprived of his base and supplies, his army could not be sustained. Baldwin asked the general if he had no redemptive ideas. He said that he did not. Unnerved by Lee's confession, Colyar would not stand by and watch. He drew up resolutions calling on Davis to appoint a three-man peace commission to be named by the House. It was not the first such resolution to be offered, but this one had wind in its sails, and Colyar and his friends had three specific peace commissioners in mind: Stephens, Hunter, and Campbell.

Naming no names, Colyar and a colleague gave Stephens a draft of the resolutions and invited him to edit them, which he gladly did.[*] They were offered to the House on January 12, the very day Blair unveiled his Mexican plan to Davis. The earlier drafts had called for negotiations based on state sovereignty, but now a new element had been added—a North-South collaboration to enforce the Monroe Doctrine, a striking coincidence at best. The resolutions were headed for adoption when the Davis men made a bargain with the cabal. The resolutions' sponsors would withdraw them and Davis would appoint on his own the same three peace commissioners they wanted. "This is substantially the truth of history," so Colyar would later say.

The truth it may be, but Davis never knew it. The president was a fighter, not a deal-maker, as his deal-making allies knew. They had struck their bargain without him, confident that they could persuade him to appoint these peace commissioners with whatever instructions *he* saw fit to give, heading off the greater evil of Congress driving the train.

After Stephens's first talk with Davis, the Cabinet endorsed the peace commission and Campbell's appointment to it, as Stephens had expected, but his other two nominees were unfavorably received. Someone suggested Hunter. Knowing that the war was unwinnable, Secretary of the Navy Stephen Mallory, an able Floridian and a former US senator, was anxious for peace talks. It was he who proposed Stephens. It would stop his maneuverings in Congress, Mallory said, and a failure to name the Confederacy's leading dove to its peace commission would "excite surprise." Davis resisted the idea, but took it under advisement.

He conferred that evening with Senator Benjamin Hill, Stephens's fellow Georgian and longtime bête noir. Hard around the eyes, Hill had once been ill-tempered enough to pitch an inkwell at Alabama's senator William Yancey and unlucky enough to hit him. In the face. Hill was young, rich,

---

[*] Stephens would later say that he did not know at the time that he and Hunter and Campbell were expected to serve on the commission. Colyar would say that he did. Both of them wrote many years after the fact.

and cocky in 1856 when he bested Little Alec in a political debate and started a lifelong feud. They had been deadly enemies, quite literally, since Hill compared Stephens to Judas Iscariot, giving Judas the better grade. When Stephens challenged Hill to a duel, Hill declined and published an explanation. To kill the little fellow would be against the laws of God and Georgia, and "a great annoyance to me afterward." Stephens was "a perfect 'Colt's Repeater' in the matter of telling falsehoods," Hill said, and had called Hill a braggart, having previously equated himself with Moses.

Their hatred for one another was grim. Now Davis asked Hill, a loyal Davis man, what he thought of the choice of Stephens to bargain for the Confederacy's life. Hill liked the idea. He would later say he insisted on it, and had urged it on Davis even before Stephens spoke with the president. Stephens had been close to Lincoln in the old Congress, Hill said (a pale compliment). Sending him to Washington "would at least check his evil-doing in the Senate," and Davis could not be blamed for a failed peace conference if Stephens led it. Persuaded by Hill's advice, which echoed Secretary Mallory's, Davis assured the senator that he would not yield their country's independence as the price of a chat with Mr. Lincoln, but if a truce could be had, he would take it. With reunion out of the question, Hill was sure that the peace talks would fail and disappoint the people. What better man to lead them than Moses?

Though Hill did not tell Davis, he had made his own deal with Stephens: Georgia's congressional delegation would support Colyar's peace resolutions, and Stephens would persuade Governor Joseph Brown to drop his threats to seek a separate peace. Hill calculated that the resolutions would pass, and produce nothing. When Davis chose Stephens to lead a doomed peace mission, the arrangement could not have been sweeter.

The chief Confederate hawk would appoint three doves as his envoys to the North. A truce just might ensue. Far more likely, nothing would come of it all but a Yankee slap in the face, discrediting Little Alec and his peace movement. And that would be satisfactory too.

Davis's Secretary of State, Judah Benjamin, was an English fishmonger's son and a former US senator. Born in the British West Indies, raised in

Charleston, educated at Yale—from which he had been separated under a cloud of uncertain character—he had taken himself to Louisiana in possession of four dollars and risen to become a leading New Orleans lawyer and a slave-holding sugarcane planter. A "short, stout man," said the *Times of London*'s William Howard Russell, with "a full face, olive-colored, and most decidedly Jewish features, with the brightest large black eyes, one of which is somewhat diverse from the other, and a brisk, lively, agreeable manner, combined with much vivacity of speech and quickness of utterance . . ." A wellborn junior officer mocked his "keg-like form and over-deferential manner, suggestive of a prosperous shopkeeper," but acknowledged his "elegantly polished speech." It was said that "the brains of the Confederacy" was a moniker Alec Stephens coveted and Judah Benjamin won. His large cast of enemies rarely missed a chance to allude to his "Hebrew origins," which had not made his accomplishments easier, despite his conversion to his wife's Catholicism, itself no advantage in Richmond. Judah Benjamin was a talented man, and closer to Jefferson Davis than any other.

It had not always been so. In 1858, the "little man from Louisiana," as Davis called him then, grew larger after Davis imputed to him in a Senate debate "an attempt to misrepresent a very plain remark." Without so much as leaving his desk, Benjamin composed an invitation to a duel and asked a colleague to deliver it. To his credit, Davis told Benjamin's second, "I will make this all right at once. I have been wholly wrong." The next day, he apologized on the Senate floor and admitted that his behavior sometimes inclined to the "dogmatic and dictatorial," as his best friends told him. Judah Benjamin was grace itself. "I shall be very happy to forget everything that has occurred between us, except the pleasant passage of this morning."

Now he brought Judge Campbell the news of his appointment as an envoy to Mr. Lincoln, much to the judge's surprise. Benjamin told Campbell who the other members were but gave him no details, and asked him to go to the president's house. When Campbell arrived, Hunter and Stephens were already there. Davis said there was great discontent in the United States with the state of things in Mexico—so much so that Mr.

Blair had brought from Washington a plan for a joint expedition to oust Maximilian from his throne. As the judge took this in, it struck him that no mention was being made of the means to be used, "nor what was to be done with Mexico should we succeed." To Campbell's increasing amazement, Davis seemed convinced that Lincoln was more concerned about the situation in Mexico than he was about the Civil War, which he was said to be willing to suspend "under some sort of collusive contract." The Confederacy's demand for independence could somehow be adjusted after things were straightened out in Mexico.

Davis told the judge that he and Mr. Stephens and Mr. Hunter had been chosen to go north to confer with Mr. Lincoln as peace commissioners. Tomorrow morning. They would run down the James by steamer to City Point. Mr. Blair had made it clear that General Grant would be expecting them and would pass them through to Washington City.

Davis gave his envoys little guidance. They were free to accept any "treaty" that did *not* include reunion. He had made it clear to Hill, and no doubt told the commissioners, that while he did not wish them to deceive Mr. Lincoln or be responsible for any false impressions, he was willing to secure an armistice even if they were satisfied that Mr. Lincoln might accept one under the mistaken impression that reunion must follow—a subtle distinction at best. Davis would later say that he gave them some suggestions, but "left much to their discretion," and advised them, if they could, "to receive rather than make propositions." Other than that, he left them to negotiate the survival of their country (not to mention their own) on the fly.

As Campbell sized them up, the commissioners' reactions ran from scornful to naive. "I was incredulous, Mr. Hunter did not have faith. Mr. Stephens supposed Blair to be 'the mentor of the Administration and Republican party'" with a plan that made perfect sense.

Having authorized them to agree to anything *but* reunion, Davis gave his envoys, "as a passport to Washington City," the letter from Lincoln to Blair inviting a proposal to bring peace to "our one common country." As the rarely sarcastic Campbell would soon have occasion to say, they "did not find their passport available" when they presented it to the enemy.

As Stephens had feared, news of their mission was on the street before they were. With secrecy gone, he sent a draft to Davis of a statement to the Associated Press: "It is understood that Judge Campbell, Senator Hunter & Mr. Stephens will at an early day go to Washington to see what can be done in the way of negotiation. It is believed this course has been adopted from what has transpired in the Blair Mission. They go with the approval of the President." Stephens gave Davis his reasoning. To say that a commission had been appointed "may put Lincoln in some difficulty or embarrassment." He had been "particular in saying he would accept agents only in an informal way." On the other hand, an "informal" interview should not be announced explicitly. The subject should be avoided.

It fell to Judah Benjamin to draft the commissioners' credentials, a letter of authorization to be shown to the federal gatekeepers that could bridge what seemed unbridgeable—Lincoln's offer to make peace for one country and Davis's demand for two. Benjamin found a way. To accompany a copy of Lincoln's "one common country" letter, he drafted a one-sentence note to the commissioners: "In compliance with the letter of Mr. Lincoln, of which the foregoing is a copy, you are hereby requested to proceed to Washington City for conference with him upon the subject to which it relates." It was neatly done. While purporting to act "in compliance" with Lincoln's letter, Davis would merely be authorizing them to confer on "the subject to which it relates," neither accepting one country nor demanding two. Everyone's face would be saved.

Benjamin's chief clerk, William Bromwell, made three copies of the secretary's draft and brought them to Davis, who reviewed one closely and glanced at the other two. "Mr. Bromwell," he said, "there is something wrong here. Mr. Benjamin says in the letter, '*on the subject.*'" No subject was mentioned in Mr. Lincoln's letter. "And again, it will never do to ignore the fact that there are *two* countries instead of but *one common country*. We can't be too particular on that point." Davis took a pen and ruined Benjamin's work: "In ~~compliance~~ **conformity** with the letter of Mr. Lincoln, of which the foregoing is a copy, you are ~~hereby~~ requested to proceed to Washington City for **an informal** conference with him upon the ~~subject to which it relates,~~ **issues involved in the existing war, and for the purpose of securing peace to the two countries**." The Confederate States of America did not act "in compliance" with Lincoln's demands; its interests happened to conform with them. The conference would be informal, though Stephens had urged Davis not to say so. One could not be too particular about two countries.

Bromwell walked Davis's revision back to Benjamin. "He has cut it up considerably," Bromwell said.

"Just like him," Benjamin replied. Then he turned to another aide. "I never saw such a man in my life."

Benjamin could see at a glance that Davis had wrecked his draft. The whole thing would break down over "two countries," he said. The federal authorities "will never permit the commissioners to pass through with such letters."

Benjamin must have known that Davis would not relent, but he went to the Executive Mansion and tried. The commissioners' instructions should be as vague and general as possible, he said, to start a dialogue, to see where Mr. Lincoln stood, to test the intentions Mr. Blair attributed to him. If the parties got to the table, anything could happen, but a meeting conditioned on "two countries" would never occur.

Davis stood his ground and signed the letters as he had edited them. If there were not two countries, he said, he had no authority in the matter. The people had made him president to preserve and defend their Confederacy. He had taken an oath to do so, not to bargain it out of existence. A purposeful sort of vagueness might imply assent to Mr. Lincoln's false premise that reunion could be had. As a matter of "personal honor," it must be clear that Mr. Lincoln had not been misled.

According to Varina Davis, everyone thought the problematic words, our "one common country," had come from Seward, "to defeat the objects of the conference," as if Lincoln would have accepted two. Benjamin later said that neither he nor Davis nor any of the commissioners gave reunion so much as a thought. The conference was a chance for a truce, out of which peace might come. "But none of us for a moment dreamed of reconstruction." Whatever Benjamin was dreaming, the commissioners kept their dreams to themselves.

That night, a State Department man by the fabled name of Washington brought over to Judge Campbell a purse for their expenses and three identical letters of appointment. As he finished reading his, the judge looked up with dismay when he came to "two countries." It did not correspond to Mr. Lincoln's letter, he said, and "might make difficulty." Washington replied that Mr. Davis and Mr. Benjamin had differed on the issue and had settled it. The subject was closed.

After wishing his commissioners well, Davis confided in an ally, Mississippi congressman Ethelbert Barksdale, and gave the lie to what he had just led Stephens to believe—that the Mexican plan could lead to reunion, "a grave question for mature consideration." Barksdale took Blair's scheme seriously until Davis assured him that he need not worry about a negotiated peace. Davis anticipated, he said, and had given the commissioners to understand, that Mr. Lincoln would demand unconditional surrender and reject anything short of it. His instruction to insist on independence fell rather far short of it. He was sending envoys to Mr. Lincoln "to satisfy a public belief," propounded by malcontents and obstructionists, that an honorable peace could be had by negotiation. To lead it he had named Mr. Stephens as "the recognized head of the peace party," leaving no room for a charge of bad faith.

Davis would later say that Stephens and Hunter, first and second in line to succeed him, were prepared to abandon the cause, were "utterly unfit" to lead it, and could not have been trusted with "the powers of negotiation." Davis had it right, from Davis's point of view. If anything, Campbell was even less enamored of the Confederacy than Stephens was, if not so indiscreet about it, and Hunter had lost his faith. In the end, Davis was sending three of his most reluctant Rebels on a mission to save the rebellion.

None of them missed the irony. Little Alec would later say privately that he considered Davis's endorsement of the conference "a humbug" from the start. Stephens told Campbell that "the old story of the monkey that took the paw of the cat to pull his chestnuts out of the fire was not without some modern illustration." Campbell thought so too, and said he did not like it. Hunter would come to believe that the people's demands for peace had grown so loud that Davis and his circle had decided to make "a show" of an effort to obtain it. Many Southerners were alarmed by talk of arming slaves, Hunter said, and "mothers, who had shrunk from nothing heretofore, were beginning to flinch" at the prospect of their sons of sixteen or younger being fed into the grinder. Years later, Hunter would suggest that Davis had appointed his peace commissioners with no expectation of success—as dupes, not as diplomats.

Events would show what diplomats could have done.

CHAPTER FOURTEEN

Is There Nothing That Will Degrade a Man?

On the cold Sunday morning of January 29, the peace commissioners met at the Richmond & Petersburg depot near the High Bridge over the James. The ice-jammed river had forced a change in plans. Instead of going down to Grant by steamer, they would take the ten o'clock train to Petersburg and present themselves at his siege line.

Alec Stephens was in his usual condition, leaning on his cane, not long out of a sickbed, his complexion "as yellow as a ripe ear of corn," cocooned in scarves and shawls, weighted down with a ponderous gray overcoat of dense Southern wool, its collar so high off his shoulders that it tipped his hat when he shrugged them. Too feeble to travel alone, he had brought his trusted valet, a slave by the name of Ben Travis.

Lieutenant Colonel William Hatch, Preston Blair's recent host, had also come along, as an aide. A handsome, thirty-two-year-old, Kentucky-born lawyer, he did what he could as Assistant Commissioner of Exchange for the suffering men and boys who passed through his hands from both sides, and both sides admired him for it. An exchanged Michigan cavalryman called Hatch "a perfect gentleman with a big heart in him." His friendships with federal officers, acquired in the course of his trade, might ease the commissioners through the lines.

As they boarded their train, the papers were full of their trip. Stephens remarked that the publicity alone would probably keep them from accomplishing anything. The *Dispatch* noted wisely that "a thousand speculations" explained their mission, "all of which, being based on no known facts, are worthless." War news was scarce, but "peace rumors were as plentiful as blackberries."

Gathered at the depot, Campbell gave Stephens and Hunter their copies of Davis's mandate to bring peace to two countries. Stephens read his as the train left the station, literally and figuratively. The very spot was set in his memory. "Upon opening and reading it as we crossed the High Bridge, I remarked to Judge Campbell, 'nothing could come of it.'" If Davis had contrived it to prevent any conference at all, it "could not have been better worded." Campbell believed he had done just that. Stephens had thought there was a chance of doing something. Now all three commissioners despaired. Convinced that Davis's letter would stop them at the federal lines, they agreed not to use it at all unless they had no choice.

As the train rattled on to Petersburg, Judge Campbell disconcerted his fellow peacemakers with the South's inability to wage war. "I knew when we started on that mission," Hunter said, that the Confederacy's resources were thin, "but the extent of our destitution I did not understand" until Campbell shared the substance of a report he was preparing for the Secretary of War. Hunter would later call it "a beggarly account of empty regiments." The commissioners knew already that the loss of their last seaport had cauterized their trade. "To the world without we were hermetically sealed by the blockade." Now Campbell let them know that their domestic supplies of food, clothing, and arms were nearly gone too.

The train ride to Petersburg was not bereft of hope. Stephens told his colleagues about his friendship with Lincoln in the old Congress and their warm correspondence in 1860. Neither Campbell nor Hunter knew much about Lincoln personally. "I knew him well," Stephens said, "and esteemed him highly." (The feeling, moreover, was mutual. Lincoln had considered offering Stephens a Cabinet post before Georgia seceded.) Little Alec recounted their protests against taking half of Mexico in 1848 and their efforts to make Zach Taylor president, hoping he would put a stop to it. "We succeeded in the election, but not in the object."

As the train made its stops, Hunter was impressed with his constituents' response, as "we were received everywhere along the line with marks of great interest and curiosity. Of course, we did nothing voluntarily to create expectations," holding scant hope of success. When they reached embattled Petersburg, an excited crowd of well-wishers greeted them, and moved them. At the head of the welcoming party, a local judge let them know if they returned "with any fair hope of peace," every man, woman, and child in the city would thank them. Hunter had arrived with a grim expectation of failure. He would go to Abraham Lincoln determined to help his people.

The commissioners waited in Petersburg while their aide, Colonel Hatch, went off to the siege line. Not long past noon, drawing cheers when his message spread, Hatch informed the enemy under a white flag of truce that three Southern dignitaries had arrived on their way to Washington, that General Grant would be expecting them, that their mission was to end the war. Given Grant's reputation in the parts from which they had come, they may not have been surprised but could not have been encouraged when Hatch came back to Petersburg with word from a federal officer that the general was away "on a big drunk," which must have dampened their joy at the celebration of their arrival.

Lee sent a message to Davis that day from his Petersburg headquarters: If Grant were reinforced (as he surely would be), Lee did not see how he could hold on. His men had had no meat for days. An eighteen-year-old South Carolinian was delivering a dispatch on horseback when A. P. Hill's barefoot infantry marched by. Their bright red tracks on the icy ground would be fresh in his memory until he was buried in his uniform in 1917.

On the Union side of no-man's-land there was meat enough for pets. "The dog mania has got hold of my staff again," General Orlando Willcox had written his wife, "and we have curs of every degree at headquarters." Willcox was a full-bearded Indian fighter from Michigan in command of the 9th Corps. A colonel informed him of the arrival of the peace commissioners and their purported understanding with Grant. Willcox knew nothing about it, and wired his superior at City Point, General John Parke. Grant was in North Carolina and had left City Point in the hands of a capable friend, General Edward Ord. Parke passed the buck to Ord, who moved it up by wire to the Secretary of War.

For a second time that day, Colonel Hatch met his Northern counterparts in no-man's-land, cheered from both sides. He was asked to return in the morning. The *Boston Evening Transcript* said a tacit truce had prevailed for days, what with rumors of peace in the press, but few had thought it "conducive to health to exhibit themselves prominently." Now every man and boy "not otherwise engaged" was crowding the parapets of both armies, craning for a look at peace. The killing had stopped, and tragedy gave way to comedy as pickets "whiled away the closing hours of the beautiful Sabbath in seemingly friendly intercourse."

Scores of ebullient letters were composed in pits and trenches, but General Willcox wrote home to his wife in a snit. General Meade had awarded him a twenty-day leave, but Willcox's immediate superior, "being zero & afraid of his shadow," had vetoed it. Willcox felt "partly compensated" nonetheless, "for Stephens, Hunter & Campbell have been seeking to come in through my lines on their way to Washington to talk of peace. . . . I suppose I shall see the three doves with olive branches in their mouths, & God grant that peace may ensue, though I must confess I fear the talk will amount to nothing quite yet."

Late that night, having first asked Lincoln for instructions, Secretary of War Stanton shot a wire to City Point in response to General Ord's report of a Rebel peace commission expecting a welcome from Grant. There was no welcome in it. One can almost hear Mars roaring. "This Department has no knowledge of any understanding by General Grant to allow any persons to come within his lines as commissioners of any sort. You will therefore allow no one to come into your lines under such character or profession until you receive the President's instructions."

It had only been a day since Blair had told Lincoln that Davis had seemed to accept "our one common country" as a premise for peace, but Lincoln had his doubts. Davis had always rejected reunion out of hand, and Lincoln would not see his envoys until he endorsed it plainly. The House would vote the next day on the amendment banning slavery. A dozen War Democrats who were leaning toward aye were wobbly already. If they thought Jeff Davis was ready to come home, they would never drive him away by banning slavery. Instead of welcoming the doves to Washington, Lincoln decided to keep them in Virginia, out of sight of the House of Representatives, until they had been vetted and the amendment had been passed.

At or about the time that Stanton was composing his orders to General Ord to keep the Rebel peace commissioners on their own side of no-man's-land, the president was chatting in the White House with Captain Robert Todd Lincoln, Harvard '64, a newly named member of Grant's staff. The president told his son he was not entirely comfortable letting generals vet peacemakers. He was going to send Tom Eckert down to see them, with orders to let them pass if they committed to reunion in writing, but not otherwise.

Meticulously dressed and groomed, Major Thomas T. Eckert, soon to be General Thomas T. Eckert, was an expert telegrapher who had never worn a uniform, but Stanton had given him a major's rank and pay, a government horse and carriage, and command of the War Department's telegraph office, which the president haunted for war news. A bureaucrat's bureaucrat, Eckert was cut from his boss's cloth. He bullied his subordinates like a drill instructor with a toothache and guarded his master like a Rottweiler. Early in the war, he was capable of misleading the president himself, so rigidly did he follow Stanton's orders to preserve secrecy. The very model of an officious civil servant, Eckert wielded his authority whenever he had it, and often when he did not. As almost no one else would do, he was known to push back against Mars himself when he thought that Stanton was wrong, never doubting that Eckert was right.

Now Lincoln told his son that Eckert would screen the Rebel peace envoys. He had "never failed to do completely what was given him to do, and to do it in the most complete and tactful manner," without deviating an inch from his orders. An "incessant worker," as Lincoln's friend Noah Brooks called him, he would shed his harness grudgingly even to get some sleep.

According to a Lincoln bodyguard, the War Department was housed in "a small, mean, two-story building" on the western edge of the Executive Mansion's lawn. With the exception of its occupant, there was nothing mean about Stanton's second-floor office overlooking the White House, and Eckert's adjoining telegraph office made him the best-informed man in the army. Stanton hovered there day and night. Most mornings and evenings, Lincoln did too, often past midnight, feeding on news of the war. Major Eckert would walk him home with a corporal's guard. On election night, the major had provided a midnight supper for Lincoln and his friends as the returns came in by wire. The commander in chief had amused his aide John Hay, going "awkwardly and hospitably to work shoveling out the fried oysters." Eckert was powerfully built and had once impressed the president by breaking four or five iron pokers over his arm while sampling a government contractor's wares and finding them wanting. In 1907, Robert Lincoln recalled that his father was so emphatic about sending Eckert in particular to examine the Rebel peace commissioners "that it made a deep impression upon me, and I never see General Eckert without thinking of it."

Sending Eckert south was the Secretary of War's idea. Stanton told Lincoln that the conference was a trap, that Davis was sending "underlings," whose commitments could be disavowed. It was beneath the president's dignity to see them. What would be the point? He had "no right" to offer them anything but surrender. Lincoln only listened. Before Eckert left, Stanton told him to "keep close to Mr. Lincoln" if peace talks ensued, to save him from being "snared."

A telegrapher named David Bates reported to Eckert obsequiously, and it seemed even to him that Lincoln might have trusted Grant instead of Eckert to screen the Rebel envoys. "But the subject was so complicated and fraught with contingent dangers, and Stanton was so strenuous in his objections to the whole scheme, that only Lincoln himself or someone fresh from his councils who possessed his absolute confidence could be trusted to meet the shrewd and wily adversaries." Having implied that Grant was no match for shrewd and wily adversaries, let alone contingent dangers, Bates lets us know what Stanton was thinking—"that Lincoln's great kindness of heart and his desire to end the war might lead him to make some admission which the astute Southerners would willfully misconstrue and twist to serve their purpose."

Grant had heard this kind of thing before. In 1862, when the general was in command in Tennessee, Stanton and his man Henry Halleck, then General in Chief of the Army, had cautioned him to keep his military plans from the president. Lincoln was so kind, they said, "so averse to refusing anything asked of him, that some friend would be sure to get from him all he knew." Grant took their advice and improved on it. "I did not communicate my plans to the President," he later recalled, "nor did I to the Secretary of War or to General Halleck."

He was about to expand his range in the art of evading Stanton.

—◆—

On Monday, January 30, Jefferson Davis's mouthpiece spoke. The president had sent able men to see Mr. Lincoln, the *Richmond Sentinel* said. In their efforts to win peace, "no means will be left untried," but if "three eminent citizens" failed, one good thing *would* happen: It would no longer be possible for "factions or the timid" to persuade the Southern people that peace could be had by any other means than "stout hearts and strong hands."

The *Examiner* took a harder view, shamed by the very thought of the South's submission to federalism but not by human bondage as an ornament of its civilization. The enemy would demand two things—abolition and submission to federal power—"and these include everything." The defeated states would be provinces of a Northern empire, "and a distinctive element of our Southern civilization" would be lost. "The enemy knows the weakness of our President." It was weak to let Mr. Blair come and go in the service of "schemes and projects unworthy of a gallant people." It had turned their thoughts to peace when they ought to be bracing for war.

The *Examiner* was not alone. On the floor of the US Senate, the Jacobin Benjamin Wade attacked Preston Blair and Jefferson Davis like an edged weapon. "We have heard of our emissary going down there to beg for peace at the footstool of those scoundrels. . . . Is there nothing that will degrade a man? May he not steep himself in crime so deep that it is damnation and contamination to communicate with him? . . . I was here when Jeff Davis and company walked up to your desk, sir, and raised their hands to God, and swore to maintain the Constitution of the United States, and I was here when that oath was forgotten and they raised their accursed arm against this Republic. . . . Is perjury no disgrace? . . . It seems it did not affect Mr. Blair in the least."

Maryland's moderate Unionist Reverdy Johnson defended his constituent. "How came he to go there?" Johnson asked, implying that he had gone with Lincoln's blessing.

"God only knows," Wade replied. "I would like to know. Yea, sir, I intend to know . . ."

"He went in a Government vessel the last time."

"Yes, I understand he went in a Government vessel." He had no more right to be on that vessel on a mission to this devil Davis than on the road "to the lower regions in a vehicle furnished by the Government." (Wade had senators laughing now.) "Sir, it is dishonor, it is futile to beg of Davis and company for compromise or peace. I know these men. They are high-spirited men, as the devil, I suppose, is high-spirited. After he went into rebellion I suppose he would not go back into heaven if they offered to reconstruct with him. His pride would forbid it." (More laughter.) Why did our president allow communication with this rebellious devil Davis? "I do not know that he does, and I hope to God he has not sanctioned any such thing, and that he never will sanction it." Break up "this nest of vipers at Richmond," and the people of the South will "flock back to the old standard with joy . . . but you must first break up these devils; you must not disgrace our nation by treating with them; for it would be disgrace, dishonor, contamination in the eyes of our own people and in the eyes of the civilized world."

On the siege line that Monday morning, three devils awaited their due. General Willcox sent a wire to his superior, General Parke. "I fully share what I know must be your regret at the delay concerning the commissioners. If the rebel government is seeking capital, this delay will be a point in their favor." If Grant, as they claimed, had authorized their passage, would it not be well to admit them through the lines and hold them on our side until the word came to pass them on? Parke replied promptly. No one was going anywhere until Washington said so.

Bearing his flag of truce, the charming Colonel Hatch appeared again in front of Fort Morton and its fourteen Northern cannon and again returned to the Rebel lines. No pass had come through. Less than seven months earlier, Colonel Sam Harriman, one of Hatch's interlocutors, had lost 145 of the 37th Wisconsin's 250 men and boys in a single day. Now he wrote home to his adjutant general. "I have but little faith in peace commissions. A piece of ten-inch shell is all the peace they can appreciate or that will help them any."

The Secretary of War sent a wire to the front at 10:30 a.m. Major Eckert was coming from Washington, it said, though the major was not named: "By direction of the President," Stanton said, General Ord was to tell the commissioners "that a messenger will be dispatched to them at or near where they now are, without unnecessary delay." The message was unspecified. Far from dropping his guard, Ord wired Parke that "the rebels may attempt something on our rear or flank." Have your men alert and "plenty of ammunition handy."

While Ord kept his powder dry, an anxious Alec Stephens wrote a note to General Grant, which Hunter and Campbell approved and Hatch delivered to the siege line.

> *Sir: We desire to pass your lines under safe conduct and to proceed to Washington to hold a conference with President Lincoln upon the subject of the existing war [Judah Benjamin's evasion restored], and with a view of ascertaining upon what terms it may be terminated, in pursuance of the course indicated by him in his letter to Mr. F. P. Blair of January 18, 1865, of which we presume you have a copy; and if not, we wish to see you in person, and to confer with you upon the subject. [Emphasis added]*

They signed themselves "Very Respectfully." Very cleverly too. The course that Lincoln had indicated in his letter to Mr. F. P. Blair was peace for "our one common country." The commissioners kept to themselves their orders to insist on two. Their request to see Grant if Lincoln would not see them was rooted in Blair's assurance that the general endorsed their mission, and their belief that Grant and Lee could end the war if Lincoln and Davis could not.

⸻

Traders dumped gold on Wall Street that day. The threat of peace had reached New York. Gideon Welles recorded the mood in Washington. "Great talk and many rumors from all quarters of peace."

Jefferson Davis's wild-eyed nemesis, the resigned Rebel congressman Henry Foote, wrote to his old friend Seward that day from a Union Army command post on the Virginia side of the Potomac, to which he had made his way after a Confederate judge had ordered him freed from his Fredericksburg jail cell, completing his escape from rebellion. Mr. Davis was the only bar to peace and reunion, he wrote. Most Southerners and many of their leaders would return to "the flag of our fathers" and endorse a ban on slavery, effective in 1900, if the North gave them amnesty and restored their Constitutional rights. Seward replied coolly, soliciting any further information that "the prisoner may think it proper to impart," and giving him a choice between repatriation to the Confederacy and a one-way trip to Liverpool. Foote chose the latter.

While Foote flailed away ineffectually, General Lee was staying abreast of Richmond's authorized peace mission. In a letter to Davis that day, he speculated that the enemy was delaying the commissioners' passage to keep them from seeing troop movements.

As Colonel Hatch and the commissioners retired for the night, unsure if their mission had failed, General Grant was on his way back to City Point on an overnight steamer.

CHAPTER FIFTEEN

You Will Not Assume to Definitely Consummate Anything

Grant admired Lincoln. His affection for the Secretary of War was limited. "Mr. Lincoln gained influence over men by making them feel that it was a pleasure to serve him," Grant said. Mr. Stanton "cared nothing for the feelings of others. In fact, it seemed to be pleasanter to him to disappoint than to gratify. He felt no hesitation in assuming the functions of the executive, or in acting without advising him." Two could play at that game.

Civilian supremacy over the military had been drilled into Grant since his plebe year at West Point. So had honesty in all things. An aide said the general always thought himself obliged to defer to Stanton, his civilian superior, whose Assistant Secretary of War, Charles Dana, said the general was incapable of chicanery. The general said otherwise. Long after peace had come, he repeatedly recalled in public, without a hint of contrition, how he had evaded the Secretary of War, defied him, even deceived him when it served.

As General Jubal Early had shown in July in his visit to Silver Spring at the head of a Rebel division, his troops in the Shenandoah Valley were a short march from Washington. Stanton insisted on keeping strong forces between Early and Pennsylvania Avenue, forgoing opportunities to attack him from the south. As Grant would blithely recall, "I determined to put a stop to this." Stanton objected when Grant chose the hyperaggressive General Phillip Sheridan, then defending Washington on the Monocacy River, to attack General Early. Unmoved by the secretary's wishes, Grant wired General Halleck, Stanton's obedient servant, and said that Sheridan must "put himself south of the enemy and follow him to the death. Wherever the enemy goes let our troops go also."

When Lincoln saw Grant's telegram he wired him directly. "This, I think, is exactly right, as to how our forces should move. But please look over the dispatches you may have received from here, even since you made that order, and discover, if you can, that there is any idea in the head of any one here of 'putting our army south of the enemy,' or of 'following him to the death' in any direction. I repeat to you, it will neither be done nor attempted unless you watch it every day, and hour, and force it."

Needing no clearer license to ignore Stanton, Grant saw it and raised it to a deception. "I replied to this that I would start in two hours for Washington, and soon got off, going directly to the Monocacy without stopping at Washington on my way." There was more. "I knew it was impossible for me to get orders through Washington to Sheridan to make a move, because they would be stopped there." He executed his plan without troubling Stanton with it. Sheridan attacked Early and routed him.

When Grant approved Sherman's march to the sea, cut off from the War Department, "the authorities" vetoed it. "Out of deference to the Government," Grant would later say, "I telegraphed Sherman and stopped him twenty-four hours, and then considering that that was deference enough to the Government, I telegraphed him to go ahead again."

As part of their running battle, Stanton instructed Grant's telegraphers to send him every word the general transmitted, and forbade any orders to be sent until he approved them. "He never disturbed himself, either, in examining my orders until it was entirely convenient for him," Grant said. "I remonstrated against this in writing, and the Secretary apologetically restored me to my rightful position of General-in-Chief of the Army. But he soon lapsed again and took control much as before." Two could play at that game, too.

No one was tougher in a fight than Grant, but the general was as soft as Lincoln on peace and reconciliation. He dismissed the Secretary of War's assessment that the president's kindness required supervision. "Mr. Lincoln was not timid, and he was willing to trust his generals in making and executing their plans. The Secretary was very timid.... He could see our weakness, but he could not see that the enemy was in danger. The enemy would not have been in danger if Mr. Stanton had been in the field."

Mr. Stanton was not in the field when Messrs. Stephens, Hunter, and Campbell presented themselves at Grant's siege line, seeking leave to come to the peace table.

On Tuesday, the last day of January 1865, the commissioners, still in Petersburg, woke up to a warming trend. By Michigan standards, General Willcox thought the weather had turned fine. The Virginian John Jones found it "bright and frosty." Early that morning, Grant returned to City Point and found it hot with peace fever. Despite "the admirably private and noiseless manner in which everything is conducted here," the *New York Times* correspondent said, the distracting news was out that peace envoys were coming, though "no one seemed to know exactly when or how." Every train pulling in from the front, every steamboat down the James, was said to bring Rebels bearing armistice papers. The end of the war was in the air, and Grant was determined to keep it aloft, the Secretary of War notwithstanding.

Resuming his command at the center of the bubble, the general was informed that three Rebel dignitaries had presented themselves at his lines two days before, and had sent him a note seeking leave to proceed to Washington for the purpose of ending the war. It was put in his hands immediately. Davis had told the commissioners that Grant would be expecting them. He waved them through on the spot with an eloquent exclamation point:

Gentlemen!

Your communication of yesterday requesting an interview with myself, and a safe conduct to Washington and return, has been received. I will instruct the commanding officers of the forces near Petersburg to receive you, notifying you at what part of the line and the time when and where conveyance will be ready for you. Your letter to me has been telegraphed to Washington for instructions. I have no doubt that before you arrive at my Head Quarters, an answer will be received, directing me to comply with your request. Should a different reply be received, I promise you a safe and immediate return within your own lines.

To deliver his note of welcome and bring his guests to City Point, Grant dispatched his twenty-nine-year-old aide, Lieutenant Colonel Orville Babcock, a battle-tested veteran and a genial favorite of Mrs. Grant's. Babcock left for the siege line on the next train.

Only after all of this was done did the general enlighten Washington, enclosing the commissioners' note. He began writing a message to the Secretary of War, then crossed out Stanton's name and addressed himself to Lincoln: "I have sent directions to receive these gentlemen, and expect to have them at my quarters this evening awaiting your instructions." Lincoln replied that afternoon, well aware that Stanton had stopped the gentlemen cold a day and a half before. "A messenger is coming to you on the business contained in your dispatch. Detain the gentlemen in comfortable quarters until he arrives, and then act upon the message he brings as far as applicable, it having been made up to pass through General Ord's hands, and when the gentlemen were supposed to be beyond our lines." The president did not inquire why Stanton's order to keep them there had been ignored.

Lincoln was encouraged when he read their note to Grant, suggesting as it did that they were ready to bring peace to our one common country. He decided to meet them halfway, far from Capitol Hill, in the person of his Secretary of State, so long as they assured Tom Eckert that they accepted his conditions. He took up a pen and sent Seward to Hampton Roads.

You will proceed to Fortress Monroe, there to meet and informally confer with Messrs. Stephens, Hunter, and Campbell on the basis of my letter to F. P. Blair, Esq., of January 18, 1865, a copy of which you have. You will make known to them that three things are indispensable, to wit: 1st. The restoration of the national authority throughout all the states. 2d. No receding, <u>by the Executive of the United States</u>

*[emphasis added], on the slavery question from the position assumed
thereon in the late annual message to Congress and in preceding documents. 3d. No cessation of hostilities short of an end of the war and the
disbanding of all forces hostile to the Government.*

*You will inform them that all propositions of theirs, not inconsis-
tent with the above, will be considered and passed upon in a spirit of
sincere liberality. You will hear all they may choose to say, and report it
to me. You will not assume to definitely consummate anything.*

Weeks later, when the president's instructions were read to the House
of Representatives, members who knew Seward would chuckle over the
last sentence.

As Lincoln was sending Seward south, his aide John Nicolay was a guest
on the floor of the House, on the verge of its vote on the Constitutional
amendment banning slavery. The outcome was considered a coin toss,
despite the president's pledge to his vote collectors on Capitol Hill:
"Whatever promise you make to those men, I will perform it." Sunset
Cox woke up that day expecting to vote aye. He had promised to support the amendment, for "high officials" had told him that all hope for
negotiation was gone, and the South was about to free its slaves to make
soldiers of them. Now there would be war until the Confederacy was
dead, and a Constitutional ban on slavery could not impede reunion. But
when Cox strolled into the chamber at half past noon, he was told that
Southern peace envoys were about to cross Grant's lines. Some said they
already had.

Congressman James M. Ashley was the amendment's floor manager, a smooth-shaven abolitionist from Toledo who had comforted John
Brown's wife on the day he hanged. Now Ashley was beset by Democrats
like Cox who had pledged to vote aye, thinking peace talks were dead.
Knowing no more than they did, Ashley confronted Nicolay. With inno-
cent sincerity, Lincoln's aide said he knew of no peace commission. It was
not good enough for Cox, who told Ashley that his vote depended on the
president's confirmation.

The president was writing his instructions to Seward when a messenger arrived with a note from Ashley: "The report is in circulation in the House that Peace Commissioners are on their way or are in the city, and is being used against us. If it is true, I fear we shall lose the bill. Please authorize me to contradict it, if not true." Honest Abe wrote his answer on Ashley's note and had it sent back up the hill: "So far as I know, there are no peace commissioners in the city, or likely to be in it. A. Lincoln." Then he finished sending Seward to meet them at Hampton Roads.

At half past one, Lincoln's note was handed to Ashley, who displayed it to Cox. Spotting the equivocation, Cox made inquiries to "other than official sources," who assured him that a peace commission from Richmond was indeed at Grant's lines. "In some inscrutable way," Cox had found, "there were men in Congress who were better advised as to their presence than Mr. Ashley or the President." Sunset Cox would vote no.

As the roll call neared, the chamber was jammed, literally from floor to rafters. Noah Brooks counted five Supreme Court justices, several Cabinet members, "Senators by the dozen," Montgomery Blair, "hosts of other prominent persons." Every seat was filled. All the standing room was taken. Anxious abolitionists fretted in the galleries. Some blacks had been admitted for the first time ever. The press gallery above and behind the Speaker "was invaded by a mob of well dressed women." The newspapermen surrendered their seats and took notes standing up.

Even now there were speeches to be made, explanations to be given. One by one, anxious Democrats took the floor and committed themselves to abolition, comforted by Lincoln's assurance that no doves were flying north. A Pennsylvanian had voted no in June. Now he had the clerk read his statement, ignorant of Cox's sources or unconvinced of their veracity: "I have been in favor of exhausting all means of conciliation to restore the Union as our fathers made it. The result of all the peace missions, and especially that of Mr. Blair, has satisfied me that nothing short of the recognition of their independence will satisfy the southern confederacy. It must therefore be destroyed. I cast my vote against the cornerstone of the southern confederacy [Alec Stephens's infelicitous phrase], and declare eternal war against the enemies of my country."

The roll was called at four, the very hour at which the commissioners had been asked to appear at Grant's lines. No one could be sure that a sufficient lot of Democrats had been pressured, cajoled, or bought. "The most intense anxiety was felt," said an Illinois Republican, and "so perfect was the silence" that the scratching of a hundred pencils could be heard as the names were called. According to Noah Brooks, "knots of members" huddled around the tally keepers, the Copperheads looking sour. The wavering James English, a Democrat from New Haven, voted aye to a burst of applause, which the Speaker gaveled down. The process was repeated when Democrats from New York cast their votes as Seward and Thurlow Weed had hoped. A Brooklyn Democrat named Moses Odell had lost his seat in November. His aye vote on the amendment and his appointment to head the Manhattan naval office may not have been coincidental.

When the names had all been called, Speaker Colfax declared in a trembling voice that the measure had been approved. The House of Representatives had agreed to banish slavery by a margin of two votes. There was "a pause of utter silence," then hundreds of congressmen, guests, and spectators leapt to their feet and cheered.

The chamber rocked for minutes. Men applauded and hurrahed, waved their hats and tossed them, threw their arms around each other's necks and wept. To an Indiana Republican, it seemed "I had been born into a new life, and that the world was overflowing with beauty and joy." When Speaker Colfax could be heard, he asked that his name be called, a pointed break with tradition. He belted out his aye and the chamber rocked again. He gaveled it to order and said he had hoped for more decorum, or so claimed the *Boston Transcript*. If he said it, the record does not reflect it, and he surely did not mean it. The House adjourned at 4:20 as artillery shook Capitol Hill. A hundred thirty miles away, Jefferson Davis's peace commissioners had just passed through the lines.

———

Two weeks later, Lincoln welcomed Elizabeth Peabody, a sixty-year-old Massachusetts abolitionist, and sat her by the fire in his office. She had been in the gallery when the roll was called. The late Nathaniel

Hawthorne had been her brother-in-law. So had Horace Mann, a pioneer in public education, also now deceased, who had served with the president in Congress. Lincoln's face grew "very sweet" when she spoke of him. "Mr. Mann was very kind to me," he said, "and it was *something* to me at that time to have him so, for he was a distinguished man in his way and I was nobody." He said it "with an unconscious dignity, and he looked down with a sweet-musing expression, as if he was remembering some interview that was pleasant." Mrs. Peabody said she was sure that Mr. Mann was rejoicing with them over the amendment. "You ought to have been in the House that day, Sir!"

Lincoln looked up brightly. "What do you think I was doing that day? I was writing my instructions to Seward! There is a little secret piece of history connected with that." When the amendment was introduced, Lincoln said, Ashley had the numbers but put off the vote to assemble a bigger majority. "And meantime that Peace Commissioner business came on." Instead of speeding it through, "I *eased* it along, and concluded to send Seward down." Ashley's converts would have recanted "had they smelt peace." Lincoln told Mrs. Peabody he had "left off" writing Seward, "and elaborately wrote that *as far as I knew* there were no Commissioners of Peace in Washington, nor did I think they would come." For his guest's entertainment, the president repeated himself—"*as far as I knew*"—much to his own amusement.

＊＊＊

The Jacobins let the president know they were watching. A friend said Lincoln never met a man he didn't like, with the exception of Charles Sumner, an unsmiling abolitionist who had once been beaten senseless on the Senate floor by a South Carolinian with a cane. His assailant was proud to say he had given the Bostonian "about 30 first rate stripes" in reprisal for a lurid antislavery speech. In their own respective sections, the incident brought glory to the attacker and the attacked. Now Sumner offered a resolution to solicit from the president "any information in his power concerning any recent personal communications with the rebel Jefferson Davis, said to have been under executive sanction." A colleague inquired delicately whether it might not be better to refer to the mission of Mr. Blair; but Sumner wished to know who was talking to traitors and why—whether Blair was involved or not—and his cane-shaped scars lent weight to his wishes.

Maryland's Reverdy Johnson recommended gentler language. Sumner would have none of it. Johnson's version referred to "the 'Confederate authorities,'" Sumner said. "In my resolution I characterize the head of the rebellion as 'the rebel Jefferson Davis.'" Declining to be out-jingoed, Johnson had "not the slightest objection" to calling a Rebel a Rebel. Sumner bristled again when a Wisconsin senator suggested that both versions be printed, letting senators make a choice the next day. "I want the information at once," Sumner said. "I should like to have the information tomorrow morning."

A few minutes later, Senator Willard Saulsbury, an overstuffed Democrat from the slave state of Delaware, took the floor in Lincoln's defense. "It is seldom, sir, that I can approve of any act of the President of the United States," but if harbingers of peace were on their way north and Lincoln was behind it, "I will take occasion here, while approving but little that he has done before, to approve his action in that respect." Not a single senator seconded him, and if Lincoln had been able to choose a champion, it would not have been Willard Saulsbury. There was no more reptilian Copperhead in the city. His approval of the president was even rarer than he professed, and his Christian love of peace was situational. In 1863, fueled by rage and whiskey, he had spewed on the Senate floor an anti-Lincoln diatribe that reminded John Nicolay of the rant of "a drunken fishwife." Vice President Hannibal Hamlin had tried to gavel him down. When the sergeant at arms approached him, the gentleman from Delaware pressed a pistol to the officer's head. "Damn you," he said. "If you touch me I'll shoot you dead."

On the floor of the US Senate, Willard Saulsbury was the president's only friend on the subject of peace talks with Rebels.

For once, the Richmond press had something good to say about them. "We are not of those that believe that peace talk and peace missions tend to demoralize the army," the *Enquirer* said that day. They would do the troops a service by defining "the exact degree of degradation to which the enemy would reduce us by reconstruction." The Southern states were not about to barter away their independence to the wiles of "Yankee cunning." Peace at the price of reunion would be "a disgraceful and ruinous failure. . . . Let us have no unmanly shrinking anywhere."

The commissioners had been waiting in Petersburg surrounded by scars of war. The local paper was called the *Petersburg Express,* and so was a gargantuan mortar brought down by train from Connecticut to batter Southern civilians as well as Southern walls. In 1894, having had thirty years to think about it, the official historian of the 108th New York entertained its paunchy veterans with a poetic bit of drollery about the terror bombing of American women and children. "This mortar threw a projectile of 300 pounds, and as it sailed majestically through the air, with its comet tail of fire, and descended into the city, its explosion produced earthquake tremors, and caused much destruction and alarming fear among the people. It is not surprising that they sought caves and cellars, and were 'not at home' to these 'Express' calls."

Sarah Pryor recalled it well. Her husband was a former US congressman and a prisoner of war in Manhattan. The children were with Sarah when the shells started falling. "There was no place of safety accessible to us," she said. "The terror and demoralization" were indescribable. Sarah's infant daughter was in her freed black nursemaid's arms in the Pryors' yard when a screaming shell dropped in and buried itself beside them. "The little creature was fascinated by the shells. The first word she ever uttered was an attempt to imitate them." Being well along in childhood, her siblings understood "it would be cowardly to complain."

Surrounded by Southern soldiers, Sarah and her children had grown fond of them, "and my boys had grown so rich in their companionship. . . . They were good, wholesome comrades, interested in our books, and in the boys' studies." Now the Pryors' house was on the battlefield, and Sarah had moved her family to a tent behind the lines. With books evacuated from home, she endowed an officers' lending library. The subscribers brought scraps from their horses' meager fodder to sustain her underfed cow.

As her husband's former colleagues were preparing to vote on abolition, the word was passed through the Southern lines that the peace commissioners were coming. A Rebel general rode over to Sarah's tent. "I thought you might come out and listen to the cheering. It is echoed by the enemy. There seems to be no doubt of the feeling on both sides." Sarah was more than interested. Her imprisoned husband, Roger, was a friend of Senator Hunter's, who might help get him freed. She asked for the use of a horse-drawn ambulance and the general obliged. With the white flags flying, the demand for ambulances had abated.

Sarah was driven to the front near the place where the commissioners would cross over. As she and her driver approached, waves of joy broke over them. "The troops of Fort Gregg and Battery 45, just in the rear of my garden, had come out and were cheering vociferously." They could hear the answering cheers from across the way.

The commissioners and the mayor had come down on the Jerusalem Plank Road, parting throngs of jubilant Rebels. When their carriage pulled up nearby, Sarah walked over to see them, aware of her beating heart. Hunter greeted her kindly and introduced her to Stephens and Campbell. "My errand is to you, dear Mr. Hunter," she said. "I entreat you, I implore you, to remember your friend General Pryor. He is breaking his heart in prison. Beg his release from Mr. Lincoln." Hunter promised to try, and so did his companions. As Sarah watched their carriage roll away toward the lines, "a mighty cheer went up from the hundreds of soldiers, Confederate and Union, who were standing on duty and looking on."

—◆—

The commissioners passed through the Rebel earthworks where a low plateau fell away. Campbell's warnings had not prepared them for the paucity of Lee's defenses—how thinly his lines were manned, how thin were the boys who manned them. Stepping down from their carriage at the appointed hour of four, they proceeded on foot to no-man's-land, escorted by Colonel Hatch. Stephens got along on the arm of his slave, Ben Travis. A captain named O'Brien bore a white flag before them. A gaggle of federal officers met them halfway, Colonel Harriman among them, keeping his thoughts to himself—that the only peace they wanted was a piece of ten-inch shell. To Harriman, Stephens and Campbell seemed "haggard and careworn," Hunter "rosy and fat." Colonel Babcock represented Grant. "The bearing of these officers was extremely courteous," said the *Petersburg Express*, their reception "graceful and becoming. They were in excellent good humor and seemed alive to the importance of the occasion."

Colonel Hatch was given leave to accompany the commissioners to Grant. A request that Mr. Stephens's "servant" be allowed to assist him was granted too. Bellmen in blue took the gentlemen's trunks, leaving Ben Travis free to keep his master ambulatory. The *Express* said they approached the Yankee lines by the Baxter Road. More colorfully, the *Times* said they crossed at Fort Hell. The cheers on both sides raised their chins. As far as one could see, "the breastworks were dark with men," some surveying the scene with spyglasses. Ladies down from Petersburg, escorted by Southern officers, were in front of the Rebel earthworks, watching from the parapets, riding horseback in the fields. A City Point telegrapher sent Stanton the *Sentinel*'s report of "prolonged and enthusiastic shouting," which the *Times* denied indignantly, saying "no such thing was heard, or even dreamt of." The *Times* was doing the dreaming.

A respectful pause interrupted the cheers as the commissioners and their escorts walked slowly across no-man's-land, Alec Stephens setting an invalid's pace. Hunter noticed how they trod on spent ammunition. The Yankees resumed their cheering when the commissioners came back into the Union.

Despite all the brotherly love, Sarah Pryor expected the war to resume once the peacemakers had crossed the lines. "In an instant we were enemies again, and I was hastening out of the range of shot and shell." Sarah was wise to hasten. The Southern general in local command put an emphasis on his point that peace would be won by "manly exertions." As soon as the commissioners were out of harm's way, the Rebels opened up with muskets and artillery. The killing continued all day and through the night.

CHAPTER SIXTEEN

I Was Never So Much
Disappointed in My Life

On the military railroad behind the Union lines, an idle locomotive with an empty car had been standing at Meade's Station for hours, giving rumormongers notice that the peacemakers were coming. By the time they arrived at dusk, a crowd of men in blue had gathered there to gawk. They cheered as the train pulled away. On the eight-mile trip to City Point, the commissioners and their escorts mixed small talk with lurching. The tracks were only temporary, and laid with little grading. From a distance, a general said, the trains looked like flies crawling over a washboard. Riders had been known to be seasick.

When the train reached City Point at about seven o'clock, another crowd was waiting, but a certain decorum prevailed at headquarters. There was no report of cheering. Having gotten to know the Southerners, the bitter Colonel Harriman entrusted them to Grant's aide Colonel Babcock and returned to the front. Stephens grasped Harriman's hand and hoped that they would meet again soon "under happier auspices." Harriman's time with the little Georgian may have softened him.

It was dark when they detrained, as it was a few weeks later when Lincoln arrived by steamer. For a presidential bodyguard, the approach to City Point was enchanting, "with the many-colored lights of the boats in the harbor and the lights of the town straggling up the bluffs of the shore, crowned by the lights from Grant's headquarters at the top. It was a busy camp, and everything was in motion." More city than camp, it bustled through the night with the comings and goings of troops, politicians, prisoners of war, and walking wounded. A horse-drawn coffee maker with a steam-powered heating plant helped keep them all awake.

Colonel Babcock brought the Southerners directly to General Grant, accompanied by other officers, including Lieutenant E. W. Clarke. Clarke had encountered the guests of honor in Washington City before the war and was not among their admirers. He wrote that night to Senator Henry Wilson of Massachusetts, a Radical Republican. "Poor Stevens [*sic*] looked weaker and sicker than ever," Clarke said, the morose Senator Hunter "much the same, only browner and not so fat and oily looking." Judge Campbell was "stiff, starchy, and pokerish as usual." Hunter smiled just once, acerbically at that, when a colonel making small talk said he would "find the country much changed hereabouts." "Not I," the Virginian told its conqueror. "I was never here before." It occurred to Lieutenant Clarke that "the bone of contention" came along with Alec Stephens "in the shape of a black man carrying a valise." If the South dropped the bone, well and good, but another four years of war would be better than "a pasteboard peace. And this I believe to be the voice of the Army."

About to come face-to-face with Grant, the scourge of the Southern nation, the commissioners' pulses must have quickened as they passed the rough-hewn cabins that served as his officers' quarters and approached a fine white house. A self-respecting scourge would have taken it for himself. Grant had assigned it to his chief quartermaster, from which to supply his men. The general's own residence was a cabin like the others, a bit larger than the ones laid out in rows on either side of his, but every bit as plain. Colonel Babcock knocked at its door, which could have been salvaged from a shed. As Stephens heard it, a "very distinct" voice called out to come in. Colonel Hatch and Ben Travis stayed outside.

The door opened directly into Grant's humble office, redolent of cigars, with a bare wood floor, a plain brick hearth, a well-fed fire, a couple of pine tables, some common wooden chairs, and two tiny bedrooms in the back. Grant was the small man in blue, seated at a table, writing by a kerosene lamp. When the general rose to greet them, Stephens "was never so much disappointed in my life," the impression being instantly favorable. "I was immediately struck with the great simplicity and perfect naturalness of his manners and the entire absence of everything like affectation, show, or even the usual military air" of a man in his position. There were no flags or aides about him. He wore no polished boots, no gold-braided uniform. He stood in low-cut shoes and a common soldier's jacket with no trappings or insignia but the three gold stars on his shoulder straps, the only man in the army who wore them.

He spoke with a natural fluency, according to Stephens, and "more of brains than tongue, as ready as that was at his command." The conversation flowed easily, and "I understood now that the report about his being on a big drunk was a canard of the Munchhausen sort," a fiction of mythic proportions. The general told his guests how sorry he was for the delay in passing his lines. He had been away, he said, and had just gotten back that morning. He had wired their note to Washington. Instructions had been received. He was sorry to have to say they must stay at City Point until a messenger arrived, which could take some time. The river might be icebound for days, and he had no quarters available to make them as comfortable as he wished. He would house them in the staterooms of his steamboat, the best accommodation he had.

He had never met his guests, but "found them all very agreeable gentlemen." He knew them by reputation, he would later recall, "and through their public services," a generous note, considering where their services had lately gone. Before the war, he had particularly admired Stephens, a fellow Stephen Douglas Democrat.

A few minutes into their chat, an orderly arrived with a dispatch. The general wrote a quick reply and asked the orderly if he knew how to get it to its destination. When the poor man confessed that he did not, Grant enlightened him patiently and confirmed that he understood. Several other dispatches came and went. The General in Chief of the Army was running the war against the Rebels in their presence. Did anyone think it bizarre?

Not long into their visit, a high-ranking officer knocked and entered, handed the general a document, saluted, and withdrew. Grant begged the enemy's pardon, took a moment to read what had been given him, and scribbled a half-page reply, "very hastily," Stephens thought. Then he folded it, wrote something on the back, took it to the door, and called for an orderly to deliver it. Quickly. It was probably the wire that Grant sent to Stanton at 7:30 p.m.:

> *On my arrival here this morning, I received a letter from Messrs. Stephens, Hunter, and Campbell, which I immediately telegraphed the contents to the President and sent at the same time a staff officer to receive the gentlemen and conduct them to my quarters to await the action of the President. The gentlemen have arrived, and since their arrival I have been put in possession of the telegraphic correspondence which had been going on for two days previous [Stanton's order to keep the gentlemen behind their lines and General Ord's obedient reply]. Had I known of this correspondence in time, these gentlemen would not have been received within our lines.*

Grant's story comes to this: His staff had let him know that morning that three of the highest-ranking men in the Confederacy had appeared at his lines two days ago, seeking leave to proceed to the White House for the purpose of ending the war. Without consulting Washington, or inquiring whether orders had been sought or received, he had waved them through immediately, telling Lincoln after the fact. No one had let him know that the Secretary of War had stopped them in their tracks and ordered them held at the lines until the president decided otherwise. According to an aide, even routine dispatches were brought to Grant instantly, but Stanton's order to keep the Rebel peace ambassadors away—received, understood, and acknowledged on Sunday night—was put in his hands on Tuesday evening, twelve hours after his return, as the objects of the attention of every man in the army sat chatting with him in his cabin.

No one ever asked him to explain himself.

The Southerners had been visiting with him for half an hour or so when Stephens thought it polite to say that if an escort could be provided, they would trespass no more on his time—a sporting gesture indeed, considering how he spent it. Grant denied any trespass but deferred to his guests. "Well, gentlemen, if you wish to go, I will escort you myself." As Stephens lets us know, Grant rose from his simple chair, "fixed his papers quickly, turned down his kerosene lamp, as I had seen many a village lawyer do, opened the door," and followed them outside. Then he turned his key in the lock, put it in his pocket like a shopkeeper closing for the night, "and led the way to the wharf." The Confederate vice president's slave Ben Travis took Stephens's feeble arm. Though Grant's rustic office had been warm, Stephens had never shed his coat.

On the rugged path to the pier, "General Grant and Judge Campbell went side by side in the lead. The night was dark, Campbell was tall," and Grant had to struggle to keep pace. Stephens found it poignant. He thought of the scene in *The Aeneid* where Aeneas flees burning Troy with his aged father on his back and his little boy in hand, working hard to keep up. When a sentry demanded, "Who goes there?" the general told him quietly.

Steep wooden stairs ran down the side of the bluff to Grant's luxurious paddle wheeler, *Mary Martin*. Stephens needed help from his slave. The word had gone forth that the peacemakers were coming, and a craning knot of spectators had gathered in a spot where a lamp lit the way. Stephens would never forget how "someone in the crowd said, quite loud enough for me to hear, 'Which is Stephens? Which is the Vice President?'"

"That one, leaning on the arm of the black man."

"My God! He's dead now, but he don't know it."

"With this ringing in my ears," Little Alec says, "I got on the boat as quickly as I could, with the assistance of my faithful servant, Ben Travis."

Grant had understood that Stephens was "a very small man, but when I saw him in the dusk of the evening I was very much surprised to find so large a man as he seemed to be." The cloth of his course gray coat "was thicker than anything of the kind I had ever seen, even in Canada. The overcoat extended nearly to his feet, and was so large that it gave him the appearance of being an average-sized man." When Stephens removed his wrappings, as Grant would later say, "I was struck with the apparent change in size, in the coat and out of it."

Mary Martin had been a Hudson River excursion boat, a beauty of her kind, elegant in white, with tasteful gold trim and a rakish cast to her bow. Julia Grant hosted Cabinet members and their wives in her well-appointed dining room and accommodated them in her staterooms. Julia was fond of berthing there herself, a welcome change from the shed.

If the commissioners had not expected the Northern cheers that had swept them across the siege line, or the gracious Northern officers who had taken them to City Point, or the deference that Grant had shown them there, their day was not yet done. They were greeted on the *Mary Martin* with something in the nature of a surprise party. Some fifty Union generals and a smattering of lucky colonels had assembled for a feast in their honor, a liberal interpretation of Lincoln's instructions to Grant to keep them safe and comfortable. History holds no record that the festivities were mentioned to the president, let alone to the Secretary of War.

After a get-acquainted reception in *Mary Martin*'s saloon, a well-appointed compartment for entertaining guests, the party moved on to the dining room for what Stephens describes as "a most sumptuous meal of the daintiest viands, consisting of fish, meat, and vegetables of many varieties with an abundance of champagne, hock, sherry, Madeira, as well as other varieties of wine and the best of French brandy, all ending in coffee and cigars." The guests enjoyed their beverages, but there was no big drunk for the host. Stephens took note that Grant presided at the head of the table, and "I was placed at his left, and I noticed particularly that while others indulged very freely in the good liquors on the board, he took no drop of anything of the sort."

By the time the board was cleared and the brandy had been poured, the smoke-filled room was a free and easy place, complete with "racy anecdotes" as Stephens would later confess, "many of them bearing upon the mutual acquaintances of the Commissioners and several of the officers at the table." It is safe to assume that the anecdotes did not grow tamer when the party moved back to the saloon and Grant withdrew for the evening. He took the commissioners aside, promised to return in the morning, and instructed the steward to give them the best staterooms. Stephens had done enough for one day, and retired to his berth with the help of Ben Travis, but sleep would not come for the tired little Georgian. The rosy-cheeked Hunter and even the austere John Campbell, no longer as sober as a judge, kept drinking with their friends until nearly 1:00 a.m., as Stephens gruffly clocked them. "At least they kept up a noise of laughing and talking that prevented me from sleeping until about that hour."

Like the Rebels on the *Mary Martin*, the Rebels on the siege line were unusually active that night, causing wary federal officers to prepare to repel an attack. While the commissioners and their friends nibbled fish and sipped Madeira, the most vulnerable Northern boys, the sick and walking wounded, were shipped to City Point, temporarily out of harm's way.

The Tuesday-night revelers awoke on Wednesday morning to an elegant breakfast and a lovely day. Content with lesser pleasures, the combatants on the front were grateful for the break in the cold. It was warm and pleasant even at Fort Hell. Walking down to the *Mary Martin*, the *New York Times* City Point correspondent got a look at Grant's guests, their dignity intact on the morning after. "I caught a glimpse of the lions this morning, on board the *Martin*," he told his readers. "One was a very thin, spare man, who was pointed out as Alexander H. Stephens, pacing the after-deck, thoughtfully, in company with a stout, burley figure, said to be Hunter of Virginia."

The newspaperman was not the only curious Yankee to stroll past *Mary Martin*. In any ordinary week, so many famous men came to visit Grant that his camp had grown used to them, but the eagerness to see the "new-comers from rebellion was quite remarkable," and the objects of all this interest had been left to roam free. No guard was put on them, no limits imposed on their movements, no pledge extracted that they would not abuse their privileges. "They were permitted to leave the boat when they felt like it," as Grant would later recall. The general had a reason to let the lions off the leash. The embarrassment of riches that the North had laid at his feet was good for them to see, their welcoming feast included. Captured at Spotsylvania in May, Private Louis Leon of the Charlotte Grays, a sharpshooter by trade, had absorbed what the commissioners were absorbing. "Look at our army," he had written, "and you will see them in rags and barefooted. But among the Yankees I see nothing but an abundance of everything." The gap had widened since then.

Hunter had a way with understatement. "It was interesting to us to know whether the other party was aware of our real situation." Spies and deserters and the broad notoriety of the South's destitution made it "impossible to suppose that the enemy were not sufficiently aware of our condition to make their knowledge in that particular an important element in the negotiation," but no one at City Point said so. When the commissioners passed through their own thin lines and emerged in a cornucopia, Hunter thought he knew why they had been left so long to wait. The Lincoln administration had little interest in a Rebel peace commission, and wanted them to know it. The North could take whatever peace it chose.

⸻

Grant called on the commissioners late that morning, giving them time, perhaps, to sleep off their consultations with his generals. He took them back to his cabin and introduced them to his wife and children, the youngsters no doubt thrilled to meet Rebels in the flesh. Julia Grant had been raised by slaves on a Missouri plantation and professed to believe they were as pleased about the arrangement as she was. When her family spoke of Yankees it was not a term of endearment. Now she gushed Southern charm, blessed the commissioners' mission, and asked to be remembered by name to several Rebel officers.

Grant took his guests to his stables and showed off his favorite mounts. To Stephens, an animal named Lexington appeared to be his favorite; Cincinnati may have been introduced; Jeff Davis probably not. The general had arranged to take the commissioners on a carriage ride, but Stephens begged off for the cold. Though the day was clear and pleasant, his colleagues demurred in deference to the vice president.

Not all of their talk with Grant was of horses and friends. According to Stephens, they spoke freely on several subjects, though "not much" on the peace mission, but Grant made it clear he was anxious for its success. Stephens inferred that the general was fully apprised of Blair's invasion of Mexico. One of Grant's subordinates watched the commissioners try to draw him out on peace, on two occasions, but Grant would not be drawn. The Southerners spoke of negotiations between "the two governments," while the general would acknowledge only one. Hunter later said the commissioners suggested what amounted to a coup—that Grant and Lee could settle things more easily than Lincoln and themselves.

"The attempt was in vain," to Hunter's regret. "Lee had too much principle probably to have yielded to such a suggestion" (it seems not to have occurred to Hunter that he was unprincipled enough to suggest it) "and if Grant would have suffered no principle to restrain him . . . he had not the ability to weigh truly his responsibility or to understand his opportunities." Regrettably, Hunter thought, Grant was no Julius Caesar.

More than twenty years later, Grant claimed no recollection of any conversation with the commissioners on the subject of their mission. "It was something I had nothing to do with. . . . As long as they remained there, however, our relations were pleasant and I found them all very agreeable gentlemen." Discretion surely tempered what he told them, but Grant found their mission as agreeable as their company. He would have a great deal to do with it.

The slender, balding, trim-bearded General Meade made a courtesy call on the peace commissioners. A contemporary described Meade, who had beaten Lee at Gettysburg and saved the war for the North, as "the tall figure, with the nervous, emphatic articulation and action, and face as of antique parchment." Some thought highly of him, but Stanton's Assistant Secretary of War Charles Dana was no friend. "I think he had not a friend in the whole army. No man, no matter what his business or his service, approached him without being insulted in one way or another, and his own staff officers did not dare to speak to him unless first spoken to, for fear of either sneers or curses."

When he called on the Southerners, there were no sneers or cursing. They talked very freely, Meade told his wife, Margaretta. "Judge Campbell asked after your family, and Mr. Hunter spoke of Mr. Wise, and said he had brought two letters with him, one of which I herewith enclose." As governor of Virginia, Henry A. Wise had hanged John Brown. Now he commanded the brigade that the commissioners had just passed through, followed by shot and shell, sent aloft pursuant to his orders. Margaretta knew him well. He was married to her sister.

Meade told the Southerners he had nearly been arrested in Chicago when the war began, for predicting it would end like the Kilkenny catfight, an old Irish yarn involving cats who bit and chewed each other until only their tails remained. "And who now will say that such an opinion was absurd?" They spoke about slavery and Richmond's desire for a truce, which Meade said would never happen. After they had chatted a while, the Southerners sidled up to the same proposition they had tried on Grant. They thought it was a pity that the matter of war and peace could not be taken from the politicians and given to the generals. Meade refused the bait as Grant had done, but not without a hint of reluctance. Things would be settled more quickly that way, he said, but "I fear there is no chance for this."

Meade told his wife that the whole thing boded "not much chance of peace. I fear we will split on the questions of an armistice and State rights. Still, I hope Mr. Lincoln will receive them and listen to all they have to say, for if it can be shown that their terms are impracticable, the country will be united for the further prosecution of the war. At the same time, the selection of three most conservative of Southern men indicates most clearly to my mind an anxiety on the part of Mr. Davis to settle matters if possible." He cautioned Margaretta that "it would not do to let it be known I had been talking with them, or what I said."

Other Northern officers came calling. Hunter found them "courteous in their comments on their enemies," complimentary toward Southern military prowess, "mindful of old acquaintanceship and old ties." Many were eager for peace, and Stephens impressed them in particular. His "complexion was sallow," a general said, "and his skin seemed shriveled upon his bones. He possessed intellect enough, however, for the whole Commission." Another Yankee officer shared his impressions of Little Alec with a friend: "The Lord seems to have robbed that man's body of nearly all its flesh and blood to make brains of them."

One federal officer let the Southerners know that Mrs. Grant thought the general should send them on to Washington—that something good would come of a meeting with Mr. Lincoln—but if Mr. Seward intervened, he would break it all up with "his wily tactics." Like her husband, Mrs. Grant was fond of peace talks and Blairs—plain-speaking Southerners with strong Missouri ties and deep Southern roots, much like herself, decidedly unlike Seward.

Candidly enough, Stephens told an officer that after bringing disaster upon them, the men who had started the rebellion could not tell their people, "We have drawn you into this war, and now that you have poured out your blood and treasure until want and woe sit by every fireside of the South, you must abandon it." Hundreds of thousands of graves would be dishonored if the South won nothing "but desolation and distress. You should not ask, you cannot think, we must abandon all and turn back to our old allegiance" with nothing but sorrow to show for it. If the North would only treat the South as a nation, a deal could be struck that would unite them in practice if not in form. Stephens made it clear that another campaign would inflict "fearful losses" on both sides. Though the North would win in the end, it would be far better for both to make an agreeable peace. "We are but one people," Stephens said, "and should have but one common interest."

——————

Like the troops at City Point, the citizens of Washington City were not overawed by celebrities, but the *Times* called them "much excited" by word that Rebel peacemakers were coming. Rumors were rife that they had already arrived. "One of them originated with a porter of a hotel, who said he was perfectly familiar with their faces." The visitors he had spotted were tourists returning from Baltimore. The Washington correspondent for a Cincinnati paper said "the impression is hourly growing stronger here" that the peace talks would succeed. Horace Greeley's *Tribune* was not so optimistic. Powerful men in Congress and the administration were "impatient of the whole olive branch business."

Having placed a bet on olive branches, sending Seward to Fort Monroe, Lincoln hedged it with arrows. He sent a wire to Grant that morning: "Let nothing which is transpiring change, hinder, or delay your military movements or plans." Grant replied forthwith: "Your dispatch received. There will be no armistice in consequence of the presence of Mr. Stephens and others within our lines. The troops are kept in readiness to move at the shortest notice, if occasion should justify it."

The president's messenger, Major Eckert, was on his way to City Point, and Lincoln had put him in Seward's charge: "Call at Fortress Monroe,

and put yourself under direction of Mr. S, whom you will find there."
Mr. S had left that morning in his traveling coat and muffler from his
office at the State Department on the eastern edge of the White House
lawn, accompanied by R. S. Chew, his elegant clerk. They took a train to
Annapolis to steam down Chesapeake Bay to Hampton Roads. Governor Augustus Bradford welcomed them at Maryland's statehouse. Seward
urged him to assemble the legislature to ratify the Thirteenth Amendment. Bradford was ahead of him. The State Senate would vote that very
day, the General Assembly on Friday. The result was not in doubt. One of
four loyal slave states, Maryland had just adopted its own ban on slavery.

With Maryland in hand, Seward and Chew were escorted to the
Naval Academy and boarded the double side-wheeler *River Queen*, already
gathering steam. Leased from a private owner, formally under Grant's
command, but known as the president's yacht, the *River Queen* reigned
over Chesapeake Bay. Less than a year old, she was built to the state of
the art; fast and clean in white; her name in black under gold-painted
half-moon wheel covers with carved, gilded eagles; her furnishings and
accoutrements fit for a head of state. In minutes, her civilian captain and
crew had her steaming toward Hampton Roads, a star-spangled navy-
blue pennant snapping from her bow, a grand American flag thrown out
to the wind from her stern.

Lincoln's Copperhead friend James Singleton debriefed him that day on
his two weeks in Richmond as a guest of the Rebel government, which had
cheerfully paid his bill from the Spotswood Hotel, a "miniature world" of
politicians, generals, speculators, and spies "as thoroughly identified with
Rebellion as the inn at Bethlehem with the gospel." No less a team of
Rebels than Jefferson Davis and Robert E. Lee had impressed upon Singleton the wisdom of peace talks between Lee and Grant. Singleton told
Lincoln that the people of the South were anxious for peace. Reunion
could be forged in the space of a sixty-day armistice. The South would
insist on the right of each state to govern itself domestically, of course,
including its labor system. Reversing its original goals, the Confederacy
was prepared to free its slaves to bolster its army, but would consider fair

compensation instead, among other liberal terms. Constitutional amendments would secure Southern rights for the future.

If Singleton had it right, Lincoln could have his three preconditions for peace—reunion, submission to federal authority, and no backward steps on slavery. Indeed, he could have the slaves, as long as they were paid for, which had always seemed reasonable to him.

———

In a joyful White House ceremony that day, Lincoln signed the House resolution submitting the Thirteenth Amendment to the states. His signature was not necessary. He signed it anyway. Blair's daughter, Lizzie, was there, and so was the Reverend Henry Ward Beecher, the celebrated brother of Harriet Beecher Stowe, down from his Brooklyn pulpit for a stern little talk with the president about rumors of peace on earth. Long-haired and smooth-shaven, a heartthrob in his youth, still a magnetic presence at fifty-one, the silver-tongued Beecher believed outspokenly in abolition, women's suffrage, religious liberalism, Darwin's new theory of evolution, and crushing the rebellion mercilessly. Before the war, he had raised cash to buy rifles for Kansans and Nebraskans resisting the spread of slavery. Beecher's Bibles, they were called. When the war broke out, his Congregational Church sent a regiment south to kill rebels. Impatient with the pace of the killing, his editorials in the *Independent*, a voice of the Christian abolition movement, had flailed against Lincoln like "a mowing machine," as their author recalled. He had heard that Lincoln read them, and they "bore down on him very hard."

The reverend did not approve of peace talks. "The war had lasted so long, and I was afraid that Lincoln would be anxious for peace, and I was afraid he would accept something that would be of advantage to the South," two sins to be deplored. En route to Washington City, Beecher had stopped in Baltimore, rousing his fellow Christians with an image of traitors "of the blackest dye" on their way to a righteous gallows. "Who would let these criminals loose?" A voice in the crowd yelled, "Blair, Blair," and turned the meeting "turbulent."

After the White House ceremony, Beecher was welcomed to the president's office, where they met alone. Lincoln's hair "was every way for

Sunday," as Beecher would soon tell friends, like "an abandoned stubble field." He wore his favorite carpet slippers, his customary footwear at home, "and his vest was what was called 'going free.'" He was weary to the bone. When he fell down into his chair, he "looked as though every limb wanted to drop off his body."

"Mr. Lincoln," the reverend began, speaking for his circle, "I come to know whether the public interest will permit you to explain to me what this Southern commission means. We are all very much excited over that," and not in a joyful way. The president went to his pigeonhole desk "and came out and handed me a little card as long as my finger and an inch wide, and on that was written, 'You will pass the bearer through the lines. A. Lincoln' (or something to that effect)."

" 'There,' he said. 'That is all there is of it. Now Blair thinks something can be done, but I don't.'" He had let the old man try, with no authority whatever but to go down to Richmond and see what he could do.

" 'Well,' said I, 'you have lifted a great burden off my mind.'"

Major Thomas T. Eckert arrived at City Point that day, descended from Washington City like the coming of the Lord. He came in civilian clothes, as always, bearing orders from Stanton instructing Grant to do what Eckert told him. It had been a long time since the General in Chief of the Army had taken direction from a major, let alone a pontifical bureaucrat who had never shed blood—his own, or anyone else's. The novelty was unwelcome.

As chief of the military telegraph, the officious Major Eckert may have run into Grant before. He ran into him forcefully now as he handed him Stanton's orders. The president had ordered a conference to be held between the commissioners *and Eckert,* "and if, on his return to you, he requests it, pass them through our lines to Fortress Monroe, by such route and under such military precautions as you may deem prudent, giving them protection and comfortable quarters while there, and that you let none of this have any effect upon your movements or plans."

With the speaking role left to a major and Grant consigned to the wings, the general was not pleased. Eckert would later say that they "came very near getting into a difficulty that would have forced me to have done something that might have caused a row, because General Grant wanted to be a party to the conference. I told him no." We can only imagine Grant's face. The major was not finished. "You are the commanding general of the army. If you make a failure or say anything that would be subject to criticism, it would be very bad. If I make a mistake I am nothing but a common businessman, and it will go for naught. I am going to take the responsibility and I advise you not to go to the conference." According to Eckert, Grant said "decency would compel me to go and see them," but the major would not have it. "I said that for the purpose of introduction I should be pleased to have him go with me, but not until after I had first met the gentlemen." Eckert, not Grant, would deal with these Rebels, and he would deal with them alone.

Eckert was eighty-two when he told his tale, forty-two years after the fact. The tone he had taken with the head of all the armies would have sharpened over time as the details faded—for one thing, Grant and the commissioners required no introduction—but the substance rings true, and so does Eckert's report that "Grant was vexed with me because I did not tell him exactly what my mission was."

One of Grant's staff said he "rarely showed vexation at occurrences great or small, which must have tried him hard. Sometimes, in great emergencies, his lips became set and his mouth rigid, his expression stern; but even then his eye rarely flashed, and his voice betrayed no emotion." His lips were surely set as the officious Major Eckert, fresh from Edwin Stanton, told the general what he could and could not do. His eye may even have flashed.

Hunter recalled it well. "And now commenced our troubles."

CHAPTER SEVENTEEN

With Evident Indications of High Gratification

Lincoln had instructed Major Eckert in writing to deliver a letter to the peace commissioners and receive their answer, also in writing, "waiting a reasonable time for it." If they accepted his terms "without further condition," the major would pass them through to Hampton Roads, Fort Monroe, and Mr. Seward. If not, he would turn them away. "And this being your whole duty, return and report to me."

Shortly after four, Grant walked Eckert down the steps to the *Mary Martin* and introduced him to the commissioners in her elegant saloon. The major and Alec Stephens had met before. Two months into the war, Eckert was passing through Atlanta when the authorized agents of a mob who had just hanged a similarly situated Yankee showed up at his hotel to greet him too. Fortuitously, Stephens had roomed with Eckert's cousin George in Congress, and Eckert had seen his name in the hotel register. They were chatting when Eckert's callers arrived. Little Alec interposed his ninety-pound frame between his fellow Georgians and the Yankee. "This man is my guest and friend, and I will be responsible for him. He is all right."

When they reunited on the *Mary Martin*, Eckert found Stephens pleasant, "more so than the others," who had not saved his life. Eckert surmised that Hunter was their spokesman, but the major addressed himself to Stephens, "his name being the first on the list of three" and Eckert being nothing if not a stickler for form. "Campbell had the least to say. He was, however, a close listener."

When the gentlemen took their seats, Stephens asked Eckert to give his best to Cousin George and inquired politely what the major had been doing since their last encounter. Then he asked if they might discuss the subject. Eckert said yes, and asked a silly question if ever there was one. "What is the subject you want to discuss?" Stephens began with a lecture—"We of the South lay great store by our State rights"—until Eckert interrupted him. "Excuse me, but we in the North never think of that, we cannot discuss that subject at all," and all of their communications must be in writing. Then he handed Stephens a letter. It bore Eckert's signature but Abraham Lincoln had written it.

GENTLEMEN: I am instructed by the President of the United States to place this paper in your hands, with the information that, if you pass through the United States military lines, it will be understood that you do so for the purpose of an informal conference, on the basis of the letter, a copy of which is on the reverse side of this sheet [Lincoln's "one common country" letter to Blair], and that, if you choose to pass on such understanding, and so notify me in writing, I will procure the commanding general to pass you through the lines and to Fortress Monroe, under such military precautions as he may deem prudent, and at which place you will be met in due time by some person, or persons, for the purpose of such informal conference; and further, that you shall have protection, safe conduct, and safe return in all events.

When the Southerners had read it, Eckert asked them point blank if they accepted it. Lincoln's "one common country" letter was nothing new to them. Davis had given them copies. They had read it, reread it, and discussed it ever since. They had probably dreamed about it. Now they played for time. They would like to consider it, they said. Lincoln's instructions having anticipated this, Eckert followed them to the letter. He would come back soon for a written reply.

The commissioners concluded that the only written answer they could give was Davis's mandate to secure "peace to the two countries." Regrettably, the time had come to reveal it. They softened it as best they could with a cover note of their own, which included this:

The substantial object to be obtained by the informal conference is to ascertain upon what terms the existing war can be terminated honorably. Our instructions contemplate a personal interview between President Lincoln and ourselves at Washington City, but with this explanation we are ready to meet any person or persons that President Lincoln may appoint, at such place as he may designate. Our earnest desire is that a just and honorable peace may be agreed upon, and we are prepared to receive or to submit propositions which may possibly lead to the attainment of that end. Very respectfully yours, Alexander H. Stephens, R. M. T. Hunter, John A. Campbell

At about six o'clock, Eckert walked back to the *Martin* with General Grant. If he tried to keep Grant away, he failed. Night had fallen, and the five men gathered in the steamer's saloon by lamplight. The commissioners presented Davis's letter, accompanied by their own, and played their hand as best they could. It was not good enough. Eckert had no bend in him, and his orders allowed none. Stripped of the gloss that his negotiators had put on it, Jefferson Davis's position was clear: Far from accepting reunion, he insisted on two countries. Eckert told his envoys they could not proceed.

The Southerners did not give up. They wanted peace, they said, and to learn how it could be had. What could be lost by finding out? Stephens tried to dodge the fatal impact of both presidents' letters, Lincoln's *and* Davis's, one country or two. "Neither letter was accurate," he said, for thirty-six countries were involved. Why not disregard the last few words of both letters? Eckert was unmoved. Since the commissioners crossed the siege line, thousands of Northern soldiers and dozens of Northern officers had been urging them on to Lincoln, but their lawyerly wits got them nowhere with Major Eckert, and their regional charm fell flat. Their position was "not satisfactory."

As the major had feared they would, they tried to go over his head to the General in Chief of the Army. Hunter said to Grant, "We do not seem to get on very rapidly with Major Eckert. We are very anxious to go to Washington, and Mr. Lincoln has promised to see us there." As Eckert later told it, he interrupted Grant when the general tried to answer.

" 'Excuse me, General Grant, you are not permitted to say anything officially at this time,' and I stopped him right there. I added, 'If you will read the instructions under which I am acting you will see that I am right.' " We can only imagine the general's face. As Eckert would have it, Grant stayed and listened for a while, then abruptly got up and left.

Alec Stephens had a more plausible recollection, recorded three decades earlier than Eckert's. When the major declared the commissioners' position unsatisfactory, Grant seemed deeply disappointed. "Mr. Stephens," he said, "can't you modify the language of your reply to Major Eckert, and put it in acceptable shape?" Stephens wrote out a note:

To Lieutenant General Grant

Sir: We desire to go to Washington City to confer informally with the President personally, in reference to the matters mentioned in his letter to Mr. Blair of the 18th of January ultimo [1865], without any personal compromise on any question in the letter. We have the permission to do so from the authorities in Richmond.

Very respectfully yours, etc.

The first few words simply asked for a meeting with Lincoln on the subject of his letter, echoing Judah Benjamin, but what did "personal compromise" mean, and was it Lincoln or the commissioners who would not be making any? Alec Stephens was a careful lawyer. He did not draft ambiguities unintentionally. He was searching for a way past Eckert.

Stephens handed the note to Grant after he and his colleagues had signed it. The general seemed pleased. "That will do," he said. It was meant as a command. The major did not obey it. He beckoned to Grant, and they left for several minutes. Grant surely argued that the gentlemen had dropped Davis's demand for two countries, even if they had not accepted one. What harm could a meeting do? Eckert no doubt replied that the gentlemen were to be sent packing unless they accepted reunion unconditionally, and this they had failed to do. With all due respect, the general had no say in the matter.

"He was angry with me for years afterward," Eckert said much later, conceding that the army's greatest general since Washington himself had "some reason for chagrin" when "a mere major" overruled him in the face of the enemy. "But at the time I gave no thought to this feature of the case, remembering only my explicit orders, written and oral, from the President."

When Eckert and Grant returned, Eckert told the Southerners that their mission was done unless they accepted President Lincoln's terms. If they changed their minds, they could tell General Grant. It was the last time they saw Major Eckert.

As Eckert left the *Mary Martin*, Seward was approaching Hampton Roads on the *River Queen*, not knowing whether the major had sent the Southerners through or not. When he disembarked at Fort Monroe, he sent a wire to Lincoln: "Arrived at 10 this evening. Richmond party not here. I remain here." He wired Grant too: "I arrived at 10 o'clock this evening, and shall remain here to meet the persons from Richmond. Send Major Eckert here, if he is with you." The Secretary of State was plainly expecting the peace commissioners, which would have emboldened Grant had he needed emboldening.

After telling the commissioners that their mission was over, Eckert composed a wire to the president, which the City Point telegrapher sent:

> *I have the honor to report the delivery of your communication and my letter at 4:15 this afternoon, to which I received a reply at 6 p.m., but not satisfactory. At 8:00 p.m. the following note addressed to General Grant was received: [The commissioners' "without any personal compromise" note was inserted] At 9:30 p.m. I notified them that they could not proceed further unless they complied with the terms expressed in my letter. The point of meeting designated in the above note [Washington City] would not, in my opinion, be insisted upon. Think Fort Monroe would be acceptable. Having complied with my instructions, I will return tomorrow unless otherwise ordered.*

Because Eckert's report barred any meeting at all, his assessment that the commissioners would meet at Fort Monroe was curious. He had seen how eager they were, and may have thought it worth noting. Then he wrote a second message, this one addressed to Stanton, twice as detailed as his wire to Lincoln:

> *In reply to the letters delivered by me to Messrs. Stephens, Campbell, and Hunter, they give a copy of their instructions from Jefferson Davis, which I think is a verbatim copy of that now in the President's possession. Am positive about the last two words ["two countries"], which differ from the ending of copy delivered by me ["our one common country"], and to which the President called my particular attention. After giving object of conference they add: "Our instructions contemplate a personal interview with President Lincoln in Washington, but with this explanation we are ready to meet any person or persons that President Lincoln may appoint at such place as he may designate. Our earnest desire is that a just and honorable peace may be agreed upon, and we are prepared to receive or to submit propositions which may possibly lead to the attainment of that end." They say the ending of letter I delivered to them is the only objectionable point, and one that, in their opinion, should be left out of both the letter they bring and the one they received, adding, if they accept the latter, and terms are not agreed upon, it would be an acknowledgment that might prejudice the interests of the people they represent.*

After writing his message to the war god, Eckert tried to send it. And now commenced *his* troubles. The telegraph line was down, so the major was told. Bad luck indeed. The line "was occasionally broken," one of Grant's staff officers said, but "generally well maintained and made to perform excellent service." The odds that it went down just when Eckert tried to use it seem small, let alone that it popped back up again when Grant sent a carefully crafted message of his own to the Secretary of War.

As the general well knew, Lincoln monitored his telegrams to Stanton religiously. He sent this one at ten-thirty, moments after Eckert was told that the wire was down:

Now that the interview between Major Eckert, under his written instructions, and Mr. Stephens and his party has ended, I will state confidentially but not officially, to become a matter of record, that I am convinced, upon conversation with Messrs. Stephens and Hunter, that their intentions are good and their desire sincere to restore peace and union. I have not felt myself at liberty to express even views of my own or to account for my reticence. This has placed me in an awkward position, which I could have avoided by not seeing them in the first instance. I fear now their going back without any expression from any one in authority will have a bad influence. At the same time I recognize the difficulties in the way of receiving these informal commissioners at this time, and do not know what to recommend. I am sorry, however, that Mr. Lincoln cannot have an interview with the two named in this dispatch [Campbell having fallen ill], if not all three now within our lines. Their letter to me was all that the President's instructions contemplated, to secure their safe conduct, if they had used the same language to Major Eckert.

As the telegrapher sent Grant's wire, Eckert was on his way to Hampton Roads on the overnight steamer *Lady Long,* leaving Grant in possession of the field. It was past ten-thirty when the general circled back to the *Mary Martin.* Campbell had gone to bed, nursing a lingering ailment, but Stephens and Hunter were up. Stephens took note of Grant's "heavy brow," and the three of them talked past midnight.

The *New York Times* correspondent was hovering by the wharf, wondering what the Southerners were up to. "It was expected that early this morning they would take their departure down the river, but up to this time of writing, midnight of the 1st, the *Mary Martin* is still at her station. This has, of course, given rise to all sorts of speculations; many wondering whether these gentlemen have, after all, come here in any authoritative capacity to act; and whether their visit is not going to terminate here."

Not if Grant could help it. He was working with Stephens and Hunter in the *Martin's* saloon. How to get past Eckert? How to get around one country, or two? How to get Lincoln to the table, where anything might happen? After midnight they had a plan and a letter. Stephens served as scrivener:

February 2, 1865
Maj. THOMAS T. ECKERT,
Aide-de-Camp

MAJOR: In reply to your verbal statement that your instructions did not allow you to alter the conditions upon which a passport could be given to us, we say that we are willing to proceed to Fort Monroe, and there to have an informal conference, with any person or persons that President Lincoln may appoint, on the basis of his letter to Francis P. Blair of the 18th of January ultimo [1865], or upon any other terms or conditions that he may hereafter propose, not inconsistent with the essential principles of self-government and popular rights, upon which our institutions are founded.

It is our earnest wish to ascertain, after a free interchange of ideas and information, upon what principles and terms, if any, a just and honorable peace can be established without the further effusion of blood, and to contribute our utmost efforts to accomplish such a result.

We think it better to add, that in accepting your passport we are not to be understood as committing ourselves to anything, but to carry to this informal conference the views and feelings above expressed.

Very respectfully, yours, etc.
Alexander H. Stephens, J. A. Campbell, R. M. T. Hunter

Grant seemed delighted with the letter and said it should satisfy Major Eckert. Then he purported to take it to Eckert, who was on his way to Fort Monroe. After a suitable interval, Grant returned with what looked to Stephens like "an anxious disquietude upon his face." He delivered the bad news first, with a straight face. Major Eckert was still not satisfied. But the good news outweighed the bad. Grant had decided on his own responsibility to send the commissioners to Fort Monroe, where Mr. Seward might agree to see them. He asked them to be ready in the morning. There was no need to pack. They would go on the *Mary Martin.*

Grant bid them good-night, taking their letter with him. Then he summoned Colonel Babcock, handed the letter to him, and told him not to wire it to Fort Monroe, but to take the commissioners there in the morning and hand their letter to Eckert, too late for the major to prevent them from arriving literally and figuratively on common ground with Seward.

On Thursday, February 2, Preston Blair's daughter teased her husband. "The world is all agog about the peace commissioners," Lizzie wrote. "There is an odd game going on which would excite you not a little if I dared write it, but as I cannot, I will only say that Father thinks you would enjoy it."

That day, Rhode Island and Michigan became the second and third states whose legislatures ratified the Thirteenth Amendment, beating Maryland to the punch.

At 9:00 a.m., the *Lady Long* arrived at Hampton Roads and delivered Major Eckert to Fort Monroe. He presented himself to Seward, handed over his correspondence with the commissioners, and declared that he had turned them away. As Eckert and Seward prepared to return to Washington, a message was on its way to Seward from Grant, who had wired it at 9:00 a.m., knowing it would take time to be transcribed and delivered: "The gentlemen here have accepted the proposed terms and will start for Fort Monroe at 9:30 a.m." The wire said no more, and the gentlemen's late-night note to Eckert was not included, leaving no way to question whether they *had* accepted Lincoln's terms, and no time to stop them before they left.

At 10:20 a.m., unaware that they were coming, Eckert wired Stanton the news he had tried to transmit from City Point—that he had sent them back to Richmond. They were on their way to Hampton Roads as the telegrapher tapped it out.

After breakfast, the president had walked over to the War Department and read Eckert's message that the commissioners' response was not satisfactory. He was about to recall Seward when he read Grant's wire to Stanton of the night before, as Grant had known he would—the one about how sorry Grant was that the president would not see them, for "their intentions are good and their desire sincere to restore peace and union." It moved him.

The Southerners had been standing with their aide Colonel Hatch on the *Mary Martin* as her boiler made steam for the run to Fort Monroe when the General in Chief of the Army came pounding down the stairway almost at a run. He was "beaming with joy" as Stephens caught sight of him, waving a ribbon of telegraph paper, shouting to his coconspirators. "Gentlemen! It's all right! I've got the authority!" In his hand was a wire from the president. Almost out of breath, Grant read it aloud on the paddle wheeler's deck. "Say to the gentlemen I will meet them personally at Fortress Monroe as soon as I can get there. A. Lincoln." The president had wired Seward as well. "Induced by a dispatch of General Grant, I join you at Fort Monroe so soon as I can come."

Lacking Grant's gift for brevity, Stephens would later say that the general congratulated them "with evident indications of high gratification." Then Hunter pushed his luck. "Well, General. How about Colonel Hatch, our secretary. Will he be permitted to go or not?" Grant reflected for a moment. Lincoln had agreed to meet "the gentlemen," the general said, by which he clearly meant the commissioners. Grant would take no more liberties with his orders. "We've had a great deal of trouble already." He turned to Colonel Hatch with the ease of a brother soldier. "We'll send these gentlemen down to Fortress Monroe to make peace while you and I go up to Varina to see about the exchange of prisoners." Varina, Mrs. Davis's coincidental namesake, was the place south of Richmond where prisoners were often traded. As Assistant Commissioner of Exchange, Hatch would soon learn that Grant wanted him out of a job. The general was willing to exchange *all* prisoners, officer for officer, man for man, until one side exhausted its supply.

Then Hunter asked to bring another uninvited guest. "How about Mr. Stephens's body servant?" Mr. Stephens was "just out of a bed of illness and cannot travel without him." The general turned to Stephens. "Is he white or colored?"

"He is colored."

"Is he slave or free?"

"He is a slave."

"Are you not afraid he will run away [and] make his escape from you?"

"Not at all. I have no apprehensions of the sort."

"Well, then," the general said, "I take the responsibility."

As the *Mary Martin* pulled away for Hampton Roads with a parting blast of her steam whistle, the commissioners' mood had shifted from despair to excitement. When they had fallen into bed the night before, their mission had been half-dead. Now something might be done, but hope was a burdensome gift. "We were no diplomatists," as Hunter would later say. In the space of less than twenty-four hours, they had been asked to end the war and had set off to try, with almost no direction from their delusional president. In their scant time alone, they had barely absorbed their task. "We had formed no particular scheme of negotiation, no definite line of policy . . ." Apart from their shared ambition to secure a truce—to give the South room to breathe and both sides time to regain their senses—they had not even reconciled their own divergent thinking.

For Hunter, the Mexican scheme was nonsense, but if Blair had it right that the North would fight on regardless of cost, the South had no chance, and neither did two countries. Hunter thought that "any limitation of the range of discussion was unwise and inexpedient," but the senator agreed with Davis that reunion was too high a price for peace. He was going to Hampton Roads to learn what the enemy was thinking and to try to get a truce. Given Davis's mandate to reject reunion, he "never supposed that we were authorized to treat for peace . . . and if we had been, none of the Confederate commissioners, in my opinion, would at that time have accepted peace on the condition of reunion. I certainly would not."

He was wrong about Campbell and Stephens.

Judge Campbell's mind was clear. The Mexican scheme was a pipe dream, the demand for two countries absurd. The war was lost, slavery was dead, reunion was inevitable. The questions were when and how. The South could be conquered and crushed or rejoin the Union with honor, though shorn of many prewar advantages. Hoping only for the latter, Campbell wished to hear Lincoln's proposals for reconstruction, "and the rights that would be secured to the Southern states in the event that one should take place." He put his hopes for peace not in Lincoln and Davis but in Grant and Lee. The Northern and Southern people would accept terms from them that they would take from no one else. Once the fighting stopped, "old habits of communion and profitable trade" would return, and a rekindling of good feeling and self-interest could produce a peaceful reunion that politicians could not achieve.

Hunter and Campbell shook their heads over Stephens's eccentricity. To Hunter, Stephens seemed "possessed" with the thought that the North might agree that the states should realign as they wished. On the way to Hampton Roads, Stephens told Campbell he had given up on the Confederacy. Its internal divisions and Davis's destructive policies were wounds that would not heal. In the end, another union might form, but not necessarily the old one, though Stephens did not oppose its reconstruction. He never had. The alignments that the states might choose were not the essential thing. What mattered was their sovereignty, and "Constitutional Liberties." Whatever civil unions they might join or put asunder were secondary. A marriage for love would vindicate all that Stephens held dear. A shotgun wedding would not.

Intrigued as he was by the Mexican idea, Stephens would bring it to Lincoln reluctantly, with only a "slight hope of doing some good." He was sure that Davis was merely using it to derail the peace resolutions in Congress. Like Hunter and Campbell, he hoped for no more than a truce, a "cooling of hot blood," a stepping stone at best to a conference of all the states, where peace could be made "upon some satisfactory basis." Once Americans stopped killing one another they would never start again. As for slavery, its profits were "but the dust in the balance" when weighed against its social and moral consequences. He would give it up for a better alternative with no regrets. So long as state sovereignty was respected, the issue was whether slavery or some other system better served both races—the "inferior" as well as the "superior."

Before the *Mary Martin* paddled off to Hampton Roads, Campbell left a letter with Colonel Hatch to take to Davis, informing him that the commissioners would meet Lincoln and Seward at Fort Monroe, enclosing their correspondence with Eckert and Grant. The judge gave their maneuverings a dubious, self-congratulatory spin: "We suppose that thus far we are entirely free from any compromise and that we have sufficiently defined our expectations and purposes, to those who may be apprehended to meet us, so that there will be no mistake."

Davis had no hope that anything good would come from Hampton Roads after Campbell let him know that Seward would be there. He told Stephens's nemesis Benjamin Hill that "Mr. Lincoln is an honest, well-meaning man," despite his misguided views, "but Seward is wily and treacherous." Unlike Jefferson Davis.

On Thursday morning, February 2, at about nine-thirty, Lincoln left the White House in the company of Charles Forbes, his twenty-eight-year-old valet, born and raised in Ireland with all of the charm of his tribe. The president called him Charlie. He was one of Tad's favorites. Lincoln's friend Noah Brooks was not especially fond of the "corps of attachés of Hibernian descent" whom the president had gathered around him, with the specific exception of Charlie, an "intelligent servant" according to Edward Neill, the 1st Minnesota Infantry's chaplain, assigned temporarily as one of Lincoln's live-in secretaries.

Neill had befriended Charlie too. He was going upstairs to his room that morning while Charlie was coming down with a carpetbag in his hand. Neill asked him where he was going. Looking back up to be sure they were alone, Charlie whispered, "Fortress Monroe," and hurried on. When Neill reached the upper hall, "I met the President with his overcoat, and going to my room, looked out of the window, and saw him quietly walking around the curved pavement which leads to Pennsylvania Avenue, while Forbes was following, at a distance of two or three hundred feet." Neill crossed the hall to John Nicolay's room. Nicolay knew nothing about it.

Montgomery Blair had left Lincoln a note asking to see him. Lincoln left a note of his own: "Mr. Blair will hereafter know that I ought not to stop now."

Charlie, the president, and his carpetbag, making up his entourage, were driven to the Washington City depot and left for Annapolis in a one-car train that the Baltimore & Ohio Railroad supplied at a moment's notice. A B&O agent escorted them. Apart from Seward, no Cabinet member knew that Lincoln had gone until he was on his way. Only Seward was pleased. Gideon Welles had grave misgivings when he heard about it. "The President and Mr. Seward have gone to Hampton Roads to have an interview with the Rebel commissioners, Stephens, Hunter, and Campbell. None of the [rest of the] Cabinet were advised of this move, and without exception, I think, it struck them unfavorably that the Chief Magistrate should have gone on such a mission."

Davis's friends at the *Richmond Sentinel* made little of it. "The less we say or think about the probable success of the deputation to Washington the better. Let us go on with our work as though no such mission was on foot, lest we make of it a snare and a peril."

A more festive mission was under way that day as General John Pegram marched his division ceremoniously past Robert E. Lee. Just turned thirty-three, Pegram was a Petersburg native and a product of West Point. His charisma moved men and his looks melted women. He had married Hetty Cary two weeks before, with the loan of a horse and carriage from two of their wedding guests, President and Mrs. Davis. No one enjoyed a Virginia lineage more luminous than Hetty Cary's. Descended from Jeffersons, Randolphs, and Pocahontas, she had famously waved a Rebel battle flag at scowling blue regiments as they marched through her native Baltimore. Now the newlyweds had been loaned a honeymoon cottage near Petersburg.

Pegram's young friend Colonel Henry Kyd Douglas had never seen so beautiful a woman as the general's auburn-haired bride. The review of the division was dedicated to her. With Lee at her side, Hetty sat her horse "like the Maid of France." As she rode off the field past a group of common soldiers, she brushed a gawking North Carolinian and nearly knocked him down. When she pulled up immediately and turned to the man to apologize, he snatched his hat from his head. "Never mind, Miss," he said. "You might have rid all over me. Indeed you might!"

———

It occurred to Seward belatedly to verify Grant's report that the commissioners had accepted Lincoln's terms. Eckert may have prompted him. He wired the general that afternoon from Fort Monroe: "You state 'The Gentlemen here have accepted the proposed terms and will start for Fort Monroe at 9:30 A.M.' Please telegraph me the form & words of their acceptance as soon as possible." With the gentlemen irretrievably on their way to Hampton Roads, Grant replied immediately: He had given their acceptance to "a Staff Officer to be delivered to you. I retained no copy of it."

———

A mutton-chopped army captain met Lincoln's private train at Annapolis. Then the captain, Charlie Forbes, and the B&O Railway man walked the president half a mile to the Naval Academy pier, where the USS *Thomas Collyer*, the fastest ship on Chesapeake Bay, was steamed up and ready. As Lincoln and Charlie went aboard, the Academy hospital band played patriotic airs. The *Collyer* pushed off immediately, nudged past the ice in the harbor, and broke into open water for the fastest run to Hampton Roads on record, just under eight hours.

In the shadow of Fort Monroe, the enormous stone-built edifice that had guarded Hampton Roads since 1834, the *River Queen* was waiting, resplendent with flags and pennants. When the *Mary Martin* approached the scene before five o'clock, hours ahead of Lincoln and the *Collyer*, the *New York Herald*'s man was watching: "General Grant's flagboat, *M. Martin*, has just arrived, bringing the rebel peace commissioners. The *River Queen*, with Secretary Seward on board, is anchored a short distance from the wharf, and as I write the *M. Martin* is just coming alongside of her." As the *Mary Martin*'s captain eased her up to the *River Queen*, sailors stepping lively threw lines from one to the other and drew the two steamboats together. The tugboats *Silas O. Pierce* and *George J. Loane* shuttled smartly between the *River Queen* and the shore, bearing messengers, fuel, and supplies.

Denied the freedom of movement they had enjoyed at City Point, the Rebel dignitaries were not invited to disembark. Their escort Colonel Babcock crossed over to the *River Queen* and handed Major Eckert the letter Alec Stephens had written to him the night before, in which, according to Grant, they had "accepted the proposed terms." The look on Eckert's face when he read its closing line can be imagined: "We think it better to add, that in accepting your passport we are not to be understood as committing ourselves to anything . . ."

Resisting the temptation to go over to the *Martin* and take his old friends by the hand, Seward stayed put on the *River Queen* and sent a wire to Stanton: "Richmond party here. President Lincoln not arrived. I do not recognize them until he comes." Recognition duly withheld, the Secretary of State sent over to the Southerners a welcoming gift—three bottles of good whiskey.

Lincoln arrived on the *Collyer* at about ten-thirty and transferred to the *River Queen,* where Seward and Eckert handed him the commissioners' letters and told him they were on the *Mary Martin* and Seward had not yet seen them. The president would soon tell Congress, careful of every word, how he came to be in this place. "I ascertained that Major Eckert had literally complied with his instructions, and I saw, for the first time, the answer of the Richmond gentlemen to him, which, in his dispatch to me of the 1st, he characterizes as 'not satisfactory.'" Fresh from the *Mary Martin,* Colonel Babcock showed the president the commissioners' midnight note to Eckert, another equivocation that Lincoln had not seen. With the gentlemen from Richmond literally tied to his ship of state, he could hardly cut them loose even if he had wanted to, which he surely did not. Grant had given him shelter.

After wondering for years what the decision makers in Richmond were thinking, Lincoln and Seward were about to sit down with three of them. If Grant had it right, there might be a chance for peace. If not, what good might come of this thing? What could be learned from these men? Lincoln and Seward surely pondered it together before they went to sleep on the *River Queen.*

Word was sent to the *Martin* that the president was fatigued from his journey and would see them in the morning on his steamboat, sealed off from the press and interlopers. An hour later, Eckert wired Stanton: "I have the honor to report the arrival of the President at 10:30 p.m., and is now with Mr. Seward on board the *River Queen*. The interview will take place in the morning. The vessels of both parties are anchored half a mile out from dock."

As the Northern leaders took their rest on the *River Queen* and the Southerners on the *Mary Martin*, the *New York Herald* set the scene. "Peacefully and fraternally these little steamers lay side by side on the placid waters of the river."

CHAPTER EIGHTEEN

There Has Been Nothing
We Could Do for Our Country

On Friday, February 3, 1865, a warm sun was shining on a brilliant spring-like day as the three distinguished Southerners were welcomed aboard the *River Queen* and shown to the floating drawing room on the vessel's upper deck. The president and Mr. Seward would be joining them soon.

Approached through a pair of French doors, the *River Queen*'s saloon had the size, shape, and feel of an elegant bowfront parlor, touched with a nautical tinge. A multipaned skylight admitted the morning sun through the low, coffered ceiling, painted beige to match the woodwork, set off by Corinthian pilasters edged with gilded trim. The compartment was lined with rows of gleaming windows with rose-colored blinds and deep green curtains tied back with tasseled cords over tufted black-leather banquettes. Turned wooden armchairs were arranged with upholstered chairs in a conversational arc on a lush Persian rug that covered the deck completely in ivories, roses, and greens. In the gravity of the moment, the splendor of their surroundings may have been lost on the peace commissioners, who did not have long to admire them before Lincoln and Seward walked into the room and extended their hands to their enemies.

Nathaniel Hawthorne described a similar entrance on a visit to the White House in 1862. "By and by, there was a little stir on the staircase and in the passage-way, and in lounged a tall, loose-jointed figure, of an exaggerated Yankee port and demeanor," dressed in an ancient black suit. Lincoln's hair was uncombed and there was "no describing his lengthy awkwardness," but his homeliness was lit by the "homely human sympathies that warmed it."

Three years of civil war had passed since then, and the president was thirty pounds underweight. As Horace Greeley would soon observe, his sunken face was "seamed with thought and trouble" like a weather-beaten mariner's. All of that said, he was six feet, four inches tall, and the saloon's low ceiling exaggerated his height. Abraham Lincoln commanded the room.

If any introductions were required, Seward could have made them, having worked and socialized with all three Southerners for years, but no more than one was necessary. Lincoln and Stephens had enjoyed a special friendship. As a Supreme Court justice, Campbell had met Lincoln and attended his inauguration. Lincoln and Hunter had served as fellow Whigs in an intimately scaled Congress for two overlapping years, Lincoln in the House, Hunter in the Senate, and had probably met. After parting as friends, it was more than a little awkward to reunite as enemies, but the tension was broken when Stephens greeted Lincoln with the warmth of an old companion and the president responded in kind. Stephens found him talkative and relaxed, in "a splendid humor." His aide John Hay said Lincoln's eye would brighten when he welcomed old friends to the White House. As he welcomed Alec Stephens to the *River Queen*, the little Georgian looked up at him warmly, grasped his hand with feeling, called him Mr. President in his childlike voice, and took it as a compliment when Lincoln called him Stephens, a familiar, manly form of address that neither recognized his title nor snubbed it, and flattered him with a presidential intimacy in the presence of his peers. It was just the right note. Stephens took the bait and relished it.

Seward brought his charm, remembered Southern friends, and inquired particularly of the health of Mr. Davis. The Southerners were gracious too. If Hunter was true to form, he presented what Mary Chesnut encountered when they met before the war at a state dinner, "a rather tumbled up appearance. His waistcoat wanted pulling down and his hair wanted brushing." But when seated between Hunter and Alabama's Senator Clement Clay, Mrs. Chesnut found Hunter the better companion. "Mr. Clay had taken me in to dinner, but he seemed quite satisfied that my other side should take me off his hands," which Hunter smoothly did "from soup to dessert," with a publishable critique of English literature. Since then, Mrs. Chesnut said, "I have always looked forward to a talk with the Senator from Virginia with undisguised pleasure."

Even the stiff Judge Campbell struck a sociable pose when the Northerners took his hand. Campbell was still convinced that Seward had used him in the Sumter crisis, but Seward was still a charmer, and no one was more engaging than Lincoln. Campbell had respected him from afar. Close up, he found himself liking him. "The naturalness was like that of a child," as the abolitionist Elizabeth Peabody would soon observe, "and had a touch of pathos in it." He seemed to be "full of feeling," with "kind, shining eyes." Campbell saw it too.

Back in Richmond, General Gorgas was thinking that the commissioners "probably reached Washington yesterday and are now pow-wowing. No one expects any results." Expectations ran stronger up North, where rumors of peace talks had matured into news. According to Noah Brooks, "the perturbation in Washington was something which cannot be readily described." In House and Senate cloakrooms the Jacobins outbid each other in their prophesies of doom. Lincoln would surrender what the war had been fought to win. The Thirteenth Amendment would be abandoned. The Emancipation Proclamation would be revoked. Freed slaves would be returned. Jeff Davis would be back in the Senate before the month was out. No one would be hanged. The president had followed Seward to Hampton Roads for fear that he would not be sufficiently craven. Moderates urged their colleagues to wait and see. Jacobins shouted them down. There was talk of impeachment. Thaddeus Stevens was bright with rage.

The president, to be sure, was not without his friends. On the floor of the House, Fernando Wood, the despised former mayor of New York, lavished blessings on his head, a fork-tongued kiss of death from the Copperhead king. Some thought it quite deliberate. In the pages of the *Washington Chronicle*, Lincoln's friend John Fourney explained the president's negotiating plans and defended their wisdom, unimpaired by the slightest knowledge of them. Concessions would be made, the *Chronicle* said, but peace was worth the price. Noah Brooks thought Fourney had taken it on himself "to prepare the public mind for the sacrifice of something vaguely dreadful, and dreadfully vague." Dread was the result among the Radicals, who knew that Fourney often spoke for Lincoln.

With the president at the peace table, the loyal *New York Times* came abruptly around. "We again advise our readers not to be sanguine in anticipating that peace will be hastened by this conference"—the *Times* had been far from sanguine—but the president should be praised "for making the most of that chance," an editorial flip-flop of Olympian proportions. Sworn to secrecy by Preston Blair, Horace Greeley could not contain himself. The *Tribune* had "received some inklings" of the conference's agenda, including "the reunion of North and South upon the grand idea of the Monroe Doctrine." The *New York Herald* praised the president for hosting the event at Hampton Roads, sheltered from the "rising storm of indignation" on Capitol Hill, and denying the rebel envoys "the freedom of Washington," full of Copperheads and leaks as it was.

In the *River Queen's* saloon, a free black steward brought in water and cigars as the gentlemen took their seats and began to reminisce. Fragrant smoke filled the air, tinged with the scent of nostalgia. Better times were recalled. Dead characters were exhumed. Amusing anecdotes were told, improving, no doubt, with the telling. There were rumbles of masculine laughter. No one seemed eager to spoil it. The business at hand could wait.

Though the day was warm and the *River Queen* well heated, Stephens stayed bundled in his wrappings well into the conversation. Recalling how small the little Georgian had been as a fellow Young Indian in the club they had formed in the House, Lincoln was amused as Stephens struggled out of his overcoat and revealed his waiflike frame, just as he had to Grant. An agricultural metaphor occurred to the president, which he took the risk of sharing. He had never seen so small an ear emerge from so much husk. Happily for diplomacy, Stephens led the laughter.

To their mutual pleasure, the Confederate vice president and the President of the United States remembered old friends. Lincoln was fond of stories, and a Georgian lets us know that when Stephens relived old times, his companions would find themselves bantering with "a happy looking schoolboy" with "a wrinkled face and wonderful eyes." Stephens spoke fondly of Truman Smith, a Young Indian from Connecticut, now older. Lincoln returned the favor with affectionate inquiries about the Georgian Robert Toombs, an outrageously entertaining Indian in 1848, a wounded Rebel general now. Stephens took credit for the making of Zachery Taylor and shared it generously with Lincoln, who recalled the connection vaguely. It began to occur to Judge Campbell that Stephens was gilding their friendship more brightly than Lincoln was, but when the president remembered Tom Flournoy, the Virginian whom Stephens had urged Davis to send in his stead, Little Alec had his moment of unspoken vindication. Adept raconteurs in their own patrician ways, Seward and Hunter shared memories of the old Senate. Campbell no doubt spoke pleasantly when spoken to.

It was Stephens who called the meeting to order. "Well, Mr. President," he said, "is there no way to put an end to the present troubles and restore the good feelings that existed in those days between the different States and sections of the country?" His words were chosen well. They had a nostalgic air, more than halfway home to our one common country.

Before Lincoln answered, Seward stepped in. It was understood, he said, that the conference would be informal. Implying but not quite saying that it would also be confidential, he observed that no stenographer had been summoned, so that everyone could speak freely. The Southerners concurred. The steward returned from time to time to replenish cigars, bring in refreshments, and straighten up the room, but no aides were present. The conferees were on their own.

Stephens repeated his question: How to end the trouble that plagued "the country" and restore the old feelings?

"There is only one way I know of," Lincoln said, "and that is for those who are resisting the National Authority and the laws of the United States to stop."

The laughter had come to an end. Judge Campbell had heard what he had expected. "Any other response would have filled me with amazement," he would later say. Instead he was filled with resignation.

Stephens was undeterred. Taken as he was with the Mexican scheme, he was confident that Lincoln and Seward had floated it south through Blair and were here to talk it through. In his Lilliputian voice and his windy Victorian style, rarely using a simple word where a convolution would do, Stephens began with some prompting. "Is there no other question," he asked, "that might divert the attention of both parties, for a time, from the questions involved in their present strife, until the passions on both sides might cool, when they would be in a better temper to come to an amicable and proper adjustment of those points of difference out of which the present lamentable collision of arms has arisen? Is there no continental question which might thus temporarily engage their attention? We have been induced to believe that there is."

If Stephens expected the Northerners to unveil it, he was promptly disappointed. Lincoln understood the allusion immediately and killed it on the spot with a force that hushed the room. His short declarative sentences hit all the harder on the heels of the little Georgian's verbosity. "I suppose you refer to something Mr. Blair has said." He wished to make it clear "at the beginning," with what Campbell perceived as "a great deal of emphasis and force," that whatever Mr. Blair had said was said on his own account. "Doubtless the old man meant well," but when he asked to go to Richmond to discuss his ideas with "some influential persons there," as Lincoln chose to call them, "I told him flatly that I did not want to hear them. If he wished to go, I would not stop him, but he had no authority to speak for me in any way whatever."

The Southerners were skeptical, though not so impolitic as to say so. Whether the Mexican scheme was his own or not, Blair was no amateur. If Lincoln had not sent him, he had let him go for a reason. After nearly four years of carnage, Lincoln must be under almost as much pressure as Davis. The commissioners had expected *some* flexibility in his position, something they could sell in Richmond. Lincoln was giving them nothing.

The president announced categorically that without immediate submission there would be no peace. Plain and simple. He warmed to the subject as he spoke, sensing that the commissioners had misled him. In a rising, high-pitched twang, he rejected any notion that *he* had come here under false pretenses. (No one had said that he had.) "The restoration of the Union is a *sine qua non* with me. I will listen to no proposal that does not include an immediate restoration of the National Authority." His letter to Mr. Blair had made that clear. The commissioners were familiar with it. They had used it to cross the lines. He had always been willing to entertain peace, but only on the conditions it recited, "and hence my instructions that no conference was to be held except on that basis." There was passion in all of this, and no give at all. An aide has let us know that Lincoln could be petulant "when overworked or weary," and "was always singularly firm in the assertion of his own fixed views or will." He was singularly firm now.

What came next was a pointed silence. The Southerners could not challenge what the president had said, but how to go on despite his having said it? He demanded what they could not give. It was they who had come under false pretenses. Grant could not help them now.

Stephens wished away what he had just seen and heard—Lincoln's disavowal of Blair's improbable scheme, his demand for immediate submission, the intensity of his convictions. To his colleagues' sheer amazement, Little Alec seemed to think that Lincoln and Seward might step away from victory, admit the simple justice of the Southern cause, and march arm in arm on Napoleon's army. For Hunter, "the extent to which he carried these opinions was strange indeed," as he now proceeded to prove.

Stephens was so fond of the Mexican fantasy, so sure he was sitting with its authors, that he came to an odd conclusion. Schooled by the crafty Seward, Lincoln might be playing a game, telling the Southerners, sotto voce, that he needed two things to put Blair's plan in motion: an ability to deny its paternity, and an agreement in advance to restore the Union after Mexico was freed. The first was easy to give. The second was the problem. Stephens collected his thoughts and played the Mexican card face up, exuding hope and verbosity.

"But suppose, Mr. President," he began, "that a line of policy should be suggested which, if adopted, would most *probably* lead to a restoration of the Union without further bloodshed. Would it not be highly advisable to act on it, even without the absolute pledge of ultimate restoration being required to be first given? May not such a policy be found to exist in the line indicated by the interrogatory propounded? Is there not now such a Continental question in which all the parties engaged in our present war feel a deep similar interest? I allude, of course, to Mexico and what is called the Monroe Doctrine, the principles of which are directly involved in the contest now waging there." Lincoln was still listening and Stephens was still talking. Richmond was under the impression that the administration in Washington was opposed to a French empire in Mexico, he said, and desired to sustain the Monroe Doctrine. These impressions came from Northern newspapers, the speeches of prominent men of the North, and "other sources." (Blair had become unmentionable.)

"Yes," was Lincoln's reply; most of the Northern people *did* feel that way.

Well, then, Stephens said, could not the North and South postpone their present strife and agree to suspend hostilities until the principle was maintained in Mexico? Might not their success in Mexico naturally and "almost inevitably" lead to a peaceful and harmonious solution to their own difficulties? Could any pledge of reunion make a permanent restoration "or reorganization" of the Union more probable, or even *as* probable as that?

But Lincoln was not interested in probabilities. Nor was he interested in invading Mexico, jointly or alone. The politician in him suspected it would be popular, but the commander in chief had had enough of killing. He had launched his career condemning the Mexican War. He would not be responsible for a second. After four years of suffering, the rebellion was all but crushed. Everyone in the room knew it. Now Stephens was suggesting that the South would "almost inevitably" consider some sort of "reorganization" if the North would stop the war, on the edge of winning it, and blithely start another.

Lincoln replied emphatically. The French intervention in Mexico was a second-tier issue for him. The settlement of "the existing difficulties" was of "supreme importance." He had fully considered a truce. There would be no truce without a satisfactory pledge that the Constitution and laws of the United States would be restored.

Stephens had seen the Mexican scheme as the only way out of the dilemma of one country or two. For him, Lincoln's demand for a pledge of reunion seemed to put an end to the conference, for the commissioners had no authority to give one, even if they had wanted to. Stephens would later say he had not expected such a demand, convinced as he was that the Northerners had hatched the Mexican idea. As a strict precondition to the meeting, Lincoln could not have demanded reunion more clearly, yet Stephens was surprised to hear that he meant it.

Judge Campbell was not. He did not believe in fairy tales. He could see that Blair had misled Davis. "We learned in five minutes that the assurances to Mr. Davis were a delusion and that union was the condition of peace. I had always supposed this to be the case, and had refused all discussions on the subject of negotiations unless that condition was first admitted." Like Stephens, Campbell had never seen reunion as unacceptable or even undesirable. For years he had thought it inevitable. But great questions remained to be resolved, and the judge had come to Hampton Roads to learn how the victors proposed to resolve them. The South would be punished, but would the rebellious states be restored as free and equal members of the Union, or subdued like vanquished tribes? Slavery was dead, but would the slaves be freed gradually or suddenly, and with compensation for their masters or not? Much of the South had been conquered already, but would its lands be restored to their owners or forfeited to their conquerors? The Confederate leaders would be deposed, but would they also be hanged (not the least of all issues for three of the men in this room)?

Performing the role that his colleagues had assigned him, Campbell probed searchingly into the Northern idea of the *manner* of reunion, accepting Lincoln's premise and his terminology too, with none of Stephens's flummery. "How would the reestablishment of the National Authority take place?" How would reconstruction be accomplished if the Confederate authorities consented? Might the North consider something like the Zollverein, the European economic union that had been drawing the independent German states together since 1818? Free trade and a renewal of good feelings might lead to something more.

It was Seward who replied. With all due respect, he would like to hear more of Mr. Stephens's thoughts about diverting the public mind from the present quarrel before they turned to Judge Campbell's inquiry. (Before these Rebels were told how unlike the Zollverein the National Authority would be, Seward wanted to hear what they were thinking. Campbell would say not a single careless word. Stephens liked to hear himself talk, as Seward and Lincoln knew. They may have agreed in advance to draw him out.)

Little Alec gladly obliged, filling the air with speech, egged on by Seward's interjections endorsing his "general views," though he needed no encouragement. If he only kept talking, something might turn up. As Hunter sat and listened, he slowly began to realize that Stephens was attempting to convince Abraham Lincoln and William Seward that secession was the most "conservative" remedy for their differences. "Never was hope more mistaken."

Stephens said he favored the taking of all of North America by "the States of the two confederacies" in a union of Southern and Northern *power*. In the course of *that* union, with trade and friendly intercourse restored, would not fraternal feelings be restored as well, and a reasonable settlement reached when the blood of "our people" had cooled? A French empire in Mexico offended the Confederate states as much as the United States, and the sovereign right of local self-government was sacred to both—the basis on which their political union should be restored when the heat of the war had dissipated. After bleeding together in Mexico, the states could be expected to reunite. Freely. In the present temper of "both nations," reunion should be desired by neither, but the law of self-interest would pull them together like the law of gravity, with no further loss of fraternal blood. The people of other North American lands would join the new union as they had the old. An "ocean-bound Federal Republic" would emerge, regulated, of course, by the sovereignty of each state.

For what it might be worth, Campbell suggested that a joint invasion of Mexico, leaving all Southern strongholds in Union hands, would inevitably lead to reunion. Stephens disagreed, the first of several splits in the face of the enemy that would play themselves out in this room. The states would adjust themselves as their interests suited them. Reunion would come if the states were so inclined, but their sovereignty did not permit them to be compelled.

"There is something superficially plausible in what you say," Seward replied, but it did not work practically. Suppose France or some other nation at war with the other states persuaded Louisiana to join it. Could the rest of the country leave the mouth of the Mississippi in hostile hands at Louisiana's pleasure?

Stephens said Louisiana was unlikely to leave the Union to ally herself with France, but if France treated her better than her sister states, she *ought* to secede. If the other states treated her fairly, she would never think of leaving.

Seward was hearing nothing new—the South had been singing the same old song throughout his long career—but he kept it going for a while. Suppose we did invade Mexico together; how would the South be governed? Who would collect the tariffs? How would they be spent?

Still convinced that the ideas Blair had shared with Davis were balloons sent south by the Lincoln administration, Stephens floated one of them back. If the parties called a truce, whatever troops remained in the South could be withdrawn to designated areas. Civilians could collect the tariffs and execute the laws. No one but the authorities in Richmond and Washington would even have to know. Confederate officials would preside, of course, and the state governments recognized by the Confederacy would be supreme.

Lincoln had heard enough. As Hunter was hearing it, all of this was received with "even less favor than I expected." Richmond wanted a truce; that much was clear. Lincoln would not give it to them. Stephens was suggesting that he recognize states "in arms against the National Government," he said, and that Lincoln would never do. He would consider no truce until "the great and vital question of reunion" was accepted. No treaty, convention, stipulation, or agreement could be made with the Confederate states, jointly or separately, on any subject at all, except on the basis of reconstruction.

Judge Campbell saw that Lincoln was declaring his terms, not negotiating them. There was nothing more to say, so Campbell said nothing. Not so Stephens.

"Well, Mr. President," he said, as commander in chief of the armies of the United States, you might enter into a *military* convention with the opposing combatants. "Everything could be effected in that way, if both sides were willing." Lincoln acknowledged that he had that authority, but he was working from a nineteenth century script. There could be no war in Mexico unless Congress declared one, he said; there could be no treaty without the Senate's consent, and, for many reasons, a joint invasion of Mexico made no military sense. He mentioned just one: If a quarrel broke out between the two armies—and they could hardly be sure of each other after four years of war—either could combine with the French to destroy the other. No, Lincoln said, for the third and last time, he would not suspend the war without a prior agreement to restore the National Authority, and surely not to achieve a "collateral objective."

Before the subject was dropped, Hunter disavowed Alec Stephens's idea that if Mexico were invaded, reunion must follow. The South might remain independent, though closely allied with the United States. In Richmond, there was a diversity of opinion on Mexico. He, for one, differed very much with Mr. Stephens. He would not pick a fight with France on the "pretense" of the Monroe Doctrine. Many Southerners thought the American people had no exclusive rights to this continent, and would not go to war over a mere question of policy, as opposed to one of "honor or right." Another nineteenth century idea.

Seeing a chance to show that the North was made of sterner stuff, Seward said the government in *Washington* was *united* on this subject. A Napoleonic army on North American soil had feelings running high in the North. The United States might invade Mexico alone. Indeed, there was cause to come to grips with France *or* to settle "the ancient grudge against Great Britain." Hunter got the message: The Confederacy was dead. The North was looking past it. The North had a war to spare. If the United States of America decided to drive the French out of Mexico—or attack the British Empire—it would need no help from Robert E. Lee.

Hunter summoned his dignity. The commissioners had no instructions to negotiate on the subject of Mexico, he said. "Nor am I, for one, prepared to do so."

As the senator spoke, one of Sherman's divisions was breaking through a critical Rebel blocking position, leaving South Carolina all but helpless to resist him.

Blair's Mexican fantasy having played itself out, Judge Campbell turned back to reality. "Supposing, Mr. President, that the Union were reconstructed with the Confederate States' assent—how would the reconstruction be accomplished?" Lincoln answered the question as simply as Campbell had asked it. "By disbanding their troops and permitting the national authorities to resume their functions."

As if that were not stark enough, Seward turned his friends to the elephant in the room. Not a word had yet been said about slavery. Its size and its smell were daunting. Now the governor led it out and put it on the table. A contemporary said he spoke unpretentiously on the Senate floor, "as though he were engaged in conversation, and the effect was always great." In an armchair with friends and cigars, the effect was greater still. The president could not express himself more plainly than he did in his message to Congress, Seward said, which clearly showed the way "by which peace can be secured to the people." The New Yorker did not speak of the Southern people or the Northern people. Peace would be secured to "the people." He then recited from memory the substance of the message's salient points, an effective bit of theater:

> In presenting the abandonment of armed resistance to the National Authority on the part of the insurgents as the only indispensable condition to ending the war on the part of the Government, I retract nothing heretofore said as to slavery. I repeat the declaration made a year ago, that "while I remain in my present position, I shall not attempt to retract or modify the Emancipation Proclamation, nor shall I return to slavery any person who is free by the terms of the Proclamation, or any Acts of Congress." If the people should, by whatever mode or means, make it an Executive duty to reenslave such persons, another, and not I, must be the instrument to perform it. In stating a single condition of peace, I mean simply to say that the war will cease on the part of the Government whenever it shall have ceased on the part of those who began it.

The consequences were simple, the governor said. There was no swagger in his tone, no arrogance on his face, but what he said was plain: Federal officials will preside over the post offices, the custom houses, the land offices, and the courts. The federal government will appoint them. "The laws will be submitted to."

Campbell replied like a former Supreme Court justice. He did not challenge what Seward had said, but the consequences of the separation and the war must be lawfully adjusted before a "harmonious restoration of the former relations" could be achieved, supposing that the South endorsed one. Both sides had seized and sold Southern property, leaving titles to be settled, compensation to be negotiated. Disbanding the Confederate Army and disposing of its supplies would be no small task. All of this would take time. The judge did not say so, but time was what the commissioners wanted to buy.

Seward was not selling any. Certainly, there were legal issues to be resolved, but that was what the courts were for. The war must end first. Congress would no doubt be liberal about confiscated property "after the passions excited by the war have been composed."

The issue of property having been raised, Stephens looked the elephant in the eye. In effect, the Emancipation Proclamation had only freed the slaves in the *occupied* South, he said. If the war ended now, how would it affect the *entire* Negro population? Would it emancipate them all, or only the slaves that the Northern army freed?

Ironically enough, it was here, on the issue of slavery—the issue of the century, the damnable issue that had started it all—where the Northerners had room to maneuver. Their demand for reunion and disarmament had been made. The chest-thumping phase was over. Now Lincoln and Seward tried to coax the Southerners home with kinder, gentler inducements, none of them inconsiderable: their lives, their fortunes, and their sacred honor.

Two of Lincoln's three conditions for peace had already been declared. The Rebels must lay down their arms and the Union must be restored. Unequivocally. But there were cards to be played in the *River Queen's* saloon on the third condition: The *president* would take no *backward* steps on slavery. Lincoln gave Stephens his first nuanced answer.

His public statements on slavery were impossible to reverse, he said, even if he wanted to. So long as he remained in his present position (he never referred to himself as president), *he* would not change the Emancipation Proclamation "in the slightest particular." The issue was what it meant, a point on which reasonable minds could differ and did. Some said it was a purely military measure that would end with the war, others that it operated only in places under Union occupation, still others that it was effective everywhere in the rebellious states. These were legal issues, to be dealt with in the courts. How they would be decided he did not pretend to know. He supposed the answer would come when someone took a slave from one place to another and the question was raised in a lawsuit.

There was no mistaking his meaning. In the *Dred Scott* case, Judge Campbell had helped decide, as a matter of *federal* law, that slaves were *not* made free when taken into free territory. It was still the law of the land. The South could not preserve its independence on the battlefield, but Lincoln was suggesting that it might preserve slavery in the courtroom, if only for a while. Even if slavery died, a palatable substitute might take its place. General Meade had told the commissioners that a system could be devised that would not be "so obnoxious as slavery." Many Northerners shared his vision of an American brand of serfdom. Lincoln himself had spoken of a transitional "apprenticeship" system.

Lincoln did not stop there. In his own opinion, he said, the Emancipation Proclamation was an exercise of his presidential war-making powers, and could only be effective as such. If the war ended now, it would only have freed the slaves in the areas under Union control. Of course that was only his opinion. The courts might see it otherwise. Then Seward laid a stick next to Lincoln's carrot. "*Up to this time*" the Emancipation Proclamation had freed only about two hundred thousand of the South's three million slaves. If the war went on, they would all be freed by force.

~

They were saying in Washington City that Jeff Davis had come through the lines and was closeted with Lincoln at City Point—or was it Fort Monroe? An unnamed Cabinet member would neither confirm nor deny it, which was reasonable enough, since no Cabinet member but Seward knew anything. Stanton had only a false inkling, Grant's message of the day before that the Southerners had accepted Lincoln's terms. The *New York Herald* said Stanton told a former congressman that "an early and amicable termination of the war" was probable, "and a feverish anticipation of the result of the pending negotiations exists among all classes."

Not among all classes. Though the price of gold had dropped, in fear of a chance for peace, the market was "but little affected," said the *New York Commercial Advertiser.* "There is such utter incredulity as to the possibility of peace coming out of the negotiations that stocks are actually strengthening . . ." It was widely assumed on Wall Street that nothing would come of it all but a keener commitment to the killing, to be followed by "a strong upward bound in prices."

On the floor of the US Senate, the old Democrat Reverdy Johnson observed that "a singular state of things is existing at the very moment I am speaking." Senators should reflect on it. Suppose the commissioners said, "We know the whole thing has been wrong; we see the horrors which have resulted from it . . . we have committed the error of our lives," and only ask a pardon. Why should we not welcome it? It was clear when they crossed the lines that despite the arts "of the traitor and the demagogue," the people's affections for each other and common love of country had not changed. "The rebel soldiers cheered, and so did ours, seeing that they should no longer do all they could to murder each other; but that the time was approaching when they could embrace each other as brethren and as American citizens."

In a musical Galway brogue, the Irish-born senator John Conness, a Republican from California, asked the senator from Maryland how he knew what the troops were cheering. Perhaps the Rebels thought their independence was at hand, while "our Army cheered because they believed the Commissioners were going to acknowledge the power of the Union and the supremacy of our flag."

Senator Jacob Collamer, a taciturn Vermont Republican, had a shorter explanation. "Perhaps they were cheering at the idea that they would be able to go home in peace."

In the *River Queen's* saloon, when the time seemed right to disclose the morning's surprise, Seward did it casually. "It might be proper to say" that the House had just endorsed a Constitutional amendment for the *immediate* abolition of slavery *throughout* the United States, which would moot the debate on the Emancipation Proclamation. Illinois, Rhode Island, and Michigan had already ratified it. Then he handed Judge Campbell the words that would render *Dred Scott* a nullity. It took just a moment to read them:

> *Be it resolved by the Senate and House of Representatives of the United States in Congress assembled: That the following article be proposed to the Legislatures of the several States, as an amendment to the Constitution of the United States, which, when ratified by three-fourths of said Legislatures, shall be valid to all intents and purposes, as a part of said Constitution, namely:*

> *ARTICLE XIII*

> *SECTION 1. Neither slavery nor involuntary servitude, except as a punishment for crime, whereof the party shall have been duly convicted, shall exist within the United States, or any place subject to their jurisdiction.*

> *SECTION 2. Congress shall have power to enforce this article by appropriate legislation.*

Judge Campbell asked the governor what significance he attached to it. Were he not William Seward, his reply would have been astonishing. "Not a great deal," he said. The amendment had passed under the revolutionary passions of war, which always recede in peace. Maryland had just banned slavery within her own borders. Her abolitionists had proposed to end it in fifty years, well into the twentieth century. A more extreme faction countered with seven. The radicals demanded abolition now, and got it. Extremists always predominate in a revolution. If the South abandoned the war, the measures the war engendered would probably be abandoned too. There were thirty-six states in the Union (the undivided Union), any ten of which could block the Thirteenth Amendment. Seward stopped short of insulting the Southern intelligence. It was needless to say that eleven of them were Confederate, or that Delaware and Kentucky had never left the Union and never abolished slavery.

It was a clever piece of positioning. Campbell's nimble mind suspected on the spot that the commissioners had been held at the lines until the amendment passed the House. It gave Lincoln and Seward leverage. The Southerners had come to Hampton Roads thinking slavery would end with the war. Now they had reason to think it might not, if the war ended now and the South rejoined the Union with its Constitutional powers restored.

Seward remarked that he thought before the war that forty or fifty years of agitation would be required to bring the public around to abolition. Now it was at hand. Campbell heard a threat in the word *agitation*, little knowing that nearly a century would pass before it was carried out. Until now, Campbell said, all of the agitation had been confined to emancipation. Did Mr. Seward think that agitation about the *political* relations between the races would end when the blacks were freed? "Perhaps not," Seward said. "Possibly not."

Now Stephens picked up the thread that Campbell had been pulling. What would happen politically if the Confederate states rejoined the Union? Would they retake their seats in Congress with all of their old rights?

Lincoln answered promptly. In his "own individual opinion," they should; *he* thought they would, but he could not stipulate to it. Only Congress had that power. That said, he was struggling to preserve the Union, and there could be no Union unless all of its states were represented. Millions of Northerners sympathized with the Southern people (a frank admission for their commander in chief to make), and the sympathy would grow if Congress kept them out. Northern voters would raise "a clamor on their behalf." He could give no guarantees, but better to rejoin the Union now than continue the war and deepen the bitterness in Congress. The time might come when the residents of the South would not be considered an erring people, to be invited back to citizenship, but defeated enemies, to be subjugated and ruined or worse.

When Stephens pressed for a specific understanding that the returning states' rights would be restored, Lincoln went back to first principles. He would never treat with armed Rebels as if they were a foreign power, he said, another government inside the one of which he was president. To do so would be to recognize their legitimacy—"what you have long asked Europe to do, in vain, and be resigning the only thing the armies of the Union have been fighting for." The only grounds on which he could rest the justice of the war, with his people and the world at large, was that it was not a war for conquest, "for the States had never been separated from the Union."

Judge Campbell suggested that if Washington would not treat with Richmond, a convention of the states would make a better peace than one imposed by conquest. His hosts were unmoved. "They left no opening for any convention," Campbell later said. "Everything was to be settled by the laws of Congress and the decisions of the courts."

Senator Hunter asked about West Virginia, carved away from his constituency while the Civil War raged, a newly created state composed of mountain folk, free-labor folk, mostly loyal to the Union. Would Virginia be restored to "her ancient limits" in a reunited country? Lincoln replied that this too was a question for Congress and the courts. In his own opinion, West Virginia should survive, but the issue was not up to him.

Typically slow to anger, Hunter was angry now, but calm enough not to say what he was thinking: that what Hunter perceived as Lincoln's demand for unconditional surrender, his refusal to treat with the South, his demand to submit to his mercy, was as cruel as it was unwise. Hunter was thinking that the two senior officers of the National Authority were treating with Rebels *now*, *because* they were in arms, but he summoned the will not to say so. Instead he cited history. Many governments had negotiated with armed rebels. In the English Civil War, Charles the First had often parlayed with them. The Confederacy must be granted "some recognition" before peace could be negotiated.

The point was astute, but Lincoln spotted its flaw. With his face lit up by what Stephens recognized as "that indescribable expression that often preceded his hardest hits," he laughed and delivered the jibe of the day. "Upon questions of history I must refer you to Seward, for he is posted in such things, and I don't pretend to be bright. My only distinct recollection of the matter is that Charles lost his head."

Stephens saw Hunter blanch. As Stephens would later say, the president had "crushed him and his precedent." To his credit, the senator hit back cleanly. Charles lost his head because he refused to *settle* with rebels, not because he negotiated with them. But Hunter had been wounded and everyone could see it. Lincoln's wit had deflated his erudition. It had also stoked his anger. In an effort to defuse the tension, Stephens said that government-to-government negotiations could be avoided entirely. If Lincoln had issued the Emancipation Proclamation under his war powers—and the Constitution could not support it on any other ground—he could use them to *end* the war by restoring the Confederate states to their former status.

Now Lincoln felt compelled to explain himself on abolition, almost apologetically, according to Alec Stephens. An aide would later recall the animation that came over him when he discussed compelling issues with people he respected, "a wonderful power of expression" that lit his homely features "by the great soul within." This was such a time.

He would never have issued the Emancipation Proclamation had he not been "compelled by necessity" to preserve the Union. He had hesitated for some time, perplexed by many questions. He had acted only when driven to it. He had always favored emancipation, but not *immediate* emancipation, even by the states themselves. It would lead to many evils. He did not intend in the beginning to interfere with slavery in the states. He had wanted to ban it in the territories. He had thought the federal government had no peacetime power over it in the states, and now that events "have taken us where we are," a gradual emancipation, perhaps over five years, would better enable the races to work out their "codes and designs for living together" than "emancipation at one sweep."

Then he paused for a moment, as Stephens would later recall, with his head "rather bent, as if in deep reflection." Everyone else was silent, waiting for him to go on. As Stephens would later tell it, Lincoln raised his head, rose from his chair, and spoke gently to his old friend, towering over the room.

"Stephens, if I were in Georgia, and entertained the sentiments I do—though I suppose I should not be permitted to stay there long with them—but if I resided in Georgia, with my present sentiments, I'll tell you what I would do if I were in your place. I would go home and get the governor of the State to call the legislature together and get them to recall all of the State troops from the war, elect Senators and Members to Congress, and ratify this Constitutional amendment prospectively, so as to take effect, say in five years. Such a ratification would be valid, in my opinion. I have looked into the subject, and think such a prospective ratification would be valid. Whatever may have been the views of your people before the war, they must be convinced now that slavery is doomed. It cannot last long in any event, and the best course, it seems to me, for your public men to pursue, would be to adopt such a policy as would avoid, as far as possible, the evils of immediate emancipation. That would be my course, if I were in your place."

According to Stephens, Seward seconded this. A gradual end to slavery would be palatable if the war ended now and the South rejoined the Union freely. If not, the Thirteenth Amendment would end it abruptly, with the Southern states excluded from the process.

It was Hunter who replied. Campbell had owned no slaves for years, and Stephens treated his own like tenants, professing to hold none against their will. But Hunter was the voice of the slaveholding aristocracy. It was the voice of the past, and he knew it. He made no case for slavery. He did condemn the "cruelty" of freeing the slaves overnight. They could not provide for themselves, he said. In places like Eastern Virginia, where many Negro men had "absconded" to the Union Army, the old and infirm and the women and children were "a tax upon their masters." They would find themselves helpless and suffering if the North freed them suddenly. They were accustomed to working only by compulsion. They would not work at all if the compulsion stopped. Slave and master would starve alike.

Lincoln looked at Seward but the governor said nothing, so the president turned to what Stephens recognized as "his chief resort in conveying his ideas upon almost every question," an endless supply of "exceedingly pointed" parables of a distinctly rustic sort and an entertainer's knack for recounting them. This one, Stephens thought, would not have made "a list of his best and most felicitous hits." Seward tried to interrupt him, impatient if not annoyed by the old familiar preamble, "This reminds me of a little story," but there was no stopping him now.

"Mr. Hunter," Lincoln said, "you ought to know a great deal better about this argument than I, for you have always lived under the slave system. I can only reply to your statement of the case that it reminds me of a man out of Illinois by the name of Case, who undertook a few years ago to raise a very large herd of hogs. It was a great trouble to feed them, and how to get around this was a puzzle to him. At length he hit on the plan of planting an immense field of potatoes, and when they were sufficiently grown, he turned the whole herd out into the field, and let them have full swing, thus saving not only the labor of feeding the hogs, but also that of digging the potatoes. Charmed with his sanguinity, he stood one day leaning on a fence, counting his hogs, when a neighbor came along.

" 'Well, well,' said he. 'Mr. Case, this is all very fine. Your hogs are doing very well just now, but you know out here in Illinois the frost comes early, and the ground freezes for a foot deep. Then what are you going to do?'

"This was a view of the matter which Mr. Case had not taken into account," Lincoln said, and butchering time for hogs was away off in December or January. He scratched his head and thought about it. " 'Well,' he eventually said, 'it may come pretty hard on their snouts,' but in the end it will be 'root hog, or die.' "

The fable fell flat. Stephens replied obsequiously—"That, Mr. President, must be the origin of the adage, 'Root pig, or perish' "—but the story came across as callous, toward the slaves and also, to Southern ears, toward the whites who would also suffer. Seward was visibly displeased. Stephens thought the parable out of place in Lincoln's repertoire, but he understood its point. The slaves and poor whites could take care of themselves when slavery was gone. Though nothing would be easy, they would survive and eventually flourish as self-made men and women, as Lincoln and Stephens had. Freedom and poverty were better than slavery and security.

But Hunter was deeply offended. For the planter elite, the "inferior race" depended on noblesse oblige. It made the system respectable to its guilt-ridden beneficiaries, the hallmark of "our Southern civilization." Lincoln's story mocked it, mocked Hunter as the senator was hearing it, for the second time that morning. His red-faced rage boiled over as he summed up the president's position.

"You offer nothing to the Confederate States and their people but unconditional submission." No treaty, no agreement, not even terms of surrender. Nothing but absolute, unconditional submission, with a "wish" of only one branch of government to avoid an unrestricted taking of *landed* property and no promises even as to that.

Seward's reply was quick. He tried to make it soothing. No words like *unconditional submission* had been used, he said, or anything implying degradation or humiliation to the Southern people. "This should be borne in mind."

Hunter demanded to know what else could be made of it. No treaty. No stipulations. No agreement with the Confederate states, or any of them—not even a promise of their safety or their status in the Union. "What is this but unconditional submission to the mercy of conquerors?"

"We are not conquerors," Seward said, "further than we require obedience to the laws." Force had only been used to preserve the federal authority to execute them. To yield to them, with Constitutional guarantees, was nothing like unconditional submission, and surely no conquest. If they chose to return to the Union, the Southern states and people would return to its Constitution, with all of their rights secured like the people of the other states.

Seward had gone further than Lincoln had, and Hunter called him on it. "But you make no agreement that these rights will be so held and secured!"

The president could not give orders to Congress or the courts, Lincoln said, but the power to enforce the penal laws was his. "Perfect reliance" could be placed on his leniency. Only Congress could restore property already seized, but the executive had the power to bar more seizures, and if peace were restored, persons subject to the law's pains and penalties might rely on a very liberal use of his power to remit them. There was no need to add that he was talking to three such persons. He told them he would use his public influence on the South's behalf as well as the power of his office. He was giving them more assurance, he said, than a victor had ever given rebels at the point of their destruction.

In what might have been a joke if a joking man had uttered it, Campbell replied that he had never thought his neck was in danger. Lincoln *was* a joking man, but his equanimity vanished. He would lose his temper only once today. Now was the time.

"There are a good many oak trees about the place where *I* live," he said, "the limbs of which afforded many convenient points from which *I* might have dangled in the course of this war." In 1860, his own party's leaders had wanted someone else there. (Seward recalled it well.) Now some very hard men in its leadership were pressing him for retribution. Indeed, the conduct of certain Rebel leaders had exposed them to "the punishment prescribed for the highest crime known to the law."

An awkward pause ensued. The Southerners may have felt their collars tighten. Then Hunter summoned the nerve to look Lincoln in the eye. "What you are saying, Mr. President, is that we of the South have committed treason, that we have forfeited our rights, and that we are proper subjects for the hangman. Is that what your words imply?"

If the gentleman from Virginia was expecting reassurance, he was disappointed. "Yes," Lincoln said. "You have stated the proposition better than I did. That is about the size of it."

There was, to say the least, another uncomfortable pause. Then Hunter broke the tension. In an odd sort of way, Lincoln's anger had cooled his own. "Well, Mr. President," he said, "we suppose that would necessarily be your view of our case, but we have about concluded that we will not be hanged as long as you are President—so long as we behave ourselves." Lincoln took it as the compliment Hunter intended. His face surely gave him away. A few days later, a friend saw it clearly when he repeated what the Virginian had said. Stephens took the chance to soften him further when someone mentioned an Illinois congressman who had gone to the Mexican War. Little Alec recalled two congressmen from that state who had differed on how to pronounce it. One said "Illi-noy," the other, "Illi-noise," and John Quincy Adams had been asked to adjudicate.

Considering the state's politicians, the crusty former president said, it ought to be called "All Noise." Lincoln enjoyed the story, as Stephens knew he would.

Now Lincoln turned to a more agreeable topic than oak trees and necks: compensation for the slaves in return for their freedom, a salve for Southern pride, an analgesic for surrender. With the war caused by slavery still raging, almost within earshot, the president told his enemies that the people of the North were as responsible for slavery as the people of the South. The North had "abetted it," he said, "traded in it, and defended it, until slavery became a vast, public question and invited war." Northern shippers brought the slaves from Africa and sold them to Southern planters. He did not add, though he knew it to be so, that Northern investors, manufacturers, and merchants had profited from slave-picked cotton and tobacco ever since, and the people of the North consumed them. He would take back nothing he had done to advance abolition as far as it had gone, but if the war ended now, with a *voluntary* emancipation, he for one "would rejoice to be taxed on my own little property" to help slave owners bear the cost, and he believed that feeling was widely shared in the North. More than merely saying that the victors should pay the vanquished to abandon the sin of slavery, the commander in chief of the triumphant Union armies was sharing the weight of the sin. Future presidents would help the people of defeated nations whose evildoing had led to war. None would share blame for the evil.

The Southerners may have been glad to hear Lincoln's confession, but they gave him no absolution. They seem to have sat in silence. Of course, Lincoln said, only Congress makes laws and appropriations. He could provide no assurances, no stipulations; he could only express his views and his understanding of those of others. But he believed that a fair compensation of $400 million could be had. He was willing to recommend it to Congress. "You would be astonished were I to give you the names of Senators and Representatives who have told me this could be done" if the war ended now, with no more expense, with a voluntary abolition of slavery. Horace Greeley supported it too.

"These observations were incidentally made," Campbell would later say, "and did not seem to have any reference to the general subject. They were not intended apparently as the ground of any proposition."

Seward took them seriously enough. What happened next was a display in the presence of the Davis administration of a fundamental rift in Lincoln's. What the president had told these Rebels was so startling that his Secretary of State bolted from his chair and paced the colorful carpet as he disavowed it, a habit in moments of intensity. "The United States has already paid on that account," he said, having spent so much on the war and suffered such losses.

Lincoln stayed calmly seated. "Ah, Mr. Seward," he said. "You may talk so about slavery if you will, but if it was wrong in the South to hold slaves, it was wrong in the North to carry on the slave trade, and it would be wrong to hold onto the money that the North procured by selling slaves to the South, without compensation, if the North took the slaves back again."

The governor threw up his hands, figuratively if not literally. The Northern people were weary, he said (another frank confession). They wanted peace and harmony. He believed they *would* pay a price for the slaves "equal to the cost of continuing the war." He was not so indelicate as to speak of the cost of winning it.*

As Stephens would later recall, rather than generating more discussion, the compensation overture produced a silent pause, "as if all felt that the interview should close." In the end, as Judah Benjamin had foretold, it had all broken down over Lincoln's demand for reunion and Davis's refusal to consider it.

Judge Campbell picked up an impression that Lincoln and Seward had sincerely hoped an agreement could be made, and were disappointed that the commissioners offered none—no terms of their own, or even a pledge to return with any. The Mexican fantasy aside, they brought nothing to the table but a vague idea that a truce and renewal of trade would shoot tendrils across the border and eventually draw the "two countries" into some sort of voluntary reorganization. It was far from good enough.

---

* Even before the war, Seward had favored federal compensation to slaveholders as an inducement for the states to legislate abolition. Lincoln had supported the idea for years.

The meeting had lasted about four hours when Stephens brought it to a close. It seemed that their mission would be entirely fruitless, he said, unless something could be done by way of a prisoner exchange. Lincoln said he favored one, and invited the Southerners to raise it with Grant when they passed through City Point on their way back to Richmond.

"Well, Stephens," Lincoln said, "there has been nothing we could do for our country. Is there anything I can do for you personally?"

"Nothing," Stephens said. And then he thought of something. "Unless you can send me my nephew, who has been twenty months a prisoner on Johnson's Island," a famously uncongenial prison camp for Southern officers on Lake Erie.

"I shall be glad to do it," Lincoln said, "if you will send back one of our young lieutenants. Let me have his name." When Stephens happily obliged, the president wrote it down and asked considerate questions about Lieutenant John A. Stephens and his family.

Little Alec was reluctant to leave without a final effort to salvage something of broader consequence than his nephew's liberation. Perhaps, he thought, Lincoln had felt constrained by the publicity the conference had generated, and might revisit the Mexican idea after things had settled down. "I wish, Mr. President, that you would reconsider the subject of an armistice on the basis which has been suggested. Great questions, as well as vast interests, are involved in it. If, upon doing so, you shall change your mind, you can make it known through the military."

As Stephens heard him, Lincoln answered "with a peculiar manner very characteristic of him" before they wished each other farewell. "Well, Stephens, I have thought it through maturely. I will reconsider it, but I do not think my mind will change, but I will reconsider." Lincoln's sympathy for the suffering Southern people had been plain to Judge Campbell, who was moved and encouraged by it. He would take it back to Richmond and build on it.

In their own brotherly parting, Hunter put a wistful question to Seward. The Capitol's magnificent dome had been under construction when he had left it four years ago. "Governor," he asked, "how is the Capitol? Is it finished?" Seward said it was, and described its grandeur with feeling.

And now the reluctant enemies "took their formal and friendly leave of each other," as Alec Stephens called it. Lincoln and Seward withdrew together first, but not before Seward took his old friend by the hand. "God bless you, Hunter," he said.

—◦—

Major Eckert wired Stanton at three o'clock. The conference was over. The presidential party was preparing to return. "We shall leave here on steamer *River Queen* at 4:30 p.m." Eckert wired Grant at the same time: "The President directs me to say that Mr. Stephens had some conversation with him on the subject of prisoners, and that he referred the matter to you, and desires that you confer with Mr. Stephens on the subject. The interview has concluded and both parties preparing to return." The major did not enlighten the general on the results.

At about dusk, the *River Queen* parted gently from the *Mary Martin* and turned toward Chesapeake Bay for the run back to Annapolis. The faster *Thomas Collyer* followed and soon overtook the *River Queen*, bearing two of Grant's generals.

Judge Campbell would soon report, as a thing to be commended, that the conference had been conducted "with gravity and without levity," but Seward could not resist a touch of levity in the end. As the *River Queen* pulled away, a black man in a rowboat approached the *Mary Martin* with a basket of champagne and a note with the governor's compliments. The Southerners waved their handkerchiefs at Seward, who stood on the deck of the *River Queen* waving back, shouting at them through a boatswain's trumpet.

"Keep the champagne! Return the Negro!"

An interior view of Fort Hell LIBRARY OF CONGRESS

Union pickets facing Fort Damnation LIBRARY OF CONGRESS

Horace Greeley NATIONAL ARCHIVES

Secretary of State William H. Seward ABRAHAM LINCOLN PRESIDENTIAL LIBRARY AND
MUSEUM (ALPLM)

Francis Preston Blair LIBRARY OF CONGRESS

Secretary of War Edwin M. Stanton LIBRARY OF CONGRESS

Congressman Thaddeus Stevens LIBRARY OF CONGRESS

Congressman Samuel S. ("Sunset") Cox LIBRARY OF CONGRESS

Justice John A. Campbell in about 1855 LIBRARY OF CONGRESS
(RESTORATION BY CHELSEA MILLER)

Senator Robert M. T. Hunter before the war LIBRARY OF CONGRESS

Confederate Vice President Alexander H. Stephens LIBRARY OF CONGRESS

The Confederate
Executive Mansion
LIBRARY OF CONGRESS

The depot at City
Point NATIONAL
ARCHIVES

Grant's City Point office
and residence were in the
large cabin on the left.
The house he assigned
to his quartermaster is
in the near background
on the right. LIBRARY OF
CONGRESS

Lieutenant General Ulysses S. Grant NATIONAL ARCHIVES

The City Point waterfront NATIONAL ARCHIVES

Major Thomas Eckert LIBRARY OF CONGRESS

Fort Monroe and the adjoining anchorage at Hampton Roads (a contemporary postcard)

The *River Queen* THE STEAMSHIP HISTORICAL SOCIETY ARCHIVES, WWW.SSHA.ORG

The ruins of Columbia, South Carolina, after Sherman captured the city NATIONAL ARCHIVES

A view from the James River of the burned-out district of Richmond, with the pillared Confederate capitol building above it NATIONAL ARCHIVES

Part III

A Suffering and Distracted Country

Photograph of Abraham Lincoln taken on Sunday, February 5, 1865, two days after the Hampton Roads Peace Conference

CHAPTER NINETEEN

It Is More Dangerous to Make Peace
Than to Make War

The *River Queen* docked at the Naval Academy pier early on Saturday morning, awash in a sea of rumors. Lincoln and Seward rebuffed a crowd of newspapermen, leaving hope to feed on gossip. On the *River Queen* herself, the crew had spread the word that a thirty-day truce was in place. No one knew for sure. Everyone wished to know—some more than others.

The B&O Railroad supplied a private car to take the president and his party to Washington City. As Major Eckert later told it, an acquaintance approached him on the platform and handed him an envelope. If he shared what he knew, there was something for his trouble inside. He took it with a noncommittal word, asked his benefactor to wait, and joined Lincoln on the train. When the envelope was opened, the major and the president beheld a certified check for $100,000, made out to Thomas Eckert—fifty years' pay for a major. Who had done this? Lincoln asked. Eckert did not feel at liberty to say, but the president might watch and see for himself. When Eckert disembarked and returned the check, Lincoln recognized its donor, a well-known player from a western state. Lincoln took Eckert's advice and let it go. No good could come of exposing it.

When the presidential train chugged into Washington City, the Hampton Roads Peace Conference, as the press had begun to call it, was widely understood to have ended the war, until Seward summoned the Associated Press to his State Department office, adorned with books and engravings and not much else. The peace talks had failed, he said. All rumors to the contrary were false. The stock market rose in New York and Lincoln's stock rose in the capital. With conquest in their grasp, the Jacobins were relieved that the president had not made peace. Some Democrats thought better of him for trying.

As soon as he was free of Lincoln and Seward, Eckert reported to Stanton and threw his hands up high. "Mr. Secretary, you are heads and shoulders above them all!"

The war had resumed in Virginia, where the *Times* reported a twelve-mile race near Petersburg on that lovely, false spring day. A company of "colored cavalry" had chased a dozen guerrillas tricked out in captured blue. All but two escaped, but their leader was dropped from his horse with an ounce of lead in his stomach. A sergeant rode up to the writhing man, one Johnny Roach by name, who shot at him and missed. When a bullet in the leg failed to take the fight out of him, the sergeant clubbed him to death with his carbine, saving the authorities the trouble of hanging him.

On the siege line that day, a Georgian named William Sharp took a bullet in the knee and lost his leg to a saw. The officer leading his company, a lieutenant named Levy, was hit too. It took him a day to die.

On the floor of the US House, Thaddeus Stevens assured his fellow Jacobins that peace was not at hand. As Sunset Cox had promised, many Democrats threw in with Lincoln and victory, the Rebels having rejected peace and reunion. Thaddeus Stevens and Fernando Wood were in the same tent, and so was Horace Greeley, but an Illinois Republican wanted more. Lincoln and Seward had barely gotten back when Congressman Ebon C. Ingersoll declared that no enduring peace could be made "which shall ever recognize the traitorous leaders of this rebellion as citizens of the United States, entitled to equal rights, privileges, and immunities with the loyal people thereof under the Constitution of the United States."

Seward wrote home to his wife in Auburn. "I wish I were able to give you an account of our conference at Hampton Roads but it is mail day today and I can only write so much as shall show that I do not forget to write to you altogether." He did let her know that the state of the South was "pitiable, but it is not yet fully realized there."

The president summoned his Cabinet for a short noon briefing. He and Seward described their encounter with the Rebel leaders. It was more than merely civil, they said. Something might yet come of it. They had surely talked it through on the long trip home. Gideon Welles had a sense that it was likely to tend to peace, which Lincoln said he thought he could negotiate better than any agent. Lincoln and Seward said the commissioners had named no terms that could bring the South back, but had not ruled it out. They had made no demands for liberty or death, Jefferson Davis style. Peace had been left dangling on a tantalizing hook. Uncle Gideon could see that Lincoln and Seward hoped to find a way to grasp it. "I have not brought back peace in a lump," the president told James Singleton, "but I am glad I went down, and hope for good results."

Alec Stephens's hopes had been vindicated. Lincoln had not given up on peace. No halfway step would do, and surely no foreign invasion, but the very idea of negotiation—giving something to the South in *exchange* for reunion instead of simply demanding it, saving thousands of young lives, all of them American, promoting the national healing that was Lincoln's dearest wish—had already been put into play. In the meantime, the pressure would be kept up. At a quarter past noon, Stanton sent a wire to Grant: "The President desires me to repeat that nothing transpiring with the three gentlemen from Richmond is to cause any change, hindrance, or delay of your military plans or operations." Grant assured Stanton he had nothing to fear: "The appearance of Mr. Stephens and party within our lines has had no influence on military movements whatever."

Later that day, a dozen Southern officers were huddled by a stove with the wind whipping off Lake Erie when a soldier in blue appeared at the bunkhouse door and called out "John A. Stephens!" When a wary Georgian replied, he was told to report to the commanding officer. He would have been handsome had he not been undernourished. Captured in the fall of Port Hudson, Louisiana, in 1863, Stephens knew the ropes. Nothing good could come of this.

His anxiety turned to amazement when the commandant handed him a telegram addressed to the officer in command of the Johnson's

Island prison camp: "Washington, D.C., February 4, 1865. Parole Lieutenant John A. Stephens, prisoner of war, to report to me here in person, and send him to me. It is in pursuance of an arrangement I made yesterday with his uncle, Hon. A. H. Stephens. Acknowledge receipt. A. Lincoln."

Alec Stephens had been a second father to John, whose natural father had a wife and six children, a failed law practice, and a weakness for whiskey. His older half brother Alec gave him lectures and loans. Neither did long-term good. In 1854, John came to live with his Uncle Alec, who enrolled him in the local academy and paid for it. When the boy's father died, Alec moved his widow and her other five children across the state, bought them a house near his, and cared for them as his own. Now he had smiled on John again. In a state of disbelief, the lieutenant gathered his meager possessions and said his ambivalent good-byes. He was led to a sleigh, wrapped in a buffalo robe, and pulled across Lake Erie by a pair of army mules to a train bound for Washington City. A celebratory jingle of bells dispelled the numbing cold.

The Reverend Henry Ward Beecher wrote to Lincoln that night from his parsonage in Brooklyn. He had read the late editions, and their meeting at the White House had eased his reverend mind. "Even your unexpected visit to Fort Monroe did not stagger me. It has been much criticized. The pride of the nation is liable to be hurt. Anything that looks like the humiliation of our Government would be bitterly felt," though "going to the rebels is an act of condescension which will stop the mouths of Northern enemies." The country's leading Christian signed off with a warning that "it is more dangerous to make peace than to make war. An address to the army, or to the nation, declaring that peace can come only by arms, if in your judgment the fact is so, would end these feverish uncertainties & give the spring campaign renewed vigor."

The commissioners had reached City Point on Friday night, several hours after the peace conference, and spent their last evening on the *Mary*

Martin commiserating with Grant. When they told him that Lincoln had encouraged a prisoner exchange, the general repeated what he had told their aide Colonel Hatch. He would approve a universal exchange immediately, with a few individual exceptions, of which General Roger A. Pryor was one. Hunter would later tell Sarah Pryor that the commissioners had remembered her husband but could not secure his freedom. He was too big a fish to catch and release.

The commissioners left City Point on a Saturday-morning train. Heading up their honor guard, Grant's staff officer Horace Porter chatted with Stephens on the jolting ride back to the front. The little Georgian "was greatly disappointed at the failure of the conference," Porter thought, but "prudent enough not to talk much about it." The artillery duel that had started on Tuesday as the commissioners crossed the lines had gone on killing sporadically as they reminisced with Lincoln and Seward on the *River Queen*. It was still in progress now, greeting them on their return as it had on their arrival, mocking them with death.

A lieutenant from Alabama returned to the trenches that day after an absence of some duration, disturbed to find "an intense feeling of insubordination among our men . . . this feeling I fear pervades the whole army. . . . The men speak openly of the 'muskets having the power' and of their determination not to submit to military authority much longer." Later that week, more than two hundred men would desert one brigade in a single night.

Arriving in Richmond on Saturday evening, the commissioners went directly to the Executive Mansion to brief Jefferson Davis and Judah Benjamin in detail. Stephens thought "everybody was very much disappointed, and no one seemed to be more so than Mr. Davis." Careful with words, Stephens is unlikely to have chosen *seemed* haphazardly. Benjamin scoffed at Lincoln's terms, dismissing out of hand "the weakness," "the folly, the suicidal folly" of any thought of accepting them. Davis concurred, and accused Mr. Lincoln of disowning the Mexican plan in bad faith. Mr. Blair had assured him it would have Mr. Lincoln's support. Davis attributed the betrayal to the fall of Fort Fisher and the closing of the last Confederate seaport after Mr. Blair's first visit to Richmond.*

Stephens disagreed. If Davis was right, and the Mexican idea was Mr. Lincoln's, there was still hope. The conference's public disclosure was enough to explain its failure without assigning bad faith to Mr. Lincoln or Mr. Blair. Nothing had been accomplished, but nothing had been foreclosed. The conference had confirmed that the United States desired peace, and the way was open for a settlement. He had asked Mr. Lincoln to reconsider. Mr. Lincoln had said he would, though he was unlikely to change his mind. He might be heard from again, quietly, through the military, after the "hubbub" subsided.

Judge Campbell told Davis that reunion and abolition were inevitable. He should send the commissioners back, or send new ones, to propose specific terms and take the best the South could get, including emancipation "upon suitable arrangements." In this he agreed with Stephens, surely thinking of Lincoln's remarks about compensation for the slaves and shared responsibility. As Campbell describes how Davis replied, one can almost see him swelling. "Mr. Davis, with the air of a sage, declared that the Constitution did not allow him to treat for his own suicide. All that he could do would be to receive resolutions and submit them to the sovereign States." His personal honor did not permit such a settlement, he said. Campbell replied that he had raised with Mr. Lincoln the idea of treating with the states, and Mr. Lincoln had rejected it.

Campbell would later say that Davis "had no capacity to control himself to do an irksome, exacting, humiliating, and in his judgment dishonoring act, however called for by the necessities of the situation. He preferred to let the edifice fall into ruins, expecting to move off with majesty before the event occurred." Now he informed his emissaries that they had "probably fallen into a trap" by accepting Seward's rule that the conference would be confidential and undocumented, leaving Seward free to lie. He would probably have his minister in Paris use the Mexican scheme

---

* When Davis and Benjamin repeated themselves to Secretary of the Navy Mallory, he deplored their rejection of a chance to make peace, knowing "we could hold out no longer than Grant chose to permit us."

"to interfere with whatever good feeling the Emperor of the French had for us."*

Davis asked the commissioners to submit a written report to Congress and the people. Stephens protested. A disclosure of the conference's *"real objects* [the Mexican scheme] could not, with propriety, then be made," and to leave them out would be misleading. Davis insisted, and the others concurred. Stephens agreed reluctantly to put his name on the report, thinking its omission would be misconstrued and do more harm than good.

Davis told his envoys that Mr. Lincoln's declarations made it plain that there could be no peace short of unconditional submission by the Southern people, with "an entire change of their social fabric." The only remaining hope of escaping calamity was to rouse them to desperate efforts to resist their degradation and save themselves and their institutions. As Stephens saw and heard it, he "seemed more determined than ever to fight it out on this line," to put everything at risk on turning Grant back from Richmond. Stephens could hardly absorb what Davis yet believed—that Grant and Sherman could be defeated in open battle, that Richmond could be defended, that the cause could be won without a change in policy.

Campbell was past believing that policy mattered. In his heart, so was Hunter, but the anger and humiliation he had borne on the *River Queen* still burned.

When Davis sent his commissioners to Lincoln, he had empowered them to agree to any "treaty" that did not include reunion. Now he told a friend that their mission had "no diplomatic character." They had merely gone informally to see "whether negotiations were possible." He told his Secretary of the Navy he was "bitterly hostile" to the terms laid down at Hampton Roads, and the Senate was strongly opposed. He would not let them say he surrendered while he had the means to resist.

After the war, Davis would tell Varina that his lack of authority to dissolve the Confederacy absolved him from any blame for rejecting

---

* It may not have occurred to Davis that he had given the emperor cause to adjust his feelings. Seward, moreover, had said that the conference would be informal and unrecorded, not confidential, and the participants on both sides promptly issued public reports.

Lincoln's terms, while "any dolt whose blunders necessitated frequent conviction, and whose vanity sought for someone on whom to lay the responsibility for his failures, could readily, and if mean enough, would now ascribe them to me." No specific dolts were named, but Little Alec matched the description. It had gotten back to Davis that Stephens had told some friends that Lincoln offered terms "not humiliating to the South." No such terms were reported to *him*, Davis said. The commissioners would have had to "conceal" them from him. Humiliation was in the eye of the beholder. As Davis beheld it, what Stephens called the "good terms of reconstruction" that Lincoln had put on the table, including a payment for the slaves, were a Yankee plan to "encourage treason" and incite the Southern people to ignore their elected leader.

Late into the night on the day the commissioners returned, Judge Campbell unburdened himself to James Seddon, his newly resigned superior as Secretary of War. In 1863, the War Department clerk John Jones had called Seddon a "dead man galvanized into muscular animation." Twenty months of suffering had passed since then. Now Campbell briefed Seddon on the peace conference. The judge thought a reasonable arrangement to free the slaves could be had—that Davis should stop the war now and lead the South back to the Union on the best terms he could get. Both men knew that there was no sensible alternative. Both men knew that Davis would not agree.

—◦—

Outside Washington City, where the 1st Wisconsin Heavy Artillery was encamped, Corporal Richtmyer Hubbell and his friends awaited the newspaper eagerly until it reported that the conference had failed. Having read that the Rebels had demanded independence, Hubbell was glad that the president had rejected it, and glad that peace talks had been tried. Their failure would persuade the people to support a more vigorous war.

A young Rebel named David Johnston had the same idea. The conference disappointed the 7th Virginia Infantry, but David and his friends had no quit in them. "There is nothing left us but to fight it out. The cry is for war, war to the knife." Brave words from a teenage boy, but some of his elders had had enough. Davis received a letter that day from "many soldiers" with the remnants of Jubal Early's beaten army in the Shenandoah Valley. They had heard about the peace talks and implored their president "to strive every way in your power to settle our troubles by arbitration. Most of us have fought our last battle. Our property has all been lost to us, our wives and children are bound to suffer, if not starve, in the next six or eight months, and we beg you to enable us to quit this war with honor." Davis inscribed their letter and sent it to Early: "It is to be hoped that this is not a fair sample of the feeling of the 'Army of the Valley.'" General George Armstrong Custer's men would find it in a wagon when they captured Early's headquarters in March.

Richmond's Sunday morning was clear and cold as Judge Campbell composed the commissioners' report. Hunter and Stephens endorsed it, and a messenger brought it to Davis. There was no invective in it, just a stark recitation of Lincoln's formal terms. No treaty could be made with the Confederate states, collectively or separately. Their sovereignty would be recognized "under no circumstances." Individuals "might rely upon a very liberal use" of the president's clemency, but the authority of the United States must be restored with "whatever consequences may follow." It was "brought to our notice" that the Congress of the United States had adopted a Constitutional amendment banning slavery.

Nothing was said of Lincoln's confession about a shared responsibility for slavery, his support for an immediate restoration of the Southern states' rights, his tolerance for a gradual emancipation, or a $400 million payment for the slaves. No mention was made of Grant's commitment to a general prisoner exchange, or Seward's observation that the South could block the Thirteenth Amendment by returning to the Union. None of the friendship, courtesy, and respect that the commissioners had been shown from the moment they crossed the siege line made it into their report—no reference to the Northern soldiers' cheers; Grant's welcoming dinner on the *Mary Martin;* Seward's gifts at Hampton Roads; Lincoln's liberation of Stephens's nephew; his promise to reconsider his position; or the many Northern leaders, military and civilian, who remembered Southern friends.

Davis was not satisfied. He sent for Judge Campbell and demanded more, to "influence the people." The report should declare that Lincoln and Seward demanded the South's immediate acceptance of abolition and insulted Southern honor. Campbell would say no such thing. So long as he remained a reluctant member of the Davis administration, he thought himself bound to follow its policies and not "encourage treason," as Davis called it, by giving any hint that reunion might be palatable or Yankees fully human, but he would not arm his president with a garment-rending screed. The report "stated the exact result of the conference," Campbell said. It described Lincoln's terms accurately, as opposed to his hopes and dreams. Stephens told some friends that Lincoln's musings about paying for the slaves were omitted so as not to damage him politically.

That evening, Stephens, Campbell, and Hunter called on Davis together. He pressed them again to embellish their report, which they refused to do. Years after the war, he would say it was too meager to explain what he called "their failure and the reasons for it."

Senator William Graham of North Carolina was a widely respected friend and ally of Campbell and of Hunter. "The situation is critical," Graham told a friend that day, "and requires a guidance beyond human ken." He would find no such guidance from the lips of Jefferson Davis. "I have a very strong conviction," the senator would soon say, "that there has been very great duplicity towards a large portion of the Southern people displayed in this little drama. It is most offensive to me."

CHAPTER TWENTY

You Are All Against Me

Lincoln held on like a drowning man to a last thin hope for peace. He had listened on the *River Queen* as the Southerners asked to be treated with rather than conquered. He had heard Hunter say that he offered them nothing but humiliation, nothing that could help them stop the killing. He had taken it in. He had talked it out with Seward. Now he spent the Sabbath at work on something he could give.

Sometime that day, he brought his son Tad to Alexander Gardner's photographic studio at Seventh and Pennsylvania with its sign hawking VIEWS OF THE WAR. Almost all of his photographs were somber. He smiled for one faintly that day, as White House messengers fanned out over Washington City with invitations to his Cabinet to assemble at seven o'clock. For reasons now unclear, Seward did not attend.

When the rest of the Cabinet had been seated around the table, Lincoln read aloud by the gaslight chandelier the product of his work, a message to his "Fellow Citizens of the Senate and House of Representatives" that sought their authorization to tender to the slave states, whether loyal or in rebellion, $400 million in government bonds, half to be paid if all resistance to the National Authority were abandoned before April 1, the other half if the Thirteenth Amendment were ratified by July 1. All political offenses would be pardoned, all forfeited property except slaves released, except where third parties had acquired it. Liberality would be recommended on all points beyond presidential control.

As Lincoln read his draft, his genial Secretary of the Interior John Usher was thinking of Robert Schenck, a radical Ohio congressman with a right arm crippled at Second Bull Run. After the word was out that

Lincoln and Seward were talking peace in Virginia, Usher's Assistant Secretary William Otto had run into Schenck, who said nothing of Lincoln but abused Seward violently. He hoped the Rebels would catch him and put him in Libby Prison. Otto had seen Schenck again this very day. "I suppose now, General, you have changed your mind." But Schenck had only repeated himself. Seward was a damned devil who ought to be put in Libby. Of Lincoln he again said nothing.

Now Usher listened hard as the president read his draft, pardoning all these traitors, giving them back their lands, paying for their human property, proposing liberality in what he did not control, promising it in what he did. If he sent that message to Congress, Usher thought, men like Schenck would turn on him. It might even weaken his ability to get men and money for the war. Usher had been his friend for twenty years. Now he sensed that Lincoln would take his plan to Congress, explosive though he knew it would be, if his own inner circle gave him any encouragement at all. "I think his heart was so fully enlisted in behalf of such a plan that he would have followed it if only a single member of his Cabinet had supported him in the project."

Not a single member did.

The president defended his proposal as a matter of fiscal policy. Apart from "all the blood which will be shed" if the killing went on, he said, "How long has this war lasted, and how long do you suppose it will still last?"

No one answered.

"We cannot hope that it will end in less than a hundred days. We are now spending three million a day, and that will equal the full amount I propose to pay, to say nothing of the lives lost and property destroyed. I look upon it as a measure of strict and simple economy."

No one agreed. According to Usher, the discussion didn't last ten minutes. With a sadness familiar to his friend, Lincoln "simply brought a long sigh" and folded up his Proclamation. "You are all against me."

Lincoln's secretaries Nicolay and Hay thought the peace offer had been "nearest his heart." After the meeting adjourned, he wrote a note to posterity on his folded draft: "February 5, 1865. To-day these papers, which explain themselves, were drawn up and submitted to the Cabinet and unanimously disapproved by them."

Gideon Welles told his diary that Lincoln's desire to conciliate was plain, "but there may be such a thing as so overdoing. . . . In the present temper of Congress the proposed measure, if a wise one, could not be carried successfully," and Welles saw no wisdom in it. "The Rebels would misconstrue it if the offer was made. If attempted and defeated it would do harm."

It had taken Stanton by surprise. Unpleasantly so. With victory in sight and the Thirteenth Amendment on its way to ratification, there was no need to bargain for peace. According to the Jacobin Charles Sumner, the only man Lincoln disliked, Stanton said "peace can be had only when Lee's army is beaten, captured, or dispersed, and there I agree with him."

Secretary of the Treasury William Pitt Fessenden, a flinty former senator from Maine, was a critic of men and ideas. "Querulous and angular," Uncle Gideon called him. Before the war, when Davis had said on the Senate floor that the South would secede if need be, Fessenden had accused him of intimidation. The stenographer recorded what followed:

> *Mr. Davis: I try to intimidate nobody; I threaten nobody; and I do not believe, let me say it once for all, that anybody is afraid of me, and I do not want anybody to be afraid of me.*
> *Mr. Fessenden: I am. [Laughter].*
> *Mr. Davis: I am sorry to hear it, and if the Senator is really so, I shall never speak to him in decided terms again.*

Jefferson Davis had spoken decidedly too often for Fessenden, who inscribed a note on his invitation to the Cabinet meeting. "It was evident by the unanimous opinion of the Cabinet that the only way to effectually end the war was by force of arms, and that until the war was thus ended no proposition to pay money would come from us." Few of the Cabinet's secrets were better kept, say Nicolay and Hay. Congress never heard that the subject had been raised.

~~~~~~

Earlier that day, Union forces crossed a stream called Hatcher's Run and attacked a Rebel wagon train near Petersburg. As Confederate troops drove them back, the handsome young general John Pegram, newly married to the stunning Hetty Cary, took a bullet in the chest. He died in the arms of a youthful wedding guest, Colonel Henry Kyd Douglas. An hour later, with Pegram laid out dead on Douglas's bed in Petersburg, Douglas glanced out his window to the sound of passing wheels. Hetty was being driven to their honeymoon cottage. No one had broken the news to her.

John Pegram had been a patron of Sarah Pryor's library and a favorite of her boys. In 1905, his death was an unhealed wound. Sarah counted him in her memoirs "among the first of those martyrs whose lives were sacrificed after the leaders *knew* there was no more life in the cause for which they died." She had never forgiven them for it.

On Monday, February 6, a young Rebel officer went straight from the Washington depot to 1600 Pennsylvania Avenue and walked unimpeded to an anteroom upstairs. An attendant asked for his card. Having none, he identified himself in ink on a slip of paper. Lieutenant John A. Stephens. His name was taken next door, and then he was shown in.

The President of the United States was draped across the Cabinet table with his elbow on its surface and his chin in his palm, conversing with his secretary of state. He pulled himself to his feet and put out his hand, the tallest man John Stephens had ever seen. Lincoln told Seward who their visitor was and offered him a chair. Then he told the young man he had recently seen his uncle and had promised to send him his nephew. His uncle was well and so were his mother and sister. "You have the freedom of the city as long as you please. When you want to go home, come back and let me know, and I will pass you through the lines."

Nearly speechless with gratitude, the lieutenant would stay in the capital another five days, gaining strength and putting on weight through the hospitality of friends.

If Lincoln's trip south had accomplished little else, it had satisfied many War Democrats. According to Sunset Cox, some Copperheads debunked it as a military intelligence operation in which Blair had been a scout.

Cox thought otherwise. He offered a resolution that day that bestowed on the president "the gratitude of a suffering and distracted country" for pursuing peace and reunion, urged him to keep it up, and asked him to enlighten the House with a report on the conference at Hampton Roads. The resolution passed easily, but thirty-one Republicans voted no. In private, Cox heard from many others who felt constrained to support it but were "furious in their opposition to any effort toward peace except through war."

Before he set sail for his banishment to England, Henry Foote, the frustrated fugitive from the Rebel Congress, wrote again to his old friend Seward. He had read about Hampton Roads. Stephens and Campbell, if not Hunter, were ready for peace on "almost any honorable terms," he said, though Davis had no doubt tied their hands. Secession had become odious to the people of the South. Davis would never give in, but the people were prepared for a "counterrevolution" and would surely respond to an appeal from President Lincoln to return to the Union with amnesty and their old political rights. Seward showed the letter to Lincoln.

The midwinter thaw on the siege line was over. There was snow and sleet and freezing rain, and a Georgian froze to death. "He was on picket duty," a brother in arms would say, "and had to keep still to keep the Yanks from seeing him."

General Meade wrote home to his wife again. General Warren had attacked the Rebels, and after much success was "compelled to retrace his steps in great disorder." It was day number two of three days of mayhem at Hatcher's Run.

As lives and limbs were being lost at Hatcher's Run, Davis sent his Congress the peace commissioners' report. An accompanying message of his own supplied the missing vitriol. For a bit of extra flavor, he stirred in flat untruths. The Yankees had insisted that the South must accept their Constitutional amendment banning slavery and the right of the federal Congress to legislate Southern race relations. It was moved in the Senate that a thousand copies be made. The number was increased to five thousand. The *Richmond Enquirer* observed that Mr. Lincoln's solicitation of negotiations followed by insults was "quite within the decency of the Yankee" and had opened everyone's eyes. Also on that day, Davis wrote to Stephens's nemesis Benjamin Hill and reported the US Congress's enactment of the Thirteenth Amendment, "which disposed of" any question of peace and made a mockery of the ill-fated conference.

Alec Stephens would soon tell Seward that "no one could have been more chagrined and mortified than I was" by the show Davis made of its failure. The day was set aside for war rallies in Richmond. As the *Examiner's* Edward Pollard said, the papers called them "a triumph, a resurrection, a regeneration of the war no longer to be doubted." Shops were closed. Business was suspended. Three speakers' stands were built in different parts of the city and a procession of distinguished orators, led by a marching band, passed through the streets to fill them. The cheering went on until dusk and started up again after supper.

The papers were saying Alec Stephens was going home to incite his fellow Georgians to continue the war. Grant sent the news to Stanton with a hint of betrayal. The papers had it wrong. Alec Stephens was going home, but not to beat the war drum. Alec Stephens was done. Bloody speeches would be made in Richmond that night, and Davis had asked him to participate, but Stephens could not urge his people to do "what I believed to be impossible, or to inspire in them hopes which I did not believe could ever be realized."

The keynote speeches were set to begin at seven-thirty at the First African Baptist Church, an old wooden building on College Street, but a multitude had gathered by noon. According to Edward Pollard, the African Church's size endeared it to politicians who had long been in the habit of appropriating it for mass meetings, "as if there was no invasion of sanctity of so lowly a house of God as that where Negroes worshiped." By five o'clock, two and a half hours early, the white folk of Richmond had taken every foot of its standing room. The balconies were so packed that fears were expressed about their collapse. After the church was filled, a crowd began to grow outside, causing many to regret that the cold and the snow had persuaded the rally's organizers not to stage it in Capital Square.

When a lane had been cleared for the speakers, they were led by Jefferson Davis, sick and gaunt in an old gray suit. His appearance was unannounced, and he found himself buoyed by cheers. With him came Virginia's eccentric governor, William "Extra Billy" Smith, an old Jacksonian postmaster who had earned extra pay expanding the rural mail service. Extra Billy spoke first, interrupted by thunderous support when he told his aroused constituents that Virginia "would sacrifice everything that remained to her, sooner than surrender."

Then Davis took the podium, proud and erect as ever. People whose spirits had been dead just days before, who had roundly despised their leader, were stomping their booted feet, shouting and clapping wildly, roiling the African Church. To his own surprise, Edward Pollard was moved by "a smile of strange sweetness" that came to his president's lips, "so feeble, he should have stayed away." Nearly disabled by the pain in his right arm, by Sherman's devastation of Georgia and South Carolina, by Lee's impending defeat, by the Confederacy's empty coffers, by the catastrophic loss of its outlet to the sea, by every other sign that the Davis administration would be its last, he held the cheering crowd "with his glittering eye," his "stricken face" tensing as he gathered himself against the pain. Even Pollard admired his courage. When the roar subsided at last, Davis began to speak with a "tuneful flow of words" and delivered the speech of his life. Alec Stephens was there, silent in the crowd. He knew Davis's gifts and had never seen him so "majestic."

Davis told his people he would be less than a man if he did not yearn to end their suffering. He had chosen his peace commission from "among our best men," to "heal the breach which severed us," to secure the independence "which no other power on the face of the earth but the Yankees would think of denying us." And now Mr. Lincoln had declared his terms. An "extravagance of insolence." Unconditional surrender. A new Constitution forcing abolition down their throats, breaking their society to fit the Yankee mold. "We are not even allowed to go back to them as we came out, but are required to take just what a conqueror may choose to give the conquered." To be sure, Davis said, Mr. Lincoln had pledged to be "liberal" in "the confiscation of our property and the hanging of our officers." The Yankee preacher Henry Ward Beecher had lately declaimed a sermon with "a long line of rebels on their way to the gallows." The length of the procession may have softened Mr. Lincoln's heart.

Stephens could not believe what he was hearing. "Brilliant though it was, I looked upon it as not much short of dementation." The person did not know him, Davis said, who thought he would consent to reunion on *any* terms. He would sooner yield all he had, yield his life a thousand times. In his correspondence with Mr. Lincoln, "that functionary" had spoken of the North and South as one country, but Davis had insisted on two, for "I can have no common country with the Yankee." The army would stand and fight. Richmond would be defended to the last man and boy. No one who had seen them could think that they would fail, but if the enemy's power "were ten times greater, and ours ten times less than it is, there are still some rights of which they could not dispossess us—the right to maintain our personal honor and the right to fill an honorable grave." If the South were overcome, happy would be "those who had fallen in the fight. The miserable would be the survivors."

Listening to his president, the wild response he drew, and his public repudiation of a limited war of maneuver and a negotiated peace, Stephens recalled the Charge of the Light Brigade, British cavalry attacking Russian cannon. Someone had said "it is brilliant; it is grand; but it is not war." Little Alec was thinking that Davis well knew that the South had nothing left "but the fragments of shattered armies."

The crowd was hearing otherwise. According to the editorialist Edward Pollard, when their leader scorned the edicts of "his Majesty, Abraham the First," the African Church's "foul air" was "rent with shouts and huzzahs, and its crazed floor shaken under applause." If their spirit only spread, Davis said, and he had no doubt that it would, "then indeed would I feel that we are on the very verge of success." By the summer solstice, the North would sue for peace, and its leaders would know that when they spoke at Hampton Roads "they were speaking with their masters."

It was then that Stephens knew that the war was truly lost. "Repeated calls were made for the Vice President," said the *Richmond Dispatch*, "but it was announced that he was not well enough to respond."

Davis told his people that the South would never surrender with an army as grand as Napoleon's, defending its own homes, every man in its ranks reared with "the habits of command," the superior of any Yankee.

Some twenty-five miles away on the siege line, a Yankee general made an entry in his journal: "One deserter, 26th Va., a squalid, half-famished wretch."

~

At midnight, Grant wired Washington that the Rebels had launched a failed attack, "leaving a part of their dead for us to bury." General Mott "buries thirty-one of the enemy, and counted twenty-two graves besides, some of which were large enough for five or six bodies each. General Smyth estimates the loss of the enemy in his front at 200."

The Northerners buried twenty-one of their own.

CHAPTER TWENTY-ONE

Thank God We Know It Now

Lincoln's Cabinet reconvened the next day. He seemed to have recovered from their rejection of his peace proposal. When Gideon Welles arrived, the commander in chief was reading aloud from the reflections of Petroleum V. Nasby, a fictional, work-averse Copperhead whose letters to the editor never failed to entertain him. Uncle Gideon observed that the stiff-chinned William Pitt Fessenden, "who came in just after me, evidently thought it hardly a proper subject for the occasion, and the President hastily dropped it."

On the floor of the House that day, a Democrat proposed that with the Confederacy melting down, half a million dollars could be trimmed from the cost of Washington City's defenses. Thaddeus Stevens disagreed. "I did expect, to be sure—I did hope that the late proceedings would have produced peace. It was very promising for a while—promised on that side of the House, promised elsewhere—but those promises have not been fulfilled, and I understand the war is to be resumed with renewed vigor."

Even as the congressman spoke, the generals were proving him right.

In South Carolina, a retreating Rebel commander sent a message to Sherman. He would stop burning cotton in the general's path if Sherman would stop burning houses. Sherman replied promptly. "I hope you will burn all cotton and save us trouble. We don't want it, and it has proven a curse to our country. All you don't burn I will." As for houses, Sherman said, his men only torched the abandoned ones, which did not speak well of their owners.

In the last day of killing at Hatcher's Run, Meade's troops attacked Lee's in a windblown snow and recovered most of the ground they had lost the day before. Meade told Margaretta that his losses had been modest, and "I hear of but few officers killed or severely wounded." The general would not have heard of a sergeant of the 60th Ohio who had lost all his limbs to a shell. With one of his last breaths, he spoke of a ring on a severed hand. "He told the boys to take this ring and send it to his wife." Lee lost over a thousand men at Hatcher's Run, taking ground and giving it back. The North lost more, and kept more coming.

Colonel Charles Francis Adams Jr., a veteran of Antietam and Gettysburg, wrote from Boston that day to his father, the American minister in London, chosen by his old friend Seward. The peace conference had "met with no favor in these parts," Colonel Adams said. "The old Puritan vindictiveness" was at work. The conference was an indispensable step toward peace, and the man in the street was ready to forgive the Rebels, but the kid glove set were "as ugly and vindictive as possible. They really don't want peace, unless with it comes the hangman." Seward "needs you in Massachusetts more than in London."

On the same day, Seward wrote to Adams too, anticipating foreign inquiries about the conference. He opened with a backhanded shot at Blair for pushing Lincoln into war, then pulling him toward peace. Both sides were kind at Hampton Roads, the governor said, but the Southerners made no offers, no "categorical demands," no "absolute refusals." They seemed to want to unite in some extrinsic scheme (which Seward left unspecified), with only vague allusions to an ultimate resolution. It amounted to a plea for a truce, which Lincoln considered and rejected. "Nevertheless, it is perhaps of some importance that we have been able to submit our opinions and views directly to prominent insurgents, and to hear them answer in a courteous and not unfriendly manner." For foreign consumption, Seward said the 13th Amendment would be quickly ratified.

The title of the *New York Times* editorial spoke for itself: A PEACE POLICY NOW TREASON. Lincoln had been wise to make a run at peace, but the Rebels had declared independence nonnegotiable. Now talk of settlement was disloyal. Having branded the doves with treason, the *Times* took a swipe at the hawks, leaving Lincoln looking reasonable in the middle. The Jacobins could rest easy. "There is no immediate danger of peace."

In accord with the *Times* on the futility of negotiations, the Richmond press competed in a venom-hurling contest. Henceforth, the *Dispatch* declared, the "dream of a reunited country will vanish even from the lunatic asylums and every eye will see in the face from which the Federal mask has been dropped . . . the undisguised features of the thug and the devil. They will have our property, our lands, our lives will they? Let them come and take them."

Snow had turned to rain in the slushy streets of Richmond when General Breckinridge took his oath as Secretary of War. Then he met with Judge Campbell to review the Confederacy's means of survival. It was a long meeting and a short list. The judge had held on as Assistant Secretary of War, but had told his subordinate, Robert Kean, that all was lost; he would stay a few weeks and go, whether Mr. Davis liked it or not. With Campbell on his way out, the War Department clerk John Jones could see that a "scramble is going on by the young politicians for the position of Assistant Secretary of War, and Mr. Kean is supposed to be ahead in the race." As if it were a prize.

Alec Stephens paid a visit to the War Department that day. "He has a ghostly appearance," Jones thought. He too met at length with Judge Campbell, "with locked doors."

That day or the next, Lincoln crossed Pennsylvania Avenue and called on Preston Blair. Lizzie knew how depressed her father was. The dreams of an old man had come to nothing more. He would soon tell a New York congressman that the Rebels in Richmond had cheated him.

On Wednesday, February 8, the Bostonian Charles Sumner introduced a resolution in the Senate calling on the president to account for the peace conference, and how such a thing had come to be. The old Puritan vindictiveness was indeed afoot. Sumner would soon spread the word that Seward had plied the Southerners with whiskey, which they "drank thirstily," and "a couple of bottles of champagne for their dinner."

Lincoln wired Grant for help. He wanted to include in his report the wire from Grant that had said he wished the President could see the commissioners, their desire for peace and reunion being clear. "I think the dispatch does you credit, while I do not see that it can embarrass you. May I use it?" Grant replied instantly. "By all means." He had meant it to be used "as you or the Secretary of War might think proper."

On a bright and frosty Thursday, February 9, the last of Richmond's war rallies began at high noon in the African Church, a blazing Viking funeral on a crisp Nordic day. John Jones was surprised to hear that Hunter would preside, for "no man living has a greater abhorrence of blood! But perhaps he cannot decline." Campbell and Stephens did, but Hunter was still angry. The Armory Band played a stirring "La Marseillaise" before his opening address, delivered "under the influence" of his humiliation at Hampton Roads, as the senator later confessed.

Mr. Lincoln had demanded submission, Hunter said, with a "cold insolence" made "monstrous" in the face of two hundred thousand Southern soldiers. He had promised to pardon leniently, but what free people would submit their lives and property to the whim of one man? Washington made treaties "with the meanest Indian tribe" but refused to treat with the Confederacy. Mr. Lincoln had not even promised that the people would have a voice in their government. He would only say he favored it. Such was the inducement held out to them. Over three million slaves "would at once be turned loose as idlers and vagabonds upon our community." Congress would regulate race relations and be hostile to the South for a generation. The people must resist, and if they were forced to yield, to make their submission dear. "With faith and diligence and courage, we shall assuredly triumph at last."

Judah Benjamin spoke next, plump, sleek, and smiling. He bowed to Hunter first, behind him in the chair, then disclosed without embarrassment how the administration had used the peace talks and its own confused vice president. No one should be surprised that "our President, whose only defect is that he is too tender-hearted," had tried to stop the bleeding. Mr. Stephens had been confident that his peace idea was feasible, "which we were not, and what better could we do" than to let him bring it to the enemy? "We knew its failure would be the signal for a grand uprising of the people, which was the only element necessary to success," but no one had dreamed that the North would make "such arrogant propositions as were brought from Fortress Monroe. Thank God we know it now."

The Speaker of the Virginia House of Delegates came last, providing comic relief. Just weeks ago, he said, many Southern men had been ready to go back into the Union "if they could carry their heads on their shoulders." Others might have "run some risks with their heads" if they could bring their stocks and bonds. And then came Blair to Richmond. "Courtesies were extended to him." Three eminent men were sent to an audience with the Northern king and his prime minister. The streets were full of talk of their grand reception in Washington, when, "lo and behold, it turned out that they were stuck in Hampton Roads . . . and no duck or dinner." The women of the South "would scorn the wretch who, with sackcloth on his loins and ashes on his forehead, asked mercy from Abraham Lincoln."

⌣

Later that day, Alec Stephens left for Georgia, to settle his affairs and live a quiet life until the federal army took him. He had told Jefferson Davis he would go home and stay there. He would make no public statements, play no part on the public stage, "but quietly abide the issues of fortune, whatever they might be." They parted, according to Stephens, "in the same friendship which had on all occasions marked our personal intercourse." Their bitter public intercourse was over. "I therefore left on the 9th of February and reached home the 20th, where I remained in perfect retirement, until I was arrested on the 11th of May."

⌣

The day after Stephens left, Hunter was collecting statistics on the South's ability to wage war when its Congress issued a proclamation of gratitude for the conference at Hampton Roads. "Thanks be to God, who controls and overrules the counsels of men, the haughty insolence of our enemies which they hoped would intimidate and break the spirit of our people is producing the very contrary effect."

From the distance of North Carolina, the Raleigh *Progress* made short shrift of Richmond's war rallies, which produced great enthusiasm, putting no one in the army. "When will these farces cease?" Their well-springs ran dry within days. A "dull, helpless expectation, a blank despondency" soon fell over even the best of Richmond's people, as Edward Pollard appraised them, while the "worst" demanded peace at any price. The "insidious" thought was spreading that the North's brutal war on the South was a military necessity, that Washington sought no more than the Union as it was, that the meeting on the *River Queen* was marked by hearty fellowship, that Lincoln and Seward made liberal propositions. The idea was growing in the Southern mind "that the Yankee was not such a terrible monster after all, that the newspapers had been practicing scarecrows on the people," that the government had exaggerated the enemy's demands and "painted the terrors of submission" falsely.

Lincoln and his Cabinet knew none of this. A negotiated peace seemed no closer to Gideon Welles than it had before. The ideologues of his party were pushing it away. "There are ultras among us who insist on terms that make peace remote," resisting every step, demanding that the South be crushed, "violent without much regard to Constitutional or State rights or any other rights indeed, except such as they may themselves define or dictate."

On Friday, February 10, Lincoln sent his report on the peace conference to Capitol Hill. It consisted by and large of the pertinent correspondence, which he literally cut and pasted into his draft. He omitted Grant's note welcoming the commissioners through the lines after Stanton ordered them stopped, and Eckert's wire to Stanton on their willingness to meet with Lincoln's designee instead of Lincoln himself. He let the rest of it speak for itself, adding only enough scant narrative to string it together, knowing very well that he who explains is losing. Mexico was not mentioned.

When the report was read aloud in the House, every member was in his seat. Noah Brooks was in the press gallery. As the clerk began to read, "no man so much as stirred his hand." The silence was broken by a murmur of applause when the House heard Lincoln say he would receive any agent proposing to bring peace to our one common country. A louder burst of approval met his three preconditions: Southern disarmament, unqualified reunion, no backward steps on slavery by the executive. A "ripple of mirth" washed over his instruction to Seward not to assume to consummate anything. The wire that Lincoln had received on January 29 was disclosed, saying peace commissioners were at Grant's lines, two days before he told the House that none were in Washington, or likely to be. If anyone noticed, the record does not say. Grant's wire telling Stanton that the commissioners were ready for reunion was read. In the end, the report declared, they had neither ruled it out nor accepted it. They had seemed to want to postpone the issue.

When the clerk had read the report, he identified its author with a flourish, and the chamber exploded in applause. The Speaker's attempt to quell it was perfunctory. Then Congressman James Brooks, a bespectacled Copperhead from New York, stood up and tried. The president's demand for "absolute submission" was deplorable, and yet he deserved thanks for making *any* effort for peace. When he left for Hampton Roads, the fanatics had opened up "in full howl upon him." It took courage to face them down. Many thousands of citizens on both sides would welcome peace on any honorable terms. The men of both armies were "panting for it," as the cheering soldiers showed when the commissioners crossed their lines, but no man in power, North or South, dared boldly to advance it.

The Illinois Republican Elihu B. Washburne, Lincoln's friend and Grant's, asked Brooks if he favored an armistice. Brooks said he did. "I am in favor of appealing from guns and bayonets and artillery to reason, to sense, to Christianity, and to civilization."

"The gentleman agrees with Jeff Davis and his commissioners upon that subject," Washburne said.

"Why, certainly I am in favor of an armistice," Brooks replied. "Someday or other this war must stop." If the two cheering armies were permitted once again to welcome a peace commission, *they* would end the war if their leaders would not.

Brooks closed with a word on Blair's secret plan, a secret no more, having passed from mouth to ear, in the strictest of confidence, a few too many times. Of "far more importance to us than slavery in the South" was the French flag in Mexico. "Then let us hush this unnatural, fraternal, civil war" until the French invasion was repelled. "Let not Mexico and Central America be enslaved to free a few Negroes here."

Then Thaddeus Stevens struck. What the gentleman had said was "but perfectly natural and just." The president had indicted the Rebels, and justice entitled them to an advocate, "one who fully enters into their views and sympathizes with their purposes." The gentleman was highly qualified, but too hard to please. The Democrats had wanted to send envoys south. On this they had "differed somewhat from the loyal people, I mean the other loyal people of the North and from the gentlemen on this side of the House." Now it had been learned that the South would insist on independence, as Stevens and his side had expected.

When Brooks pointed out that Lincoln's report did not say that the Rebels had demanded independence, Stevens cited their war rallies, as Campbell and Stephens had known he would. "They met in the African Church. I do not know what to understand by that. They have got very low when they can do that. However, that is a passing remark." Then he quoted Jeff Davis: "Sooner than we should be united again, I would be willing to yield up everything I have on earth; and if it were possible, I would yield up my life a thousand times rather than succumb." Then Stevens pointed to his left at Brooks, rhetorically if not physically: "And yet a man calling himself a patriot and an American rises upon this floor and sends forth to the country a denunciation of the President of the United States for not entering into negotiations with men holding these doctrines and entertaining these views. I will apply no epithets to such a man; I do not know that I could use any which would be sufficiently merited."

Stevens praised Lincoln for trying peace, then warned him indirectly not to try again. A truce would have been an admission that Southern independence was possible. If the president had agreed to one, he should have been impeached.

Sunset Cox took the floor and recalled how the Jacobins had opposed the very idea of a peaceful reunion. Their goal was bloody revenge. One should read between the lines of the peace commissioners' notes included in Lincoln's report. Negotiations should resume. If peace were not achieved, "the fault, I will not say the crime, of failure will lie at the door, if not of the President, of the radicals whose incessant pressure is always at his back."

If Blair had not briefed Cox, someone else had. Lincoln's "one common country" letter was familiar to him, he said. He wished the House knew *everything* that was said at Hampton Roads. According to Lincoln's report, the commissioners only wished to postpone the reunion question while another course was pursued. "What that other course was, we are only left to conjecture. Perhaps it had reference to a union of our armies for a common object, perhaps in Mexico," but whatever it was, the commissioners had clearly seen reunion as feasible. A truce would merely suspend the war while reasonable men talked peace.

After five days in Washington, Alec Stephens's nephew John went back to the White House that day for the papers he would need to get home. Lincoln made time to chat again, spoke kindly of his uncle, reminisced about their friendship, shared some impressions of the peace conference. Then he took a sheet of paper and wrote to his old friend:

Executive Mansion,
Washington, Feb. 10, 1865
Hon. A. H. Stephens

According to our agreement your nephew, Lieut. Stephens, goes to you bearing this note. Please, in return, to select and send to me that officer of the same rank imprisoned at Richmond whose physical condition most urgently requires his release.

Respectfully, A. Lincoln

Folding the note in half, forgetting to blot the ink, he handed it to his guest and asked him to bring it to his uncle. Then he drew from one of the pigeonholes in his upright desk a postcard-size photograph of himself, signed it, and handed it over too. "Suppose you take this along with you. I don't expect there are many of them down South."

More grateful than he could say, Lieutenant Stephens went home to Georgia and got himself back in the war.

A new White House guard had been given the midnight shift. As he paced the long corridor through the family quarters, he passed the president's room, adjacent to Mrs. Lincoln's. "I could hear his deep breathing. Sometimes, after a day of unusual anxiety, I have heard him moan in his sleep. It gave me a curious sensation." With Lincoln "defenseless in his sleep, it made me feel the pity that would have been almost an impertinence when he was awake. I would stand there and listen until a sort of panic stole over me. If he felt the weight of things so heavily, how much worse the situation of the country must be than any of us realized! At last I would walk softly away, feeling as if I had been listening at a keyhole."

CHAPTER TWENTY-TWO

To Serve a People in Spite of Themselves

After Hunter incited the crowd at the African Church, a "considerate friend" approached him and changed his heart and mind. "He told me that he had never listened to me with so little pleasure, and thought me wrong all the while." Knowing that the war was lost, he should not have urged his people to resist a reasonable peace.

It was a hard thing to hear, and Hunter defended himself at the time, but he knew he had made a mistake. He would regret it the rest of his life, consoling himself with his efforts to correct it. "I did not utterly abandon my duty to the people," he said, and tried to soften their fall.

Hunter faced the truth. Reunion and abolition were inevitable. An effort should be made "to save as much as possible from the wreck. Upon this Mr. Davis and I differed." Not long after the war rallies, Hunter paid a call on Davis with two respected colleagues, both of them prewar Unionists, Senator James Orr of South Carolina and Senator William Graham of North Carolina. Sherman was burning his way up through Orr's constituents as they spoke. He would soon be starting on Graham's. Hunter's would be reached in a month or so. However slim their chances, they would try to persuade their leader to endure the unendurable and negotiate a peaceful reunion.

According to Edward Pollard, no one could match Davis for receiving his critics "with such a well-bred grace, with a politeness so studied as to be almost sarcastic, with a manner that so plainly gave the idea that his company talked to a post." And so, no doubt, he received these senators. In the manner of his considerate friend, Hunter told his president what he did not want to hear. He spoke, as he thought, in confidence. If Davis believed, as Hunter did, that any chance of success was gone, it would become him to consider something better than waging war until all that was left was defeat. Even if he failed to achieve an honorable, peaceful reunion after further resistance had become pointless, he owed it to himself and "a gallant people" to leave some evidence of having tried.

Acquainted with Davis's pride, Hunter had found a way out for him. Knowing how hard it would be for the president to tell the Senate that the end had come, the Senate might tell *him*. Hunter said he thought he could promise that it would. If Davis would pledge his utmost to get the best terms possible, the Senate would ask him to do so, and take the burden from his shoulders. If necessary, Hunter would introduce the resolutions himself. "We could draw them together," he said, to be sure that Davis could live with them. The senator was offering to go down in Southern history as the man who had scuttled his country, sparing its president the humiliation and second-guessing.

Davis cast him into the void. It was then, "for the first time, my faith in Mr. Hunter was impaired; and confidence is a plant which will not bear topping." Hunter had joined the cabal.

Davis asked his visitors to send him a Senate resolution and promised a prompt reply. He suggested a consultation with Robert Woodward Barnwell, Orr's fellow senator from South Carolina, a wealthy, sixty-three-year-old Harvard man and a trusted Davis ally whose father had served in the Continental Congress. Hunter was intrigued, thinking Barnwell had so much influence that if he and Davis would call for a peaceful reunion, the movement would be irresistible.

Davis summoned his Cabinet as soon as the senators left, and disclosed what he saw as their treachery, which "I would not have permitted to be held confidentially." Then he went alone to Senator Barnwell, who lived nearby and was ill, and revealed it to him too. As Davis clearly explained, he wanted the resolution to be "so unequivocal that my issue with the cabal should be distinctly understood by the people."

Then Barnwell behaved unexpectedly. He asked Senator Hunter to come to his home and inquired what he thought were the odds for a palatable peace. "I could not say," Hunter replied. He quoted Lincoln's declaration that he would not treat with Rebels in arms, but the pressure for peace was so great that if Richmond proposed another talk, he doubted that Lincoln could say no. At any rate, if an effort to make peace should fail "through the cruelty or vengeance of our enemy, the fact of our having made the attempt would relieve our Government, and particularly the President, from much responsibility that would otherwise attach to us."

Hunter had the impression that Barnwell disagreed, but the South Carolinian was wavering. He and Hunter, Orr, and Graham went to see Judge Campbell together. Davis was making a legal argument, they said, that the president had no authority to act, that only the states could authorize reunion. A mere abstraction, Campbell said, whatever its merits might be. Some of the states were occupied, some were cut off, and the rest were under pressure. But no one in the room could have thought that Davis would move.

Knowing him as he did, Hunter had tried to save his people with little hope of success. "I scarcely expected to hear more." But he soon heard it "bruited all over Richmond that I had been thoroughly conquered, had submitted, and was disposed to make peace on any terms, with many other disparaging remarks." And now he was boxed in. Duty, he thought, prevented him from explaining himself, for his belief that the South was beaten was based on its destitution, "which could not be revealed to the world without doing much mischief."

So Hunter spoke of peace no more. "If I did not know it before, I was destined to learn how necessary it was to have a great man at the head of a government, to serve a people in spite of themselves."

In the opinion of General Fitzhugh Lee, the demigod's mortal nephew, no Southern peace commission could have ended the war without winning independence. "Had Mr. Davis agreed with the commissioners that peace should be restored upon any other basis, the soldiers in the field would have marched over him and them to battle." Only one man could have done it. "But Robert E. Lee was in accord with his civil chief on that question, and was determined to fight and risk the last defiance of fortune."

Hunter has told us otherwise. Not long after the senator's peace initiative failed, Lee came alone to his boardinghouse under cover of darkness. They were old friends, and they talked through most of the night. Lee told his fellow Virginian that if any chance remained to negotiate a fair reunion in place of a rank surrender, he thought it Hunter's duty to *insist*. He mentioned no duty of his own.

Hunter told Lee about his overture to Davis, and how he had been mocked for it. He would not try again. "It would do no sort of good, for any effort I might make would be misrepresented and laid before the public as soon as it was made, with a view to injure my influence, in which it would probably be successful." He would share no more confidences with Mr. Davis unless Mr. Davis cleared his name.

Lee insisted that for *him* to seek peace talks in public would be almost the same as surrender. That was so, Hunter said, but if Lee thought the situation desperate, he ought to tell the president. Lee did not reply. He did not tell Hunter that the South had no chance, "but the tone and tenor of his remarks made that impression upon my mind." He spoke of Hatcher's Run, where his men had repelled the enemy in a furious storm. "The next day, as he rode along the lines in the snow," he said, "one of the soldiers would thrust forth his bare foot and say, 'General, I have no shoes.' Another would declare, as he passed, 'I am hungry; I haven't enough to eat.' These and other circumstances betraying the utmost destitution he repeated with a melancholy air and tone which I shall never forget."

Not long after Hunter's long night with Lee, the new Secretary of War John Breckinridge came to see him and repeated Lee's advice in so nearly the same words that Hunter wondered if they were working together. Hunter told his old rival Breckinridge about his offer to Davis and what had come of it. He saw no hope for peace, he said, unless the president would cooperate, which he hardly thought Davis would do.

Judge Campbell did his best to save his people too, more persistently than Hunter. He had joined the administration in the first place—a burden, not an honor—to mitigate the evils that infected his new country. "I cannot make you feel how large they were." The very idea of reunion was unspeakable in Richmond. It could only be whispered behind locked doors. As a premise for negotiations, even the peace movement's leaders said the states must align themselves as they saw fit. Richmond's peace men denied Unionist sentiments even when they held them, a mortal political sin of which their detractors freely accused them. When Campbell tried to find a responsible leader to face the inevitable and take the responsibility for reunion, he found himself surrounded by duty-shirking men with "a superstitious dread" of negotiation. Though they knew or should have known that reconstruction was inevitable, they responded with a "sort of hesitation, timidity and dread of responsibility" resulting in nothing at all.

First Campbell went to Lee, who repeated, in substance, his late-night speech to Hunter. He would do his military duty, he said, and would not assume to counsel the civil authorities on their responsibility to make peace or war, let alone usurp it.

Then the judge went to Davis, who repeated himself as well. He lacked the Constitutional authority to dissolve the Confederacy and would not assist its suicide. The people had elected him to establish it, not abolish it. He had sworn to preserve, protect, and defend it. He could only submit the issue to the states, which was impractical. Even if he had the power, he could not accept Lincoln's terms without personal dishonor, which was unthinkable. His Secretary of the Navy Stephen Mallory thought he dreaded being charged, as several militants in the Senate stood ready to charge him, with cowardice and treason.

Then Campbell tried the peace movement's leaders in Congress. They said it was Davis's duty to steer the ship of state, not theirs. If the Senate had faced the truth, so Mallory would later say, peace would have come, and countless miseries been prevented, but "its members dreaded the responsibility and were disposed to see Mr. Davis act alone."

In the end, Campbell said, the captain of the ship stood upright at her helm and watched her hit the shoals. Campbell and Hunter and a few other courageous senators who tried to help him got nowhere. "The idiosyncrasy of one man defeated the design." Davis and his circle kept the war drum beating, denying their people the truth.

On Saturday, February 11, General Meade wrote his wife about Hatcher's Run. "I see the *Tribune*, with its usual malice, charges the recent movement as a failure, and puts the blame on me." Her brother Willie's regiment "was in the thickest of the fight and suffered severely," the general said, "but I believe behaved very well." Leaving Margaretta to surmise that Willie was in one piece, the general let her know that her status had its rewards. An artist was in camp, "of the name of Simmons, who is sculpturing a life-size head of me, of which he intends casting a medallion in bronze. His work is pronounced excellent, and he promises to present you a copy, so you will have your Meade art gallery increased."

In response to the peace that Lincoln and Seward offered, General Lee called for "new resolution" in a message to the Southern people. His soldiers, he said, required no exhortation. "The choice between war and abject submission is before them. To such a proposal brave men, with arms in their hands, can have but one answer. They cannot barter manhood for peace, nor the right of self-government for life or property." Fresh from his night with Hunter, Lee assured his people that "our resources, wisely and vigorously employed, are ample, and with a brave army, sustained by a determined and united people, success, with God's assistance, cannot be doubtful."

He did not inspire Sarah Pryor. "I am afraid we were too faint from want of food to be as courageous as our noble commander expected."

Judge Campbell had started taking lives out of harm's way. His clerk John Jones could make no sense of it. He was "furloughing, detailing, and discharging men from the army," Jones wrote that day, "and yet he thinks the country is pretty nearly exhausted of its fighting population! His successor is not yet appointed; the sooner the better, perhaps." Three days later, Jones lamented that Davis was "immovable in his determination not to yield to the demand for new men in the government, and the country seems to have lost confidence in the old. God help us, or we are lost!"

On Saturday, February 18, Judge Campbell had a private talk with Jones's superior, Robert Kean. What did Kean think of the state of things?

"We will all be fugitives" by the end of March, Kean said.

"What then?"

"The second stage of the war, as some call it," Kean replied. "The boldest will be bushwhackers. The struggle will be outside the laws of war."

"Do you think that is work for a patriot?"

"The enemy in your Conference have left us nothing else. I don't think a patriot could consent to carrying on the war a day after the struggle has become hopeless, provided any door for terms is open."

Campbell concurred in Kean's view of patriotism, but it was not the North that had closed the door. Lincoln and Seward had seemed disappointed on the *River Queen*, he said. They had plainly expected an offer. The speeches at the African Church could only have hardened them. Their people had been disappointed, too, "until the speeches made here went North." Campbell recalled how Davis had pressed the commissioners to misquote Lincoln and Seward. The judge seemed proud of their refusal but very much dissatisfied about the peace conference. "It *ought not* to have been dropped when it was." The commissioners should have returned with a proposal for reunion. Kean reminded him how Lincoln had spoken of oak trees and necks when Campbell discussed the difference between conquest and negotiation. "He said this was true, and shook his head and spoke in a low tone of despair."

The judge confessed his forebodings to a clerk named Wattles too. "We are now arrived at the last days of the Confederacy." A second peace commissioner was in the same place. Jones told his diary that "Mr. Hunter seems more depressed today than I have ever seen him. He walks with his head down, looking neither to the right nor the left."

Sickness had slowed Alec Stephens on his journey back to Georgia, but he got home to Liberty Hall toward the end of February. His enemy Benjamin Hill soon wrote to Davis, attacking his fellow Georgian for refusing to enflame the people after "his failure" at Hampton Roads. "He has been a weight for two years and seems determined to remain one." Some time ago, Stephens had said in a published letter that the South had the means to win and only lacked the brains. Now Hill was glad that Stephens had been sent to talk peace with Lincoln. "His failure has at least *silenced* his pernicious tongue about '*brains*' and has made active patriots of many of his heretofore deluded followers."

Instead of inciting his neighbors, Stephens assembled his slaves. "I told them they were now free, at which I was perfectly contented and satisfied; that I might and probably should be taken away from them soon and perhaps hung; that I wished them, if they saw fit, to remain there and finish the crop," and take half the harvest. If he survived, he said, and the authorities allowed, he would come back and divide the plantation into farms that they could tend and live on if they wished, paying rent from the fruits of their labors. Then he went home to Liberty Hall and sat down with Harry, his black plantation manager, who had put his private earnings in Stephens's care. They amounted to $662. In exchange for that sum, Stephens sold Harry all of his horses and mules, "to which he was attached." They were worth more. Then he taught him how to manage in the event of his master's arrest.

Little Alec told friends at dinner that Davis sent envoys to Lincoln because Stephens and his followers pressured him. Lincoln's terms were not "utterly bad," but Davis denounced them and the peace process died. Stephens had gone home to avoid a public rift. The great trouble with Davis was not that Lincoln had insulted the South but that Lincoln had insulted Davis, who could not abide the thought that his office was ignored, that the Confederacy and its president would never be more than "a name and a dream." When Lincoln had said that he would not recognize the Confederacy and would make no treaty with its government, Davis had heard that there would be no recognition of *him*, no treaty with *Jefferson Davis*. His military blunders had shattered his plans to dictate peace "from the head of Lee's legions at the gates of Washington City." Now the South could get no more than Lincoln's overture at Hampton Roads: payment for its slaves and its rights restored in the Union. It was not much, but it was the best one could hope for with the Confederacy on its deathbed.

Stephens told a fellow Georgian that he knew Lincoln well in Congress, a fair and reasonable man who usually voted with him. If the commissioners had returned, he would have accepted a truce (undeclared, to save Northern pride), a joint invasion of Mexico, and secret arrangements to slip cotton to Europe through the blockade for the common account of the North and South. Blair had told Davis that all of this was possible. Though Lincoln dared not write it down, for fear of Northern opinion, Stephens knew Blair, whose word was "voucher enough" for him. But now it was too late.

Poor, deluded Stephens.

Friends urged him to say publicly that Davis had sabotaged peace, but Stephens chose not to "divide our people." Instead, "I stayed at home, not wishing by absence to seem to be avoiding arrest, which from the time I left Richmond, I considered my ultimate fate." He would not get out of the way of Northern troops, he said, but neither was he disposed to get *in* their way. In the meantime, it pained him to see Davis and his circle use the failure at Hampton Roads to incite a still more hopeless war. *Quos Deus vult perdere, prius dementat,* he thought. Whom God would destroy, He first renders demented.

On February 22, Senator William A. Graham of North Carolina wrote a friend that Davis was telling people that he "never intended to commit himself officially against negotiations on the basis of reunion—that his speech at the African Church was but the expression of his individual opinion. What do you think of the distinction, or of the specimen it affords of the wisdom with which the world is governed?"

CHAPTER TWENTY-THREE

It Is the Province of Statesmanship
to Consider of These Things

On February 23, a Rebel officer sent a wire to Richmond from the siege line. Was it meant to be sardonic? "I have nothing to report this morning of unusual interest. Sixteen of Gracie's, nine of Wallace's, and ten of Wise's brigade deserted to the enemy." On February 24, a resolution declaring the unalterable determination of the Southern people never to unite with the North again was adopted by their Congress. Unanimously. It was not good enough for Judah Benjamin. Two days later, he denounced as cowards and traitors "these Representatives and Senators who are still hankering after peace."

Senator Graham fit the bill. Five of his sons were fighting for the South, and a niece was Stonewall Jackson's widow, but for Benjamin and Davis, the silver-haired North Carolinian, an antebellum Unionist, had gone over to the cabal. Having accompanied Hunter and Orr on their fruitless mission to Davis, he asked Judge Campbell whether Lincoln would negotiate, and what would be the legal consequences, apart from abolition and reunion, if the South were defeated in battle? On February 24, Campbell replied in a letter, which he urged Graham to share with his "brother Senators."

Lincoln would not treat with the Confederacy, Campbell said, but only with individuals, to whom he would "declare" his terms, which ought to be no worse than the ones he endorsed at Hampton Roads. Congress might have to approve some of them, but the commander in chief had broad authority, and the statutes that directed him to seize Southern property allowed him to make exceptions. In the judge's legal opinion, the president could intercede in confiscations prospectively *and* retrospectively. With reunion as a premise, negotiations could proceed on the status of West Virginia, paying the Confederacy's debts, disbanding its armies, readmitting its states "into fellowship" with the North, addressing the slavery issue and other "internal affairs." True Northern statesmen should prefer negotiation to conquest. As for their Southern counterparts, the terms that Lincoln had floated on the *River Queen* should have been taken, if none better could be had. The Confederacy was in disarray. There was no communication across the Mississippi. Hood's defeat at Nashville had opened the west to the enemy. The war had been reduced to the defense of Richmond. Grant had Lee pinned. Sherman was storming north. Another federal army was on its way. The South could neither support the troops it had, nor recruit new ones. There were three times as many Southern men in Northern prisons as there were in Lee's army.

The facts were plain, the conclusions unavoidable. Graham shared Campbell's letter with his colleagues, along with the judge's summary of the conference at Hampton Roads.

A few days later, expanding his dolorous litany, Campbell submitted a report to the Secretary of War, premised on the necessity "that accurate views of our situation be taken. It is not the part of statesmanship to close our eyes upon them." The Treasury was four or five hundred million dollars in debt, "paralyzed by want of credit." Its authority to issue paper money had expired on December 31. The Secretary of the Treasury had been selling gold ever since. When the gold was gone, the Treasury would cease to exist. Campbell would soon observe that there was no treasure with which to fill it, "or even to veil its nudity." Paper money was trading at sixty to one against gold and silver.

The condition of the army was scarcely less dire. The supply of foreign weapons was barred by the blockade. All of the South's munitions factories were vulnerable or gone. So many deserters were at large, an estimated 100,000, that the crime had lost its stigma, and "the criminals are everywhere shielded by their families, and by the sympathies of many communities." Lee had just reported 1,200 new desertions. The conscription pool was exhausted. North Carolina, South Carolina, and

Georgia had withdrawn from it. An effort to draft 20,000 slaves as team-sters and laborers had driven as many black men to the enemy's ranks as had reinforced the South's. If everything went well, the army could not be sustained. These "embarrassments" had so much accumulated that the problem of sustaining Lee was beyond solution. Permitting himself an understatement, Campbell allowed that the morale of the Army of Northern Virginia was "somewhat impaired." Elsewhere things were worse. Hood's decimated troops, now back under General Johnston, could "scarcely be recognized as an army." Tasked with resisting Sherman, only a fraction of General William J. Hardee's command was fit to fight. (His son would soon be killed at Bentonville, North Carolina, in the last, losing effort to stop Sherman. He was sixteen years old.)

The political situation was no better. Georgia was in a state of insurrec-tion. North Carolina did not support the war as Virginia did. The less said about the entire length of the Mississippi, the better. When Richmond was evacuated, as it surely would be, Virginia must be abandoned. "The war will cease to be a national one from that time." The Southern people's hopes, affections, and treasure had long been devoted to Virginia. "When this exchequer becomes exhausted, I fear that we shall be bankrupt, and that the public spirit in the South and Southwestern States will fail."

The judge concluded eloquently. "It is the province of statesman-ship to consider of these things. The South may succumb, but it is not necessary that she be destroyed. I do not regard reconstruction as involv-ing destruction, unless our people should forget the incidents of their heroic struggle and become debased and degraded. It is the duty of their statesmen and patriots to guard them in the future with even more care and tenderness than they have done in the past. There is anarchy in the opinions of men here, and few are willing to give counsel, and still fewer are willing to incur the responsibility of taking or advising action. In these circumstances I have surveyed the whole ground, I believe calmly and dispassionately." Campbell did not ask that his views be accepted, "but that a candid inquiry be made with a view to action." He proposed that General Lee's opinion be solicited (a canny suggestion), and that the president submit the subject to the Senate or the whole Congress and invite *them* to act.

Campbell presented his report with a memorandum on the Hampton Roads Peace Conference, a reminder of a direction in which to go. Then Lee submitted a report of his own, complying with Secretary Breckinridge's request to all department heads. The consequences of Grant's superior resources, it said, had already been "postponed longer than we had reason to anticipate." The other reports were as grim.

Campbell was convinced that Lincoln and Seward had disclosed enough at Hampton Roads to warrant an expectation that terms could be had "which would avoid some of the evils of conquest and subjugation," and so he told Graham and anyone else who would listen. A few days later, Graham told him that Davis would send no more peace commissions.

Campbell spoke of what befalls a party that "knows not when it is beaten." Then he wrote to a friend, the former US senator and Alabama governor, Benjamin Fitzpatrick. Richmond would soon be evacuated, Campbell said. Lee's army would be no more. The cause was lost. The governor should be prepared to lead Alabama back to the Union.

———

With steel-blue eyes and a full brown beard, the South Carolinian James Longstreet was Lee's right arm. His own right arm was in a sling, a souvenir of the Battle of the Wilderness. He was one of Lee's best generals. He was one of Grant's best friends.

They had bonded at West Point over twenty years earlier. Some would even call them family. Fresh from the Academy, they were serving with the elite 4th Infantry at Jefferson Barracks, Missouri, when Longstreet rode out to see his uncle Fred Dent and his cousin Julia Dent and brought Grant with him. When Grant married Julia, Longstreet was one of three fellow officers who stood up for him, future Rebels all. Since 1861, he and Grant had been in contact only in battle. The conference at Hampton Roads had come and gone since Grant told the Bishop of Arkansas that he would like to be a peacemaker and have a talk with Lee. He had not abandoned his vocation since the failure on the *River Queen*.

Grant's confidant General Edward Ord, who had been in command at City Point when the peace commissioners arrived, was another friend of Longstreet's. On February 20, Ord sent Longstreet a note, purporting to be concerned about commerce between pickets (a pastime as old as the war), and proposing to discuss it. Longstreet was sure that his friend had something else in mind. When they met the next day on neutral ground, Ord asked to see Longstreet alone. It may have taken two minutes for Longstreet to suggest how to stop the fraternization and Ord to accept it. Then they turned to other things.

Longstreet had been called Old Pete since his youth, an allusion to St. Peter's rocklike character, and Longstreet says Ord brought up the conference at Hampton Roads. Northern politicians were afraid to talk peace, Ord said. The only way to start was through the officers. On Ord's side of the lines they thought "the war had gone on long enough; that we should come together as former comrades and friends and talk a little." In response, Longstreet made it clear that he and Lee knew the war was lost. It would be a "great crime" to prolong it. "Mr. Davis was the great obstacle to peace. . . ." Then Ord suggested a truce—that "General Grant and General Lee should meet and have a talk."

Ord had more to say. Longstreet's wife and Mrs. Grant were friends. Mrs. Longstreet should visit Mrs. Grant at City Point with an escort of Southern officers. Mrs. Grant would return the call in Richmond, accompanied by Northern officers. While Grant and Lee were talking, their officers and ladies would be talking too, "until terms honorable to both sides could be found." Longstreet said he would report the idea to Lee and the civil authorities. Then he wired his wife at Lynchburg and asked her to come to Richmond.

Horace Porter, another member of Grant's inner circle, understood the idea. The officers' chivalry would arouse goodwill, and "everywhere lead to demonstrations in favor of peace between the two sections of the country." But according to Porter it was Longstreet's idea, too visionary to be taken seriously, though drowning men catch at straws. Perhaps they do, but the notion that Longstreet proposed it is challenged by a witness in a position to know, apart from Old Pete himself.

Julia Grant stepped out of her bedroom and into her husband's office one afternoon and found Ord there with him. "See here, Mrs. Grant," her husband said. "What do you think of this?" (He knew very well what she would think of it.) General Ord had brought a suggestion that peace might be had "through you." Ord explained that he had gone to see Pete Longstreet—that pickets were trading newspapers for tobacco, running races together, and generally "on good terms"—and he thought it ought to stop. And then he had said to Longstreet, "Why do you fellows hold out any longer? You know you cannot succeed. Why prolong this unholy struggle?" To the best of Julia's memory, many years later, Ord said it was *he* who had proposed the exchange of female visits. The idea delighted Julia, but she was sure it was not her husband's. She was eager to see Louise Longstreet and help make peace, but her husband only smiled and said no. The whole thing was unseemly. "It is simply absurd. The men have fought the war and the men will finish it."

Grant's protests notwithstanding, it is all but inconceivable that Ord made an overture to the enemy for peace talks between Grant and Lee without Grant's knowledge, let alone a proposal that Grant's wife should receive Longstreet's and a bevy of Rebel officers at his headquarters. It would not have been the first time Ord protected Grant's flank.

Longstreet and Lee were called to Richmond to discuss Ord's overture. They met at night at the Executive Mansion with Davis and Breckinridge. They talked it through for hours and agreed that another meeting should be arranged. Longstreet urged Lee to ask to see Grant on "some irrelevant matter," and "once they were together they could talk as they pleased." Breckinridge was keen on the part assigned to the ladies.

On February 27, Grant sent Ord a message: He wanted to see Longstreet himself, but Ord should revisit him first. "[G]o tell him that you will try to arrange for an interview. . . ." Ord replied that night. A meeting had been set with Longstreet to discuss an exchange of civilian prisoners, and "had I not better have some definite proposition. . . ." Grant responded immediately: Since the meeting's "ostensible" purpose was a prisoner exchange, Ord should negotiate one. When Ord met again with Longstreet, Old Pete let him know that he and Lee were anxious for peace, but "nothing could be done with J. Davis." Ord said Lee should write Grant and propose a meeting, so that "old friends of the military service could get together and seek out ways to stop the flow of blood."

Lee wrote to Grant on March 2, saying Longstreet had spoken with Ord about "a satisfactory adjustment of the present unhappy difficulties by means of a military convention." Ord had said that Grant would agree to see him if Lee had authority to act. Lee said he did. "Sincerely desiring to leave nothing untried which may put an end to the calamities of war," he proposed to meet at a time and place of Grant's choosing. Displaying some eagerness, he suggested eleven o'clock on Monday morning, at the place where Ord met Longstreet.

Even before Grant reported Lee's note to Washington, he ordered a subordinate to tell Longstreet that his reply would be delivered at noon the next day. Then Grant wired Lee's note to Stanton, and deceived him again. Ord and Longstreet had met at *Longstreet's* request, Grant said, to arrange a prisoner exchange. "A general conversation ensued on the subject of the war, and has induced the above letter. I have not returned any reply, but promised to do so at 12 tomorrow. I respectfully request instructions." Grant did not deny Lee's claim that Grant wanted to see him about ending the war.

The president was signing bills in his Capitol office with Seward, Stanton, Nicolay, and Hay when Stanton handed him Grant's telegram. According to Nicolay and Hay, he spoke not a word and wrote a dispatch to Grant, which he showed to Seward and handed to Stanton. An alternate account said Lincoln was thrilled by the thought of Grant making peace with Lee, until Stanton spoke: Tomorrow was Inauguration Day, and the president had better not take the oath if he would hand to the generals his responsibility to make peace. Whichever way it happened, Lincoln wrote a message to Grant for Stanton's signature:

> *The President directs me to say to you that he wishes you to have no conference with General Lee, unless it be for the capitulation of General Lee's army or on some minor and purely military matter. He instructs me to say that you are not to decide, discuss, or confer upon any political question. Such questions the President holds in his own hands, and will submit them to no military conference or conventions. Meantime you are to press to the utmost your military advantages.*

Telling Grant that the president had written it, Stanton fired the message off with a sharp cover note, as if Lincoln's were not sharp enough. "I will add that General Ord's conduct in holding intercourse with General Longstreet upon political questions not committed to his charge is not approved. . . . You will please in future instruct officers appointed to meet rebel officers to confine themselves to the matters specifically committed to them." A newspaperman close to Grant said he took it as "an open rebuke." It did not make him fonder of Stanton.

Lincoln's negativity on generals negotiating peace was more than merely driven by the principle of civilian control. In the opinion of Gideon Welles, far from fearing leniency, he suspected that his generals preferred to prolong the war, and "exact severe terms." There was cause for such suspicions. Sherman was crushing the Southern people, not just their troops. U. S. Grant, also known as Unconditional Surrender Grant, resented Lincoln's soft-hearted pardons of deserters. General George Stoneman said Lincoln predicted one night that his head would ache the next evening. "Tomorrow is hangman's day and I shall have to act upon death sentences." Stoneman never forgot the look that came over him. Grant had no such headaches.

But Lincoln had misread his man. Grant betrayed his eagerness to see Lee in a dispatch to a subordinate, before he heard from Stanton: "You may say to General Longstreet that I will send my reply to General Lee's communication as early as possible, but may not be able to do so today." When Stanton's wire arrived, quashing the whole thing, Grant replied to Lee and clarified "a misunderstanding" on the issue of exchanging prisoners charged with capital crimes. Then he turned to the issue of generals making peace, another misunderstanding:

> *I have no authority to accede to your proposition for a conference on the subject proposed. Such authority is vested in the President of the United States alone. General Ord could only have meant that I would not refuse an interview on any subject on which I have a right to act, which, of course, would be such as are purely of military character, and on the subject of exchanges which has been entrusted to me.*

Then Grant wired Stanton: He had written to Lee; a copy would be sent to Stanton. "I can assure you that no act of the enemy will prevent me from pressing all advantages gained to the utmost of my ability. Neither will I, under any circumstances, exceed my authority or in any way embarrass the Government. It was because I had no right to meet General Lee on the subject *proposed by him* [emphasis added] that I referred the matter for instructions."

Stanton's reply was conciliatory. No imputations had been intended. The president had merely wished to make it plain that "the enemy had a purpose in desiring to enter into political negotiations with military officers." Stanton did not specify the nefarious purpose in question.

Grant's rejection of a parlay with Lee was published in Richmond immediately. Judge Campbell's friend Robert Kean thought it was made public "to follow up the Hampton Roads business, and make our people desperate."

In Washington City, the 38th Congress adjourned and went home on Saturday, March 4, Inauguration Day. The 39ths, still more hostile to a generous reconstruction, would not arrive until December, leaving Lincoln alone on the stage for nine months. Having given his inaugural address "with malice toward none, with charity for all," he was bent on luring the South back in a reconciling mood before Congress could stop him.

In Richmond, General Gorgas was in no such mood, and despised men who were. "The Senate, it is now said, are ready for *any* terms—the cowards. Pity a few could not be taken out and hung or shot." If a soldier may be shot for cowardice, "why may not the craven Senator be made to yield his dastard life in the same way?"

Like his nemesis Alec Stephens, Benjamin Hill had left for Georgia, where he filled the great void left by Stephens's silent tongue. On Saturday, March 11, Hill assembled an array of women, children, old men, and crippled veterans and scorned the Yankee offer made at Hampton Roads. The army would not be degraded, not with half a million men under arms east of the Mississippi (a wild exaggeration). "Support the President," he told the helpless crowd, "support the generals; supply the army; drive off the traitors; confound the critics; and then you will be able to defy the enemy; arrest disasters; and win independence."

As for South Carolina, where the rebellion had begun with whoops and cheers and blood-red sashes over dashing gray uniforms, Mary Chesnut mourned what Sherman had done to her capital. "Columbia is but dust and ashes, burned to the ground. Men, women and children are left there houseless, homeless, without a particle of food." Among other soft targets, Sherman's men had torched a convent. Socialites were subsisting on scraps of scattered corn left behind on the ground by his horses.

In early March, Lee told Davis that his army must retreat within weeks. Richmond would fall when it did, which would cripple his men's morale. The loss of its factories would be devastating too, but the government could regroup, arms could be made elsewhere. Davis asked Lee if he should not withdraw at once, but the general said his underfed horses were too weak to pull wagons and artillery through the mud. He must wait for the roads to firm up. He proposed to withdraw to Danville, Virginia, when the time came. He might be able to fight his way to Johnston. As Davis saw the vision, Lee's shattered troops would combine with Johnston's to be "hurled upon Sherman in North Carolina, with the hope of defeating him before Grant could come to his relief." Deserters would return, Grant would be drawn into a hostile population, and "Virginia be delivered from the invader."

Days later, Lee had to change his plans. With Grant almost ready to turn his right flank, he proposed to attack Fort Stedman on his left. If he succeeded, Grant's connections to City Point would be threatened. If he failed, which was likely, he would force Grant to shift his forces "and delay the impending disaster for the more convenient season for retreat." Davis approved the disaster-delaying plan.

Sarah Pryor's husband had enjoyed a colorful career as an American diplomat in Greece, a US congressman, a target of Thaddeus Stevens, and a Confederate congressman turned general. He resigned when Davis denied him a higher command, reenlisted as a scout, and was captured and imprisoned in New York Harbor as a suspected spy. Horace Greeley and other Northerners persuaded Lincoln to release him. Grant had wanted him held. Stanton had wanted him hanged. The fulfillment of Hunter's promise to try to get him freed may have saved his life.

Now Pryor and two friends who had worked for his release came to the White House and asked the president to reprieve John Yates Beall, Pryor's recent cellmate, who had plotted to derail passenger trains carrying Rebel prisoners through upstate New York. Lincoln said he grieved for the young man and his family but must yield to the officer in command in New York, who said a hanging was necessary to deter terrorism.˙ Moved by the loss of another young life and a need to deny responsibility for it, Lincoln turned the conversation to the conference at Hampton Roads. If Mr. Davis had accepted reunion and abolition, his people might have been paid for their slaves and enjoyed a general amnesty, but Mr. Davis had demanded independence. Now he would be responsible for the futile, wicked loss of every drop of blood to be shed for the rest of the war, when its outcome was clear to every sane man. Lincoln could not believe that Mr. Davis's "senseless obstinacy" reflected his people's sentiments.

Pryor took it as a plea. He would soon tell his wife how he pleaded too, with Hunter and other sane men in Richmond, "but with one voice they assured him that nothing could be done with Mr. Davis, and that the South had only to wait the imminent and inevitable catastrophe."

˙ Lincoln's eyes would later moisten when he spoke of the condemned young man to Seward and a friend. "They tried me every way. . . . I even had to turn away his poor sister when she came and begged for his life, and let him be executed, and can't get the distress out of my mind yet."

CHAPTER TWENTY-FOUR

With Cheerful Confidence in the Result

Born in 1793, the Confederacy's gray eminence, William Cabell Rives, had deep-set eyes, an intelligent forehead, and a formidable résumé. Thomas Jefferson had taught him the law. James Madison had been his friend. He had long since dismissed the notion of slavery as a positive good as an "obsolete and revolting" idea. He had served with distinction as Jackson's minister to Paris, a US senator, and a delegate to the Washington peace convention of 1861. He had followed Virginia out of the Union like a mourner in a funeral procession. Now Lee had lately told him that "true policy required us to close the war on the best terms we could." As chairman of the House Foreign Affairs Committee, he had long supported Davis but had recently resigned, pleading age and ill health.

Toward the middle of March, Judge Campbell asked Rives to draft for the Senate a resolution urging Davis to offer reunion on reasonable terms. It was Hunter's old idea, but with Rives as its author it could not be ignored. While cherishing the cause, Rives wrote, the Senate had concluded that the Confederacy must yield, "as the proudest and most valiant of nations have done in like circumstances, to the stern law of necessity and the apparent decree of Heaven," to avoid pointless bloodshed "and avert the horrors of a savage and relentless subjugation by a triumphant armed force of every race and complexion."

At Campbell's request, Senator Graham agreed to submit the resolution, with no time to lose. He returned it to the judge that night. Senators had said there was no point. Davis would ignore it if it passed.

A few days later, the Confederate Congress expired with the War Department's reports of its extremity clutched in its dying hands. "It is

not the part of statesmanship to close our eyes upon them," Judge Campbell had said. Davis did just that. He sealed them and sent them in secret
to Congress without comment, accompanied by a *public* message that
politely accused the House and Senate of incompetent neglect and proposed emergency legislation to help win the war. Allowing that "our country is in danger," its president declared that the war could be waged "with
cheerful confidence" in the result, and with no honorable alternative. Mr.
Lincoln had decreed at Hampton Roads that no treaty would be made,
that "in the event of our penitent submission, he would temper justice
with mercy," that the victors would decide whether the South would have
self-government. Mr. Lincoln had rebuffed the peace commissioners' suggestion that Grant could treat with Lee, but had promised to reconsider.
Davis had thought General Ord's overture to General Longstreet was the
result, but that door too had closed, and the people of the Confederacy
"could be but little known to him who supposed it possible that they
would consent to live in a country garrisoned by its own Negroes and
governed by its conqueror, in degradation and slavery."

Davis's supply of unconscious irony was inexhaustible, but his rhetoric had weight. Lincoln and Seward had left him too much running room.
The hints of conciliation they had dropped at Hampton Roads were not
enough to stop him from inciting a longer war or to give his opposition a clearly marked roadmap to peace. On March 18, Davis gathered in
his office the entire Virginia congressional delegation, his Cabinet, and
General Lee, who recounted the army's destitution but made no recom-
mendation. "He was a soldier," said a congressman who was there, "and
doubtless felt that it was not his province to volunteer advice to the political department." All fifteen legislators said Virginia stood ready to do
what was asked of her.

The Confederate Congress adjourned that day in the moral wreck-
age of Richmond, never to reconvene. Among its last acts, it adopted a
resolution, with one dissenting vote, to keep fighting until independence
was won. "Failure," it said, "will compel us to drink the cup of humiliation
even to the bitter dregs of having the history of our struggle written by
New England historians." Edward Pollard would soon submit that Congress had abandoned its post like cowards, unwilling to witness the end,

but not before a Senate committee lashed back at Davis, consuming precious time and no little paper to support the proposition that the Southern people's president, not their Congress, had waged the war ineptly. A record had been left in the ruins. *

The wildly whiskered Senator Louis T. Wigfall, a South Carolinian by birth, a Texan by choice, an arsonist by disposition, had been a Davis ally in the old Senate, but had long since adjudged him "an amalgam of malice and mediocrity." On the day the Confederate Congress left Richmond for good, Wigfall amused Judge Campbell with a copy of a Virginian's speech in the House proposing the ludicrous notion of an alliance with the United States to eject the French from Mexico. Wigfall said he intended to read it between his conviction for treason and his execution, "thinking it would tend to reconcile me to death." Knowing more than Wigfall did, Campbell said he would postpone reading it until after his execution.

The judge told a friend that he understood he was "in high disfavor" in the Davis administration, regarded as a sort of leader of the opposition for his efforts to "put backbone" into Mr. Hunter and Mr. Graham. High disfavor was the least of it. In the eyes of his cornered president, Campbell had joined the cabal.

On Thursday, March 23, Lincoln and his family left Washington on the *River Queen*, bound for City Point, invited by General Grant, escorted by the aptly named *Bat*, a captured blockade runner, one of the fastest ships in the navy. "There is no doubt he is much worn down," Gideon Welles told his diary; "besides, he wishes the War terminated, and, to this end, that severe terms shall not be exacted of the Rebels." He had leapt at the chance to escape the capital and plan the war's end from a vantage point closer to the scene than Major Eckert's telegraph office. It was no joyful news for Stanton, who was not invited. The Secretary of War assigned a captain to shadow the commander in chief.

---

* As late as 1957, a respected Southern historian described as treasonable the underground congressional movement to accept a peaceful reunion. Hunter, Orr, and Graham were a small group of "whipped Senators." Congress had gone out of existence "with at least the satisfaction of never having begged for mercy."

No better quarters being available, the Lincolns stayed on the *River Queen*, snug but no hardship. The president saw Grant for the first time since the peace conference. They mourned its failure together. If the commissioners had agreed to reunion and abolition, Lincoln said, "he was almost willing to hand them a blank sheet of paper with his signature attached for them to fill in the terms upon which they were willing to live with us in the Union and be one people."

Now it was almost too late.

On Saturday, March 25, hours before the attack on Fort Stedman that Davis had approved as a desperate throw of the dice, Lee spoke with General John B. Gordon, who would lead it. Knowing how slim were its chances, they agreed that another peace overture was the better course, on whatever terms the South could get. Uneasy with his conscience, Gordon asked Lee if he had so advised the government. Lee replied that he was a soldier. His duty was to obey orders, and advise the civilian government on military matters. "It is enough to turn a man's hair gray to spend one day in that Congress," he said. Its members "will neither take the responsibility of acting nor will they clothe me with authority to act. As for Mr. Davis, he is unwilling to do anything short of independence, and feels that it is useless to try to treat on that basis." Lee felt free to add that Mr. Davis was "very pertinacious in opinion and purpose."

Gordon's troops took Fort Stedman before dawn. Within hours, led by General John F. Hartranft, Northern troops took it back, inflicting some 4,800 Southern casualties, bringing pain to some 4,800 Southern families, costing Lee 10 percent of his army. The South had nothing to show for them.

Generals Hartranft and Gordon called a truce to recover their dead and wounded. Colonel Henry Kyd Douglas, the dead General Pegram's friend, oversaw the Southern work. "Men ran over the field from each side and gathered up their comrades." A federal officer noticed an unusually large number of shattered legs and thighs. As the stretcher bearers worked, other men traded and gossiped with their enemies, and Douglas and Hartranft discovered that they had both gone to Franklin and

Marshall College. Douglas gave the Northerner a letter to send to his Virginia home, now in federal hands. He would later learn that Hartranft, a future Pennsylvania governor, had added a kind note of his own. As they took each other's hands, a Northern major made a partial delivery for which Douglas wrote out a receipt. It was found among Hartranft's papers when he died: "Received of Major Bertolette: 120 dead and 15 wounded in the engagement of the 25th March 1865."

Two days later, General Sherman and Admiral David Dixon Porter, a heavily bearded man who had joined the navy at the soft age of ten, arrived at City Point to confer with Lincoln and Grant in the *River Queen's* saloon, three weeks after the peace conference. As Sherman and Porter later told it, Lincoln was ready for peace on almost any terms. "Must more blood be shed? Cannot this last bloody battle be avoided?" Once the Rebels went home, "they won't take up arms again. Let them all go, officers and all. I want submission, and no more bloodshed. Let them have their horses to plow with and, if you like, their guns to shoot crows with. I want no one punished. Treat them liberally all round. We want those people to return to their allegiance to the Union and submit to the laws." When asked what to do with captured civilian leaders, Lincoln told a story about an Irishman who had sworn off liquor but told a barman he would take a spiked lemonade, so long as the brandy went in "unbeknownst to meself." The officers inferred that Davis and his circle should be left to flee the country, unbeknownst to Abraham Lincoln.

Johnston must soon surrender, Sherman said. As Sherman would later have it, Lincoln let him know that Johnston should be given almost any terms that would induce him. "Only don't let us have any more bloodshed if it can be avoided." His generals said they would do their best, but a last big battle might have to be fought.

In 1898, Julia Grant recalled a chat with Lincoln at City Point while the peace talks were in progress, a conversation that never happened. When the conference took place, Lincoln was not at City Point and Mrs. Grant was not at Hampton Roads. She seems to have mixed two memories, thirty-three years after the fact—her disappointment when she learned that the conference had failed in February, and a discussion with Lincoln in March or April. "Why, Mr. President," she recalled telling him, "are you not going to make terms with them? They are our own people, you know."

"Yes, I do not forget that," Lincoln said, and read her the terms he had proposed. Julia was amazed that they were not accepted. Her memory had faded years later, but she had the essence right.

⁓

After Lee's attack on Fort Stedman failed, Davis put his wife and children on a train to Charlotte, much against their wishes. Varina could see that it nearly killed him. He would soon be in the field, he told her, where their presence would be a worry, not a comfort. "Mr. Davis gave me a pistol," Varina later recalled, and showed her how to use it. "He was very apprehensive of our falling into the hands of the disorganized bands of troops roving about the country." He told her to make every effort to escape, but now that she was armed, "You can at least, if reduced to the last extremity, force your assailants to kill you."

⁓

On Saturday, April 1, in a charge led by General Sheridan, Union forces took Five Forks, a vital crossroads near Petersburg, cutting off the Danville train, Richmond's lifeline and Lee's, inflicting three thousand casualties. That and the next day's attack on Lee's center left him helpless to hold on. He sent word to Davis that his army would withdraw that night. Richmond would be taken within hours. In a message to Congress five months earlier, Davis had proclaimed that "not the fall of Richmond, nor Wilmington, nor Charleston, nor Savannah, nor Mobile, nor all combined" could destroy the Confederacy. His theory would be tested now. With the single exception of Mobile, they were all in federal hands, and so was Mobile Bay.

Davis and his Cabinet moved to Danville on the last open rails, to continue the war from there. Judah Benjamin told a French diplomat it was "simply a measure of prudence. I hope that we will return in a few weeks." The Frenchman could not tell whether the remark was delusional or mendacious. Either would have been in character. After a frantic afternoon of panic and packing, Davis and his Cabinet, the Confederacy's critical papers, and what remained of its gold were loaded onto cars marked STATE DEPARTMENT, WAR DEPARTMENT, and the rest. The train was rolling south before midnight. When a crowd cheered their president at the Clover station, he smiled and waved, "but his expression showed physical and mental exhaustion."

In the words of Gideon Welles, every senior Confederate official but one had fled, "with heavy hearts and light luggage." Judge Campbell alone remained, to "renew my obligations to the United States" and "abide the fate of Richmond." His son, two sons-in-law, and a nephew, all of them soldiers, had left with Lee's army. Every effort he had made to advance a peaceful reunion having failed, "I could only await the ruin certain to arrive." No other Southern leader had the courage to remain in the fallen capital, represent his people before their conquerors, and do what he could for them. He knew he was draping a noose around his neck.

— — —

What was left of the Army of Northern Virginia vanished in the night and started moving west toward food, supplies, and Johnston. The next morning, before the blue army walked into Petersburg, the *New York Herald's* correspondent rode in ahead of them and encountered some old men whose flag of truce "looked suspiciously like a dirty tablecloth." They gave him an awkward salute and tried to surrender the city to him. Sarah Pryor soon watched a column of bony prisoners being marched down the street like walking scarecrows, "a forlorn body of ragged, hatless, barefoot men." Brokenhearted women stood in their doorways as the beaten men passed, giving them all they had, "smiles and encouraging words."

Up in Richmond, military stores that could not be carried off were opened to the people. Thousands of hungry, threadbare citizens snatched them up. Before the army left, warehouses storing cotton, tobacco, and ammunition were torched, to deny them to an enemy with an affluence of all three. Mounds of government papers were set alight in the streets.

Enraged by the discovery of speculators' hoards of food and supplies, shouting people looted them and set fire to the empty hiding places. Some fifty square blocks of homes and businesses were soon in flames, the *Enquirer,* the *Examiner,* the *Sentinel,* and the *Dispatch* among them.

Having burned the heart of their capital, the Confederacy's fleeing leaders left its eighty-year-old mayor to drive out the next morning with a letter addressed "to the General Commanding the United States Army in front of Richmond," respectfully requesting that he take possession of it, "to preserve order and protect women and children and property," endangered as they were by fire and mobs of drunken felons escaped from unguarded prisons.

When the victors marched in, Richmond was a city of ghosts, veiled in smoke and ash. Hardly a white man of military age remained. Almost all of their families were behind closed doors, leaving the streets to liberated slaves. The 4th Massachusetts Cavalry was the first to clatter down Main Street, well mounted and well fed. An interval ensued and on came regiment after regiment of infantry. Within hours the old flag was flying everywhere.

In the words of a Rebel officer, the behavior of the occupying army was "beyond all praise." To the astonishment of the city's defenseless people, Northern bucket brigades subdued the fires; homeless citizens were sheltered and fed; a guard was posted at the home of General Lee; conquerors in blue treated the conquered with respect; officers made courtesy calls at the homes of old friends, meeting sisters, wives, and daughters dressed in mourning. A Richmond lady said they "could not be made to understand that their presence was painful."

Two days after he fled—with nothing much left but his life, and that in imminent peril—Jefferson Davis released a message to his people. "We have now entered upon a new phase of the struggle. Relieved from the necessity of guarding particular points, our army will be free to move from point to point, to strike the enemy in detail far from his base. Let us but will it, and we are free." Richmond, for the moment, was lost, but Virginia was not. "If, by the sheer stress of numbers, we should ever be compelled to a temporary withdrawal from her limits, or those of any other border state, we will return until the last baffled and exhausted enemy shall abandon in despair his endless and impossible task of making slaves of people resolved to be free."

—⁓—

Spring had come to Richmond on Wednesday, April 4, a gorgeous, sun-kissed day, but for the smell of burning. "I walked around the burnt district this morning," said the War Department clerk John Jones. "Some seven hundred houses, from Main Street to the canal, comprising the most valuable stores, and the best business establishments, were consumed." So were hundreds of homes and much of the meager food supply. Thousands of helpless civilians were homeless and hungry. Most whites were despondent. Many blacks, delighted as they were with their freedom, had not yet absorbed their circumstances.

In command of the occupying army, General Godfrey Weitzel was responsible for their welfare. A West Point cadet when Lee was superintendant, Weitzel had grown close to him, and had spent much time in his home. He was handsome and full-bearded, with a receding hairline and penetrating eyes. Not yet thirty, the general was acquainted with suffering. Three weeks after their wedding, his young wife had burned to death when her dress caught fire as she walked by a hearth. Now some 25,000 citizens of Richmond had no food and many had no homes. From his headquarters at the Executive Mansion, Weitzel ordered rations distributed to anyone who took an oath of allegiance. Early that morning, Judge Campbell went over to see Weitzel's chief of staff, General George Foster Shepley of Maine, who had argued before him in the Supreme Court. The judge was the supplicant now. He surrendered himself to Shepley as the only senior Confederate official still in Richmond, and said he would be pleased to see President Lincoln. Shepley said the president was at City Point. Campbell said he would be pleased to go there. Shepley let the judge go home, and told him he would seek General Weitzel's consent to wire the president for instructions.

—⁓—

On that same Wednesday morning, April 4, Lincoln sailed up the James to Richmond on the *River Queen* with Tad, preceded by Admiral

Porter on his flagship *Malvern,* a captured blockade runner converted to a gunboat. The president walked a mile uphill to the Executive Mansion on a hot, dusty day with his son at his hand, the admiral at his side, and an armed knot of sailors, fanning himself with his stovepipe hat. Porter would later say that the street was as empty as a city of the dead until they came upon some black men digging a ditch. Their foreman recognized Lincoln, dropped his spade, and ran to him, hailing "the great Messiah," falling on his knees, kissing the president's feet. "Do not kneel to me," Lincoln told him gently. "You must kneel to God only, and thank Him for the liberty you will hereafter enjoy." The rest of the way up the hill, waves of newly freed slaves broke over him, joined by some cheering whites. "The streets seemed to be suddenly alive with the colored race," Porter said, the elderly singing hymns, children turning somersaults, everybody shouting. Some poor whites joined in. The admiral needed his guard to keep the president from being overwhelmed. Silent white citizens stood at open windows as Lincoln's party passed.

When the president reached the Executive Mansion, he climbed the stone steps to the seat of the rebellion, cheered by freed slaves and black and white Union troops. He asked for a glass of water and sat in Davis's chair. General Shepley gave him welcome and lunch. General Weitzel asked him how he should treat the people. "If I were in your place," Lincoln said, "I'd let 'em up easy—let 'em up easy."

Escorted by Admiral Porter and the Fifth Massachusetts, a unit of black cavalry, the president and Tad took a carriage ride to Capitol Square. Jefferson had designed the pillared temple that housed the Rebel government. Now it showed signs of disorderly flight. Tables were overturned. Bales of Confederate money lay abandoned and unmissed. Drifts of documents were scattered across the floor.

When Stanton learned that Lincoln was in Richmond, he sent Assistant Secretary Charles Dana after him, with orders, as Dana recalled them, "to keep as close as possible to Mr. Lincoln for the purpose of watching and reporting." Having heard about Weitzel's largesse, Stanton fired off a wire demanding to know "under what authority he is distributing rations to the people of Richmond." Dana told him Grant had authorized it. For feeding desperate Americans, the War Department would be reimbursed from the sale of captured property.

The *Whig* was the only paper with an office still standing. In its last edition under Rebel management, the *Whig* had said, "It is ultimately impossible for the people of the South to embrace the Yankees. Even to recognize them as fellow creatures." An "acre of blood" would separate them forever. On the day of Lincoln's coming, the *Whig* reopened its doors as a voice of the occupation, led by a Unionist Virginian.

— —

Judge Campbell was told that Lincoln had come to Richmond to confer with his generals and would see him at the presidential mansion. "A staff officer came for me," Campbell says. Northern newspapermen noticed the dignified figure sitting sadly in an anteroom.

When the judge was led into Davis's familiar parlor, accompanied by a friend by the name of Gustavus Myers, Abraham Lincoln greeted him, with Weitzel and Shepley in their jarring blue uniforms. It must have seemed strange. Campbell gave the president a courtly bow. He soon picked up an impression that Lincoln was expecting some authorized communication. The judge disabused him of that. Campbell had told Secretary Breckinridge he would stay in Richmond and try to see President Lincoln, he said. He had asked for authority to discuss peace but received no reply. He had stayed on his own, "to perform my duty to my country." The war was over, "and all that remained to be done was to compose the country." He described the city's desolation and asked the president and his generals to preserve order but impose no restraints on the people, make no requisitions on them, demand no oaths of allegiance, leave their churches alone. Lincoln set his mind at ease and so did Weitzel and Shepley.

Campbell felt compelled to speak for Virginia "what would have been more appropriate for a Virginian" if a Virginian were here to say it. The war was under way when Virginia rallied to the South, he said. She had played no part in starting it. The president should summon her influential men, who would surely help restore peace and order, reconstruct the state's political system, renew her membership in the Union, meet "the new and extraordinary conditions of society." For the South as a whole, "a large, liberal, and magnanimous policy" would serve the Northern people as well as the Southern. If Virginia were treated harshly, other Southern states would be taught to resist instead of submit. Campbell quoted from *Henry V* as nearly as he recalled: "When lenity and cruelty play for a kingdom, the gentlest gamester is the soonest winner."

He had expected the collapse for some time, he said, had tried to bring about peace, but no one would take the responsibility. After Hampton Roads, he had spent the rest of the winter in search of the man who would accept the inevitable and lead the South through it. He had gone to Mr. Davis, to Congress, to General Lee. Everyone had pointed to someone else. But now that the end had come, Virginia's public men would restore her to the Union and "aid in the work of pacification." If Lincoln called them together, "the work would be nearly done."

The president asked whom Campbell meant by Virginia's public men. Among others, the judge named General Lee, Senator Hunter, William Cabell Rives, and John B. Baldwin, who had met with Lincoln privately in 1861 to try to find a compromise. The war had been a contest between "close communities." The party that had fought for independence had meant to stay close to the North had it won. Now the winner should make its success "as little aggravating to the other as possible."

Lincoln replied that Campbell's principles were right; "the trouble was how to apply them." He said he was impressed by what the judge had said about finding someone to help him make peace. (He did not cite his own difficulties.) He "wanted to have another talk," and would stay overnight to do so. He invited Campbell to call again tomorrow, and told him "I might bring with me citizens of the place." Nothing was said about oak trees or necks.

Before the judge left, a distinguished old Virginian came to see the president. When Campbell introduced him, Lincoln knew his name. "You fought for the Union in Mexico."

"Mr. Lincoln," he replied, "if the Union will be fair to Virginia, I will fight for the Union again. Younger men than I, Mr. President, will give you that pledge."

"He looked at me hard," the old Virginian recalled, "and shook my hand, and there wasn't any need for him to say anything."

A day or two later, Julia Grant and some other generals' wives steamed up the James on the *Mary Martin* for a sightseeing trip to Richmond. She regretted it immediately.

A carriage had been hired to drive them around the city. One or two carriages bore other privileged tourists, "and occasionally an old colored servant would pass along, looking on us as intruders, as we all felt we were." The city was otherwise deserted, the streets near the public buildings strewn with paper. Julia returned to the *Martin* and slept. Darkness had fallen when she awoke. On the paddle wheeler's deck, she listened to the peeping frogs, looked out at the blackened city, and cried.

Robert E. Lee and what was left of the Army of Northern Virginia, some 30,000 famished men and boys and a few thousand half-dead horses, were still moving west, pursued by Grant and 120,000 healthy troops. Hardship had purged them of their quitters. Many had deserted when the army began its retreat, but a veteran would later recall that "not one of us who remained despaired of the end we sought." They discussed where their miraculous stand would be made, and wondered where the seat of government would be.

For security's sake, Lincoln was persuaded to spend the night on Admiral Porter's *Malvern*, anchored in the James. According to Porter, the captain of the warship *Clinton* came aboard and said he was short of rations. He had given some away to pleading women, "destitute of food." Porter chastised the captain for his profligacy with government property until Lincoln made a gesture with both hands. "Give them all the provisions they want. Give them all they want."

The admiral was embarrassed by the *Malvern*'s accommodations— only one substantial stateroom and a small cabin aft with a sofa and four chairs. "I could not sling a cat around by the tail." Lincoln enjoyed it thoroughly. What pleased him most, he said, was that no one could get at him but those he chose to see. He declined Porter's offer of his stateroom and slept in the small cabin. He would soon tell the admiral that his brief time on the *Malvern* was one of the pleasantest of his life. With peace at hand after four years of war, he would always consider it the holiday of his administration.

He had less than two weeks to live.

CHAPTER TWENTY-FIVE

Allow Judge Campbell to See This, But Do Not Make It Public

It was warm in Richmond on Thursday morning and the ruins still smoldered. On the *Malvern*, Lincoln was preparing to see Judge Campbell, but the South had gambled away a shrinking stack of chips since they met at Hampton Roads. When they spoke on the *River Queen* in February, the Rebels had a capital, Lee was checking Grant, and Sherman had just begun his assault on South Carolina. When they met on the *Malvern* in April, Lee was on the run, Sherman was moving north, Lincoln presided over Richmond, and Davis and his Cabinet were fugitives. With only Campbell left to talk to, Lincoln came back to the table nonetheless.

Having seen Lincoln's interest in the idea that Virginia's leading men could help them make peace, Campbell tried to gather such men to accompany him, but most of them had fled and others declined to come. Even when Campbell shared his proof of the South's inability to fight on, the stigma of conciliation was too much for some, the humiliation too much for others. To meet with Abraham Lincoln, Judge Campbell could find no one more consequential than Gustavus Adolphus Myers, the friend who had accompanied him yesterday. The judge called Myers "an established member of the bar." The acerbic John Jones called him "a little old lawyer" and an influence peddler. He was more than that. A longtime member and sometime chairman of the city council and a leader of Richmond's Jewish community, he had made his home on Governor

Street a literary salon and served as Britain's attorney in the Rebel capital. Still, Campbell had hoped to bring to the President of the United States a weightier leading man than a Richmond city councilman.

Campbell and Myers met Weitzel at the Executive Mansion and the three of them took a carriage to Rockett's Wharf, "no other Gentlemen having appeared," as Myers put it. They boarded the *Malvern* at 10:00 a.m. and the president greeted them cordially in the warship's modest cabin with its sofa and four chairs, acknowledging that they came in no official capacity. Lincoln had drafted a memorandum of terms for peace, which he read line by line, with no less conviction than he had shown at Hampton Roads, pausing to comment on each of his three conditions before moving to the next.

The document said that the National Authority must be restored. Lincoln added that he and the good people of the North had had enough of war. He hoped "in the Providence of God" there would never be another.

The document said that there would be no armistice short of a permanent peace. Lincoln added that he would do all he could to save every Southern life if the Confederacy laid down its arms.

The document said that the executive would not retreat from any of his previous positions on slavery. Lincoln added that all existing presidential acts "must pass for what they are worth"; he would not take them back; he could not do so in good faith even if he had wanted to; "but this would not debar action by other government authorities.'"

His conditions had not changed since Hampton Roads, but his freedom of movement had. The conquest of Richmond and the imminent end of the war had strengthened his hand, and neither Congress nor his Cabinet were there to tell him no. Instead of increasing the pressure, he eased it back. On the *River Queen*, he had refused to treat with Rebels in arms. On the *Malvern*, he repeated to Campbell his refusal to negotiate until the Rebels stopped fighting, but his memorandum said that all

---

* According to Duff Green, a Southern editor, politician, and entrepreneur, Lincoln told Green and Campbell, in a separate conversation that day or the day before, "If you wish to keep your slaves" after coming back into the Union (echoing what Lincoln and Seward had suggested on the *River Queen*), "vote against the amendments to the Constitution. I cannot recall my [emancipation] proclamations. Whether they are binding or not will be a matter for the courts."

propositions consistent with his preconditions "will be respectfully considered and passed upon in a spirit of sincere liberality."

There was more. Lincoln had told Grant that if the commissioners had written "reunion" on a sheet of paper at Hampton Roads, they could have written almost anything else, and the commissioners had been telling whomever would listen that Davis should have sent them back to Lincoln with reasonable terms for reunion. With Richmond at his feet, Lincoln's memorandum implored the fleeing Rebels to do just that, despite what he said to Campbell about refusing to negotiate with Rebels in arms:

> *I now add that it seems useless for me to be more specific with those who will not say they are ready for the indispensable terms, <u>even on condition to be named by themselves.</u> If there be any who are ready for those indispensable terms <u>on any condition whatever</u> let them say so, and state their conditions, so that such conditions can be distinctly known and considered. [Emphasis added]*

This was not just an offer to treat with armed Rebels. It was barely short of a plea.

There was more. On the *River Queen*, Lincoln had said he would use his executive powers to forgo *future* confiscations of property if the war ended now, Seward had added that a forgiving Congress (a laughable oxymoron) might restore what was already taken, and Lincoln had said he would consider such restorations liberally. On the *Malvern*, Lincoln pledged, in writing, that *all* existing confiscations, other than "supposed property in slaves" and property that third parties had acquired, would be "remitted to the people of any State" that stopped resisting the federal government. If they prolonged the war instead, its costs would be allayed by the sale of that property.

Lincoln spoke to Campbell of the Southern leaders too. "It would not be proper to offer a pardon to Mr. Davis," he said. Besides, he went on, perhaps with a crooked grin, Mr. Davis had said he would not take one, and he did not believe in forcing one on anybody. But almost anyone who wanted one could have it for the asking. In a kind, almost teasing way, the president said he would "save any repentant sinner from hanging." If Campbell enjoyed a moment of relief, he did not say so.

The judge's legal mind saw no material difference between the terms he was hearing now and the terms he had heard at Hampton Roads. They should have been accepted then, he thought. They must be accepted now. But the political differences were crucial. No longer could it be said that Abraham the First offered nothing but subjugation and a refusal to treat with the South. On the *River Queen* he had given the Southern peace commissioners nothing in writing. On the *Malvern,* when he finished reading his memorandum inviting Southern leaders to accept his essential terms "on any condition whatever," he handed it to Campbell to publish as he wished. Had he done so at Hampton Roads, Davis could not have suppressed it.

But how to act on it now? Davis and his Congress were gone. With the exception of Judge Campbell, so was the cabal. With no authority to do more, the judge urged the president to suspend the war. The result would be "peace on your own terms." Lincoln agreed to consider it, despite the written rejection of any truce that he had just handed over.

With nothing left to hide, Campbell told Lincoln that Lee could be sustained no more, and slavery was dead. Everybody knew it. Over the winter, he said, talk of compromise had been heard in Richmond from men who had previously spurned it, though no one could be found to make peace. But with Lee on the edge of capture and Richmond occupied, there would be no hesitation to accept the president's terms. The judge handed Lincoln a copy of a document he had given to Davis and Breckinridge, proposing terms of reunion. Lincoln promised to consider it. He had been "meditating a plan," he said, but had not fixed on it, and would make no decision until he returned to City Point. When he was satisfied, he would write General Weitzel in a day or two.

And then he astonished the judge. Pointing uphill to the white-pillared capitol that Jefferson had designed, he said he was inclined to assemble "the very Legislature that has been sitting up yonder," to come back and restore Virginia to the Union and recall her soldiers from the war. He already had a government in Virginia, he said, but it had "a very small margin," and he was not disposed to increase it.* Reconvening the legislature to recognize federal authority was "desirable in many points of view," Lincoln said. He likened it to a tenant caught between contesting landlords and acknowledging the one who had shown the better title. He would like to give the legislature leave to come to Richmond and go home again if it reached no conclusion. Campbell had the impression that he expected it to ratify the Thirteenth Amendment in a show of healing.

Campbell had merely asked to assemble some prominent men. Lincoln had gone much further. The judge was delighted by his willingness to give the defeated state governments "some tolerance." Far more than that, he was talking about giving them some power. Campbell said he thought it "not impossible" that the reassembled legislature would repeal Virginia's secession and withdraw her troops.**

Lincoln asked Gustavus Myers, who had been sitting there quietly, about the composition and sentiments of "the gentlemen who comprise the Legislature," and whether they would come back to Richmond if called. Myers vouched for them.

Further on the subject of Virginia's leading men, Lincoln told Campbell he would like to see Mr. Hunter. They might agree on some proposition to bring the sections together. Based on their talk on the *River Queen*, he said, he believed that Mr. Hunter's intentions were honest, and valued his influence with his people. But Hunter had gone home to Essex County, and Lincoln was leaving for City Point in a few hours. Nothing came of his wish.

Myers told Lincoln that the occupying army's behavior had calmed Richmond's fears and produced kind feelings, but if the people were forced to take an oath of allegiance it would all be spoiled. Lincoln replied

---

* In June 1861, Unionists in northwest Virginia, where slaves and secessionists were scarce, purported to establish a Restored Government of Virginia, an alternative to Richmond's, with Francis H. Pierpont as governor and negligible support in the rest of the state. Its statewide reputation was not enhanced when it consented to detach West Virginia from the Old Dominion. Pierpont's government sat in Alexandria, across the Potomac from Washington, within Union lines and with scant effect.

** North Carolina's legislature seemed ready to do the same. Her Senator William Graham was prepared to advise Davis to send the peace commissioners back to Lincoln to accept his terms and settle things. Graham had told Campbell that if Davis refused, he would urge the legislature in Raleigh to make a separate peace.

that the people should be *encouraged* to take an oath, but he had never attached much importance to demanding one. Then the president turned to Weitzel. The decision would be his. On the carriage ride to the *Malvern*, Weitzel had said he did not believe in forcing principles under oath. He said it again now.

Then Campbell read a paper proposing a military convention between Grant and Lee. Lincoln asked to take it with him, fueling the judge's hopes.

Campbell would later say that this conversation with Lincoln "impressed me favorably and kindly to him," as it had on the *River Queen*, and they parted with mutual good wishes. Admiral Porter had already surmised that their meeting had been cordial, "to judge from their laughter."

At three o'clock that day, the Rebel War Department clerk John B. Jones made a timed and dated entry in his deathwatch on the Confederacy. "I feel that this Diary is near its end."

Eager to join Lincoln, Seward arranged for a revenue cutter to take him to Richmond, then went for a ride in his two-horse carriage with his son Fred, his daughter Fan, and her friend. When the horses suddenly bolted on Vermont Avenue, startled by a slamming coach door, Seward tried to stop them and was thrown to the street like a sack of mail. He was carried unconscious to his home, his battered face unrecognizable, his jaw and right arm broken. His recovery was said to be doubtful.

The Secretary of War was summoned to Seward's side. "Stanton wiped his lips," Fan said, "spoke gently to him," read to him, returned every day to nurse him "like a woman." Seward's jaw was so smashed up it could barely be wired together. His agony kept the household in tears for days. When he tried to bless Stanton, emotion overcame him.

Late that morning, unaware of Seward's suffering, Lincoln returned to City Point on the *Malvern*.

Lincoln wrote to General Weitzel the next day. Having worked past midnight to focus his thoughts, he had limited Virginia's legislators to a de facto sort of recognition and confined them to a single task:

It has been intimated to me that the gentlemen who have acted as the Legislature of Virginia, in support of the rebellion, may now desire to assemble at Richmond, and take measures to withdraw Virginia's troops and other support from resistance to the General Government. If they attempt it, give them permission and protection until, if at all, they attempt some action hostile to the United States, in which case you will notify them, give them reasonable time to leave, and at the end of which time arrest any who remain.

Even now, with their ruined capital taken, if they returned and renewed their treason, Lincoln would let them leave. He closed with a testament of trust in a friend. "Allow Judge Campbell to see this, but do not make it public."

Weitzel sent for Campbell, read him Lincoln's letter, and invited him to write a supporting note to leading Virginians. If Campbell noticed how narrow Lincoln's order was, he did not say so. He asked if influential persons other than legislators could be called to Richmond without fear of arrest. Weitzel said they could, and went the judge one better: The army would provide transportation and accommodations. Campbell composed an appeal to Southern pride and Southern duty and handed it to Weitzel to publish. Despite the North's superior resources, it said, the spirit of the South was unbroken and the war could be prolonged. It was "the province of statesmanship" to prevent this. The "agencies of the Confederate States" were unwilling to negotiate. "Hence the necessity to call upon the Legislature and suspend hostilities" and "bring the minds of the people to consider of peace."

Then Campbell wrote a letter to an honor roll of Virginians, reciting Lincoln's peace terms and his intention to let the legislature assemble if it would accept the Constitution and laws of the United States. "I understood from Mr. Lincoln, if this condition be fulfilled, that no attempt would be made to establish or sustain any other authority." In this the judge took a giant step too far. Nevertheless, when Campbell read his draft to General Shepley, his staff, and Stanton's eyes and ears in the person of Charles Dana, none of them objected. But when Dana wired the War Department, Stanton told him to order General Weitzel not to follow the president's instructions to summon the legislature until further notice.

Then Campbell met with five Virginia legislators. He gave them copies of the memorandum that Lincoln had handed him on the *Malvern*, the presidential instructions to Weitzel to let the legislature withdraw from the war, and Campbell's own letter to influential men. It was for the government of Virginia to decide what to do, he said.

Then he wrote to Weitzel. The spirit of the people was not broken. They were capable of "a prolonged and embarrassing resistance. Humanity as well as patriotism requires that such a contest, which must be in the end fruitless, should be averted." The Confederacy had "made no provision for the possibility of its failure. Its functionaries don't understand how they can negotiate for the subversion or overthrow of their Government." While "reflecting persons" knew that the cause was lost, and were ready for fair terms, the difficulty lay in finding a lawful authority to accept them. The legislature would provide one. In Virginia and other states, elected officials could resolve with their federal counterparts the issues of confiscated property, amnesties, representation in Congress, "the condition of the slave population."

All that was needed was a "very grave, important, and patient inquiry" between the elected representatives of the United States government and the separate state governments, Campbell said, unknowingly echoing Gideon Welles, who thought that the rebellious states could be peeled away one by one, ending the war themselves, leaving Jefferson Davis to preside over nothing.

Grateful for Weitzel's enlightened occupation of the city, Campbell encouraged him to persevere in the "patience, moderation, forbearance, and conciliation that has marked your conduct since you entered Richmond." But when Stanton's man Charles Dana asked Weitzel on Friday evening about letting the churches open on Sunday, the general replied injudiciously. They could hold their services on three conditions. There would be no disloyal invocations. The clergy would not pray for Jefferson Davis. They would pray for Abraham Lincoln.

The President of the United States, who had wished to let Richmond up easy, would be treated like a conquering caliph.

Campbell asked Weitzel's chief of staff, General Shepley, to intervene. Banning prayer for Davis was one thing, Campbell said, ordering prayer for Lincoln was another. Shepley brought the issue to Weitzel. Convinced that the judge was right, but loath to reverse himself, Weitzel sent Shepley to Dana to ask him to amend the order, on Stanton's authority, but the war god had issued no commandments on public worship, and Dana would not interfere. Then Campbell went personally to Weitzel, who sent Shepley back to Dana. Weitzel had meant to ban prayer for Davis, Shepley said. Dana had ordered prayer for Lincoln. Dana had given no such order, and said so. Weitzel must act on his own judgment. Recalling Lincoln's advice, the general revoked his edict compelling the people to bless their conqueror.

Dana would later say that on Richmond's first Sabbath in captivity the sermons were "devout and not political." When Dana reported to Stanton that freedom of religion had been restored, Mars wired Weitzel in the fullness of his wrath. Lincoln smoothed it over in a telegram to Weitzel. He did not recall discussing prayer in Richmond, "but I have no doubt that you have acted in what appeared to you to be the spirit and temper manifested by me while I was there."

Before Lincoln left City Point to comfort Seward, he wired Grant, still dogging Lee's heels, about his meeting with Campbell and his hope that Lee might be recalled to Richmond and be ordered to bring his fellow Virginians, the faintly beating heart of his army, taking them out of the war. "I do not think it very probable that anything will come of this; but I have thought best to notify you, so that if you should see signs, you may understand them." In the meantime, he said, Grant was removing Virginia's troops from the war pretty well on his own. "Nothing I have done, or probably shall do, is to delay, hinder, or interfere with you in your work."

Rumors reached Capitol Hill that Lincoln was letting the Virginia legislature assemble. A fellow Jacobin had never heard "such force and fitness" in Senator Benjamin Wade's swearing. Idle talk had been heard of assassinating Lincoln, Wade said. If the rumors were true, "the sooner he was assassinated the better."

CHAPTER TWENTY-SIX

The Rebels Are Our Countrymen Again

On Saturday morning, April 8, Judge Campbell met at the Executive Mansion with some Northern and Southern dignitaries: Stanton's man Dana, generals Weitzel and Shepley, Gustavus Myers, some Virginia legislators and minor officeholders, and the editor of the defunct *Enquirer.* Dana could see that the other Southerners shared Campbell's views. Though not as bright and articulate as he, they were "thoroughly conscious that they were beaten, and sincerely anxious to stop all further bloodshed and restore peace, law, and order."

The Virginians read to the victors an assortment of memoranda, some less submissive than others, and were told that nothing recognizing Confederate authority would be entertained. If they wanted to compose a message advising their people to stop fighting and obey the laws of the United States, the means would be provided to circulate it. If they chose to call a convention to restore Virginia to the Union, horses would be loaned for the purpose. Make no mistake, they were told; none of this should be misread as overlooking any offenses that any of them had committed. High treason was their unspoken crime. Campbell said he had stayed in Richmond to accept the consequences of his actions and to help restore peace and order. He would gladly perform any labor asked of him but did not wish to participate prominently in a convention.

After Dana left, he was sitting in the lobby of the Spotswood Hotel, whose carpets had been ripped up for Rebel army blankets, when a familiar voice called his name. It was Vice President Andrew Johnson. He drew Dana aside and warned him heatedly not to take the Rebels back unpunished. Their sins had been enormous. They might be dangerous.

They could turn on us again. Campbell later heard that when his letters calling on Virginia's leaders to assemble were read in Johnson's presence he counted himself "strongly and profanely hostile."

In the company of Grant, the hot-blooded Phil Sheridan was pursuing Lee, nipping at his heels, killing and capturing his troops, taking casualties in return. With hundreds of lives and limbs being lost every day to the death throes of the Confederacy, Lincoln wanted the Virginia legislature to assemble immediately. He told Stanton that Sheridan seemed to be getting Rebel soldiers out of the war "faster than this Legislature could think."

On the bright and beautiful Sunday of April 9, in the bucolic village of Appomattox Court House, in the parlor of Wilmer McLean, a sugar broker who had moved his family to safer ground after a shell fell through his chimney at Bull Run, Lee surrendered the Army of Northern Virginia to Grant, who had finally boxed him in. The story of Grant's compassion has been told ever since. Lee and his officers and men were amnestied and allowed to go home. Having eaten next to nothing for over a week, they were given federal rations. The officers kept their sidearms. The cavalry and artillerymen kept their horses. Lee said it would "do much toward conciliating our people." Grant forbade celebration. "The rebels are our countrymen again." The universal amnesty he had given Lee and his army was broader than the one that Lincoln had specifically authorized, which did not apply to generals or senior Rebels who had resigned from Congress, the federal bench, or the US military. Far from repudiating it, the president embraced it.

Several Confederate armies more or less worthy of the name were still in the field, most notably what was left of General Johnston's in North Carolina, another in Texas, a third in Alabama. Smaller organized forces and guerrilla bands were scattered across the South. Grant told Lee that he hoped their own transaction would lead to the end of the war and prevent any further loss of life. Lee said little.

Unaware of the momentous event, Lincoln returned to Washington late that afternoon on word of Seward's accident and went straight to the governor's home, sacrificing his fervent wish to welcome Grant back to City Point whenever Lee surrendered. He stretched himself out on Seward's bed, brought his head up close to his friend's, reached behind him to hold Fan Seward's hand, and talked about touring a hospital that day, shaking hands with hundreds of wounded men. He felt as if he had been chopping wood, he said, trying to raise a smile. Seward could barely speak.

When the news of Lee's surrender arrived that night, Stanton threw his arms around the president and ordered illuminations. Graciously enough, GRANT was displayed in gaslight across the War Department's facade. It was Grant who had subtracted the Virginians from the war after all. At daybreak, the hollow boom of cannon awakened Washington and Richmond, bringing joy to one, despair to the other. Gideon Welles made an entry in his diary. "Guns are firing, bells ringing, flags flying, men laughing, children cheering, all are jubilant." In Richmond, a citizen wrote, "God help us, we must take refuge in unbelief."

When Uncle Gideon went to see him in the morning, the president was effervescent. There would be no final battle of annihilation. The Army of Northern Virginia was no more. The war would sputter out.

The news reached Jefferson Davis as he dined with his Cabinet in Danville. An officer handed him a note. He read it and passed it down the table, and "a great silence prevailed for a moment." Judah Benjamin told a friend he would never be taken alive. Far from condemning Lee, Davis believed that a leader "less resolute, an army less heroically resisting fatigue, constant watching, and starvation, would long since have reached the conclusion that surrender was a necessity." Lee had reached it months ago. He had turned and fought repeatedly on his hopeless retreat from Petersburg, leaving thousands of men and boys dead and twice as many maimed on his fields of Southern honor.

On the day after the surrender, Grant and his staff rode over to Lee's camp and were stopped by armed men. "The force of habit is hard to overcome," a Northern officer said. A message was sent to Lee, who rode out with his own aides. They raised their hats to one another and the officers withdrew in blue and gray semicircles around their chiefs. Grant said he hoped the war would end soon. Lee said he had been anxious to stop it for some time, and trusted that everything would be done to conciliate the people. He could not predict what the other armies or President Davis would do, but he thought they would follow his example. Prolonging the war would be pointless. He would devote himself to pacifying "the country" and bringing his people back. His own heart had always been for the Union, he said. He could "find no justification for the politicians who had brought on the war," the extremists on both sides.

Grant said no one had greater influence in the South than Lee. He might use it to urge the other commanders to make peace. He could not do it, Lee said, not without consulting President Davis. Grant urged him to do so. It was not his place, Lee said. The civilian authorities would surely conclude as he had. The generals exchanged a few more words, raised their hats to one another again, and parted.

Lincoln asked "Governor" Francis Pierpont to the White House that day to discuss the transplantation of his ersatz government of Virginia from Alexandria to Richmond. The president spoke of his meetings with Judge Campbell, their discussion about the legislature, how Campbell had tried to find a leader willing to make peace. Lincoln said Pierpont's government and its legitimacy were "fully in my mind" when he spoke with Campbell. He had authorized the Rebel legislature to perform a single act—to withdraw Virginia's forces from the war—"and with this act I expected their powers as legislators to cease. They had put the army in the field, why not take it out and quit?" But "if I had known that General Lee would surrender so soon I would not have issued the proclamation."

On Tuesday, April 11, Grant and his senior officers got back to City Point before dawn. He signed a few dispatches, then rose and turned wryly to an aide. "On to Mexico."

A festive breakfast was improvised. Someone at the table said the general should go to Richmond for a triumphal tour. He waved the idea away. His wife said he should go, and persisted when he said no. Then the general leaned in close. "Hush, Julia. Do not say another word on this subject. I would not distress these people." They were feeling their defeat bitterly. She would not have him twist their wounds. No doubt recalling her own forlorn visit to the beaten Rebel capital, Julia urged no more. Instead, the Grants and some senior officers took the *Mary Martin* up the Potomac. There was triumph enough in Washington.

On a misty, overcast day in Richmond, after fire had destroyed its newspapers, after Lee had surrendered its leverage and its government had fled, thirty-three Virginians—including the *Enquirer*'s editor, the *Examiner*'s publisher, eight legislators, and Richmond's aged mayor—came together and issued an "Address to the People of Virginia." Written by Campbell and signed by the others, it "earnestly" summoned twenty-two other leading Virginians, Hunter among them, and called for the governor and the legislature to reconvene on April 25, not only for a "free deliberation" on the restoration of peace in Virginia, but also for "the adjustment of questions involving life, liberty, and property that have arisen in the State as a consequence of the war," a steep jurisdictional step beyond Lincoln's mandate to let the legislature withdraw Virginia from the rebellion. The US Army would guarantee their freedom and provide transportation. The people were assured that their persons and property were safe. Campbell submitted the document to Weitzel and Shepley. It was sent after Shepley made revisions.

In Washington City, the Cabinet met that day without its suffering Secretary of State. According to Gideon Welles, the subject was cotton. The reassembly of the Virginia legislature was touched upon only briefly.

Stanton and Attorney General James Speed spoke ill of the idea. No one but the president had a good word to say.

⌁

In "a mean room" in Greensboro, North Carolina, to which they had fled, Davis and some Cabinet members met that day with generals Johnston and Pierre Beauregard, the victor at First Bull Run. No one could be sure whether they despised their commander in chief more than he despised them. His Secretary of the Navy called their dealings with Davis "smothered quarrels."

Davis held forth on "future operations" like a man in an opium dream. He would later say he understood the gravity of the Confederacy's position, "seriously affected" as it was by the fall of its capital, the surrender of Robert E. Lee, the loss of the Army of Northern Virginia, and the resulting "discouragement," but "I did not think we should despair" with three armies still standing "and a vast extent of rich and productive territory both east and west of the Mississippi, *whose citizens had evidenced no disposition to surrender*" [emphasis added]. Varina said of her husband that even in the darkest hours before Richmond fell, "his piety held out the hope that God would miraculously shield us." He had summoned his generals now, not to discuss a peace negotiation, but to solve a military problem. In the mind of Jefferson Davis, many of Lee's deserters had gone home to continue the struggle deeper south, and "I had reason to believe that the spirit of the army in North Carolina was unbroken."

Had Davis stayed in his capital, it would have been he, not Campbell, who sat in his parlor with Lincoln, with Lee still armed and dangerous, and received Lincoln's offer to consider peace and reunion on "any condition whatever." As it was, Lee was out of the war and Davis was with his generals in a mean room in Greensboro. He could look neither man in the eye, staring at a torn strip of paper, twisting it in his hands. In the mind of Jefferson Davis, "the war had now shrunk into narrow proportions." General Johnston, he thought, "seemed far less than sanguine."

When he asked for Johnston's views, he got a straight answer: "Sir, my views are that our people are tired of the war, feel themselves whipped and will not fight." His men were stealing artillery horses to facilitate desertions. His remaining North Carolinians would desert if he left their state. It would be "the greatest of human crimes for us to attempt to continue the war . . . to complete the devastation of our country and ruin of its people." Johnston proposed that Davis should "exercise at once the only function of government still in his possession and open negotiations for peace." General Beauregard, Secretary of War Breckinridge, and two other Cabinet members concurred. Davis and Judah Benjamin did not. Davis thought that even from "the gloomiest view"—that reunion was inevitable—they could get better terms with armies in the field, a thought he might have had in February, when Lee still had one. But Davis would later say he "yielded to the judgment of my Constitutional advisors," of whom only Benjamin had the stomach and poor judgment to keep fighting. He gave Johnston leave to propose to Sherman that the civil authorities should meet and negotiate peace.

———

A crowd assembled on the White House lawn on the night of Lee's surrender. They cheered themselves hoarse when Tad leaned out of the center window and waved the captured Rebel battle flag that someone had given him at City Point. When a keeper pulled him back by the seat of his pants, his father appeared in his wake, turning the buoyant crowd into "an agitated sea of hats, faces, and men's arms." He spoke for just a moment and drew an appreciative laugh when he said he would speak more formally soon: "I shall have nothing to say then if it is all dribbled out of me now."

He honored his pledge on the following night and appeared once again at the window. A lamp was produced to illuminate him. The ovation took minutes to subside. He delivered "a carefully prepared speech," according to Gideon Welles, "intended to promote harmony and union." Tad crouched this time at his feet, gathering the pages as he dropped them one by one, calling for another, thrilled by his part in the show.

Lincoln thanked Grant, his officers and men, and "He from Whom all blessings flow." Then he spoke of the problem of healing. Whether the wayward states had truly gone out of the Union or had never really left it was a "pernicious abstraction." They had surely departed from "their proper, practical relation" to it. The object was to get them back in. There had been no war between independent nations; there was no legal government with which to treat, no one with authority to give up the rebellion for any other man, no one with whom to speak but "disorganized and discordant elements. Nor is it a small additional embarrassment that we, the loyal people, differ among ourselves as to the mode, manner, and means of reconstruction." He added a note of mystery. It might become his duty "to make some new announcement to the people of the South. I am considering, and shall not fail to act, when satisfied that action will be proper." He alluded, no doubt, to the thought that he had vetted with Judge Campbell and was still turning over in his mind—the prospect of inviting the Southern state legislatures to recall their troops voluntarily and freely rejoin the Union. He may not have abandoned entirely the possibility of fair incentives.

Standing in the crowd was the actor John Wilkes Booth, up close to the portico with a psychopathic admirer named Lewis Powell, a burly Rebel veteran of Gettysburg. Beside them was another angry Southerner, close enough to marvel at the president's height.

Lincoln touched on the issue of whether "the colored man" should be given the vote. "I would myself prefer," he said, "that it were now conferred on the very intelligent and those who serve our cause as soldiers."

Booth turned to his twisted friends. "That means nigger citizenship. That's the last speech he will ever make. Now, by God, I'll put him through."

CHAPTER TWENTY-SEVEN

I Am as One Walking in a Dream

Lincoln needed someone to talk to, and Seward's jaw was broken. He was having second thoughts about reconvening the Virginia legislature. He summoned Gideon Welles and asked for his opinion. Stanton and the others didn't like it, Welles said. Welles doubted its wisdom himself. To assemble a Rebel legislature would recognize their legitimacy, and they might "conspire against us."

Fresh from Richmond, Lincoln had no fear of that. The Rebels were beaten and done, he said. It would be better for the Virginians to "undo their own work." He felt sure that they would. Lee had quit the war, mooting any need to withdraw his Virginians from it, but self-government must be reestablished as soon as possible. It would be best for Virginia's leaders to turn themselves and their neighbors into good Union men again. On the other hand, with his Cabinet against him, perhaps he had made a mistake. He was ready to correct it if he had.

Welles said Virginia's "so-called Legislature" would probably offer terms that seemed reasonable but were not; why let that happen when we are now in charge?

Lincoln said he wanted conciliation and cared less about form than results. The Rebels had been in error. They had resorted to arms and fought well. Now they were beaten and humbled. It was best to meet them as fellow countrymen, reasonable, intelligent men with "rights that we are willing and disposed to respect."

Welles stood his ground. We never recognized them when they were in arms against us, he said. Why now? The legislature might be defiant, refuse to urge their people to submit. And then there was Pierpont's government in Alexandria. How can we renounce it and recognize the rival it helped us resist?

Lincoln said again that the Rebels were whipped. He had seen it himself. There might be something in the other concerns—Pierpont's government, the taint of a Rebel legislature—but he did not think much of them. Pierpont's was the only *legal* government, but public sentiment must not be overlooked. (Most Virginians out of reach of Northern bayonets thought the Alexandria government was a sham.) Lincoln had never intended to treat the Rebel legislature as legitimate, he said—a thought he had not shared with Campbell—but its members were the leaders of their counties, and their influence should be used in this transition.

As he spoke, indignation crept in. He was surprised to be so misconstrued, he said. The Confederacy would disintegrate if its states embraced reunion. The very act of Rebel legislators dissolving their own body would have a good influence. All of that said, it might be best to abandon the idea. He could not move it forward "with all of you opposed." Welles could see that Lincoln's friends had disappointed him yet again, Uncle Gideon most of all, an old states' rights Democrat, but Lincoln gave it up. More or less.

He sent General Weitzel a wire: "Is there any sign of the rebel Legislature coming together on the understanding of my letter to you? If there is any such sign, inform me what it is. If there is no such sign you may as [well] withdraw the offer." The wobble in his message was plain. The president needed stiffening. Stanton worked on him for hours in the morning in the White House and well into the afternoon at the War Department. When Weitzel replied to Lincoln's wire, he sensed its ambivalence too: "The passports have gone out for the Legislature," he wrote, "and it is common talk that they will come together." Then the general reminded the president about letting the people up easy.

Stanton kept pressing Lincoln. To empower the legislature "would be giving away the scepter of the conqueror." Congress would not stand for it. There was no further need to remove Virginia's troops; Lee had done that. A legislature of beaten Rebels would deny the vote to Negroes, whom men had died to free. They would have no rights, no hope, no more than a change of title. To hand power back to the traitors as if nothing had happened would squander the lives and sacrifices that had won the war. Stanton was "full of feeling," a witness said, and the president listened silently, "in profound thought."

In the end Lincoln buckled. He had never authorized an open-ended mandate for a reconvened legislature. Nonetheless, he sat at Stanton's desk and composed a message to Weitzel. He had just seen Judge Campbell's letter, it said, which falsely assumed that he had recognized the legislature and empowered it "to settle all differences with the United States. I have done no such thing. I spoke of them as 'the gentlemen who have acted as the Legislature of Virginia in support of the rebellion,'" and authorized them only to withdraw Virginia's troops. Now Grant had captured those troops. Judge Campbell had mistaken his meaning and was pressing for a truce despite his refusal to grant one. The authorization to recall the legislature should be withdrawn, along with the paper he had given to Judge Campbell.

Lincoln handed what he had written to the Secretary of War. "There," he said, "I think this will suit you." Stanton told him no. The legislators were on their way to Richmond. Weitzel should keep them out. Lincoln added a final sentence: "Do not allow them to assemble; but if any have come, allow them safe-return to their homes." He handed it back to the secretary. "Exactly right," Stanton said. As Mars later crowed, he had won his battle to "exclude the Southern leaders from any participation in the restoration of the Union."

The news did not please Grant. Mistakenly believing that Stanton had countermanded the summoning of the legislature on his own, Grant called him "a man who never questioned his own authority, and who always did in wartime what he wanted to do." Indeed he had, but not on his own authority. He had worn Lincoln down.

Hunter was back in Richmond, to meet with the Virginia legislature and add his stature to Campbell's in their stand for reunion. He was ordered to leave within twenty-four hours.

Before he complied, he and Campbell joined forces one last time and went to see General Ord, the new man in charge in Richmond

(Weitzel had been relieved) and told him they would like to see President Lincoln. For Campbell, the Confederacy's leaders had been paralyzed by the necessity to accept reunion. Now every man was "making his separate treaty," swearing allegiance to the old flag in return for food and amnesty.

On Thursday, April 13, General Ord wrote to Campbell by instruction of the president. Since the gentlemen of the "insurrectionary government of the Legislature of Virginia" had been allowed to reconvene, their meeting had become unnecessary. The president wanted the authorizing paper withdrawn. Campbell sent Ord the only paper he had—the term sheet Lincoln had given him on the *Malvern*. He had acted on the authority of the president and General Weitzel, he said, to bring peace to Virginia on the president's terms, by the agency of the very authorities that had fought the United States. Lee's surrender would "preclude the possibility of failure." There could be no better plan. Ord issued a public order rescinding it.

On Friday, April 14, Stanton unveiled to the Cabinet a memorandum on the fate of Virginia and North Carolina, a glimpse of the Southern future. Grant was there to see it, at the president's invitation. Lincoln said he had not reviewed it but was glad to have it. A plan should be in place before Congress returned in December. He asked Stanton to read it aloud. Its essence was simple: The prodigal states would be ruled by martial law. Self-government and readmission to the Union would come, but only in deliberate due course.

The president played for time. He wanted his advisers to think hard on it and deliberate later, he said, for "no more important issue could come before us or any future Cabinet." He had not had time to study the plan. Mr. Stanton had given it to him only yesterday. "We should probably make modifications." Stanton said it was only a draft.

Gideon Welles agreed that immediate action must be taken, and thanked the Secretary of War for his work, but objected to the element of military control. Having defended the Pierpont administration as Virginia's lawful government, "how can we now abandon it?" Lincoln called

Welles's exceptions well taken—some of them, at least. He said he had once been willing to have General Weitzel summon Virginia's "leading Rebels" (no longer its leading men), but they were not the legitimate legislature. The Pierpont legislature was. Ever bristling when challenged, Stanton said again that his plan was just a draft.

Lincoln said it was nothing less than providential that the rebellion had been crushed just as Congress adjourned, leaving none of "the disturbing elements of that body to hinder and embarrass us." If the Cabinet acted wisely, the Southern states could be "reanimated" before Congress returned. Congress had the right to admit or exclude its members—he could not control that—but he could recognize state governments that renewed their loyalty whether Congress liked it or not. He could give them federal judges, marshals, post offices, all the other accoutrements of normalcy. There were men who objected to these views, but those men were not here, "and we must make haste to do our duty before they come here." He could not join in their vindictiveness. He wanted no persecutions, no "bloody work." No one should expect *him* to hang these Southern men, even the worst of them. He threw up his hands and shook them. "Frighten them out of the country," he said, "let down the bars, scare them off. Enough lives have been lost."

Jacob Thompson, who had served with Stanton as Secretary of the Interior in Buchanan's Cabinet and was one of Davis's agents in the Niagara Falls fiasco, had lately been plotting in Canada to torch Northern cities, a hanging offense if ever there was one. Late that afternoon, Charles Dana, who was back at the War Department, received a wire from a federal official in Maine who had learned that Thompson would arrive that night in Portland to board a ship for England. "What are the orders?" When Dana took the news to the Secretary of War, Stanton did not hesitate. "Arrest him!" But as Dana turned to leave, the secretary thought better of it, no doubt recalling what Lincoln had said about letting down the bars. "No, wait. Better go over and see the President."

Dana crossed the lawn. It was Good Friday. The business day was done and the White House was eerily empty. He walked upstairs to the president's office, encountering not a soul. As he turned to leave, Lincoln called out from an anteroom. He was washing his hands.

"Halloo, Dana! What is it? What's up?" Dana read him the telegram about Thompson's impending escape.

"What does Stanton say?"

"He says arrest him, but I should refer the question to you."

"Well," said Lincoln slowly, wiping his hands as he spoke. "No, I rather think not. When you have an elephant by the hind leg and he's trying to run away, it's best to let him run."

When Dana returned, Stanton was not pleased. "Oh stuff!" he is said to have exclaimed. Or words to that effect.

As Thompson the Rebel arsonist prepared to sail for Britain, blissfully unaware of his surreptitious pardon, his benefactor was dressing for the theater.

At a little past eight, the president and Mrs. Lincoln got into a closed coach beneath the White House portico. Charlie Forbes, the president's Irish valet, his traveling companion to Hampton Roads, gave a hand to Mrs. Lincoln, who called him "my friend Charles." Then Charlie climbed up on the box, folded the president's plaid shawl over his arm, and nodded to the coachman. Two cavalrymen followed. They stopped on the way for the Lincolns' guests, Major Henry Rathbone and his fiancée Clara Harris, a senator's daughter. General and Mrs. Grant had declined the honor. Julia could not abide Mary Lincoln for an evening.

When the carriage arrived at Ford's Theatre, Charlie handed the passengers down with a smile and a friendly word. After they were seated in the presidential box, he closed the door to its passageway and sat down outside it in a wooden chair. Charlie was unarmed.

Lincoln's friend Simon P. Hanscom, the *National Republican*'s editor, had been lounging around the White House, consistent with his habit, when a sergeant came over from the War Department with a sealed telegram. It might be news of Johnston's surrender. Hanscom volunteered to walk it over to the president. Charlie Forbes knew him and waved him into the box. When Hanscom opened the door, Clara Harris turned around in alarm, then settled back in her chair. The telegram was from General Ord. Mr. Hunter had arrived in Richmond, it said. "He and Judge Campbell wish a permit for their visit to you at Washington, I think, with important communication." Lincoln read it and put it aside. He would deal with it tomorrow.

At about the same time, Lewis Powell, the burly thug in the thrall of John Wilkes Booth, talked his way into Seward's house, tried to shoot his son Fred, pistol-whipped him when the gun misfired, pushed his screaming sister aside, burst into Seward's room when a male nurse opened the door, slashed the nurse with a Bowie knife, knocked him to the floor, and hacked at the governor's face and throat as he lay there helpless in bed. Oddly aware that the blade was cold, Seward was engulfed in a "rainfall" of blood. His neck brace saved his life—that, and his presence of mind. He rolled off the bed in agony with his shattered jaw and arm while his nurse and another son struggled with the assassin, enduring his slashing knife until he broke away. He stabbed a State Department messenger on his way out to Lafayette Square.

A few minutes later at Ford's Theatre, John Wilkes Booth strolled casually down the dress-circle aisle to the presidential box and presented his card to Charlie Forbes, who knew his famous name. It was Charlie who let him in.

Gideon Welles wrote a passage in his diary. "At the White House all was silent and sad." His wife had stayed with Mary Lincoln all night, exhausted and hysterical as she was. Mary's friend Eliza Blair Lee would all but live in the White House for days. When Welles and his wife went down the central staircase with Attorney General Speed, Lincoln's boy Tad had been looking out a window at the foot of the stairs.

"Oh, Mr. Welles," he said, "who killed my father?"

"Neither Speed nor myself could restrain our tears," Uncle Gideon says, "nor give the poor boy any satisfactory answer."

The new president met with his Cabinet that day. "President Johnson is not disposed to treat treason lightly," Welles told his diary, "and the chief

Rebels he would punish with extreme severity." The Jacobin senator Benjamin Wade proposed to exile or hang "a baker's dozen." Johnson wanted to hang many more.

On the day Johnson met with his Cabinet, the Confederate Secretary of War John Breckinridge, in Charlotte with Davis's traveling entourage, on the run from federal cavalry, informed him of Lincoln's assassination. Davis spoke to some Rebel troopers who had ridden into town. He made no mention of Lincoln's murder. He would not despair of the cause, he said, but "remain with the last organized band upholding the flag." He would later say of Lincoln that for "an enemy so relentless in the war for our subjugation, we could not be expected to mourn," yet his death was "a great misfortune to the South." He had power over the Northern people and no "personal malignity toward the people of the South." His successor "was without power in the North, and the embodiment of malignity toward the Southern people, perhaps the more so because he had betrayed and deserted them in the hour of need." His crime had been staying loyal when his home state of Tennessee seceded.

General Sherman, the curse of the South, sat down with General Johnston that day at a farmhouse west of Durham. They liked each other immediately. Months earlier, Sherman had told the mayor of Atlanta and two of his city councilmen that peace would be won by unrelenting war, but "when peace does come, you may call on me for anything. Then will I share with you the last cracker, and watch with you to shield your homes and families against danger from every quarter." Now he granted Johnston breathtaking terms.

Rejecting Johnston's proposal of a peace negotiation between two countries, for the Confederacy *was* no country, Sherman offered him the same terms Grant had given Lee; but Johnston said the generals could make a broader peace, "as other generals had done" (none of them American). When they met again the next day, Breckinridge was there, having ridden out to join them from Davis's side. Sherman invoked the generous sentiments that Lincoln had expressed to him and Grant and Porter on the *River Queen*, and went much further than Grant had gone to implement them, further than a general could go. Invoking the *executive* author-ity, albeit conditioned on the executive's approval, he allowed Johnston's army to return their arms to their state arsenals, guaranteed the Southern people's political rights, recognized their state governments, gave them a general amnesty, and effectively restored them to the Union, which Alec Stephens would later call "the whole professed object of the war."* Then Sherman produced a bottle and shared it with his new Southern friends.

When the news arrived in Washington on the day Lincoln's funeral train left, Stanton was appalled, and Stanton was not alone. With his Cabinet's unanimous support, the new president nullified what Sherman had done. Grant brought the word to Sherman himself. When General Johnston was told, he wired the news to Breckinridge and proposed to disband his army, "to prevent devastation to the country." On Davis's behalf, Breckinridge replied that if it came to that, Johnston should escape and come to Davis's rescue with whatever mounted forces he could bring, while the infantry slipped away with their weapons. Johnston wired back. Escape was "impracticable," he said. "We have to save the people, spare the blood of the army, and save the high civil functionaries. Your plan, I think, can only do the last." And then he surrendered all over again, on terms such as Grant gave Lee. Only disconnected remnants of Rebel forces remained, in Texas, Alabama, and pockets of senseless rage.

On May 2, Davis met with Breckinridge, General Braxton Bragg, and five cavalry commanders in Abbeville, South Carolina. Once the panic had passed, he said, the three thousand men they could muster would be enough for the people to rally around until the country recovered its will. The officers looked at each other. It was not possible, they said. There was nothing left to fight with. They would risk his modest escort to defend his personal safety but would not put a single man in jeopardy or "fire another shot" to keep the war going. The truth hit Davis then. He stood up to leave, so ashen that Breckinridge offered him his arm. "Then all is indeed lost."

---

* The document Sherman signed was prepared by Davis's postmaster general, who had ridden out with Breckinridge. Sherman would later claim that when Lincoln met with Porter, Grant, and Sherman on the *River Queen,* he had authorized the terms that Sherman gave Johnston, but the evidence is strong that Lincoln had merely spoken in magnanimous generalities. He would not have ceded his executive powers to Sherman or anyone else.

Davis would later say that if Johnston had refused to surrender, he could have reached his commander in chief with his cavalry, light artillery, and many mounted infantry. Together they could have cut their way to the Mississippi, gathered men who had deserted "to escape surrender," and revived "the drooping spirits of the country." Once they had crossed the great river (how, he does not say, controlled as it was by Union gunboats), they could have joined with men who had the means, the will, and the space to fight. And then, Davis said, the foiled Yankee nation should have agreed, "on the basis of a return to the Union, to acknowledge the Constitutional rights of the States, and by a convention, or quasi-treaty, to guarantee security of person and property. To this hope I persistently clung, and, if our independence could not be achieved, so much, at least, I trusted might be gained."

On the *Malvern*, Lincoln had offered to negotiate more than that, with whomever could speak for the South, "even on condition to be named by themselves," and had put it in writing in his own hand. Had he done it at Hampton Roads—given it to the peace commissioners to publish, staked his presidency on the South's return to the Union with compensated emancipation and its Constitutional rights, taken the issue to the people over the heads of the Jacobins—history might have been different. Tens of thousands of young Americans had died since then. Many thousands more had been crippled, physically or emotionally. They would suffer for decades to come.

In lieu of Lincoln's lenient reconstruction plan, the essence of Stanton's was adopted. As Judge Campbell would later say, the defeated states were converted into military departments, "designated by Arabic numerals. Under such rule the most dishonest, despicable, and debased governments were established that ever existed on this continent." Due in large part to defiant Southern racism, all but one of the seceded states (President Johnson's Tennessee was readmitted in 1866) were excluded from the Union for three to five years. A century of bitterness followed.

On May 4, General Gorgas made an entry in his Richmond diary. "The calamity which has fallen upon us in the total destruction of our government is of a character so overwhelming that I am as yet unable to comprehend it. I am as one walking in a dream, and expecting to awake. I cannot see its consequences, nor shape my own course, but am just moving along until I can see my way at some future day. It is marvelous that a people that a month ago had money, armies, and the attributes of a nation should today be no more, and that we live, breathe, move, talk as before—will it be so when the soul leaves the body behind it?"

Epilogue

The Southerners after the War

JEFFERSON DAVIS

On May 10, 1865, the 4th Michigan Cavalry captured Davis and his party near Irwinville, Georgia. He tried to escape. His own escorting cavalry were absent, scouting nearby, but federal troopers fired on each other in confusion. Two more men lost their lives to Jefferson Davis's refusal to surrender.

He was charged with treason and imprisoned at Fort Monroe in a cell overlooking Hampton Roads. His jailers tacked a huge American flag to the wall. He fought them physically when they shackled him. Preston Blair asked President Johnson to ease his treatment. Thaddeus Stevens offered his legal services, which Davis declined, not for lack of confidence in the Jacobin congressman's abilities, but because he proposed to argue that the Confederacy was a conquered principality, and captured princes are not hanged for treason. "That would have been an excellent argument for me," Davis said, "but not for my people."

After two years in jail, he was freed on a bond that Horace Greeley helped raise. The charges were later dropped. True to his word, he refused to seek a pardon or swear allegiance to the United States, and never regained his citizenship. "He had not changed his beliefs in the least degree," Varina said, and "could not honestly express the contrition he did not feel." He accepted the presidency of the Carolina Life Insurance Company, traveled in Europe, wrote a bitter, carping memoir and *A Short History of the Confederate States of America.*

When Alec Stephens's book on the war assigned the failure of the Hampton Roads Peace Conference to him, Davis called Hunter "my hope for truth and justice." After Hunter's account appeared, Davis dismissed it as lies, senility, and "sophomorian twaddle," and condemned its "injustice to the heroic mothers" of the South, who would not have flinched at sacrificing their sixteen-year-old sons. Hunter replied that Davis knew little about mothers.

Years after the fact, Davis still smarted over Lincoln's reception of his envoys on a riverboat instead of at the White House. He faulted the commissioners for it. He had instructed them to "proceed to Washington City," and this they had failed to do.

Reviled in the South during his presidency, he was glorified in defeat. He spoke at many Confederate memorial ceremonies, not including the dedication of a statue of Lee in 1883. He canceled his appearance when he learned that General Johnston would chair the event. "I could not with due self-respect appear before a meeting over which he was to preside."

In 1878, an Episcopal minister wrote to Davis from Virginia, still struggling with the outcome of the war: "I know that we were right," he said, "and I know that God permitted our overthrow, but I do not know how to reconcile these facts." Davis had heard it many times before. God's favor required not only that a cause be righteous, he replied, but also that it be righteously defended. "Had we succeeded, how well and wisely we would have used our power was made questionable by various manifestations in the last twelve months of the war. . . . Perhaps the furnace to which we have been subjected was necessary for our purification. Has it not been shown by the result that we were more right than even our own people knew? And the world may now learn how faithless, dishonest, and barbarous our enemies were."

The Jefferson Davis Highway still connects Washington to Virginia, one of many such monuments to his name. He died at the age of eighty-one, in 1889. "In the greatest effort of his life," Varina said, he failed from the predominance of some of his "noble qualities . . . his courage, integrity, and devotion to duty. . . . His family who survive him were engulfed in the common disaster and utter ruin, but are proud of his record, and hopefully await the verdict of posterity."

VARINA DAVIS

Educated in Philadelphia, Varina Davis was fond of saying that her grandfather had been Governor of New Jersey and her mother a Virginian, which made her a proud "half breed." Left widowed with scant resources, she declined a house politely when the city of Richmond offered her one, and moved with a daughter to Manhattan. She composed a graceful memoir of her life with Jefferson Davis, submitted charming essays to Joseph Pulitzer's *New York World,* and made a good living with her pen. In an article published in the *World* in the first year of the twentieth century, she called Ulysses S. Grant a humanitarian and "a great man" and declared that God "in his wisdom" had decreed the survival of the Union. After meeting her by chance at a Hudson Valley resort, she befriended Julia Grant "with the sympathy of one who has suffered in a like way."

A sought-after figure in the city's social life, she enjoyed a daily carriage ride through Central Park and died in 1906 in a room overlooking it, but chose to be buried in Richmond, where her tombstone reads, "At Peace."

JOHN CAMPBELL

Three weeks after Lincoln's assassination, Grant had Campbell arrested on suspicion of abetting it. An officer's letter to Davis implicitly offering to kill Lincoln had been found in the Confederate archives. Davis had sent it to Judah Benjamin, who forwarded it to Campbell, who sent it "for attention" to the adjutant general, who reviewed all officers' letters. The judge was arrested at home in the night and taken out in irons in the presence of his terrified wife. No one told him why. He was cleared of the assassination but accused of leading General Weitzel into "the grave misconduct" of recalling the Virginia legislature. Lincoln, it was said, had intended no more than to gather individuals to help restore order.

Campbell wrote to Attorney General Speed from his prison cell in Georgia. General Weitzel was with him on the *Malvern,* he said, and heard the president speak. "It never entered into my imagination to conceive that he used the word 'legislature' to express a convention of individuals." The notion was in fact absurd, and his friends Justice Curtis and Justice Nelson persuaded President Johnson to release him. "I have retained a strong regard for him," Curtis wrote, "founded on his purity and strength of character, his intellectual power, his great attainments, and his humane and genial nature. . . . "

After Campbell was freed, he wrote in gratitude to Curtis, making no attempt to glorify his attempts to stop the war. "I do not pretend to have done more than to accept conditions that were inexorable," he said; and as for the war's results, "I concur in the policy of abolishing negro slavery throughout the United States. I regard the revolution as the most radical and momentous that has ever occurred in any country."

The judge moved his family to New Orleans, where he built a successful law practice and returned to the Supreme Court to argue several cases. In 1878, he ran into Jefferson Davis on a New Orleans street. Davis wrote home to Varina about it. Judge Campbell had "hesitated as if about to speak," Davis said. "I looked over his head and passed on. I want no controversy with any one, but, hating treachery, must repel a traitor."

Campbell died in 1889 at the age of seventy-seven. No highways are named for him.

ROBERT M. T. HUNTER

Unlike Alec Stephens, Hunter had not charmed Grant, who ordered him arrested with other "particularly obnoxious political leaders in the State." General Halleck objected: "Hunter is said to be at his home advising all who visit him to support the Union cause." Lincoln had recommended against disturbing him. "I would prefer not to arrest him unless specifically ordered to do so." Grant saw the wisdom of Halleck's view, and acquiesced in Hunter's liberty, but Hunter was soon arrested and imprisoned with Campbell nonetheless, at Fort Pulaski in Georgia, and charged with treason.

Campbell told Hunter that Lincoln had expressed admiration for him on the *Malvern,* and respect for his influence in the South, and had thought aloud to Campbell that he might have hammered out with Hunter "some proposition which would bring the warring sections together," had they been able to reconvene. "Whether this is the case or not, I do not know," Hunter later said, "but I have always regretted that circumstances prevented our meeting at that time."

In July 1865, Hunter wrote to a daughter from his cell (another teenage daughter had recently died of consumption): "Mr. Seward wrote to me that he would soon call the attention of the President to my case.... Your mother says very little of the farm and nothing of the mill.... Perhaps there was nothing pleasant to say, but still I would like to hear." Two days earlier, his youngest son had drowned at the age of fifteen, swimming with other boys.

A month later, Seward took Mrs. Hunter to see the president, who ordered her husband's release. He devoted himself to farming and his studies, barely making a living. A friend said, "Mr. Hunter regarded it as his duty to accept the union in good faith" and wished to help restore it. "It was deeply unfortunate that this sentiment was not at once recognized and acted on by the dominant party, instead of adopting, as they did, the policy of hate, military rule, and disenfranchisement."

In 1870, James M. Mason, a grandson of the founding father George Mason, wrote to Davis, teasing Hunter in absentia for his somnolent retirement. "He is buried at his plantation on the lower Rappahannock, entirely out of the world and difficult to disinter," but he might be dug up for a reunion with Davis. No record survives that Davis showed any interest.

The legislature made him Treasurer of Virginia in 1874. He was defeated for reelection in 1880. In the following year his mill burned down, his youngest daughter died, and the rebuilt mill burned down again. He was seventy-two years old. Grover Cleveland made him Collector of the Port of Tappahannock, Virginia, in 1885. It gave him a bare living. He died two years later, at the age of seventy-eight. Friends solicited contributions to move his remains to Richmond and build a monument at his tomb. For lack of public interest, they failed to raise the money.

Over half a century later, in 1942, the United States Navy launched the liberty ship USS *Robert M. T. Hunter*, which served in World War II and Vietnam.

ALEC STEPHENS

At a family reunion in Georgia soon after the tragedy at Ford's Theatre, John Stephens showed his uncle the letter that Lincoln had written, returning his nephew to him. "I almost wept over the letter when I saw it," Alec said. On May 11, 1865, federal troops came for him at Liberty Hall. His last conversation with Davis took place on a steamer taking prisoners to Hilton Head. Stephens found Davis "far from cordial." They shared some empty pleasantries.

Stephens was jailed in Boston Harbor, not knowing if his life would be spared. Purporting to express "the universal opinion of the army,"

General Custer had just called for "the extermination" of all senior Rebel leaders. Little Alec's old friend Lincoln had promised mercy. Now his old friend was dead. Stephens kept a prison diary. "My whole conscious- ness, since I heard of President Lincoln's assassination, seems nothing but a horrid dream." Frightened but well treated, he received kindly visi- tors from Boston, flowers from his jailor's daughter, courage from Gen- eral Richard Ewell, a one-legged prisoner hobbling on crutches who said he was waiting to see if he would hang before he bought a pros- thesis, in which case he did not care to go to the expense. On the first day of summer, Stephens recalled from behind bars Jefferson Davis's prediction at the African Church that Lincoln and Seward would know by the summer solstice that when they spoke at Hampton Roads they were speaking to their masters. Now, Stephens wrote, "I am, with him and thousands of others, a victim of the wreck."

Released after five months, with help from Grant and Seward, Ste- phens led a reconciliation movement and was sent back to Congress in 1872. According to a newspaperman, not much had changed. "An immense cloak, a high hat, and peering somewhere out of the middle a thin, pale, sad face. How anything so small and sick and sorrowful could get here all the way from Georgia is a wonder. If he were laid out in his coffin, he needn't look any different, only then the fires would have gone out in the burning eyes." He served five postwar terms and spoke at the same podium with Congressman James Garfield, a Union war hero and a future martyred president, at the presentation in the Capitol of a painting of Lincoln signing the Emancipation Proclamation with his Cabinet about him, Seward in the most prominent place, Montgomery Blair behind him, Uncle Gideon looking stern in his bad white wig. The painting hangs there still.

Most of Stephens's former slaves stayed on as tenant farmers. His law-breaking decision to teach them to read and write was rewarded in their letters. A daughter of Harry, his freed plantation foreman, wrote him soon after he returned to Congress. "My Dear Master Alex," she began. "My dear friend. I am ashame of my self for not writing to you before now. I was waiting to get over my crying spell. The reason I did not write to you it was not because I had forgot you, it was because it made me feel so sad to think that you was so far from home. . . . I wish you was hear. . . . With much love I remain your friend, Dora Stephens."

An elderly former slave wrote a letter to him in 1878, recounting the infirmities of several of her peers: "Dear old Master. I am well at this time and hope this letter may fine you the same. . . . I want to see you mighty bad if I never see you no more I hope to meet you in heaven where sickness and trials are done away with. . . . I will close by saying God bless is my pray. Your truly friend, Jane Colborne."

Stephens was elected governor of Georgia in 1882. "The one criticism recorded of his administration," an early biographer said, was his "excessive use of the pardoning power." He died in office in 1883 at the age of seventy-one. After one final illness.

JOHN L. STEPHENS

After Lincoln sent him home, John Stephens became an aide to a Rebel general. He practiced law after the war. When his uncle became governor, John was appointed adjutant general. For the rest of his life, he displayed in a frame in his parlor Lincoln's letter sending him home to his uncle, with its unblotted ink and its autographed picture. They passed to his descendants.

WILLIAM HATCH

Colonel William Hatch, the commissioner's aide at City Point, represented Missouri's First District in Congress between 1879 and 1895, serving part of that time with Stephens. He was an architect of the federal land grant college system.

JUDAH BENJAMIN

Judah Benjamin fled with Davis and his party as far as Georgia, then split off from the pack, too unfit or too clever to keep riding with the prey of every federal cavalryman in the state. He made his way to London, became a distinguished barrister, wrote the standard legal treatise on the sale of personal property, and served as Queen's Counsel. He died in France in 1884, having never returned to America.

ROBERT E. LEE

Lee never recovered emotionally from the war. He urged the Southern people to renew their American citizenship and embrace the Union, rejected lucrative offers for the commercial use of his name, and served for little pay as president of Washington College in Lexington, Virginia, now Washington and Lee University. He recruited Northern boys to be educated there, with simple expectations. "We have but one rule here, and it is that every student be a gentleman." He was once heard to say that the error of his life had been to choose a military education. He died at the age of sixty-three, in 1870. His last delirious words were said to be of General A. P. Hill, as Stonewall Jackson's had been. "Tell Hill he must come up. Strike the tent."

SARAH PRYOR

In the 1880s, Sarah Pryor was living in Manhattan, where her husband had become a judge. When former president Grant and Mrs. Grant came by for an unexpected visit, she served them tea, toast, and oysters, and showed the general a relic that her sons had found: two bullets that had fused in midair. He asked her if they had found it at Petersburg.

"Yes," she said, "but not when you were shelling the city. It was picked up on our farm after the last fight."

"He looked at me with a humorous twinkle in his eye. 'Now look here,' he said, 'don't you go about telling people I shelled Petersburg.'"

SLAVES AND THE SIEGE LINE

After the war, desperately poor freed slaves took up residence in the abandoned earthen forts on the Petersburg siege line and sustained a bare existence selling relics to tourists. By 1867, their inventory had been depleted. "Bullets are risen in value now," a visiting Englishman said. "I bought three of a little nigger for five cents; one was genuine, the other two had been expressly cast for sale by the little nigger's father."

The Northerners after the War

FRANCIS PRESTON BLAIR

On the day Lincoln was shot, Preston Blair came into the city from Silver Spring to be there for the end of the war. He went to bed a happy man. When the awful news arrived, the family let him sleep while soldiers ringed the house. The Sage of Silver Spring lived another eleven years and died at the age of eighty-five, having added Andrew Johnson and Ulysses S. Grant to his roster of mentored presidents. In the end, he and his sons became Democrats again. His descendants include the actor Montgomery Clift, a great-grandson of Montgomery Blair.

WILLIAM SEWARD

The attempt on his life left Seward in shock, and his doctors and family kept him ignorant of Lincoln's death. On Easter Sunday, two days after the conspirators' bloody work, his bed was wheeled to a window for a view of Lafayette Square. He turned to his nurse in tears when he saw the War Department's flag. "The president is dead! He would have been the first to call on me, but he has not been here, nor has he sent to know how I am, and there is the flag at half-mast." A few days later, Gideon Welles told his diary that Seward was said to have "sat up in bed and viewed the procession and hearse of the president, and I know his emotion. Stanton, who rode with me, was uneasy and left the carriage four or five times."

With a face deeply scarred, Seward survived the wounds he had suffered on the night of Lincoln's death. He stayed on as Johnson's secretary of state and welcomed a hundred Southern dignitaries to his home within months of the end of the war. In December 1865, he certified the ratification of the Thirteenth Amendment, which eight occupied states had endorsed, some more legitimately than others. In 1866, Seward put pressure on Napoleon III to withdraw French forces from Mexico, gave a diplomatic dinner party honoring Madame Benito Juarez, whose husband the French had deposed, and suggested in a toast that Juarez would reenter Mexico City within the year. Napoleon's minister to Washington advised Paris to take this no more seriously than any of Seward's other indiscretions, typically served up with dessert.

In 1867, he advanced his dream of expanding the United States throughout North America, persuading President Johnson and Congress to buy Alaska from the Russians for $7.2 million. Lincoln's former secretary of the treasury, the acerbic William Pitt Fessenden, a senator once again, promised to support the acquisition of the frozen waste ("Seward's Folly," as his critics were soon calling it), but only if "the Secretary of State be compelled to live there, and the Russian government required to keep him there."

Seward died at seventy-one in 1872, after traveling the world in retirement, to wide acclaim. The former White House aide John Hay recalled that "the only word of regret at Lincoln's superior fortune I ever heard from the Secretary was a noble and touching one. . . . 'Lincoln always got the advantage of me, but I never envied him anything but his death.'"

ULYSSES S. GRANT

Soon after the war, Seward squelched Grant's proposal to enforce the Monroe Doctrine in Mexico. Grant got it done in his own irrepressible way. "I sent Sheridan with a corps to the Rio Grande to have him where he might aid Juarez in expelling the French from Mexico. These troops got off *before they could be stopped,* and went to the Rio Grande, where Sheridan distributed them up and down the river. . . ." [Emphasis added] A weakening of Napoleonic will ensued. Two days after the last French soldier left, Napoleon's surrogate, the Archduke Maximilian, surrendered to Juarez, who responded to Seward's messages urging mercy by presenting the Austrian nobleman to a firing squad.

After a short stint as Secretary of War under President Andrew Johnson, replacing Edwin Stanton, Grant succeeded Johnson in 1869. His presidency was spoiled by scandal. None of it touched him personally, but his aide Orville Babcock, who had escorted the Southern peace commissioners to Hampton Roads, was brought down. Swindled out of his savings after he left the White House, Grant faced destitution before Mark Twain convinced him to write his memoirs and published them. He finished them a few days before he died at the age of sixty-three. They left his widow comfortable for life.

JULIA GRANT

Julia Grant entertained lavishly as first lady, brought an unprecedented level of opulence and style to the White House, forbade everyone but her husband to smoke there, and ordered "colored visitors" to be admitted to her Tuesday afternoon receptions, to which the public was invited. (The staff excluded them anyway.)

The widowed Mrs. Grant wrote her own important memoirs and rejected lucrative offers to publish them. Candid as they were, she preferred to let "several generations" pass before they were unveiled. They first saw print in 1975. A doyenne of Washington society, the former first lady befriended the wives of Presidents Harrison, Cleveland, and Roosevelt, as well as Varina Davis, attended the dedication of Grant's tomb, and was laid at his side in 1902.

EDWIN STANTON

In 1868, Andrew Johnson was impeached, primarily for removing Stanton as Secretary of War and replacing him with Grant in defiance of the Tenure of Office Act, a congressional usurpation of presidential powers. The Senate acquitted Johnson by a single vote. In 1869, knowing that Stanton was dying, President Grant appointed him to the Supreme Court, his life's ambition. He died four days after the Senate confirmed him.

THOMAS ECKERT

A month after the Hampton Roads Peace Conference, Major Eckert was appointed Assistant Secretary of War and promoted to brevet brigadier general, jumping three grades in a single bound. A subordinate thought Eckert and Eddie Stanton, another Assistant Secretary, "imitated Stanton's arrogance, and both were petty tyrants instead of big ones, like their model."

On April 14, 1865, still impressed by the major having broken several pokers over his arm, Lincoln asked Stanton to have Eckert accompany him as a bodyguard to Ford's Theatre. Stanton said no. So did Eckert. He was said to be too busy.

In 1867, Stanton got Eckert a job at Western Union. He rose to become its president in 1893 and chairman of the board in 1900, still telling friends how he had stopped General Grant "right there" when he challenged Eckert's authority at City Point.

HORACE GREELEY

In 1872, the Democrats and Liberal Republicans nominated Greeley to challenge Grant for the presidency. Alec Stephens called it a choice between hemlock and strychnine. Greeley lost all but six Southern and Border States, each of which might have voted for Crazy Horse had he run against Grant. Before the month was out, Greeley suffered a mental breakdown and died in an institution.

WILLIAM TECUMSEH SHERMAN

After the last Rebel army surrendered, Sherman declared himself "sick and tired of fighting—its glory is all moonshine . . . 'tis only those who have never heard a shot, never heard the shriek and groans of the wounded and lacerated . . . that cry aloud for more blood, more vengeance, more desolation." He succeeded Grant as Commanding General of the United States Army in 1869, presided over the Indian wars of the late 1860s and1870s, and unleashed vengeance, desolation, and blood on the Sioux after Custer's annihilation at Little Bighorn. Politics were anathema to him. Recruited to seek the Republican nomination for the presidency in 1884, he issued the classic line, "I will not accept if nominated and will not serve if elected."

He died on February 14, 1891. His worthiest Rebel adversary, General Joseph Johnston, refused to wear his hat at the funeral in New York, saying Sherman would not have worn his, had their roles been reversed. Catching a cold that progressed to pneumonia, Johnston died a few weeks later.

EDWARD ORD

General Edward Ord, Grant's collaborator in the peace overtures to General Longstreet, earned much of the credit for running Lee down and was present at his surrender. At Grant's direction, Ord investigated the Lincoln assassination and concluded that the Confederate government and its leaders had not been complicit in it. He died of yellow fever in 1883. In the Spanish American War, Ord's son and namesake led Teddy Roosevelt's Rough Riders up San Juan Hill and was killed at the summit.

THADDEUS STEVENS

In increasingly ill health, carried about the capitol in a chair, Thaddeus Stevens led the way for a punitive reconstruction; helped prevent the hanging of any Rebel leaders; championed the adoption of the Fourteen Amendment prohibiting state and local governments from discriminating in matters of life, liberty, or property; and spearheaded the impeachment of Andrew Johnson after he resisted the civil rights legislation that Stevens introduced. He died in 1868. Having demanded to be buried in a racially integrated cemetery, he caused that rare distinction to be carved on his tombstone as a monument to the "equality of man before his creator."

SUNSET COX

After his Ohio constituents removed him from Congress in 1864, Cox moved to Manhattan, whose residents returned him there in 1868. He was said to be one of the only honest men in the shadow of Boss Tweed and explained that he had voted against the Thirteenth Amendment in 1865 because slavery was already "dead by the bullet," and the Southern peace commission ought not to be driven away. In an age that valued solemnity, he was criticized for his witticisms on the House floor, "more anxious to annoy his opponents than to extinguish them." In 1885, Grover Cleveland made him the Ambassador to the Ottoman Empire, replacing Lew Wallace. He died in 1889.

MARY, TAD, AND ROBERT TODD LINCOLN

Tad died of heart failure at the age of seventeen, the third of Mary Todd Lincoln's four sons to pass away in childhood. That and her husband's murder in her presence left her all but mad. In 1875, she was institutionalized temporarily by Robert Todd Lincoln, her only surviving son, who served as Secretary of War under presidents James Garfield and Chester A. Arthur, ambassador to the Court of Saint James's under President Benjamin Harrison, and president of the Pullman Palace Car Company. He became a wealthy man, and participated in the dedication of the Lincoln Memorial in 1922.

JOHN HAY

Lincoln's young aide John Hay wrote postwar editorials for the *New York Daily Tribune,* admired by his friend Mark Twain as the only man who ever worked for Horace Greeley and was not afraid of him, a distinction that "could not be made too conspicuous." He served as Secretary of State under presidents William McKinley and Theodore Roosevelt.

A diarist to the end, Hay made an entry in 1905, less than three weeks before he died: "I dreamt last night that I was in Washington and that I went to the White House to report to the President, who turned out to be Mr. Lincoln. He was very kind and considerate, and sympathetic about my illness. He said there was little work of importance on hand. He gave me two unimportant letters to answer. I was pleased that this slight order was within my power to obey. I was not in the least surprised by Lincoln's presence in the White House. But the whole impression of the dream was one of overpowering melancholy."

Acknowledgments

In the fall of 2008, the late David Herbert Donald, the eminent Lincoln historian, took the time to prepare a thoughtful answer to my letter inquiring whether a book on the Hampton Roads Peace Conference might be worth writing, since no one had done it before. I hope it is worthy of his encouragement.

Alice Martell, my brilliant literary agent, believed in this project from the start, made *me* believe in it, and brought it to fruition. These are debts I cannot repay. The editor of this book, Janice Goldklang, recommended it to her editorial board, labored over its ponderous early drafts, and guided my efforts to make it better. I am grateful to her; to Lyons Press; to Meredith Dias and Lauren Brancato, the book's accomplished project editors; to Sharon Kunz, its diligent publicist; and to Melissa Hayes, its meticulous copyeditor.

Most of the book was researched at the Boston Athenaeum, a stunning place in which to work and write, with a uniformly helpful and knowledgeable staff. I owe particular thanks to Chloe Morse-Harding, who assembled many books and materials from the Athenaeum's collection and other libraries. The staffs of the Manuscript Reading Room at the Library of Congress, the Historical Society of Pennsylvania, and the libraries of Manhattanville College of the Sacred Heart, Emory University, and Duke University were unfailingly courteous and helpful.

I am grateful to my law partners for looking the other way as I worked on this project. My secretary, Karalee Hart, was as helpful and attentive as she always is.

My parents gave me a deep love of history and a lifelong ambition to contribute to it, in which this book has its origins.

My daughter, Erin Hennessy Conroy, read the book's first draft, improved it with incisive questions and comments, proofread the final draft, helped gather the illustrations and their attributions, and inspired me as she always has. By coauthoring a successful book of his own at the age of twenty-six, my son, Scott Conroy, shamed me into writing this one, introduced me to Alice Martell, and contributed many thoughts and much encouragement after reading early drafts.

My wife of forty years, Lynn Conroy, put up with me and my absence, physical or mental, on weekends, nights, holidays, and vacations for the four and a half years that this undertaking consumed (significantly longer than it took to fight the Civil War), and served as a resonant sounding board. Without her, neither *Our One Common Country* nor its author would have amounted to anything.

NOTES

PROLOGUE

xvii. Lincoln's departure from the White House and his trip to Hampton Roads: See chapter 17.

xvii. The military situation in the winter of 1865: e.g., Mark Grimsley, "Learning to Say 'Enough'" in Mark Grimsley and Brooks Simpson, *The Collapse of the Confederacy* (Lincoln: University of Nebraska Press, 2000) ("Grimsley and Simpson"), pp. 40–79; Shelby Foote, *The Civil War: A Narrative*, 3 vols. (New York: Random House, 1958–1974), vol. 3, *Red River to Appomattox* ("Foote"), pp. 735–70; Alfred Hoyt Bill, *The Beleaguered City, Richmond 1861–1865* (New York: Alfred A. Knopf, 1946) ("Bill"), p. 266 (50,000 men under Lee versus 110,000 under Grant).

xvii. *General Robert E. Lee was praying for their success:* See, e.g., Robert E. Lee, *Lee's Dispatches* (New York: G. P. Putnam's Sons, 1915) ("Lee's Dispatches"), pp. 305 and 331; John B. Gordon, *Reminiscences of the Civil War* (New York: Charles Scribner's Sons, 1905) ("Gordon"), pp. 389–93; Jefferson Davis and Dunbar Rowland, ed., *Jefferson Davis, Constitutionalist: His Letters, Papers and Speeches*, 10 vols. (Jackson: Mississippi Department of Archives and History, 1923) ("Rowland"), vol. 8, pp. 30–31; Josiah Gorgas and Sarah Woolfolk Wiggins, ed., *The Journals of Josiah Gorgas, 1857–1878* (Tuscaloosa: University of Alabama Press, 1995) ("Wiggins"), p. 136; Jefferson Davis and Hudson Strode, ed., *The Private Letters of Jefferson Davis, 1823–1889* (New York: Harcourt, Brace & World, 1966) ("Strode"), pp. 469–70; Robert McElroy, *Jefferson Davis: The Unreal and the Real*, 2 vols. (New York: Harper & Brothers, 1937) ("McElroy"), pp. 424 and 435; and Alan T. Nolan, *Lee Considered: General Robert E. Lee and Civil War History* (Chapel Hill: University of North Carolina Press, 1991) ("Nolan"), pp. 112–33.

xviii–xxii. Life on the siege line and the peace commissioners' arrival: *The War of the Rebellion: A Compilation of the Official Records of the Union and Confederate Armies*, 73 vols. (Washington, DC: US Government Printing Office, 1880–1901) ("*OR*") ser. 1, vol. 46, part 2, pp. 290, 317, and 347; Hezekiah Bradds, "With the 60th Ohio Around Petersburg," *National Tribune* (Washington, DC: April 8, 1926) ("Bradds"), p. 5; William J. Bolton and Richard A. Sauers, ed., *The Civil War Journal of Colonel William J. Bolton, 51st Pennsylvania* (Conshohocken, PA: Combined Pub., 2000) ("Bolton"), pp. 242–44; Orlando B. Willcox and Robert Garth Scott, ed., *Forgotten Valor: The Memoirs, Journals & Civil War Letters of Orlando B. Willcox* (Kent, OH: Kent State University Press, 1999) ("Willcox"), p. 604; *War Papers* (Portland, ME: Lefavor-Tower Company, 1902) vol. 2, pp. 105–07; George H. Allen, *Forty-Six Months with the Fourth R.I. Volunteers in the War of 1861–1865* (Providence: J. A. & R. A. Reid, 1887) ("Allen"), pp. 322 and 334–36; William P. Hopkins and George B. Peck, *The Seventh Regiment Rhode Island Volunteers in the Civil War 1862–1865* (Providence: Snow & Farnham, 1903) ("Hopkins and Peck"), pp. 232–33, 241, and 273; Régis de Trobriand, *Four Years with the Army of the Potomac* (Boston: Ticknor and Company, 1889) ("de Trobriand"), pp. 639–40; Joseph Gould, *The Story of the Forty-Eighth* (Philadelphia: Alfred M. Slocum Co., 1908) ("Gould"), pp. 280–81 and 285; Sumner Garruth et al., *History of the Thirty-Sixth Regiment Massachusetts*

Volunteers (Boston: Mills, Knight & Co., 1884) ("Garruth"), pp. 278 and 319; Thomas H. Parker, *History of the 51st Regiment of P.V. and V.V.* (Philadelphia: King & Baird, 1869) ("Parker"), pp. 601–04 (No other source confirms Parker's tale that two of the peace commissioners met him in no-man's land, and the other evidence refutes it); DeWitt Boyd Stone, ed., *Wandering to Glory: Confederate Veterans Remember Evans's Brigade* (Columbia: University of South Carolina Press, 2002); Theodore Lyman and George R. Agassiz, ed., *Meade's Headquarters, 1863–1865: Letters of Colonel Theodore Lyman from the Wilderness to Appomattox* (Boston: Atlantic Monthly Press, 1922) ("Lyman"), p. 181; George C. Eggleston, *A Rebel's Recollections* (New York: Hurd and Houghton, 1870) ("Eggleston"), pp. 239 and 242; Julia Dent Grant and John Y. Simon, ed., *The Personal Memoirs of Julia Dent Grant* (New York: Putnam, 1975) ("Julia Grant"), p. 141; Sara Agnes Rice Pryor, *My Day: Reminiscences of a Long Life* (New York: Macmillan, 1909), p. 213; Sara Agnes Rice Pryor, *Reminiscences of Peace and War* (New York: Macmillan, 1905) ("Pryor, *Reminiscences*"), p. 328; "In a Charge Near Fort Hell" ("Charge Near Fort Hell") at www.angelfire .com/ca4/forthell and www.craterroad.com/Christmas.html. W. R. Scott's dark rendition of the peace commissioners' arrival can be found at http://dmna.ny.gov/historic/reghist/ civil/artillery ("Scott"); Bill, p. 265; Noah Trudeau, *The Last Citadel: Petersburg, Virginia, June 1864–April 1865* (Boston: Little, Brown, 1991) ("Trudeau"); Earl J. Hess, *In the Trenches at Petersburg: Field Fortifications & Confederate Defeat* (Charlotte: University of North Carolina Press, 2009); *Boston Daily Evening Transcript*, February 1 and 2, 1865; *The Daily Constitutional Union*, February 3, 1865; *The New Orleans Daily Picayune*, February 12, 1865; *The New York Times*, February 2, 3, 6, 7, and 8, 1865, and December 31, 1916, p. E2; *The New York Herald*, February 4, 1865; *The Philadelphia Inquirer*, February 2, 1865; and *The Petersburg Express*, February 2, 1865.

xviii. Contemporary photographs of Fort Hell and other fortifications on the siege line: *Gardner's Photographic Sketch Book of the War* (Washington, DC: Philip & Solomons, 1865–66) and at www.craterroad.com/fortphotos.html.

xxiv. Meade's letter to his wife: George Meade and George Gordon Meade, ed., *The Life and Letters of George Gordon Meade, Major-General of the United States Army*, 2 vols. (New York: Charles Scribner's Sons, 1913) ("Meade"), pp. 258–60.

xxiv. "*Sanguinary war*": *Personal Memoirs of U. S. Grant*, 2 vols. (New York: C. L. Webster, 1885–1886) ("Grant"), vol. 2, page 119.

xxiv. *old at fifty-five:* William O. Stoddard and Michael Burlingame, ed., *Inside the White House in War Time: Memoirs and Reports of Lincoln's Secretary* (Lincoln: University of Nebraska Press, 2000) ("Stoddard"), p. 149.

xxiv. Lincoln's distress during the Wilderness Campaign: F. B. Carpenter, *The Inner Life of Abraham Lincoln* (Boston: Houghton Mifflin, 1894) ("Carpenter"), p. 30. For Lincoln's persistent sadness, see also *id.*, p. 218.

xxiv. Casualties: Civil War casualty figures are imprecise, especially on the Confederate side. The classic battle-by-battle estimates are in Thomas L. Livermore's *Numbers and Losses in the Civil War in America, 1861–65* (Boston: Houghton Mifflin, 1900) ("Livermore"). The 95,000 figure for Union casualties incurred in early May through early July 1864 is in James M. McPherson, *This Mighty Scourge: Perspectives on the Civil War* (Oxford: Oxford University Press, 2007) ("McPherson"), p. 170.

CHAPTER 1

Much of this chapter is drawn from Paul D. Escott, *After Secession: Jefferson Davis and the Failure of Confederate Nationalism* (Baton Rouge: Louisiana State University Press, 1994) and professor Escott's more recent book, *"What Shall We Do with the Negro?": Lincoln, White Racism, and Civil War America* (Charlottesville: University of Virginia Press, 2009) ("Escott"); William C. Davis, *Jefferson Davis: The Man and His Hour* (New York: HarperCollins, 1991) ("Davis, *Davis*"); William James Cooper Jr., *Jefferson Davis, American* (New York: Alfred A. Knopf, 2000) ("Cooper"); Brian R. Dirck, *Lincoln & Davis: Imagining America, 1809–1865* (Lawrence: University Press of Kansas, 2001) ("Dirck"); Jay Winik, *April 1865: The Month that Saved America* (New York: HarperCollins, 2001) ("Winik"); and Varina Howell Davis, *Jefferson Davis, Ex-President of the Confederate States of America: A Memoir by His Wife*, 2 vols. (New York: Belford, 1890) ("Varina Davis").

2. Russell's interview with Davis: William Howard Russell, *My Diary: North and South* (London: Bradbury and Evans, 1863) ("Russell"), pp. 249–50.

2. Davis's antebellum career: A chronology of Davis's life, followed by a brief autobiography, is in Rowland, vol. 1, pp. xiii–xxxi.

2. *Ambitious as Lucifer and cold as a lizard:* Foote, *Civil War*, vol. 1, p. 13.

3. *A superstitious reverence:* Rowland, vol. 1, p. 379.

3. *no risk of Pollard overlooking it:* E. A. Pollard, *Life of Jefferson Davis* (Philadelphia: National Publishing Company, 1869) ("Pollard"), p. 52. John S. Wise, *The End of an Era* (Boston: Houghton Mifflin, 1899) ("Wise"), p. 402 (*Examiner* tortured Davis).

3. *its president grasped the need; peals of public outrage:* e.g., George C. Rable, *The Confederate Republic: A Revolution Against Politics* (Chapel Hill: University of North Carolina Press, 1994) ("Rable"), *passim;* Dirck, pp. 84–87.

3. *A Virginian expressed the common view:* Frank Ruffin, quoted in the introduction to Robert Garlick Hill Kean and Edward Younger, ed., *Inside the Confederate Government: The Diary of Robert Garlick Hill Kean* (New York: Oxford University Press, 1957) ("Kean"), p. xxxi. See also Stephen Russell Mallory, "Diary and Reminiscences of Stephen R. Mallory" (Typescript), Wilson Library, University of North Carolina ("Mallory"), vol. 2, pp. 205–07.

3. *devotion to General Braxton Bragg:* Grady McWhitney, "Jefferson Davis and His Generals," in Grady McWhitney, *Southerners and Other Americans* (New York: Basic Books, 1973), p. 93.

4. The South's dire condition: Rable, *passim;* Grimsley and Simpson, *passim;* William W. Freehling, *The South vs. The South: How Anti-Confederate Southerners Shaped the Course of the Civil War* (Oxford: Oxford University Press, 2001) ("Freehling"), pp. 188–95; James G. Randall and Richard Current, *Lincoln the President: Last Full Measure* (New York: Dodd, Mead, 1955) ("Randall and Current"), pp. 322–23; Bill, pp. 244–51 and 256–61; Edward C. Kirkland, *The Peacemakers of 1864* (New York: Macmillan, 1927) ("Kirkland"), pp. 207–08 and 213–22.

4. *One tubercular draftee:* Bill, p. 235.

4. *eat rats; twelve- and-fourteen-year-old-sons:* John B. Jones, *A Rebel War Clerk's Diary of the Confederate States Capital,* 2 vols. (Philadelphia: Lippincott, 1866) ("Jones"), vol. 2, p. 175.

4. *"born to command":* Pollard, p. 66.

4. *dealt Jeff a sibling:* Dirck, pp. 19–23 and 66.

4. *"repellent manner":* Varina Davis, vol. 2, p. 163.

4. *husband was easily persuaded: Id.,* vol. 2, p. 921.

4. *"could not comprehend": Id.,* vol. 1, p. 171.

4. *"consciousness of my own rectitude":* Rowland, vol. 1, p. 378.

5. *"path of safety":* Pollard, p. 41.

5. *his military genius:* Mallory, vol. 2, p. 205.

5. *"to bear the criticisms of the ignorant":* OR, ser. 1, vol. 29, pt. 2, p. 639; Strode, p. 132.

5. *excuse himself to his study:* T. C. De Leon, *Four Years in the Rebel Capitals* (Mobile, AL: Gossip Print Co., 1892) ("De Leon"), pp. 153–54.

5. *capable of grace and a winning smile:* Wise, p. 400; Elizabeth Keckley, *Behind the Scenes* (New York: G. W. Carleton & Co., 1868), pp. 68–69.

5. *"full of tags":* Varina Davis, vol. 2, p. 919.

5. *"he would let me be bad":* Dirck, p. 18.

5. *"Poor creature":* Varina Davis, vol. 2, p. 921

5. *"death in life": Id.,* vol. 2, p. 5.

5. *final speech to the Senate: Congressional Globe,* January 21, 1861, p. 487; Varina Davis, vol. 1, pp. 697–98; Dirck, pp. 175–76.

5. Davis and his slaves: Escott, pp. 183–84; and Winik, p. 326; Cooper, pp. 50, 78, 229, and 235–36; Dirck, pp. 66–67.

6. *from heathen darkness:* Rowland, vol. 1, p. 219.

6. *unfit for slavery: Id.,* p. 212.

6. *"self-immolating devotion to duty":* Varina Davis, vol., 2, p. 923.

6. *no place for reconciliation in his psyche: Id.,* pp. 11 and 80.

6. *"possible to treat of peace":* Rowland, vol. 6, pp. 143–46.

6. Casualties at Chancellorsville: Livermore, p. 98.

6. *"What will the country say?":* Noah Brooks, *Washington in Lincoln's Time* (New York: The Century Co., 1895) ("Brooks"), p. 7.

6. Jacques in Richmond: James R. Gilmore, *Personal Recollections of Abraham Lincoln and the Civil War* (Boston: L. C. Page & Co., 1898) ("Gilmore, *Recollections*"), pp. 163–66 and 233; James D. Richardson, ed., *A Compilation of Messages and Papers of the Confederacy, Including Diplomatic Correspondence 1861–1865,* 2 vols. (Nashville: United States Publishing Company, 1905) ("Richardson"), vol. 2, pp. 664–70.

6. Chickamauga casualties: Livermore, *Numbers and Losses,* p. 105.

6. 55,000 Northern casualties: *Id.,* pp. 110–116.

6. Revolutionary War casualties: John A. Shy, *A People Numerous and Armed: Reflections on the Military Struggle for American Independence* (New York: Oxford University Press, 1976), pp. 249–50.

6. Lee's casualties: Livermore, pp. 110–15.

7. *"half wild" with letters:* Quoted in Rowland, vol. 10, p. 6.

CHAPTER 2

8. Voting on the siege line: *New York Daily Tribune*, November 11, 1864.

8. *a margin of three to one:* McPherson, p. 179; Randall and Current, p. 261.

8. *"It is unnecessary to say":* New York Daily Tribune, November 11, 1864.

9. *"the rebels"; "the other fellow"; "this great trouble":* Noah Brooks and Michael Burlingame, ed., *Lincoln Observed: Civil War Dispatches of Noah Brooks* (Baltimore: Johns Hopkins University Press, 1998), pp. 44, 180, and 211.

9. *"brutes"; "hyenas"; "lost sheep":* Dirck, pp. 172–73, 192–200, 210–19, and 226–40.

9. *issued a proclamation:* Abraham Lincoln and Roy B. Basler, ed., *Collected Works of Abraham Lincoln*, 9 vols. (New Brunswick, NJ: Rutgers University Press, 1953–1955) (*"CW"*), vol. 7, pp. 431–32.

9. *We are fighting for the Union:* e.g., Charles H. Ambler, *Francis H. Pierpont* (Chapel Hill: University of North Carolina Press, 1937) ("Ambler"), p. 258.

9. *he would look the other way:* Gideon Welles, "Lincoln and Johnson: Their Plan of Reconstruction and the Resumption of National Authority," 13 *Galaxy* (April 1872) (Welles, "Lincoln and Johnson"), p. 522; Carpenter, p. 284; Brooks, *Lincoln Observed*, p. 178; Allen Thorndike Rice, *Reminiscences of Abraham Lincoln by Distinguished Men of His Time* (New York: North American Publishing Co., 1886) ("Rice"), pp. 97–98.

9. The Jacobins: See Fawn Brodie, *Thaddeus Stevens* (New York: W. W. Norton & Co., 1959) ("Brodie"), and Hans Trefousse, *The Radical Republicans: Lincoln's Vanguard for Racial Justice* (New York: Knopf, 1969).

9. *"as England governs India":* Edward Bates and Howard K. Beale, ed., *The Diary of Edward Bates* (Washington: US Government Printing Office, 1933), p. 383.

9. *"tolerably capable":* Charles Francis Adams, *Diary of Charles Francis Adams, 1807–1886* (Cambridge: Belknap Press of Harvard University Press, 1964–1986), p. 115.

9. *"drawn a blank"; "ill-fitted both by education and nature":* Michael Burlingame, *Abraham Lincoln: A Life,* 2 vols. (Baltimore: Johns Hopkins University Press, 2008) ("Burlingame"), vol. 1, pp. 76, 79, and 629.

10. *the "patent leather kid glove set":* John Hay and Michael Burlingame, ed., *At Lincoln's Side: John Hay's Civil War Correspondence and Selected Writings* (Carbondale: Southern Illinois University Press, 2000) ("Hay, *At Lincoln's Side*"), p. 111.

10. *"the punishment due to their crimes":* Burton J. Hendrick, *Lincoln's War Cabinet* (Boston: Little, Brown, 1946) ("Hendrick, *Lincoln's War Cabinet*"), p. 440.

10. *"feasting and dancing":* Id., p. 278.

10. Running his campaign: David H. Donald, *Lincoln* (New York: Simon & Schuster, 1995) ("Donald"), p. 532; Randall and Current, p. 237; McPherson, p. 169. Raymond also wrote Lincoln campaign literature. See Henry J. Raymond, *History of the Administration of President Abraham Lincoln* (New York: J. C. Derby and N. C. Miller, 1864).

10. *reduce its people to peonage: New York Times*, August 5, 1865.

10. Governor Andrew on Lincoln: Randall and Current, p. 225.

11. The Democrats and their views of Lincoln: e.g., Brodie, *passim;* and *Congressional Globe,* January 6, 1865, pp. 150 and 154; January 8, 1865, p. 216; and January 11, 1865, p. 225.

11. Horace Greeley: The biographies from which many of this book's references to Greeley are drawn are Mitchell Snay's *Horace Greeley and the Politics of Reform in*

Nineteenth-Century America (Lanham, MD: Rowman & Littlefield, 2011) ("Snay"); Robert C. Williams's *Horace Greeley: Champion of American Freedom* (New York: New York University Press, 2006) ("Williams"); and Glyndon G. Van Deusen's *Horace Greeley, Nineteenth-Century Crusader* (Philadelphia: University of Pennsylvania Press, 1953). Greeley's autobiography is *Recollections of a Busy Life: Reminiscences of American Politics and Politicians* (New York: H. B. Ford and Co., 1868) ("Greeley, *Recollections*").

11. *"drive Lincoln into it":* Donald, p. 414.

11. *"Go west, young man":* Josiah Bushnell Grinnell, *Men and Events of Forty Years* (Boston: D. Lothrop Company, 1891), p. 86.

11. *wary respect for his power:* See, e.g., Carpenter, p. 153; Williams, p. 254.

11. Pigeonhole desk slots: Brooks, *Washington in Lincoln's Time*, p. 264.

11. *an amused admirer:* C. W. Holden, "Horace Greeley," 3 *Holden's Dollar Magazine* (January 1849), p. 34.

12. *for wildly erratic reasons:* See, e.g., McPherson, pp. 169–70 and 173–74.

12. Greeley's Niagara Falls peace offensive and its fallout: See Randall and Current, pp. 158–165; and Williams, pp. 251–55. A Confederate participant's account is in Rowland, vol. 7, pp. 327–31. Hay's account is in John Hay and Michael Burlingame and John R. Turner Ettlinger, eds. *Inside Lincoln's White House: The Complete Civil War Diary of John Hay* (Carbondale: Southern Illinois University Press, 1997) ("Hay Diary"), pp. 224–29. Lincoln's letter to Greeley is in *CW*, vol. 7, p. 435.

12. *as Davis would tacitly confess:* Jefferson Davis, *The Rise and Fall of the Confederate Government*, 2 vols. (D. Appleton and Co., 1881) ("Davis, *Rise and Fall*"), vol. 2, p. 611. See Williams, pp. 171–72 and 249–50; Lynda Lasswell Crist, ed., *The Papers of Jefferson Davis*, 12 vols. (Baton Rouge: Louisiana State University Press, 2003) ("Crist"), vol. 11, pp. 24–30; Randall and Current, *Lincoln*, p. 161.

12. *"To Whom It May Concern":* **CW*, vol. 8, p. 63.

13. *he had thought it astute; Rebels released it to the press:* Donald, pp. 366, 423, 502, 532 and 568; Escott, pp. 130–31.

13. The letter's repercussions: *Id.*, pp. 523–24; McPherson, pp. 172–76.

13. *a writer friend of Greeley's:* Williams, p. 256.

13. Gilmore and Jacques with Davis: Gilmore describes the mission in James R. Gilmore, "Our Visit to Richmond," 14 *Atlantic Monthly* (September 1864) ("Gilmore, 'Visit to Richmond,'"), pp. 372–83, in "A Suppressed Chapter of History," 59 *Atlantic Monthly* (April 1887), pp. 435–47, and in "Our Last Day in Dixie," 14 *Atlantic Monthly* (December 1864), pp. 715–26. Davis tells the story, consistently with Gilmore's, in Davis, *Rise and Fall*, pp. 610–11, Judah Benjamin's rendition is in *Official Records of the Union and Confederate Navies in the War of the Rebellion*, 30 vols. (Washington: US Government Printing Office, 1894–1922), ser. 2, vol. 3, pp. 1190–95.

13. *Atlantic Monthly* article: Gilmore, "Visit to Richmond"; McPherson, pp. 174–75.

CHAPTER 3

This chapter draws on Walter Stahr, *Seward: Lincoln's Indispensable Man* (New York: Simon & Schuster, 2012) ("Stahr"); Glyndon G. Van Deusen's *William Henry Seward* (New York: Oxford University Press, 1967) ("Van Deusen"); and Doris Kearns

Goodwin, *Team of Rivals* (New York: Simon & Schuster, 2005) ("Goodwin"), which contributes depth on Seward's relationship with Lincoln. The insights of Seward's rival, Lincoln's Secretary of the Navy, Gideon Welles, are in Gideon Welles, *Lincoln and Seward* (New York: Sheldon & Company, 1874) ("Welles, *Lincoln and Seward*").
14. Henry Adams on Seward: Henry Adams, *The Education of Henry Adams* (Boston: Houghton Mifflin, 1918) ("Adams"), pp. 103–04. For more on Seward's appearance, see "Brooks, *Lincoln Observed*"), p. 46. Brooks says Lincoln always called Seward "governor," *Id.*, p. 85.
14. *Seward hated slavery "and all its belongings":* Greeley, *Recollections*, p. 311.
14. *refused to extradite . . . three black seamen:* Stahr, p. 65.
14. *"garbage and putrefaction":* *Congressional Globe*, June 13, 1856, pp. 1401–02.
14. *"a degradation to name":* Quoted in Bruce Chadwick, *1858: Abraham Lincoln, Jefferson Davis, Robert E. Lee, Ulysses S. Grant and the War They Failed to See* (Naperville, IL: Sourcebooks, 2008), ("Chadwick") p. 189.
15. *"I thought you must be an Episcopalian":* Brooks, *Washington in Lincoln's Time*, p. 50.
15. *Underground Railroad:* Stahr, p. 154.
15. *his suits were said to be twenty years old:* *Id.*, p. 200. A Lincoln aide was amused to see Seward enter the president's office "with the knot of his cravat nearly under his left ear and carrying an unlighted cigar . . . ," Stoddard, p. 83.
15. *beguiled like everyone else:* Chadwick, p. 186.
15. *raise his hat to tourists:* Van Deusen, p. 335.
15. *called him* très sage: Hay Diary, p. 127.
15. *"Hopelessly lawless":* Quoted in Stahr, p. 213.
15. *damp feet by the fire:* Van Deusen, pp. 260–61.
16. *recipe for poaching a codfish:* Hay Diary, p. 211.
16. Thurlow Weed: e.g., Hendrick, *Lincoln's War Cabinet*, pp. 17 and 132–33.
16. *Seward shared him with Lincoln:* e.g., Gideon Welles and Howard K. Beale and Alan W. Brownsword, eds., *Diary of Gideon Welles, Secretary of the Navy Under Lincoln and Johnson*, 3 vols. (Boston and New York: Houghton Mifflin, 1911) ("Welles Diary"), vol. 2, pp. 171–72; Hay Diary, p. 234; Donald, p. 366.
16. *"get a feller to run you":* Hay Diary, p. 26; Van Deusen, pp. 338–39.
16. *"I could fill a volume":* Welles, *Lincoln and Seward*, p. 68.
16. *"a wolf in sheep's clothing":* Varina Davis, vol. 1, p. 431.
16. *"heartily liking him"; "Your man out-talked ours":* *Id.*, vol. 1, pp. 574–83.
17. Seward averted a duel between Davis and Chandler: Stahr, p. 174.
17. *Even Davis showed him sympathy:* *Id.*, p. 195.
17. Seward's humiliation: Hendrick, *Lincoln's War Cabinet*, p. 30.
17. South Carolina would rescue New York: *New York Times*, December 24, 1860.
17. *to a fully assembled Senate:* Hendrick, *Lincoln's War Cabinet*, pp. 143–44; Welles, *Lincoln and Seward*, p. 14.
18. Seward as Cabinet member: *Id.*, pp. 50, 165–66; Welles Diary, e.g., vol. 2, pp. 58, 86, 91–93, 106–07, 120, 130–31, 160, 166, 171–73, 195, and 203; Stahr, pp. 366–67; Goodwin, *passim*.

18. *"man of no decorations":* Charles A. Dana, *Lincoln and His Cabinet* (New York: Souvenir of the Thirteenth Annual Lincoln Dinner of the Republican Club of New York, 1899) ("Dana, *Lincoln and His Cabinet"), pp. 18–19.
18. *Uncle Gideon:* e.g., David Dixon Porter, *Incidents and Anecdotes of the Civil War* (New York: D. Appleton and Co., 1885) ("Porter, *Incidents"), p. 15; Crook, William H., Margarita Spalding Gerry, ed. *Through Five Administrations: Reminiscences of Colonel William H. Crook* (New York: Harper & Brothers, 1910) ("Crook, *Five Administrations"*) p. 29; Brooks, *Lincoln Observed,* p. 48.
18. *"fortune-tellers are his delight":* Welles Diary, vol. 2, p. 126.
18. *"a certain mysterious knowledge":* Welles, *Lincoln and Seward,* pp. 49–50.
18. *"hypocrite"; "sneak":* Van Deusen, pp. 336–37.
18. *"like a skein of thread":* Keckley, pp. 130–31; Hendrick, *Lincoln's War Cabinet,* p. 187.
18. *Portuguese guide:* Van Deusen, p. 338.
18. *"limited to a couple of stories":* Abraham Lincoln, Don E. and Virginia Fehrenbacher, eds., *Recollected Words of Abraham Lincoln* (Stanford: Stanford University Press, 1996), pp. 125–26.
18. *sent him memos:* Van Deusen, p. 337.
19. *"Seward was the first man who recognized this":* Hay, *At Lincoln's Side,* p. 129.
19. *committed to reconciliation:* e.g., Stahr, pp. 329, 383, and 446; Van Deusen, pp. 386–89.
19. *"that is all past and settled":* Hendrick, *Lincoln's War Cabinet,* p. 371.

CHAPTER 4

20. *"the Old Gentleman":* Hay Diary, p. 123.
20. *built a potent brand:* This chapter relies heavily on Elbert B. Smith, *Francis Preston Blair* (New York: Free Press/Macmillan, 1980) ("Smith, *Francis Preston Blair"*). Also helpful are William E. Parrish, *Frank Blair: Lincoln's Conservative* (Columbia: University of Missouri Press, 1998); and William Ernst Smith, *The Francis Preston Blair Family in Politics,* 2 vols. (New York: Macmillan, 1933) ("Smith, *Blair Family"*). The Blair Family Papers are on microfilm in the Manuscript Division of the Library of Congress, Washington, D.C. See also Keckley, p. 78, on Elizabeth Blair Lee.
21. *The teeth were not false but real:* Quoted in Smith, *Francis Preston Blair,* p. 229.
21. *awkward, homely, and repellent:* Brooks, *Lincoln Observed,* pp. 48–49.
21. *a nascent form of baseball:* Smith, *Francis Preston Blair,* p. 313.
22. *"the spirit of clan":* Hay Diary, p. 123.
22. *"servants"; put them on wages:* Smith, *Francis Preston Blair,* p. 362.
22. *The Blairs' influence with Lincoln had slipped:* See Smith, *Blair Family,* vol. 2, p. 189.
22. *testing new ideas:* Ward Hill Lamon, D. L. Teillard, ed., *Recollections of Abraham Lincoln, 1847–1865* (Washington: The Editor, 1911), p. 205.
23. *Canadian fishing trip:* Stahr, p. 167.
23. *Billy Bowlegs:* Hendrick, *Lincoln's War Cabinet,* p. 203. More charitably, Nathaniel Hawthorne described Seward's "decided originality of gait . . . ," Rufus Rockwell Wilson, ed., *Intimate Memories of Lincoln* (Elmira, NY: Primavera Press, Inc., 1945) ("Wilson"), p. 463.
23. *"contrive some apology for me":* Smith, *Francis Preston Blair,* p. 275.

23. *Blair's rant "electrified":* Welles Diary, vol. 1, pp. 13–14.

23. *"ye can't [fool] the old man":* Hay Diary, pp. 238–39.

24. *Lincoln was under their thumbs:* Hendrick, *Lincoln's War Cabinet,* p. 387.

24. *"in the inner circle of public affairs":* Greeley to Blair, December 15, 1864, Blair Family Papers, Library of Congress.

24. Blair's visit to Greeley: Smith, *Francis Preston Blair,* p. 363; Blair to Lincoln, July 21, 1864, Lincoln papers, Library of Congress.

24. Blair's talk with McClellan: Smith, *Francis Preston Blair,* p. 344.

24. *"the original gorilla":* Stahr, p. 305.

25. *Seward's son and namesake:* Id., pp. 402–03.

25. *within sight of the capitol dome:* Foote, vol. 3, pp. 446–61; Randall and Current, pp. 198–202; Smith, *Francis Preston Blair,* pp. 358–60.

25. *the president . . . Union parapet:* Wilson, pp. 527–29.

25. The Davises at Montgomery's cottage: Strode, pp. 102–03, Crist, vol. 6, p. 242 n. 3.

25. The women and Lizzie's son: Smith, *Francis Preston Blair,* p. 343.

25. The looting of Silver Spring and *"a home to me":* Elizabeth Blair Lee, Virginia J. Lass, ed., *Wartime Washington: The Civil War Letters of Elizabeth Blair Lee* (Urbana: University of Illinois Press, 1991) (*"Elizabeth Blair Lee"*), pp. 413–14 and 414 n. 3 (The original letters are in the Blair and Lee family papers, Manuscripts Division, Department of Rare Books and Special Collections, Princeton University Library); Smith, *Francis Preston Blair,* pp. 343–44 and 358–60.

26. *dashing John Breckinridge:* Smith, *Francis Preston Blair,* pp. 224, 228, and 263; Smith, *Blair Family,* vol. 2, pp. 272–74; Michael B. Ballard, *A Long Shadow: Jefferson Davis and the Final Days of the Confederacy* (Jackson: University Press of Mississippi, 1986) ("Ballard"), p. 38.

26. *He took it now:* Smith, *Francis Preston Blair,* p. 360; *Elizabeth Blair Lee,* pp. 404–05 and 412–13.

26. *A note had been left on the library mantel:* Smith, *Francis Preston Blair,* pp. 359–60; *Elizabeth Blair Lee,* p. 405.

27. *"made more fuss about things":* Elizabeth Blair Lee, p. 405.

27. *procession of blue-ribbon committees:* Carl Schurz, *Reminiscences of Carl Schurz,* 3 vols. (New York: McClure Company, 1907–08), vol. 3, pp. 103–04 ("Schurz"); Randall and Current, *Lincoln,* pp. 210–16.

27. *"an old shoe":* Welles Diary, vol. 2, p. 112.

27. *"been driven many times upon my knees":* Brooks, *Lincoln Observed,* p. 210.

CHAPTER 5

28. *"an impossibility":* Randall and Current, *Lincoln,* p. 213; McPherson, p. 177.

28. *Lincoln thought Weed was right:* John G. Nicolay and John Hay, *Abraham Lincoln: A History,* 10 vols. (New York: Century Company, 1917) ("Nicolay and Hay"), vol. 9, p. 251; Stahr, pp. 405–06.

28. *letter from a Wisconsin editor: CW,* vol. 7, pp. 499–501; McPherson, pp. 176–77.

28. *tide was setting against him; Lincoln would lose Illinois:* Randall and Current, *Lincoln,* pp. 213–14; McPherson, pp. 177–78; Donald, *Lincoln,* pp. 523–30.

29. Raymond and Lincoln's instructions: *CW,* vol. 7, p. 517; Nicolay and Hay, vol. 9, pp. 217–21.

29. *Lincoln steadied them:* John Nicolay and Michael Burlingame, ed., *With Lincoln in the White House: Letters, Memoranda, and Other Writings of John G. Nicolay, 1860–1865* (Carbondale: Southern Illinois University Press, 2000), pp. 152–54; McPherson, pp. 177–78.

29. *"I will keep my faith":* Carl Sandburg, *Abraham Lincoln,* 6 vols., Sangamon Edition (New York: Charles Scribner's Sons, 1941) ("Sandburg"), vol. 5, pp. 211–12.

29. *"All Yankeedoodledom":* Quoted in Russell S. Bonds, *War like the Thunderbolt* (Yardley, PA: Westholme, 2009) ("Bonds"), p. 291.

29. Johnston and Sherman: Grant, vol. 2, pp. 344–45; Michael Fellman, *Citizen Sherman: A Life of William Tecumseh Sherman* (New York: Random House, 1995) ("Fellman"), p. 176.

29–30. *John Bell Hood: Id.;* Foote, vol. 3, pp. 475–530; Bonds, *passim;* Pollard, p. 384; Chadwick, p. 230.

30. *Davis shrugged it off: Id.,* pp. 384–87; Richardson, pp. 482–88.

30. *"No hope . . . no fear":* Mary B. Chesnut, *A Diary from Dixie* (New York: D. Appleton and Company, 1905) ("Chesnut"), p. 326.

30. *"doubts as to its authenticity": Philadelphia Inquirer,* October 10, 1864; Crist, vol. 11, p. 66 n. 24; Rable, pp. 274–75.

30. *"Spartan mothers of old":* Crist, vol. 11, p. 61.

30. Announcing Hood's plans in advance: Grant, vol. 2, pp. 347–48.

30. *"names of a quarter of a million deserters":* Crist, vol. 11, p. 71.

30. *"Give us Johnston":* Bonds, p. 330.

30. Speech to the Alabama legislature: Rowland, vol. 6, pp. 345–47; Crist, vol. 11, pp. 74–75.

30. Taylor's talk with Davis: Richard Taylor, *Destruction and Reconstruction: Personal Experiences of the Late War* (New York: D. Appleton and Co., 1879), pp. 204–06.

31. *"a fixed, ineradicable distrust":* Crist, vol. 11, p. 59.

31. *The "infernal Hydra": OR,* ser. 4, vol. 3, pp. 707–10; Crist, vol. 11, p. 78.

31. Speech in Columbus: *Id.,* p. 76.

31. Speech in Augusta: McElroy, p. 423.

31. Speech in Columbia: Crist, vol. 11, p. 85.

31. *"no reason to doubt": OR,* ser. 4, vol. 3, pt. 1, p. 799.

32. *Shock waves:* e.g., Freehling, p. 194.

32. *coldest in recent memory:* Henry S. Foote, *War of the Rebellion* (New York: Harper & Bros., 1866) ("Foote, *War of the Rebellion"*), p. 375; Bill, p. 250.

32. Richmond's condition: Warren Akin, Bell Irvin Wiley, ed., *Letters of Warren Akin* (Athens: University of Georgia Press, 1959) ("Akin"), p. 105; Sallie A. Brock, *Richmond During the War* (New York: G. W. Carleton & Co., 1867) ("Brock"), pp. 315 and 341; Wise, pp. 392–95; Thomas Conolly and Nelson D. Lankford, ed., "The Diary of Thomas Conolly, M.P., Virginia, March–April 1865, 95 *The Virginia Magazine of History and Biography* (January 1987) ("Conolly"), pp. 75–112; Bill, pp. 244–45.

32. Seward's letter to his wife: Frederick W. Seward, *Seward at Washington, as Senator and Secretary of State,* 2 vols. (New York: Derby and Miller, 1891) ("Seward, *Seward at Washington"*) vol. 2, p. 248.

CHAPTER 6

33. Celebrations and parade: *The Daily National Republican*, November 11, 1864; Brooks, *Lincoln Observed*, p. 140.

33. *"the pet of the house"; a lovable boy:* William H. Crook, "Lincoln As I Knew Him," 114 *Harper's Magazine* (June 1907) ("Crook, 'Lincoln As I Knew Him'"), pp. 113–14; Keckley, p. 117; Stoddard, p. 187; Hay, *At Lincoln's Side*, pp. 109, 111–13, 135–36 (Tad "had a very bad opinion of books and no opinion of discipline," and his father "idolized" him); Dana, *Lincoln and His Cabinet*, p. 42; Wilson, p. 400.

34. *few . . . would recognize him now:* Brooks, *Lincoln Observed*, p. 211.

34. *worth the sting:* Noah Brooks, "Lincoln's Reelection," 49 *The Century Magazine* (April 1895), p. 866.

34. *"nothing touches the tired spot":* Brooks, *Lincoln Observed*, pp. 43 and 213; Carpenter, p. 217.

34. *McClellan had carried three; incoming Congress:* Goodwin, pp. 665–66; Donald, p. 544.

34. *the crowd cheered for minutes:* *The Daily National Republican*, November 11, 1864.

34. Lincoln's speech: *CW*, vol. 8, pp. 100–01.

34. *high-pitched Western twang . . . carrying over the crowd:* See Waldo W. Braden, *Abraham Lincoln, Public Speaker* (Baton Rouge: Louisiana State University Press, 1988) ("Braden"), pp. 97–101.

34. *"Not very graceful":* Hay Diary, p. 248.

34. Seward's speech and revelers: *Daily National Republican*, November 11, 1864; *New York Times*, November 10, 1864; Seward, *Seward at Washington*, pp. 249–50.

35. *Rome, Georgia, was lit by arson:* OR, ser. 1, vol. 39, pt. 1, p. 771.

35. Sherman's march: Fellman, *Sherman*, pp. 186–89.

35. *"I am going into the very bowels":* Id., p. 188.

35. *James W. Singleton:* Hay Diary, pp. 279–80 n. 71; Crist, *Davis Papers*, vol. 11, p. 387 n. 5 and p. 480 n. 9; Ludwell H. Johnson, "Beverley Tucker's Canadian Mission, 1864–1865," 29 *The Journal of Southern History* (February 1963) ("Johnson, 'Mission'"), pp. 88–99; Burlingame, vol. 2, pp. 754–55.

35. *the idol of his friends:* Hay Diary, p. 279 n. 71.

35. *"a miracle of meanness":* Id., p. 19.

36. *it was nothing personal:* Id., p. 279 n. 71.

36. Singleton on Clay, Tucker, and peace: Orville Hickman Browning, Theodore C. Pease, and James G. Randall, eds., *The Diary of Orville Hickman Browning*, 2 vols. (Springfield: Illinois State Historical Library, 1925–1933) ("Browning"), vol. 1, p. 694.

36. *If anyone could influence "those people":* Burlingame, vol. 2, p. 755.

36. *"heavy on his mind":* Welles Diary, vol. 2, p. 179.

37. *"the responsibility all rested upon him":* Rice, p. 96.

37. *"who will he treat with":* Welles Diary, vol. 2, p. 179.

37. *"but the States are entities and may be . . . treated with":* Id.

37. *The president should invite the rebellious states":* Id., p. 190.

37. *Lincoln sometimes called him Mars:* David Homer Bates, *Lincoln in the Telegraph Office* (New York: Century Co., 1907) ("Bates,"), p. 400.

37. *Davis called him venomous:* Davis, *Rise and Fall,* vol. 2, p. 689. See Crook, "Lincoln As I Knew Him," p. 110. Stanton was "a great man" but "a martinet . . . a very bitter cruel man."

37. Stanton on peace overtures: Welles Diary, vol. 2, p. 179.

38. *But how was he to know; Governor Francis Pierpont:* Ambler, pp. 257–58.

38. *In an effort to reach them, Southern papers ran notices:* Bill, p. 245; e.g., *Richmond Enquirer, passim.*

38–39. Lincoln's annual message: *CW,* vol. 8, pp. 136–53.

40. Thaddeus Stevens: The definitive biography is Brodie, *Thaddeus Stevens.* See Schurz, vol. 3, p. 214, for a tart recollection of Stevens.

40. *"Glad to hear it":* James M. Scoville, "Thaddeus Stevens," 61 *Lippincott's Magazine,* (April 1898), p. 549.

40. Stevens on Lincoln's annual message: *Congressional Globe,* January 5, 1865, p. 124.

40. *a priority that Lincoln embraced but had always ranked second:* E.g., Escott, pp. 54–55 and *passim.*

CHAPTER 7

Much of the discussion of John A. Campbell in this chapter is drawn from Robert Saunders Jr., *John Archibald Campbell, Southern Moderate, 1811–1889* (Tuscaloosa: University of Alabama Press, 1999) ("Saunders"); and Henry G. Connor, *John Archibald Campbell* (Boston: Houghton Mifflin, 1920) ("Connor"). A chronology of Campbell's life is in Wiggins, pp. 262–63. The Campbell family papers are at the University of North Carolina at Chapel Hill in the Southern Historical Collection. See also John A. Campbell, "Open Letters: A View of the Confederacy from the Inside," 38 *The Century Magazine* (October 1889) ("Campbell, 'Open Letters'"), pp. 950–54.

41. *"You have Mr. Lincoln's ear":* Greeley to Blair, December 1, 1864, Abraham Lincoln Papers, Library of Congress; Smith, *Francis Preston Blair,* p. 363.

41. A friend of Seward's: Stahr, p. 172.

41. Efforts of Campbell, Nelson, and Seward to avert the war: *Id.,* pp. 120–47. Campbell's account is in "Reply of Judge Campbell," 7 *The Southern Magazine* (February 1874) ("Campbell, 'Reply'"), pp. 22–28. See Alexander Stephens, *A Constitutional View of the Late War Between the States,* 2 vols. (Philadelphia: National Publishing Co., 1870) ("Stephens, *CV*"), vol. 2, pp. 346–51.

42. *"unworthy of a practical man"; "At times he is pleasant":* Connor, pp. 9–10.

42. Supreme Court appointment: Strode, p. 468.

42. *Support of the* New York Times: Quoted in *Connor,* p. 17.

42. *argued controversially:* John A. Campbell, "Slavery in the United States," 12 *Southern Quarterly Review* (July 1847), pp. 91–134.

42. *illegal African slave trade:* Connor, pp. 103–4.

42. *He owned house slaves and laborers:* Saunders, pp. 66–68.

42. *infamous* Dred Scott v. Sandford *decision:* 19 Howard 393, 15 L. Ed. 691 (1857); see E. I. McCormac, "Justice Campbell and the *Dred Scott* Decision," 19 *The Mississippi Valley Historical Review* (March 1933), pp. 565–71.

42. *against his stern advice:* Campbell, "Reply," p. 27.

42. Seward, Campbell, and Davis's peace envoys: Rowland, vol. 5, pp. 98–99; Saunders, pp. 147–52; Connor, pp. 129–48.

42. *an opinion he would later change:* Campbell, "Reply," p. 28.

43. *"to follow the fortunes of my people":* Connor, p. 112.

43. *"His is one of the hardest cases":* Chesnut, p. 77.

43. *a subordinate role:* Campbell to Nathan Clifford, August 1, 1865, Andrew Johnson Papers, Library of Congress; Campbell, "Open Letters," pp. 950–51; Kean, pp. 162–63; Connor, pp. 159–60.

43. *Judge Campbell, as everyone called him:* e.g., *Id.*, pp. 195–97; Jones, vol. 2, p. 410; Robert M. T. Hunter, "R. M. T. Hunter, The Peace Commission of 1865," 3 *Southern Historical Society Papers* (April 1877), pp. 168–76 ("Hunter 'Peace Commission'"), p. 172.

43. *Hunter of Virginia had suggested it:* Kean, p. 182.

43. *Kean thought the letter too formal: Id.*

43. Letter shown to Hunter, then Seddon: Crist, vol. 11, p. 322 n. 20; Connor, p. 164.

43. James Seddon: Roy W. Curry, "James A. Seddon: A Southern Prototype," 63 *Virginia Magazine of History and Biography* (April 1955); Burton J. Hendrick, *Statesmen of the Lost Cause: Jefferson Davis and His Cabinet* (Boston: Little, Brown, 1939) ("Hendrick, *Statesmen of the Lost Cause*"), pp. 326–27; Ernest B. Furguson, *Ashes of Glory: Richmond at War* (New York: Alfred A Knopf, 1996) ("Furguson"), p. 88.

43. *Yankees had burned Seddon's rural Virginia home:* Smith, *Blair Family*, vol. 2, p. 275.

44. *in his grave a full month:* Jones, vol. 1, p. 312.

44. *Davis, who let the attempt be made:* Connor, p. 164; Campbell, "Open Letters," p. 951.

44. *Campbell's letter to Justice Nelson:* The letter is in Connor, pp. 161–63.

44. *Campbell had no illusions:* Kean, p. 182.

44. Grant's conversation with the Bishop of Arkansas: *Id.*, pp. 180 and 186.

45. *Confederate signal service sent Campbell's letter:* Connor, p. 163.

45. *[Campbell] never got an answer:* Campbell, "Open Letters," p. 951.

45. *"In lieu of this . . . there came [Blair]": Id.*

45. Greeley's December 15 letter: Greeley's letter, in the Lincoln Papers at the Library of Congress, is in Smith, *Blair Family*, vol. 2, pp. 301–02.

45. McMullen's resolution: *New York Times*, January 12, 1865.

45. Grant's wire to Sherman: Adam Badeau, *Military History of Ulysses S. Grant* (New York: D. Appleton and Co., 1885) ("Badeau"), vol. 3, p. 357.

45. Blair's letter to Greeley: Horace Greeley Papers, New York Public Library. The letter is in Smith, *Blair Family*, vol. 2, p. 302.

45. Blair's relationship with Davis: Davis, *Rise and Fall*, vol. 2, p. 616; Crist, vol. 11, p. 319 n. 1; Smith, *Blair Family*, vol. 2, p. 323; Elizabeth Blair Lee, pp. 9, 14, 15 n. 3, 18, 47, 110, 459, and 460 n. 2.

46. *"our Oakland cronies": Id.*, pp. 459 and 460 n. 2.

46. *"That's the Blairs' carriage":* Smith, *Francis Preston Blair*, p. 258.

46. *"my heart aches for them":* Elizabeth Blair Lee, p. 9.

46. *Mrs. Davis had sent a baby's dress:* Chesnut, p. 68.

46. Baby clothes for Francis Preston Blair Lee: Crist, *Davis Papers*, vol. 11, p. 320 n. 3.

47. *Jeff [Davis] wrote his mother:* Strode, p. 103.

47. *One of the greatest who ever lived:* John Bigelow, *Retrospections of an Active Life,* 5 vols. (New York: Baker & Taylor, 1909–13) ("Bigelow"), vol. 4, p. 50.

47. Lincoln's office and its view: Brooks, *Lincoln Observed,* pp. 84–85; Goodwin, plates 38 and 41; Crook, "Lincoln As I Knew Him," p. 112.

47. *"I might do something towards peace":* Crist, vol. 11, p. 315.

47. *"Come to me after Savannah falls":* Nicolay and Hay, vol. 10, p. 94.

47. *that took two days to reach him:* William T. Sherman, *Memoirs,* 2 vols. (New York: D. Appleton & Co., 1891) ("Sherman"), vol. 2, p. 231.

48. *a captured Savannah mansion:* Fellman, p. 192.

48. *He sent a wire to the War Department:* OR, ser. 1, vol. 44, pp. 798–99.

48. *leaving Sherman an open path:* Grimsley and Simpson, pp. 43–44.

48. Browning's meeting with Lincoln: Browning, vol. 1, p. 699; Johnson, *Mission,* p. 95; Charles B. Flood, *1864: Lincoln at the Gates of History* (New York: Simon & Schuster, 2009) ("Flood"), pp. 412–15.

48. Christmas and the Episcopalian orphanage: Varina Davis, "Christmas in the Confederate White House," *New York World,* December 13, 1896 ("Davis, 'Christmas'"), p. 26.

49. *"Great commotion":* Jones, vol. 2, p. 364.

49. *counted vacant chairs:* Brock, p. 341.

49. *equal to the holiday wardrobes:* Pollard, p. 488.

49. *"The truth is we are prostrated":* Kean, p. 181.

49. *precious sweet potatoes:* Davis, "Christmas," p. 26.

49. *Lincoln sent [Sherman] a wire:* CW, vol. 8, pp. 181–82.

49. *thousands of columns of smoke:* Fellman, p. 225.

50. *"people whined like curs":* Id., p. 231.

50. Sunset Cox: Davis Lindsey, *Sunset Cox: Irrepressible Democrat* (Detroit: Wayne State University Press, 1959); Samuel Sullivan Cox, *Three Decades of Federal Legislation, 1855 to 1885* (San Francisco: Occidental Publishing Col, 1885) ("Cox, *Three Decades*"); Samuel Sullivan Cox, *Eight Years in Congress, from 1857 to 1865* (New York: D. Appleton and Co., 1865) ("Cox, *Eight Years*").

50. *"miscegenation plot":* Sidney Kaplan, "The Miscegenation Issue in the Election of 1864," 34 *Journal of Negro History* (July 1949), pp. 274–343.

50. Cox and Stuart visit Lincoln: Cox, *Three Decades,* p. 310.

51. Cox visits Seward: *Id.,* pp. 310–11.

51. Benjamin's letter to Slidell: Richardson, vol. 2, pp. 694–97; Nicolay and Hay, vol. 10, p. 155.

51. *Europe was not interested:* Richardson, vol. 2, p. 717.

51. *"some black-hearted artillery man":* History of Thirty-Fifth Regiment Massachusetts Volunteers (Boston: Mills, Knight & Co., 1884) ("*35th Massachusetts*"), p. 318.

CHAPTER 8

52. Lincoln's meeting with Blair and Blair's pass to Richmond: CW, vol. 8, pp. 188; Nicolay and Hay, vol. 10, p. 94; Stephens, CV, vol. 2, p. 600; Davis, *Rise and Fall,* vol. 2, p. 613; Rice, pp. 250–51.

52. *The president expected little: Id.*
52. *the rest of the Cabinet was not told:* Welles Diary, vol. 2, pp. 219 and 231–32.
52. *"indefinite understanding":* G. P. Lathrop, "The Bailing of Jefferson Davis," 33 *The Century Magazine* (February 1887) ("Lathrop"), p. 640.
52. Private George Deutzer: Gould, p. 282.
53. *toothache and . . . weakness; guests . . . leftovers:* Smith, *Francis Preston Blair,* p. 364.
53. *The Blairs had struck a bargain:* See *New York Daily Tribune,* January 4, 1865; *Richmond Dispatch,* January 13, 1865, reprinted in *New York Times,* January 16, 1865; *Richmond Examiner,* January 6, 1865, reprinted in *New York Times,* January 11, 1865; Smith, *Francis Preston Blair,* p. 364.
53. Departure on the *Baltimore: Id.*
53. Jamestown: Hay Diary, p. 249.
53. City Point: Horace Porter, *Campaigning with Grant* (New York: Century Co., 1897) ("Porter, *Grant*"), pp. 212–13; 233, 329–30, 368, 377, and 425; Hay Diary, p. 250; www.nps.gov/pete/historyculture/united-states-military-railroad.htm.
53. Grant: Modern biographies include Jean Edward Smith, *Grant* (New York: Simon & Schuster, 2001) ("Smith, *Grant*"); William S. McFeely, *Grant: A Biography* (New York: Norton & Company, 1981) ("McFeely"); H. W. Brands, *The Man Who Saved the Union: Ulysses Grant in War and Peace* (New York: Doubleday, 2012); Geoffrey Perret, *Ulysses S. Grant, Soldier and President* (New York: The Modern Library, 1999) ("Perret"); and Brooks D. Simpson's two treatments, *Ulysses S. Grant: Triumph Over Adversity, 1822–1865* (Boston: Houghton Mifflin Harcourt, 2000) and *Let Us Have Peace: Ulysses S. Grant and the Politics of War and Reconstruction, 1861–1868* (Chapel Hill: University of North Carolina Press, 1991) ("Simpson, *Grant*"). Grant's memoirs are cogent and informative. Julia Grant's are also interesting. See also Ulysses S. Grant and John Y. Simon, ed., *The Papers of Ulysses S. Grant* (New York: G. P. Putnam's Sons, 1975) ("Grant Papers").
53–54. Dana's impressions of Grant: Charles A. Dana, *Recollections of the Civil War* (New York: D. Appleton and Company, 1898) ("Dana, *Recollections*"), p. 61; Charles A. Dana, *The Life of Ulysses S. Grant* (Springfield, MA: Gurdon Bill & Company, 1868) ("Dana, *Grant*"), *passim.*
54. Physical description of Grant: Brooks, *Lincoln Observed,* p. 104; Dana, *Grant,* p. 403.
54. *"He talks bad grammar":* Lyman, p. 156.
54. *"carved from mahogany":* Benjamin Perley Poore, *Perley's Reminiscences of Sixty Years in the National Metropolis,* 2 vols. (Philadelphia: Hubbard Brothers, 1886) ("Poore") vol. 2, p. 150.
54. *blue-gray eyes, lion's eyes:* Dana, *Grant,* p. 403.
54. *"blushed like a girl":* Badeau, vol. 3, p. 142.
54. *"no noise or clash":* Dana, *Grant,* pp. 403–04.
54. *Now he welcomed the Blairs; awed by the might:* Elizabeth Blair Lee, pp. 459–60.
54. *had [the letters] sent up the James immediately:* See Davis, *Rise and Fall,* vol. 2, p. 612.
54. The letters: Both letters are in Rowland, vol. 6, pp. 432–33.
55. Both letters reached Davis that day: See Davis, *Rise and Fall,* vol. 2, p. 612.
55. Davis's memoirs mischaracterize them: *Id.*

55. *a blustery New Year's Eve: 35th Massachusetts*, p. 318.

55. Seddon's letter to Blair: Blair Family Papers, Library of Congress; Crist, vol. 11, p. 320 n. 3.

55. *word got around the War Department:* Kean, pp. 185–86.

55. *Late on New Year's Day:* Howard C. Westwood, "Lincoln at the Hampton Roads Peace Conference," 81 *Lincoln Herald* (Winter 1979) ("Westwood, 'Hampton Roads Conference'"), p. 244; Welles Diary, vol. 2, p. 221.

55. *Preston had left for home:* Grant Papers, vol. 13, pp. 209–10; *Elizabeth Blair Lee*, p. 459.

55. *"very pleasant trip"; "in the finest spirits possible": Id.*

56. *"Affairs are gloomy enough":* Jones, vol. 2, p. 373.

56. *rumors of Blair's journey were afoot:* Cox, *Three Decades*, p. 330; Kean, pp. 185–86; *New York Daily Tribune*, February 2, 1865.

56. *"without the knowledge of high officials":* New York Times, January 2, 1865.

56. *"Old Mr. Blair" sitting in an adjoining room:* Welles Diary, vol. 2, p. 219.

56. *His appointment with the President was canceled:* Davis, *Rise and Fall*, p. 613; Crist, vol. 11, pp. 316 and 320 n. 3.

56. *Blair had already briefed Horace Greeley:* See *New York Daily Tribune*, January 4, 1865, and *Congressional Globe*, January 5, p. 125.

56. Suspicion of Stanton: See *Id.*

56. Montgomery's review of Stanton: Hendrick, *Lincoln's War Cabinet*, pp. 259–60.

56. *others had come to his attention:* Welles Diary, vol. 2, p. 158 n. 1; Dana, *Recollections*, pp. 231–32.

56. Article in the *Tribune:* New York Daily Tribune, January 4, 1865, quoted in *Congressional Globe*, January 5, 1865, p. 125.

56. *By the time the story ran:* Grant's Papers, vol. 13, p. 209; *Elizabeth Blair Lee*, p. 460 n. 3, Davis, *Rise and Fall*, vol. 2, p. 612.

56. *Greeley duly ate crow in the* Tribune: New York Daily Tribune, January 7, 1865.

57. *"Father sets out tomorrow": Elizabeth Blair Lee*, p. 460, n. 3.

57. Fox's wire to Grant: *OR* ser. 1, vol. 46, part 2, p. 29.

57. *Fox had arranged to send: Id.,* Welles Diary, vol. 2, p. 221.

57. *"a diligent search" had found him:* OR ser. 1, vol. 46, part 2, p. 30; John L. Johnson, *The University Memorial* (Baltimore: Turnbull Brothers, 1871), pp. 673–75.

58. *"propagators of the truth":* New York Times, January 5, 1865.

58. *galleries were filled:* Brooks, *Washington in Lincoln's Time*, pp. 204–12.

58. *"devoid of music":* Schurz, vol. 3, p. 214.

58. *"the ablest man":* Brooks, *Washington in Lincoln's Time*, p. 17.

58. Stevens as demonic: George M. Drake, July 24, 1867, editorial in Alabama's *Union Springs Times*, quoted in Brodie, *Thaddeus Stevens*, p. 18.

58. Greeley and Blair admitted to the floor: *Congressional Globe*, January 5, 1865, p. 125.

58. *"as though each one weighed a ton":* Brooks, *Washington in Lincoln's Time*, p. 17.

58. Stevens's speech: *Congressional Globe*, January 5, 1865, p. 124.

59–60. Stevens's exchange with Cox: *Id.*, pp. 124–25.

CHAPTER 9

This chapter and much else in this book rely heavily on the most recent and best biography of Alexander Stephens, Thomas E. Schott's *Alexander H. Stephens of Georgia: A Biography* (Baton Rouge: Louisiana State University Press, 1987) ("Schott"). Also helpful is Rudolph R. Von Abele's *Alexander H. Stephens: A Biography* (New York: Knopf, 1946) ("Von Abele"). Stephens writes about his life and career in Stephens, *CV*, and in Myrta Lockett Avary, *Recollections of Alexander Stephens* (New York: Doubleday, Page & Company, 1910) ("Avary, *Recollections*"). Stephens's contemporary biographers were reverential friends, but they provide informative letters, speeches, and insights: Richard M. Johnston and William H. Browne, *Life of Alexander Stephens* (Philadelphia: Lippincott, 1884) ("Johnston and Browne"); and Henry Cleveland, *Alexander Stephens, in Public and Private, with Letters and Speeches, before, during, and since the War* (Philadelphia: National Publishing Co., 1866) ("Cleveland"). Useful articles include John R. Brumgardt, "The Confederate Career of Alexander H. Stephens: The Case Reopened," 27 *Civil War History* (March 1981), pp. 64–81, and James Z. Rabun, "Alexander H. Stephens and Jefferson Davis," 58 *The American Historical Review* (January 1953) ("Rabun"), pp. 290–321. Stephens's papers are in the Library of Congress, and in the libraries of Manhattanville College of the Sacred Heart ("Manhattanville Library"), Emory University, Duke University, and the Historical Society of Pennsylvania.

61. Lincoln's letter to his partner: William H. Herndon and Jesse W. Weik, *Abraham Lincoln: The True Story of a Great Life* (New York: D. Appleton, 1917) ("Herndon and Weik"), p. 268.

61. Lincoln and Stephens on the Mexican War: Dirck, pp. 103–07; Von Abele, p. 102.

61. *Young Indians:* Isaac Newton Arnold, *The Life of Abraham Lincoln* (Chicago: Jansen, McClurg & Co., 1885) ("Arnold"), pp. 77–78, quoting Stephens. See Donald, pp. 126–27.

62. *never weighed as much as a hundred pounds:* Schott, p. 21. See Avary, *Recollections,* p. 46.

62. *called him Little Alec:* Schott, p. 20.

62. *"refugee from a graveyard":* Von Abele, p. 203.

62. Ailments and afflictions: Schott, pp. 20–21; Von Abele, pp. 66, 69–70, 77, 120, and 136.

62. *"two weeks' purchase on life":* Robert Toombs, quoted in Avary, *Recollections,* p. 46.

62. *may have been an alcoholic:* Schott, *Stephens,* p. 21.

62. *"shrill but musical":Id.,* p. 88.

62. *"cease to be annoyed":* Quoted in Cleveland, p. 102.

63. *"only feel that he is right":Id.,* p. 32.

63. *The Senate's great men:Id.,* p. 103.

63. *"anterior to the war":* Stephens, *CV,* vol. 2, p. 266.

63. *"suffered from a look":* Quoted in Von Abele, p. 135.

63. *If Rembrandt could only paint him:* Quoted in Cleveland, p. 112.

63. *a well-preserved mummy:* Schott, p. 213.

63. *"lizards and watches":* Avary, *Recollections,* pp. 232–33.

63. *lonely, self-pitying man:* Von Abele, pp. 76, 120, and 135–36.

63. *"I have borne it all my life"*: Hendrick, *Statesmen of the Lost Cause*, p. 60.
63. *"half-finished thing"*: Schott, p. 20.
63. *taking comfort in his rectitude: Id.*, p. 134.
64. *"political filth"*: Von Abele, p. 89.
64. *"proud, independent, unyielding": Id.*, p. 73.
64. Encounter with Judge Cone: *Id.*, pp. 110–15; Cleveland, pp. 88–90; and Schott, pp. 91–93.
65. Adams's poem: The poem is in Von Abele, p. 103.
65. *"extending to my head"*: Stephens, *CV,* vol. 2, p. 277.
65. Speech to the Georgia legislature: *Id.*, pp. 278–307; Cleveland, pp. 694–713.
65. Correspondence with Lincoln: The correspondence is in Stephens, *CV,* vol. 2, pp. 265–71 and in Cleveland, between pp. 150 and 151.
65. Selection as vice president: Schott, pp. 327–29; Rabun, p. 291.
65. *"accused him of looking back"*: Chesnut, p. 49.
65. *"never believed in this thing"*: Mary Chesnut and C. Vann Woodward, ed., *Mary Chesnut's Civil War* (New Haven: Yale University Press, 1981), p. 520.
65. Stephens on secession: Stephens, *CV,* vol. 2, pp. 425–27; Rabun, p. 301.
66. *"how I came to make the mistake"*: Schott, p. 355.
66. *"the little pale star"*: Benjamin Perley Poore, "Reminiscences of Washington," 46 *Atlantic Monthly* (December 1880), p. 805.
66. *adjudge him an imbecile, and . . . a despot: OR* ser. 4, vol. 3, pp. 278–82; Hendrick, *Statesmen of the Lost Cause*, p. 418.
66. *Davis was a nationalist:* See, e.g., Stephens, *CV,* vol. 2, pp. 568–75; Dirck, pp. 85–87; Rable, pp. 166–67.
66. Davis's relationship with Stephens: Schott, pp. 330–31, 346–47, 357, 392, 397, 418, and 448; Rable, pp. 165–67, 251, and 256–61; Dirck, pp. 222–24; Rabun, *passim.*
66. Speech to the Georgia legislature: The speech is presented in full in Cleveland, pp. 761–86.
66. The *Southern Recorder inquired:* Schott, p. 411.
67. *"children in politics and statesmanship"*: Hendrick, *Statesmen of the Lost Cause*, p. 419; Rable, pp. 166–67.
67. *Davis offered to resign:* Rowland, vol. 8, p. 213.
67. *visiting Richmond only briefly:* Hendrick, *Statesmen of the Lost Cause*, p. 416.
67. *"as simple and genial in his manners as a child"*: Quoted in Cleveland, p. 34.
67. *paid for the educations:* Von Abele, p. 324.
67. *"I ever afterward assisted"*: Avary, *Recollections*, pp. 226–27.
67. Liberty Hall: Von Abele, engraving between pp. 112 and 113.
67. *Liberty Hall's mealtimes: Id.*, p. 43; Von Abele, p. 324; *New York Herald,* September 26, 1860, cited in Cleveland, p. 27.
67. *"He is kind to folks"*: Avary, *Recollections*, p. 42.
67. Slaves at Liberty Hall: *Id.*, p. 87.
67. *"free will and consent": Id.*, p. 208.
67. Stephens's land and slaves: Schott, p. 45.
68. *did odd jobs and played:* Avary, *Recollections*, p. 87; Schott, pp. 65 and 175.

68. *"got in trouble with a white woman": Id.,* p. 65.
68. Harry and Eliza's wedding: Avary, *Recollections,* p. 87.
68. *"subordination of the inferior African race": Id.,* p. 173.
68. *"The Cornerstone Speech":* The speech is presented, with Stephens's edits, in Cleveland, pp. 717–79; Avary, *Recollections,* pp. 173–74. See also Cleveland, pp. 168 and 717; Schott, pp. 334–35.
69. Stephens's trip to Fort Monroe in 1863: *OR,* ser. 2, vol. 6, pp. 74–76, 79–80, 84, and 94–95; Stephens, *CV,* vol. 2, pp. 538 and 558–68; Welles Diary, vol. 1, pp. 358–60; Cleveland, p. 170–71, 180; Kirkland, pp. 210–12.
69. *"psalms to a dead horse":* Cleveland, p. 180.
69. Stephens's communications with Sherman: *Id.,* pp. 196–97.

CHAPTER 10

72. General Gorgas: "A Sketch of the Life of General Gorgas, Chief of Ordnance of the Confederate States," 13 *Southern Historical Society Papers* (1885), pp. 216–28; see also Wiggins, pp. xxxiii–xxxix.
72. Party at Judge Campbell's: Josiah Gorgas and Frank E Vandiver, ed., *The Civil War Diary of General Josiah Gorgas* (Tuscaloosa: University of Alabama Press, 1947) ("Gorgas").
72. *"the striking girl in pink":* Wise, p. 403.
72. *"Is the cause really hopeless?":* Gorgas, p. 164.
72. Campbell's report to Seddon: Kean, p. 189.
72. *Seddon said he had none: Id.,* p. 187.
73. *roll call vote was required:* Grimsley and Simpson, p. 136.
73. *Alec Stephens had returned:* Johnston and Browne, p. 475.
73. *"walked with bent heads":* Pollard, p. 393.
73. Stephens's secret speech: Stephens, *CV,* vol. 2, pp. 587–89; Nicolay and Hay, vol. 10, p. 109; Stephens to Linton Stephens, February 18, 1865, Manhattanville Library.
73. Hunter in Campbell's office: Jones, vol. 2, p. 379.
73. *talk of Davis and Stephens both resigning:* Kean, p. 185.
73. *"In a letter from Georgia":* Crist, vol. 11, p. 293.
74. Singleton's pass: *CW,* vol. 8, p. 200.
74. *six hundred bales of cotton:* Crist, vol. 11, p. 480 n. 10; Browning Diary, vol. 1, p. 693 n. 3 and 699, vol. 2, pp. 1–2; Johnson, "Mission," p. 96; Flood, p. 413.
74. Singleton and Lincoln's instructions to him: Duff Green, *Facts and Suggestions, Biographical, Historical, Financial, and Political* (New York: C. S. Wescott & CC's Union Printing Office, 1866) ("Duff Green"), p. 232; Randall and Current, pp. 330–31; Grimsley and Simpson, pp. 82–83.
74. Lizzie's letter to Phil: *Elizabeth Blair Lee,* pp. 460–61 n. 1.
74. SOMETHING WICKED THIS WAY COMES: *Richmond Examiner,* January 6, 1865, reprinted in *New York Times,* January 11, 1865.
75. *"richly deserve hanging":* Richmond Whig, January 6, 1865, reprinted in *New York Times,* January 11, 1865.

75. *"We will stand on our guard":* Richmond Sentinel, reprinted in *New York Times,* January 11, 1865.

75. *"a respectable demagogue":* Executive Documents of the House of Representatives 1871–72, *Special Report on the Customs-Tariff Legislation* (Washington, DC: US Government Printing Office, 1872), p. 135.

75. Cox's speech: *Congressional Globe,* January 12, 1865, p. 242.

75. *a hard rain fell on Blair House: Elizabeth Blair Lee,* p. 460.

75. Blair departs on the *Don: New York Times,* January 9, 1865; Crist, vol. 11, p. 320 n. 3; *Richmond Dispatch,* reprinted in *New York Times,* January 16, 1865; Grant Papers, vol. 13, p. 210.

76. Blair shared his plan with Grant: Bigelow, vol. 4, p. 51; Stephens, *CV,* vol. 2, pp. 597–98; Westwood, *Hampton Roads Conference,* p. 248. See Lathrop, p. 640, third footnote.

76. *seventy-five presidents:* Hendrick, *Statesmen of the Lost Cause,* p. 108.

76. Mexico's situation: *Id.,* pp. 106–38, and Van Deusen, pp. 366–69 and 486–97.

76. *Seward had a dream: Id.,* pp. 487–88.

76. Austrians in Mexico: Stahr, p. 440.

76. *Grant's conscience:* Bruce Catton, *Grant Takes Command* (Boston: Little, Brown, 1969), p. 489.

76. Grant's conversation with Seward on Mexico: Porter, *Grant,* p. 256. See Hay Diary, p. 211, and Stahr, p. 441.

77. Pickets in view of each other: *35th Massachusetts,* p. 319.

77. *"black-mouthed bulldogs":* San Francisco Bulletin, February 14, 1865.

77. *clear and pleasant weather:* Jones, vol. 2, p. 382.

77. Blair's trip to Richmond: *New York Times,* January 19, 1865; *New York Times,* January 21, 1865.

77. Blair and Henry wait to be cleared: Crist, vol. 11, p. 318.

77. *goodwill was exhibited all around:* Blair manuscript, Lincoln Papers, Library of Congress, reproduced in Crist, vol. 11, p. 318; *Richmond Dispatch,* January 13, 1865, reprinted in *New York Times,* January 16, 1865.

78. Stephens on Blair's visit: Stephens, *CV,* vol. 2, p. 590.

78. *General Lee made a public plea:* Gorgas, p. 148.

78. *Blair "fared sumptuously":* Elizabeth Blair Lee, p. 463.

78. *guest of Robert Ould:* Jones, vol. 2, p. 386; *New York Daily Tribune,* January 16, 1865, quoting *Richmond Dispatch,* January 13, 1865; *New York Tribune,* January 17, 1865, quoting *Richmond Dispatch,* January 14, 1865.

78. Ould brought Yankee delicacies back: Bill, p. 213.

78. Ould's appearance: Francis T. Miller, ed., *The Photographic History of the Civil War* (New York: Review of Reviews Co., 1911), vol. 7, p. 101.

78. Ould a friend of Frank Jr.'s: *Elizabeth Blair Lee,* p. 463.

78. Ould as Washington DA: Jon L. Wakelyn, *Biographical Directory of the Confederacy* (Westport, CT: Greenwood Press, 1977) ("Wakelyn"), p. 336.

78. Blair's conversation with Ould: Rowland, vol. 8, p. 601.

78. Henry Foote: Rowland, vol. 7, p. 395 n. 1; Smith, *Blair Family,* p. 313; Wilfred B. Yearns Jr., "The Peace Movement in the Confederate Congress," 41 *The Georgia*

Historical Society Quarterly (March 1957) ("Yearns, Peace Movement"), p. 18; James P. Coleman, "Two Irascible Antebellum Senators: George Poindexter and Henry S. Foote," 46 *Journal of Mississippi History* (February 1984), pp. 17–27; John Edward Gonzales, "Henry Stuart Foote: Confederate Congressman and Exile," 11 *Civil War History* (December 1965), pp. 384–95; Dirck, p. 62. See also *New York Daily Tribune*, January 14 and January 24, 1865, and Foote's telling of his own story in Foote, *War of the Rebellion;* and *Casket of Reminiscences* (Washington, DC: Chronicle Publishing Company, 1874) ("Foote, *Casket of Reminiscences*").

79. Peace resolutions: Charles W. Sanders Jr., "Jefferson Davis and the Hampton Roads Peace Conference: 'To Secure Peace to the Two Countries,'" 63 *The Journal of Southern History* (November 1997) ("Sanders"), p. 808; Yearns, "Peace Movement," pp. 14–15; Kirkland, pp. 218–20; Rable, pp. 280–81.

79. Campbell blames Blair's arrival for killing his overture to Nelson: Campbell, "Open Letters," p. 951.

79. *nothing could be done until the scheme was tried:* Connor, pp. 163–64. See Westwood, *Hampton Roads Conference*, p. 248, on the likelihood that Lincoln was informed about Campbell's letter.

CHAPTER 11

80. Confederate White House: Furgurson, pp. 87–88 and map after p. xi; Varina Davis, vol. 2, pp. 198–201.

80. The Davises greet Blair: *Elizabeth Blair Lee*, p. 463; Jones, vol. 2, pp. 383 and 400.

80. *"emaciated and altered as not to be recognized":* Edward L. Pierce, *Memoirs and Letters of Charles Sumner,* 4 vols. (Boston: Roberts Brothers, 1893) ("Pierce"), vol. 4, p. 205.

80. *"noticed every shade of expression":* Varina Davis, vol. 2, p. 920.

80–86. Blair's meeting with Davis: Less than a week after his January 12 meeting with Davis, Blair preserved his memory of it in a memorandum dictated to Montgomery (Crist, vol. 11, p. 319). Nicolay and Hay published it in "Abraham Lincoln: A History," 38 *The Century* Magazine (October 1889), pp. 838–57, with the memorandum that Blair read to Davis. Both are in Nicolay and Hay, vol. 10, pp. 97–106, with some omissions. Blair's memorandum of the conversation, showing his edits, is in Crist, vol. 11, pp. 315–19. The originals are in the Blair Family Papers in the Library of Congress. Blair's memories of the conversation are further preserved in Lathrop, pp. 640–41, and Bigelow, vol. 4, pp. 50–51. Blair added details in a February 8, 1865, letter to Lincoln, in the Blair Family Papers in the Library of Congress, described by Westwood in "Hampton Roads Conference," p. 254, n. 20. In *Rise and Fall*, pp. 612–16, Davis included his "two countries" letter to Blair, recounted their conversation, and added his lightly edited memorandum of it. The salient parts of the unedited original are in Crist, vol. 11, pp. 323–25. Some of what Davis told Stephens about the conversation is in Johnston and Browne, p. 484; Stephens, *CV,* vol. 2, pp. 591–92; and Crist, vol. 11, p. 322 n. 21. The Richmond press had speculated that Davis was discussing a colonial relationship with England and France. (See William A. Graham, Max R. Williams, ed., *The Papers of William Alexander Graham,* 8 vols. [Raleigh, NC: State Department of Archives and History, 1976] ["Graham"], vol. 6, p. 225).

81. Davis thought Blair spoke for Lincoln: Stephens, *CV*, vol. 2, p. 592; Jefferson Davis, "Jefferson Davis: The Peace Commission," 4 *Southern Historical Society Papers* (November 1877), pp. 208–14 ("Davis, 'Peace Commission'"), p. 210.

81. *not to be believed: Richmond Sentinel*, February 10, 1865, reprinted in *New York Times*, February 13, 1865.

84. Napoleon would attack Virginia to build a navy: Blair to Lincoln, February 8, 1865, Lincoln Papers, Library of Congress; *Elizabeth Blair Lee*, p. 473.

84. *"Eu-rope," as he pronounced it:* Russell, p. 250.

86. *"never to say aught against him":* Crist, vol. 11, p. 322 n. 19. Seward had saved Varina's life by sending his sleigh to take her to a doctor in a medical emergency (Chadwick, p. 36).

86. Jones spots Blair in a carriage: Jones, vol. 2, p. 386.

87. *nothing "escaped from the Executive closet":* Stephens, *CV*, vol. 2, pp. 589–90.

87. *Blair kept the secret too:* Woodward, "Hampton Roads Conference," pp. 253–54 n. 14.

87. *"utmost cordiality": Richmond Dispatch*, January 13, 1865, reprinted in *New York Times*, January 16, 1865.

87. *Mrs. Stanard's:* Smith, *Blair Family*, vol. 2, pp. 304–05; Von Abele, p. 236; *Elizabeth Blair Lee*, p. 463.

87. *"wonderfully persuasive with the other sex":* Mrs. Burton Harrison, *Recollections Grave and Gay* (New York: Charles Scribner's Sons, 1911) ("Harrison"), pp. 159–60.

87. *a good Union woman:* Smith, *Francis Preston Blair*, p. 374.

87. *a style she could ill afford: Elizabeth Blair Lee*, pp. 463 and 462 n. 3; Smith, *Francis Preston Blair*, p. 374.

87. Lyons's encounter with Blair and Stephens: Rowland, vol. 8, pp. 211–12.

88. *Jackson's "long-sighted spectacles":* Elizabeth Blair Lee, pp. 463 and 464 n. 2.

88. *The Enquirer* on Blair and legislators: *Richmond Enquirer*, January 14, 1865, reprinted in *New York Times*, January 17, 1865.

88. Hunter on Blair's impact: Robert M. T. Hunter, "R. M. T. Hunter, The Peace Commission: A Reply," 4 *Southern Historical Society Papers* (December 1877) ("Hunter, 'Reply'"), p. 303.

88. *"weak in the knees":* Kean, p. 188.

88. *"it made some soldiers angry":* Jefferson Davis, "The Peace Conference of 1865," 77 *The Century Magazine* (November 1908) ("Davis, 'Peace Conference'"), p. 69.

88. Grant sends Wallace to Mexico: *OR*, ser. 1, vol. 48, pt. 1, pp. 512–13.

88. *the Rebel general endorsed the idea "heartily": New York Times*, May 7, 1865.

89. Davis gave Blair a memorandum: Crist, vol. 11, p. 322 n. 21.

89. Davis's memorandum: Davis presents it in *Rise and Fall*, vol. 2, pp. 615–16.

89. Davis's conversation with Blair: Seventy years ago, in *Blair Family*, vol. 2, p. 318, Smith quoted a memorandum of this conversation, apparently prepared by Blair, also reproduced in Crist, vol. 11, p. 328. By 1979, the original had disappeared (Westwood, *Hampton Roads Conference*, p. 254 n. 21).

89. Davis's letter: The letter is in Davis, *Rise and Fall*, vol. 2, at pp. 615–16, in *CW*, vol. 8, p. 275; in *OR*, ser. 1, vol. 46, pt. 2, p. 506; and in Nicolay and Hay, vol. 10, p. 107.

90. Blair left in jubilation: *Id.;* see Blair to Greeley in Smith, *Blair Family*, vol. 2, p. 311.

90. Blair's trip back to the *Don: New York Daily Tribune*, January 17, 1865.

90. *"dreams of the dotard":* Quoted in Furgurson, p. 290.
90. Singleton and Blair on the same boat: Randall and Current, p. 331.
90. *All of Richmond knew of [Singleton's] coming:* Jones, vol. 2, p. 387.
90. Singleton's meetings in Richmond: Grimsley and Simpson, pp. 82–83; Randall and Current, pp. 330–31; Kirkland, p. 236 n. 57.
90. *"Conceive the worst":* Crist, vol. 11, p. 329. For the bungled defense of South Carolina, see Grimsley and Simpson, pp. 43–48.
90. *"Men feel peace in their bones":* New York Tribune, January 14, 1865.
90. Fall of Fort Fisher: Foote, vol. 3, pp. 740–47, 754, 763, and 791.
90. *breathing through a quill:* Stephens, *CV*, vol. 2, pp. 619–21.
91. *"carnival of death":* New York Times, January 20, 1865.
91. *On the same clear day:* Jones, vol. 2, p. 387.
91. The army is a mob: Crist, vol. 11, pp. 332–33.
91. *Wealthy [Georgia] families: Id.,* p. 333.
91. *This, too, is injurious:* Jones vol 2, p. 400.

CHAPTER 12

92. *"a remarkably good humor":* New York Daily Tribune, January 17, 1865.
92. *laid on the table and died: Congressional Globe,* January 16, 1865, p. 275.
92. Lizzie's letter to Phil: *Elizabeth Blair Lee,* pp. 463–64.
93. They *"did not draw well together":* Bigelow, p. 51.
93. Lincoln's disclaimer: Smith, *Francis Preston Blair,* p. 366.
93. Lincoln's intentions on Mexico: See Nicolay and Hay, vol. 10, pp. 107–08.
93. *"There has been war enough":* Wilson, pp. 580 and 585.
93. *Lincoln must have told him he would consider it:* See Westwood, "Hampton Roads Conference," pp. 246–47.
93. Blair's report to Lincoln: Nicolay and Hay, vol. 10, pp. 103–07.
93. *Arrangements were made that night: OR,* ser. 1, vol. 46, pt. 2, p. 158.
93. *The Cabinet was assembled:* Welles Diary, vol. 2, pp. 226–27.
94. the Times *(which often spoke for Seward):* Randall and Current, p. 349; Stahr, *passim.*
94. The Times *article: New York Times,* January 17, 1865.
94. Addressed to Blair, to be shown to Davis: *CW,* vol. 8, pp. 275–76.
94. *"informally" was penciled in:* Lincoln Papers, Library of Congress, document 40574.
94. *Lincoln was inciting a Gray Revolution:* At least one historian has written that Lincoln may have interpreted Davis's willingness to bring "peace to two countries" as suggesting that two might become one, through a Mexican invasion or otherwise (Westwood, "Hampton Roads Conference," p. 247).
95. Blair's letter to Greeley: Horace Greeley Papers, New York Public Library. The letter is in Smith, *Blair Family,* p. 311.
95. *its Secretary of War left his post:* Kean, p. 189; Kirkland, pp. 217–18.
95. Davis's endorsement of Lee as general in chief: Ballard, pp. 14–15.
95. *"I think I am the person to advise Mr. Davis":* Pollard, p. 437.
96. Stanton's report to the Cabinet: Welles Diary, vol. 2, pp. 228–30.

96. *"a pack of sneaks in Savannah": Richmond Whig,* January 25, 1865, quoted in *New York Times,* January 28, 1865.
96. *Philadelphians who contributed to their relief:* Randall and Current, p. 324.
96. Blair and Henry leave on the *Don: New York Times,* January 21, 1865.
96. *A trusted Southern officer would be waiting: OR,* vol. 46, pt. 2, p. 261.
96. A leak on the *Don:* Elizabeth Blair Lee, p. 467.
96. *"afraid to trust me with a dinner":* Burlingame, vol. 2, p. 753.
97. *"dark and malignant passions": Richmond Sentinel,* January 20, 1865, reprinted in *New York Daily Tribune,* January 24, 1865.
97. *"Davis and the Sanhedrim": New York Times,* January 10, 1865.
97. *"portion of a European capital": New York Times,* January 23, 1865.
97. *Hostetter's Celebrated Stomach Bitters: New York Times,* January 25, 1865.
97. *on the verge of a vote of no confidence:* Wilfred B. Yearns, *The Confederate Congress* (Athens: University of Georgia Press, 1960) ("Yearns *Confederate Congress*"), p. 231.
97. *"spare nothing":* Sherman's Memoirs, vol. 2, pp. 184–85.
97. Cobb's letter to Davis: *OR,* ser. 1, vol. 53, pp. 393–94; Crist, vol. 11, p. 343.
98. General Brown's note to Davis: *Id.,* p. 342.
98. Campbell's resignation: *Id.,* pp. 342–43.
98. *"not a man of small details":* Jones, vol. 2, p. 401.
98. *"an opportunity to escape":* Kean, p. 190.
98. Campbell's resignation rejected: Campbell, "Open Letters," p. 951.
98. *Grant was away when Blair passed through City Point: OR,* ser. 1, vol. 46, pt. 2, p. 134.
98. The *William Allison* carrying Blair and prisoners: *New York Times,* January 26, 1865.
98. Arrived on January 22: Crist, vol. 11, p. 323 n. 21.
98. Blair lodged with Hatch: *Richmond Dispatch,* reprinted in *New York Times,* January 26, 1965.
98. Blair dines with the Davises: *Richmond Dispatch,* reprinted in *New York Times,* January 28, 1865.
98. Blair's conversation with Davis: *CW,* vol. 8, p. 276; *Congressional Globe,* February 10, 1865, p. 729; Nicolay and Hay, vol. 10, pp. 108–11 and 111 n. 1; *Rise and Fall,* pp. 616–17, Crist, vol. 11, p. 323 n. 21.
98. *Lincoln had not rejected it:* Nicolay and Hay say Lincoln never gave the Mexican idea "an instant's consideration," but they do not substantiate their claim that Blair told Davis it was dead (*Id.,* p. 108). As will be seen, Davis later told his colleagues that Lincoln favored it, or at least had not rejected it, and Davis sent his envoys to him thinking it viable. It seems likely that when Blair put the idea to Lincoln, the latter did not rule it out, at least not out loud to Blair, hoping, perhaps, to keep the prospect of peace talks alive. There is no firsthand evidence that Blair told Davis that the Mexican plan was dead. Lincoln may have been noncommittal on it merely to let Blair down gently. See Westwood, "Hampton Roads Conference," pp. 246–47.
99. Prospect of Grant-Lee talks: Davis, *Rise and Fall,* vol. 2, pp. 616–17; Stephens, *CV,* vol. 2, p. 591.
99. Blair was optimistic: See Blair to Greeley, January 27, 1865, Greeley Papers, New York Public Library.

99. Blair sent Davis word that Lincoln would not allow Grant-Lee talks: See Westwood, "Hampton Roads Conference," p. 246; Davis, *Rise and Fall*, pp. 616–17.

99. Vance's letter to Davis: Varina Davis, vol. 2, pp. 454–61.

99. Blair went calling in a cold rain: Willcox, p. 601, regarding cold rain; Davis, *Rise and Fall*, pp. 618–19; Hunter, "Peace Commission," p. 169.

99. Blair's conversations with dissidents: Yearns, "Peace Movement," pp. 13–14.

99. *"The mystic Blair"*: *The Richmond Enquirer*, January 23, 1865, reprinted in *New York Times*, January 27, 1865.

99. *The* Whig *on peace talks*: *Richmond Whig*, January 23, 1865, reprinted in *New York Times*, January 27, 1865.

100. Meade's letter to his wife: Meade, pp. 258–60.

100. Stephens on Blair's return: Quoted in Schott, p. 440.

100. *objectionable and divisive*: Davis's letter is in Rowland, vol. 6, pp. 403–6. See also Crist, vol. 11, pp. 161–68.

100. Campbell tells Kean that peace men will propose reunion: Kean, p. 191.

100. Rives's conversation with Kean: *Id.*, pp. 192–93.

100. The Rives family: See Donna M. Lucey, *Archie and Amelie: Love and Madness in the Gilded Age* (New York: Harmony Books, 2006), pp. 82–83; and Lyon G. Tyler, *Encyclopedia of Virginia Biography*, vol. 3 (New York: Lewis Historical Publishing Company, 1915).

101. *Lee issued a public plea for weapons and saddles*: *Richmond Dispatch*, reprinted in *New York Times*, February 7, 1865.

101. *"They do us no good"*: Gorgas, p. 166.

102. *making no one rich*: Browning Diary, vol. 2, pp. 4–6 and 12–15; *CW*, vol. 8, pp. 353 and 410; Crist, vol. 2, p. 480 n. 10; Johnson, *Mission*, pp. 98–99; Flood, p. 415.

102. The Rebel flag-of-truce boat appeared with Blair: *OR*, ser. 1, vol. 46, pt. 2, p. 261.

102. *Admiral Lee had pressed for more ships*: Elizabeth Blair Lee, p. 469.

102. *her husband had been known to indulge her*: Julia Grant, pp. 129–30 and 135.

102. Blair gets home in the cold: *New York Times*, January 27, 1865, reprint from *Baltimore American*.

102. *looking weary*: Elizabeth Blair Lee, p. 468.

102. Blair's letter to Greeley: Horace Greeley Papers, New York Public Library.

102. *"Great was the excitement"*: Brooks, *Washington in Lincoln's Time*, p. 223.

103. *"a total failure"*: *New York Times*, January 28, 1865.

103. Lincoln's note on the back of the letter: *CW*, vol. 8, p. 276.

103. Blair's list of requests: Lincoln Papers, Library of Congress; Smith, *Francis Preston Blair*, p. 374.

103. *must have given Lincoln some encouragement*: See Westwood, "Hampton Roads Conference," p. 247.

103. Brooks thought Lincoln had no faith: Brooks, *Washington in Lincoln's Time*, p. 224.

103. Welles's speculations: Welles Diary, vol. 2, pp. 231–32.

CHAPTER 13

Hunter's biographers are his daughter and a fellow Virginian: Martha T. Hunter, *A Memoir of Robert M. T. Hunter* (Washington, DC: Neale Publishing Company, 1903) ("Hunter, *Hunter*"), and Henry H. Simms, *Life of Robert M. T. Hunter* (Richmond, VA: The William Byrd Press, 1935) ("Simms").

104. *[Not given to] "gossiping intercourse":* Hunter, *Hunter,* p. 78.

104. *"tardy and sluggish":* Foote, *Casket of Reminiscences,* p. 311.

104. *any plain Virginia farmer's:* L. Quinton Washington, quoted in Hunter, *Hunter,* p. 162; Simms, p. 27.

105. *financial strain: Id.,* p. 19.

105. *tableau vivant of temperaments:* Pollard, pp. 31–32.

105. *Hunter listening quietly:* Jones, vol. 1, pp. 64–65.

105. Condescending, Davis made him Secretary of State: Rowland, vol. 8, p. 124; Simms, p. 188.

105. Resignation as Secretary of State: Hendrick, *Statesmen of the Lost Cause,* p. 186.

106. Death of Hunter's son: Hunter, *Hunter,* pp. 88 and 115.

106. *"ruin stared him in the face": Id.,* pp. 122 and 162.

106. *who found himself nudging:* Graham, p. 224.

106. *"great exposure and suffering":* Willcox, p. 603.

106. *burgled their neighbors' coal bins:* Brock, p. 341.

106. Hunter hurrying down the street: Jones, vol. 2, pp. 400–01.

106. Davis sent Hunter for Stephens: Stephens, *CV,* vol. 2, p. 590; Stephens to Linton Stephens, January 26, 1865, Manhattanville Library.

106. Hunter went to see Campbell: See Jones, vol. 2, p. 400.

106. Davis was home with neuralgia: Crist, vol. 11, p. 356.

106. Stephens had not spoken to Davis since 1863: See Schott, p. 440; Graham, p. 225.

106. The scathing Davis-Stephens correspondence preceding their meeting is in *OR,* ser. 4, vol. 3, pt. 1, pp. 840, 934, and 1000–04. For more on the exchange, see Rowland, vol. 6, pp. 439–45; Stephens, *CV,* vol. 2, pp. 583–84; Avary, *Recollections,* pp. 75–77; and Schott, pp. 433–35. It was hot gossip in Richmond. See Kean, pp. 188–89.

106. Davis sought Stephens's judgment: Stephens, *CV,* vol. 2, pp. 590–91.

107–108. Stephens's conversation with Davis: Stephens recounted it in Stephens, *CV,* vol. 2, pp. 591–94, and described it to his authorized biographers in Johnston and Browne, p. 484. It is also mentioned in the *Augusta Chronicle & Sentinel,* June 7, 1865, reprinted in *New York Times,* June 26, 1865 ("*Augusta Chronicle and Sentinel, in New York Times, June 26, 1865*"), purportedly based on an interview with Stephens, who denied he had given it but verified some of the article's contents (Avary, *Recollections,* pp. 264–65, 271, 275, 280–81, and 373). The accurate elements are discernible by Stephens's failure to deny them, and their consistency with other sources.

108. *"whither, of course, it was not proper for me to go":* Davis, "Peace Conference," p. 68.

108. *The ice had been broken:* Crist, vol. 11, p. 310. n. 11.

108. *"Can't find a thermometer"; "many smiling faces":* Jones, vol. 2, pp. 401–02.

108. Breckinridge a rival in the old concern: *Id.,* p. 401.

108–109. Stephens's second conversation with Davis: Stephens recounts it in Stephens, *CV*, vol. 2, pp. 594–95. See also Crist, vol. 11, pp. 355–56.

109. *a crippled negotiation was better than none:* Stephens, *Augusta Chronicle and Sentinel,* in *New York Times, June 26, 1865.*

109. Arthur Colyar, John Baldwin, and peace resolutions: Colyar tells the story in Rowland, *Davis*, vol. 8, p. 30. See also Westwood, "Hampton Roads Conference," p. 248; Rowland, vol. 8, p. 27; Foote, *Casket of Reminiscences*, p. 298; Foote, *War of the Rebellion*, p. 375; Schott, pp. 438–39; "Arthur St. Clair Colyar 1818–1907," *The Tennessee Encyclopedia of History and Culture*, http://tennesseeencyclopedia.net.

109. *a fact-finding committee: Journal of the Congress of the Confederate States of America, 1861–1865*, 7 vols. (Washington, DC: US Government Printing Office, 1904–05) (*"Journal of the Congress"*), vol. 7, pp. 393–94.

110. *It was not the first such resolution to be offered: Id.,* pp. 360 and 363–64.

110. Stephens's edit of Colyar's draft: The edited version is in Johnston & Brown, pp. 480–82; an explanation of the various drafts is in *id.,* pp. 482–83 and in Von Abele, p. 233 n. 93. The version reported to the House on February 12 is in *Journal of the Congress,* pp. 451–52.

110. North-South collaboration to enforce the Monroe Doctrine: *Id.,* pp. 451–52.

110. *They had struck their bargain without him:* Davis responds to Colyar's story in Rowland, vol. 8, p. 27, and denies no part of it. At bottom, he merely says he knew nothing about it and expresses surprise that Stephens did not address it in *CV*. Stephens told a friend that Davis appointed the commissioners to preempt a congressional demand (Johnston and Browne, *Stephens*, p. 486). Davis discusses his choice of commissioners in Davis, "Peace Commission". See also Schott, pp. 432–38 and Von Abele, p. 233.

110. The Cabinet chooses the commission: Crist, vol. 11, p. 379 n. 2; Mallory, vol. 2, p. 208; Rowland, vol. 8, pp. 27–28. In the North, no leading Rebel had a stronger reputation as a peacemaker than Stephens. Greeley had told Blair he was "looking for" Davis's death, since Stephens would succeed him, and "I guess that would soon end the war" (Greeley to Blair, December 23, 1864, Blair Family Papers, Library of Congress).

110–111. Benjamin Hill and his relationship with Stephens: Benjamin Harvey Hill Jr., *Senator Benjamin H. Hill of Georgia: His Life, Speeches and Writings* (Atlanta: H. C. Hudgins, 1891) ("Hill"), pp. 19–30; Schott, pp. 216–21, 500–01; Haywood J. Pearce, *Benjamin H. Hill: Secession and Reconstruction* (Chicago: The University of Chicago Press, 1940) ("Pearce"), pp. 104–05, footnotes 50–52.

111. Davis confers with Hill on Stephens's appointment: *Atlanta Constitution*, April 22, 1874, letter to the editor from Hill; Crist, vol. 11, p. 379 n. 2.

111. Hill's own deal with Stephens: Schott, p. 441; Pearce, pp. 102–05.

111. Judah Benjamin: A profile of Benjamin, from which some references to him in this chapter and elsewhere in the book are drawn, is in Hendrick, *Statesmen of the Lost Cause,* pp. 157–87.

112. The *Times of London* on Benjamin: Russell, pp. 252–53.

112. *A wellborn junior officer:* Wise, pp. 401–02.

112. *"the brains of the Confederacy":* Hendrick, *Statesmen of the Lost Cause,* p. 153.

112. Benjamin's relationship with Davis: *Congressional Globe*, June 9, 1858, p. 2823, Hendrick, *Statesmen of the Lost Cause*, pp. 174–75 and *passim;* Mallory, vol. 2, p. 206; Bill, pp. 207 and 243.

113. Davis's conversation with the commissioners: Campbell tells the story in John A. Campbell, *Reminiscences and Documents Relating to the Civil War during the Year 1865* (Baltimore: John Murphy & Co., 1877) ("Campbell, *Reminiscences*"), pp. 3–4, in Campbell, "Open Letters," p. 951, and in "The Hampton Roads Conference, Letter of Judge Campbell," *The Southern Magazine*, November 1874, vol. 8, pp. 187–90, ("Campbell, 'Hampton Roads Conference, *Southern Magazine*'"), p. 187. Stephens recalls the conversation in Stephens, *CV*, vol. 2, pp. 619–22. Davis's comments to Senator Hill are in Hill, p. 409. See also Graham, p. 235, and Johnston and Browne, p. 484.

113. *"did not find their passport available":* Campbell, "Hampton Roads Conference," *Southern Magazine*, p. 187.

114. Stephens's draft statement to the Associated Press: Stephens to Davis, Duke University Library, Charles Colcok Jones Papers, Georgia Portfolio; Crist, vol. 11, pp. 357–58. See Schott, pp. 442–43.

114. Drafting and revising credentials: Benjamin's draft and Davis's are in *Rise and Fall*, vol. 2, p. 617, and in Crist, vol. 11, p. 356, with a narrative of the events. Davis and Benjamin give their versions of those events in Davis, "Peace Commission," pp. 210–11 and Rowland, vol. 7, pp. 570–71. Bromwell gives his in William Bromwell, "Peace Conference," *Southern Bivouac*, December 1886, vol. 2, no. 7, p. 424.

115. *"to defeat the objects of the conference":* Strode, p. 469.

115. *"But none of us . . . dreamed of reconstruction":* *Richmond Sentinel*, February 10, 1865, reprinted in *New York Times*, February 13, 1865.

115. *not to bargain it out of existence:* Strode, pp. 468–69.

115. *it must be clear that Mr. Lincoln had not been misled:* Rowland, vol. 7, pp. 570–71.

116. *Washington replied that . . . The subject was closed:* Campbell, *Reminiscences*, pp. 8–9.

116. Davis's conversation with Barksdale: Rowland, vol. 8, p. 247, which includes Barksdale's rebuttal of Colyar's account and assessment.

116. *"utterly unfit"; could not have been trusted with "the powers of negotiation":* Strode, p. 483.

116. *three of his most reluctant Rebels:* See Fitzhugh Lee, "Failure of the Hampton Roads Conference," 52 *The Century Magazine* (July 1896) ("Lee, 'Failure'"), pp. 476–77; Sanders, pp. 815–17; Randall and Current, pp. 329 and 333.

116. *a "humbug" from the start:* Schott, p. 442.

116. *"the monkey that took the paw of the cat":* Stephens, *Augusta Chronicle and Sentinel, in New York Times, June 26, 1865.*

117. Hunter's assessment of Davis's motives: Hunter, "Peace Commission," pp. 169–70. Intelligent analysts have debated whether Davis's choice of commissioners was made cynically or in good faith (e.g., Davis, *Davis*, pp. 591–92; James M. McPherson, *Battle Cry of Freedom: The Civil War Era* (New York: Harper Collins, 1991), p. 591; Westwood, "Hampton Roads Conference," pp. 248 and 255 n. 52; and Sanders, *passim*. In the author's view, the weight of the evidence favors cynicism.

CHAPTER 14

118. *cold Sunday morning:* Jones, vol. 2, p. 402.

118. *depot near the High Bridge:* Furgurson, map of Richmond after page xi.

118. *met at the Richmond & Petersburg depot . . . change in plans:* Fragment written by Stephens ("Stephens Fragment"), Stephens Papers, Library of Congress, p. 23; *Richmond Dispatch,* January 30, 1865, reprinted in *Philadelphia Inquirer,* February 3, 1865; handwritten article written by Stephens for the *Philadelphia Times,* in the Stephens Papers at the Library of Congress ("Stephens Manuscript"), pp. 3–4.

118. *not long out of a sickbed: Id.,* pp. 19–20.

118. Yellow complexion: Porter, *Grant,* p. 385.

118. *ponderous gray overcoat: Id.*

118. Ben Travis and Colonel Hatch: Stephens Manuscript, pp. 4 and 11; Samuel Harris, *Yankees in Rebel Prisons* (Chicago: Samuel Harris & Co., 1900), p. 21; Schott, p. 445; *Biographical Directory of the United States Congress,* www.bioguidecongress.gov. ("Biographical Directory").

118. *the publicity alone:* Stephens, *CV,* vol. 2, p. 621.

118. *"plentiful as blackberries":* Richmond Dispatch, January 29, 1865, quoted in *Philadelphia Inquirer,* February 3, 1865.

119. *Campbell gave Stephens and Hunter their copies:* Campbell, *Reminiscences,* p. 9.

119. *"nothing could come of it":* Stephens Fragment, p. 23, which contradicts Stephens's public, postwar repudiation of the idea that Davis tied the commissioners' hands and sabotaged the peace conference (e.g., Stephens, *CV,* vol. 2, p. 577), as do Stephens's private conversations with friends (e.g., Rowland, *Davis,* vol. 10, pp. 20–22; Johnston and Browne, pp. 484 and 486; *Augusta Chronicle and Sentinel,* reprinted in *New York Times,* June 26, 1865).

119. *Campbell believed he had done just that:* See Strode, p. 468.

119. *Stephens had thought there was a chance of doing something:* Schott, p. 442.

119. *Now all three commissioners despaired:* Stephens Fragment, p. 23. See Campbell, *Reminiscences,* pp. 4–5 and 8–9; Hunter, "Peace Commission," p. 170; Hunter, "Reply," pp. 304–05 and 317; and Jones, vol. 2, p. 402.

119. *"the extent of our destitution I did not understand":* Hunter, "Reply," p. 306

119. *"a beggarly account":* Hunter, "Peace Commission," p. 168.

119. *"hermetically sealed":* Hunter, "Reply," p. 306.

119. *"I knew him well":* Stephens, *CV,* vol. 2, p. 266.

119. *considered offering Stephens a Cabinet post:* Avary, *Recollections,* p. 61; Julian S. Carr, *The Hampton Roads Conference* (Durham, NC: 1917) ("Carr, Hampton Roads Conference"), p. 7.

119. *"but not in the object":* Stephens, *CV,* vol. 2, p. 266.

119. Hunter's reaction to public sentiment: Hunter, "Peace Commission," p. 170.

120. *General Grant would be expecting them:* Bolton, p. 243; Willcox, p. 604; *Boston Daily Evening Transcript,* February 1, 1865.

120. *"on a big drunk":* Stephens Fragment, p. 23.

120. Lee's message to Davis: *Lee's Dispatches,* p. 330; McElroy, p. 435.

120. *Their bright red tracks:* Ulysses R. Brooks, *Butler and His Cavalry in the War of Seces-sion, 1861–1865* (Columbia, SC: The State Company, 1909), p. 385.
120. *"curs of every degree":* Willcox, p. 600.
120. Reports of the commissioners' arrival: *Id.,* pp. 603–04; *OR,* ser. 1, v. 46, pt. 2, 290; Bolton, p. 243; see Henry C. Houston, *The Thirty-Second Maine Regiment of Infantry Volunteers: An Historical Sketch* (Portland, ME: Southworth Brothers, 1903), p. 444; *Daily Constitutional Union,* February 3, 1865.
120. City Point in the hands of General Ord: Howard C. Westwood, "The Singing Wire Conspiracy," 19 *Civil War Times Illustrated* (December 1980) ("Westwood, *Singing Wire Conspiracy*"), p. 32.
120. *Parke passed the buck to Ord: OR,* ser. 1, v. 46, pt. 2, pp. 290, 290, 292, and 302–03.
120. Hatch was advised to come back in the morning: *Id.,* pp. 291–92.
121. *"in seemingly friendly intercourse": Boston Daily Evening Transcript,* February 2, 1865.
121. *"zero & afraid of his shadow":* Willcox, p. 603.
121. Stanton's order to stop the commissioners: *OR,* ser. 1, v. 46, pt. 2, p. 292; CW, vol. 8, p. 277. Stanton's January 29, 1865, note seeking Lincoln's instructions: Lincoln Papers, Library of Congress.
121. *until they had been vetted:* Elizabeth Peabody and Arlin Turner, ed., "Elizabeth Peabody Visits Lincoln, February 1865," 48 *New England Quarterly* (March 1975) ("Peabody"), pp. 119–20.
122. Lincoln's conversation with Robert: Bates, pp. 328–29.
122. *had never worn a uniform: Id.,* p. 403.
122. *major's rank; government . . . carriage; command of . . . telegraph:* Kirkland, p. 235.
122. *which the president haunted for war news:* Bates, pp. 7–8; Crook, "Lincoln As I Knew Him," p. 110.
122. *bullied his subordinates; guarded his master; wielded his authority:* Benjamin P. Thomas and Harold M. Hyman, Edwin M. Stanton: *The Life and Times of Lincoln's Secretary of War* (New York: Alfred A. Knopf, 1962) ("Thomas and Hyman, *Stanton*"), p. 574; Bates, pp. 103–05, 136–37, 315–18, and 327–28; Hay, *At Lincoln's Side,* p. 109.
122. *misleading the president: Id.,* pp. 95–97.
122. *"in the most complete and tactful manner": Id.,* p. 328.
122. *"incessant worker":* Brooks, *Washington in Lincoln's Time,* p. 30.
122. *"a small, mean, two-story building":* Crook, "Lincoln As I Knew Him," p. 110.
122. *Stanton hovered there day and night: Id.*
123. *midnight supper for Lincoln:* Welles Diary, vol. 2, p. 178; Hay Diary, p. 246.
123. *iron pokers: Id.,* p. 131; Jim Bishop, *The Day Lincoln Was Shot* (New York: Bantam, 1956) ("Bishop, *The Day Lincoln Was Shot*"), p. 77.
123. *Sending Eckert was the Secretary of War's idea:* Frank A. Flower, *Edwin McMasters Stanton* (Akron, OH: Saalfield Publishing Company, 1905) ("Flower"), pp. 249 and 257–58.
123. *"I never see General Eckert without thinking of it":* Bates, p. 329.
123. *reported to Eckert obsequiously: Id., passim.*
123. *"shrewd and wily adversaries": Id.,* p. 328.
123. *what Stanton was thinking: Id.,* p. 338.

123. *"I did not communicate my plans"*: Grant, vol. 2, p. 123.
124. *"stout hearts and strong hands"*: Richmond Sentinel, January 30, 1865, reprinted in *New York Times*, February 2, 1865.
124. *"unworthy of a gallant people"*: Richmond Examiner, January 30, 1865, reprinted in *New York Times*, February 2, 1865.
124–125. Wade's exchange with Johnson: *Congressional Globe*, January 30, pp. 495–96.
125. Willcox's exchange with Parke: *OR*, ser. 1, v. 46, pt. 2, p. 301.
125. Hatch appeared and returned: *Id.; New York Times*, February 2, 1865. Fort Morton and its fourteen guns are in Trudeau, pp. 55–57.
125. Harriman's regiment's losses: E. B. Quiner, *The Military History of Wisconsin* (Chicago: Clarke & Co., 1866).
126. *"A piece of ten-inch shell"*: New York Times, December 31, 1916, p. E2. For Colonel Harriman, see Dictionary of Wisconsin History, www.wisconsinhistory.org/dictionary ("Wisconsin Dictionary").
126. *"a messenger will be dispatched"*: OR, ser. 1, v. 46, pt. 2, p. 302.
126. *"plenty of ammunition handy"*: Id., p., 297.
126. The commissioners' note to Grant: *Id.*; Stephens Manuscript, p. 5.
126. *Traders dumped gold on Wall Street*: Baltimore Sun, February 1, 1865.
126. *"Great talk and many rumors . . . of peace"*: Welles Diary, vol. 2, p. 231.
127. Foote's letter to Seward: Foote, *War of the Rebellion*, pp. 387–401 and 405; Kirkland, p. 236 n. 57.
127. *keep them from seeing troop movements*: McElroy, p. 436.

CHAPTER 15

128. Grant on Stanton: Grant, vol. 2, pp. 536–37.
128. *obliged to defer to Stanton*: Badeau, vol. 3, p. 157.
128. *incapable of chicanery*: Dana, *Grant*, p. 406.
128. *"I determined to put a stop to this"*: Grant, vol. 2, p. 317.
129. Grant's wire to Halleck: *Id.*, pp. 317–18.
129. Lincoln's reply to Grant's wire: *Id.; OR*, ser. 1, vol. 37, pt. 2, p. 582.
129. *"without stopping at Washington on my way"*: Grant, vol. 2, p. 319; see Smith, *Grant*, pp. 379–80.
129. *Sheridan attacked Early and routed him*: Grant, vol. 2, pp. 331–32.
129. *"deference enough to the Government"*: Paraphrased by Grant's friend Mark Twain in Mark Twain and Harriet E. Smith, ed., *Autobiography of Mark Twain*, vol. 1 (Berkeley: University of California Press, 2010), p. 382.
129. Stanton's control over Grant's telegraphed orders: *Grant*, vol. 2, pp. 103–05.
129. Grant's struggles with Stanton over control of the telegraph: Grant, vol. 2, pp. 103–05.
129. Grant's softness on reconciliation: e.g., Grant Papers, vol. 14, p. 433; McFeely, *William S. Grant: A Biography* (New York: Norton & Company, 1981), pp. 197–98.
129. *"Mr. Lincoln was not timid"*: Grant, vol. 2, p. 537.
130. Willcox and Jones on the weather: Willcox, p. 604; Jones, vol. 2, p. 404.
130. *Grant returned to City Point*: OR, vol. 46, pt. 2, pp. 311–12.

130. *Every train pulling in:* New York Times, February 4, 1865.
130. *It was put in his hands immediately:* OR, ser. 1, v. 46, pt. 2, pp. 311–12; see Badeau, *Grant,* vol. 3, p. 136.
130. *Grant would be expecting them:* See Willcox, pp. 603–04; *Boston Daily Evening Transcript,* February 1, 1865.
130–131. Grant's note to the commissioners: OR, ser. 1, v. 46, pt. 2, p. 312; Grant Papers, vol. 13, p. 334.
131. Colonel Babcock: Julia Grant, pp. 140 and 199 n. 16.
131. Babcock left on the next train: OR, ser. 1, v. 46, pt. 2, p. 317.
131. Grant's wire to Lincoln: OR, ser. 1, v. 46, pt. 2, p. 311; originally addressed to Stanton, Grant Papers, vol. 13, p. 333.
131. Lincoln's reply to Grant: *Id.*
131. *Lincoln was encouraged:* Brooks, *Lincoln Observed,* p. 159; Nicolay and Hay, vol. 10, p. 114.
131. Lincoln's instructions to Seward: *CW,* vol. 8, pp. 250–51.
132. *members who knew Seward would chuckle:* Brooks, *Lincoln Observed,* p. 163.
132. *Nicolay was a guest on the floor:* Cox, *Three Decades,* p. 327.
132. *a coin toss:* Nicolay and Hay, vol. 10, p. 85.
132. *"Whatever promise you make . . . I will perform it":* Dana, *Lincoln's Cabinet,* pp. 57–59.
132. Cox was told peace envoys about to cross or already had: Cox, *Three Decades,* p. 327.
132. The exchange between Ashley, Nicolay, and Cox: *Id.*
133. *"So far as I know": Id.; CW,* vol. 8, p. 248.
133. *"In some inscrutable way";* Sunset Cox would vote no: Cox, *Three Decades,* pp. 327–28.
133. *the chamber was jammed:* Brooks, *Washington in Lincoln's Time,* p. 205.
133. Congressmen's statements: *Congressional Globe,* January 31, p. 523.
134. *The roll was called at four, the very hour:* Nicolay and Hay, vol. 10, p. 85; Stephens, *CV,* vol. 2, p. 596.
134. *"intense anxiety"; "knots of members"; burst of applause; Manhattan Naval Office:* Arnold, p. 365; Brooks, *Washington in Lincoln's Time,* pp. 205–06; Randall and Current, pp. 310–13.
134. Announcement and cheers: Brooks, *Washington in Lincoln's Time,* pp. 207–09.
134. *"I had been born into a new life":* George W. Julian, *Political Recollections* (Chicago: Jansen, McClurg & Company, 1884), p. 251.
134. *he had hoped for more decorum: Boston Daily Evening Transcript,* February 2, 1865.
134. *artillery shook Capitol Hill:* Arnold, p. 365; Randall and Current, p. 313.
134. *peace commissioners had just passed through the lines:* Stephens, *CV,* vol. 2, p. 596.
134–135. Mrs. Peabody's story: Peabody, *passim.*
135. Lincoln didn't like Sumner: Crook, *Five Administrations,* p. 35.
135. *"about 30 first rate stripes":* David H. Donald, *Charles Sumner and the Coming of the Civil War* (New York: Alfred A. Knopf, Inc., 1960), pp. 289–311.
135. Sumner's resolution and dialogue with his colleagues: *Congressional Globe,* January 31, 1865, p. 511.
136. Senator Saulsbury's remarks: *Congressional Globe,* January 31, 1865, p. 519.
136. *"If you touch me I'll shoot you dead":* Goodwin, p. 503.

136. The *Enquirer's* view: Reprinted in *New York Times*, February 3, 1865.
137. *"were 'not at home' to these 'Express' calls"*: George H. Washburn, *A Complete Military History and Record of the 108th Regiment New York Volunteers* (Rochester, NY: Press of E. R. Andrews, 1894), p. 87.
137. *Sarah Pryor recalled it well:* "Pryor, *Reminiscences*", pp. 280–83.
137. *"good, wholesome comrades"*: *Id.*, pp. 319–20.
138. Arrival of the commissioners and the mayor: Von Abele, p. 237; Charge near Fort Hell, p. 1.
138. *parting throngs of jubilant Rebels:* Parker, p. 604.
138. Sarah Pryor's encounter with the commissioners: Pryor, *Reminiscences*, pp. 327–29.
138. *where a low plateau fell away:* Charge near Fort Hell, p. 1.
138. *the paucity of Lee's defenses:* Hunter, "Peace Commission," p. 171.
138. The commissioners' passage through the lines: *Petersburg Express*, February 2, 1865; Stephens, *CV*, vol. 2, p. 596; *Daily Constitutional Union*, February 3, 1865; *New York Times*, December 31, 1916, p. E2; *New York Times*, February 3, 1865; *New York Daily Tribune*, February 3, 1865; Willcox, p. 604.
139. *Colonel Hatch was given leave:* OR, ser. 1, v. 46, pt. 2, p. 317.
139. *Stephens's "servant" be allowed to assist him:* *Petersburg Express*, February 2, 1865, reprinted in *New York Times*, February 6, 1865.
139. *to keep his master ambulatory:* Id.
139. *by the Baxter Road:* Id.
139. *they crossed at Fort Hell:* *New York Times*, February 1, 1865.
139. *raised their chins:* *Daily Constitutional Union*, February 3, 1865.
139. *"dark with men"; spyglasses:* *Petersburg Express*, February 2, 1865, reprinted in *New York Times*, February 6, 1865.
139. *Ladies down from Petersburg:* Id.; Parker, p. 604.
139. *"prolonged and enthusiastic shouting"*: OR, ser. 1, v. 46, pt. 2, p. 317.
139. *"no such thing was heard"*: *New York Times*, February 8, 1865.
139. *A respectful pause:* *Petersburg Express*, February 2, 1865, reprinted in *New York Times*, February 6, 1865; Parker, p. 605.
139. *they trod on spent ammunition:* Hunter, "Peace Commission," p. 171.
139. *The Yankees resumed their cheering:* *New Orleans Daily Picayune*, February 12, 1865; Meade, p. 260.
139. *"In an instant we were enemies again"*: Pryor, *Reminiscences*, p. 329.
139. *The killing continued:* Bolton, p. 244; *Richmond Enquirer*, February 4, 1865.

CHAPTER 16

140. *an idle locomotive:* Scott, p. 3; *New York Herald*, February 3, 1865.
140. *a crowd of men in blue:* *Daily Constitutional Union*, February 3, 1865; *New York Times*, December 31, 1916, p. E2.
140. *laid with little grading:* Porter, *Grant*, p. 212; Trudeau, p. 298.
140. *at about seven o'clock:* *New York Times*, February 4, 1865.
140. *no report of cheering:* *New York Herald*, February 4, 1865.
140. *"under happier auspices"*: *Daily Constitutional Union*, February 3, 1865.

140. *It was a busy camp:* Crook, *Five Administrations*, p. 42.

141. *A horse-drawn coffee maker:* Edward P. Tobie, *History of the First Maine Cavalry* (Boston: Emery & Hughes, 1887), p. 378.

141. *accompanied by other officers:* New York Times, February 4, 1865.

141. Letter from E. W. Clarke to Senator Henry Wilson, January 31, 1865: Henry Wilson Papers, Library of Congress.

141. *a cabin like the others:* Porter, *Grant*, pp. 212, 329, and 369.

141. *salvaged from a shed:* The door is displayed today at the City Point Visitors' Center.

141. *a "very distinct" voice:* Stephens Manuscript, p. 6.

141. *Grant's humble office:* Porter, *Grant*, pp. 233 and 329–30; Badeau, vol. 3, pp. 135–36. The cabin is still at City Point.

141. *"never so much disappointed":* Stephens, CV, vol. 2, pp. 596–97; Stephens Manuscript, p. 7.

142. *The conversation flowed easily:* Id., pp. 7–8.

142. *"all very agreeable gentlemen":* Grant, vol. 2, pp. 421–22.

142. *a fellow Stephen Douglas Democrat:* Id., pp. 121–22 and 421–22; Schott, pp. 302–03 and 309.

142. *dispatches came and went:* Stephens Manuscript, pp. 8–10.

142. *a half-page reply:* Id., p. 8.

143. *Grant's wire to Stanton:* OR, ser. 1, v. 46, pt. 2, pp. 311–12. Grant's wire was sent at 7:30 (*Id.*, p. 311). The Stephens Manuscript (p. 6), written a dozen years later (see Westwood, "Hampton Roads Conference," p. 253 n. 2), says the commissioners reached City Point at nearly 8:00, but a newspaperman on the scene marked their arrival at about 7:00 (*New York Times*, February 4, 1865).

143. *even routine dispatches were brought to Grant instantly:* Badeau, vol. 3, p. 136.

143. *"I will escort you myself":* Stephens Manuscript, p. 10.

144. *Stephens had never shed his coat:* Grant, vol. 2, p. 422.

144. *On the rugged path to the pier:* Stephens Manuscript, p. 10.

144. *"With this ringing in my ears":* Id., p. 11.

144. *"in the coat and out of it":* Grant, vol. 2, p. 422.

144. *well-appointed dining room:* Id., p. 420; New York Herald, February 5, 1865; Porter, *Grant*, p. 383.

144. *Julia was fond of berthing there:* See Julia Grant, pp. 132–34 and 139–40; Sylvanus Cadwalader, *Three Years with Grant* (New York: Alfred A. Knopf, 1955) ("Cadwalader"), p. 281.

145. *a feast in their honor:* Stephens Manuscript, p. 12. See *Augusta Chronicle and Sentinel*, reprinted in *New York Times, June 26, 1865* and *Richmond Examiner*, February 6 and 7, 1865, reprinted in *New York Times*, February 10, 1865.

145. *"a most sumptuous meal":* Stephens Manuscript, p. 12.

145. *"racy anecdotes"; "a noise of laughing and talking":* Id., pp. 12–13.

146. *the most vulnerable Northern boys:* Philadelphia Inquirer, February 6, 1865; New York Tribune, February 4, 1865.

146. *a lovely day:* Willcox, p. 604.

146. *Content with lesser pleasures:* Hopkins and Peck, p. 241.

146. *"I caught a glimpse of the lions"; "new-comers from rebellion":* New York Times, February 4, 1865.

146. *"when they felt like it":* Grant, vol. 2, p. 421.

146. *"an abundance of everything":* Lewis Leon, *Diary of a Tar Heel Confederate Soldier* (Charlotte, NC: Stone Publishing Co., 1913), p. 61.

146. *"It was interesting to us to know":* Hunter, "Peace Commission," p. 171.

147. *[Mrs. Grant] asked to be remembered:* Stephens Manuscript, pp. 13–14.

147. *Julia Grant had been raised by slaves:* Julia Grant, p. 2.

147. *his favorite mounts; his colleagues demurred:* Stephens Manuscript, p. 14.

147. *Grant made it clear he was anxious for its success:* Stephens, *CV*, vol. 2, p. 598.

147. *Grant would not be drawn:* Porter, *Grant*, p. 382.

148. *Grant was no Julius Caesar:* Hunter, "Peace Commission," p. 175. See Nicolay and Hay, vol. 10, p. 116.

148. *"I found them all very agreeable gentlemen":* Grant, vol. 2, p. 421.

148. *Meade made a courtesy call:* Meade, p. 258.

148. *"the tall figure":* Quoted in Randall and Current, p. 149.

148. *Some thought highly of [Meade]:* e.g., Cadwalader, pp. 342–44.

148. *"I think he had not a friend":* Dana, *Recollections*, pp. 226–27.

148. *They talked very freely:* Meade, pp. 258–59.

148. *He was married to her sister:* McFeely, p. 200.

148–149. *the Kilkenny catfight:* Hunter, "Peace Commission," p. 171.

149. *"I fear there is no chance for this"; "it would not do to let it be known":* Meade, pp. 259–60.

149. *"mindful of old acquaintanceship":* Hunter, "Peace Commission," p. 171.

149. *His "complexion was sallow":* Porter, *Grant*, p. 383.

149. *"The Lord seems to have robbed that man's body":* Id.

149. *"his wily tactics":* Hunter, "Peace Commission," p. 172.

150. *"We are but one people":* Philadelphia Inquirer, February 6, 1865.

150. *tourists returning from Baltimore:* New York Times, February 2, 1865.

150. *"hourly growing stronger here":* Cincinnati Commercial, February 2, 1865, reprinted in New Orleans Daily Picayune, February 12, 1865.

150. *"the whole olive branch business":* Id.

150. *"Let nothing which is transpiring":* CW, vol. 8, p. 252; OR, ser. 1, v. 46, pt. 2, p. 341.

150. *"There will be no armistice":* Id.

150. *"Call at Fortress Monroe":* CW, vol. 8, p. 252.

151. *traveling coat and muffler; his elegant clerk:* New York Herald, February 3, 1865; New York Daily Tribune, February 4, 1865; Lincoln Papers, Library of Congress, Seward to Lincoln, January 31, 1865. The dapper Mr. Chew is depicted in the painting, *Signing the Treaty of Cessation,* reproduced at www.library.state.ak.us/hist/cent/020-0181.jpg.

151. *Governor Augustus Bradford welcomed them:* Philadelphia Inquirer, February 6, 1865; New York Times, February 2, 1865; New York Tribune, February 3, 1865; Toews, Rockford, Lincoln in Annapolis, February 1865 (Annapolis: Maryland State Archives, 2009) ("Toews"), p. 11. www.lincolninannapolis.blogspot.com. See Brooks, Noah, *Lincoln Observed,* p. 138.

151. *With Maryland in hand:* Toews, pp. 11 and 44 n. 12, citing *Baltimore American*, February 2, 1865.

151. *the* River Queen *reigned:* Wayne C. Temple, *Lincoln's Travels on the* River Queen *during the Last Days of His Life* (Mahomet, IL: Mayhaven Publishing, 2007) ("Temple"), pp. 9–13.

151. *The Spotswood Hotel:* Quoted in Furgurson, p. 52.

151. Singleton's report to Lincoln: Browning, vol. 2, p. 5; *New York Daily Tribune*, February 1, 2, 4, and 6, 1865; Randall and Current, pp. 330–31. See Burlingame, vol. 2, p. 755.

152. *which had always seemed reasonable to him:* Escott, pp. 34–35, 55, 60, and 96–97; Debby Applegate, *The Most Famous Man in America: The Biography of Henry Ward Beecher* (New York: Doubleday, 2006) ("Applegate"), p. 339.

152. *a stern little talk:* CW, vol. 8, pp. 253–54 and 318–19; Crist, vol. 11, p. 388 n. 12; Elizabeth Blair Lee, p. 471.

152. *"bore down on him very hard":* Rice, pp. 248–49.

152. *"Who would let these criminals loose?":* New York Daily Tribune, February 2, 1865.

153. Beecher's conversation with Lincoln: *Id.*, pp. 249–50.

153. *bearing orders from Stanton:* OR, ser. 1, v. 46, pt. 2, p. 302.

153. *He ran into him forcefully:* Eckert relates his confrontation with Grant in Bates, pp. 334–38.

153. Lincoln's instructions to Grant: OR, ser. 1, v. 46, pt. 2, p. 302.

154. *"rarely showed vexation":* Badeau, vol. 3, p. 142.

154. *"And now commenced our troubles":* Hunter, "Peace Commission," p. 171.

CHAPTER 17

155. Lincoln's instructions to Eckert: *CW*, vol. 8, pp. 220–21, 246, and 248.

155. *Grant walked Eckert:* See *OR*, ser. 1, v. 46, pt. 2, p. 342.

155. *The major and Alec Stephens had met before:* Bates, pp. 125–29; Nicolay and Hay, vol. 10, p. 115 n. 1; Justin T. Turner, "Two Words," 2 *Autograph Collectors' Journal* (April 1950), p. 4.

155. *When they reunited on the* Mary Martin: Bates, p. 335.

156. *Lincoln had written it:* Westwood, "Singing Wire Conspiracy," p. 33.

156. *I am instructed by the President:* CW, vol. 8, pp. 277–78.

156. *Eckert asked them point blank:* Bates, p. 335.

156. *Davis had given them copies:* Campbell, *Reminiscences*, p. 8.

156. *He would come back soon:* Bates, p. 335.

156. *the only written answer they could give:* Campbell, *Reminiscences*, p. 9.

157. *The substantial object to be obtained:* OR, ser. 1, vol. 46, p. 512.

157. *At about six o'clock:* OR, ser. 1, v. 46, pt. 2, p. 342.

157. *Eckert told his envoys they could not proceed:* Bates, pp. 336–37.

157. *What could be lost by finding out:* Campbell, *Reminiscences*, p. 9.

157. *disregard the last few words of both letters:* OR, ser. 1, v. 46, pt. 2, pp. 341–42; *CW*, vol. 8, pp. 281–82 n. 19.

157. *Their position was "not satisfactory":* OR, ser. 1, v. 46, pt. 2, p. 342; Nicolay and Hay, vol. 10, p. 116.

157. *they tried to go over his head:* Bates, pp. 336–37.
158. *a more plausible recollection:* Stephens Manuscript, p. 15. Stephens recounted his memory in the late 1870s (Westwood, "Hampton Roads Conference"), Eckert in 1907 (Bates, p. 334).
158. The commissioners' note to Grant: *OR,* ser. 1, v. 46, pt. 2, p. 342; Stephens Manuscript, p. 15.
158. *"That will do":* Id., p. 16.
158. *He beckoned to Grant, and they left:* Id.
159. *"He was angry with me for years":* Bates, p. 337.
159. *The last time they saw Major Eckert:* Stephens Manuscript, p. 16; Bates, pp. 337–38.
159. Seward's wire to Lincoln: *CW,* vol. 8, p. 280.
159. Seward's wire to Grant: *OR,* ser. 1, v. 46, pt. 2, p. 342.
159. Eckert's wire to Lincoln: *Id.; CW,* vol. 8, p. 281.
160. Eckert's wire to Stanton: *OR,* ser. 1, v. 46, pt. 2, pp. 341–42.
160. *The telegraph line was down:* Id., p. 342. Howard C. Westwood, whose study of the record uncovered it, tells the story in "Singing Wire Conspiracy," pp. 30–35. See also McFeely, p. 205.
160. *The line "was occasionally broken":* Porter, *Grant,* p. 233.
160. *Lincoln monitored his telegrams to Stanton religiously:* e.g., Grimsley and Simpson, p. 84.
160. *He sent this one at ten-thirty:* OR, ser. 1, v. 46, pt. 2, p. 342.
161. *Campbell having fallen ill:* Campbell's *Reminiscences,* p. 9.
161. Grant's wire to Stanton: *CW,* vol. 8, p. 282; *OR,* ser. 1, v. 46, pt. 2, pp. 342–43.
161. *Eckert was on his way to Hampton Roads:* Westwood, "Singing Wire Conspiracy," p. 34.
161. *Campbell had gone to bed:* Campbell's *Reminiscences,* p. 9.
161. *Grant's "heavy brow":* Stephens Manuscript, p. 16.
161. *the three of them talked past midnight:* Westwood, "Singing Wire Conspiracy," p. 34.
161. *"It was expected that early this morning":* New York Times, February 4, 1865.
161. *Not if Grant could help it:* See Campbell's *Reminiscences,* p. 9; Westwood, "Singing Wire Conspiracy," p. 34.
162. *Stephens served as scrivener:* Stephens Manuscript, pp. 16–17.
162. The commissioners' note to Eckert: *OR,* ser. 1, v. 46, pt. 2, p. 512; *CW,* vol. 8, p. 284. Stephens dated the note February 2, after midnight, having dated his two, pre-midnight notes February 1. *OR,* ser. 1, v. 46, pt. 2, pp. 342. and 512 and Westwood, "Singing Wire Conspiracy," p. 34.
162. *Grant's charade:* Id.; McFeely, p. 205; Stephens Manuscript, p. 18.
163. *Grant's instructions to Babcock:* McFeely, p. 205; see *OR,* ser. 1, v. 46, pt. 2, pp. 352 and 512; *CW,* vol. 8, p. 283.
163. *"The world is all agog":* Elizabeth Blair Lee, p. 472.
163. *Rhode Island and Michigan:* Nicolay and Hay, vol. 10, p. 88.
163. *the Lady Long arrived:* OR, ser. 1, v. 46, pt. 2, p. 353.
163. Grant's wire to Seward: *Id.,* p. 352.
163. *Eckert wired Stanton:* Id., pp. 341–42.

164. *It moved him:* Nicolay and Hay, vol. 10, p. 117.

164. *"beaming with joy"; waving a ribbon:* Stephens Manuscript, pp. 18–19.

164. *"Say to the gentlemen":* CW, vol. 8, p. 282.

164. *"Induced by a dispatch":* Id.; OR, ser. 1, v. 46, pt. 2, p. 352.

164. *"with evident indications"; He turned to Colonel Hatch:* Stephens Manuscript, p. 19.

164. *[Grant] was willing to exchange* all *prisoners:* Grant's Papers, vol. 13, p. 454; *New York Times*, February 12, 1865.

164. *"How about Mr. Stephens's body servant":* Stephens Manuscript, pp. 19–20.

165. *"We were no diplomatists":* Hunter, "Peace Commission," p. 172.

165. *their shared ambition to secure a truce:* Stephens, CV, p. 603; Johnston and Browne, p. 484.

165. Hunter's frame of mind: Hunter, "Reply," pp. 303 and 305–06.

166. *"in the event that one should take place":* Campbell, *Reminiscences*, p. 16.

166. *"old habits of communion":* Hunter, "Peace Commission," pp. 172–73.

166. *Stephens seemed "possessed":* Hunter, "Peace Commission," p. 172; Campbell, *Reminiscences*, p. 6.

166. *wounds that would not heal:* Campbell, *Reminiscences*, p. 67.

166. *A shotgun wedding would not:* Avary, *Recollections*, p. 198; Stephens, CV, vol. 2, p. 593; Johnston and Browne, pp. 471 and 486–87.

166. *"slight hope of doing some good":* Id., p. 484; Avary, *Recollections*, p. 77.

166. *"upon some satisfactory basis":* Cleveland, p. 198; Avary, *Recollections*, p. 374.

166. *they would never start again:* Bradley T. Johnson, "The Peace Conference," 27 *Southern Historical Society Papers* (1899) ("Johnson, 'Peace Conference'"), p. 376.

166. *the "inferior" as well as the "superior":* Avary, *Recollections*, pp. 198–200.

167. *"thus far we are entirely free":* Crist, vol. 11, pp. 370–71.

167. *"but Seward is wily and treacherous":* Hill, p. 409; *Atlanta Constitution*, April 22, 1874, letter from Hill.

167. *in the company of Charles Forbes:* Stephen M. Forman, *A Guide to Civil War Washington* (Washington, DC: Elliott & Clark Publishing, 1995) ("Forman"), p. 150; Association for the Preservation of Historic Congressional Cemetery, Newsletter, Winter 1983. See *New York Herald*, February 4, 1865.

167. *He was one of Tad's favorites:* Crook, "Lincoln As I Knew Him," pp. 113–14.

167. *with the specific exception of Charlie:* Brooks, *Lincoln Observed*, p. 49.

167. Chaplain Neill's encounter with Forbes: Edward D. Neill, in *Glimpses of the Nation's Struggle* (St. Paul: St. Paul Book and Stationery Company, 1888) ("Neill"), p. 331; Sandburg, vol. 6, pp. 37–38.

168. *Mr. Blair will hereafter know:* Lincoln Papers, Library of Congress.

168. *making up his entourage:* New York Herald, February 3, 1865; *New York Daily Tribune*, February 3, 1865, *Baltimore American*, February 3, 1865, reprinted in Toews, p. 30. According to a serially inaccurate February 5, 1865 *New York Herald* article, Andrew Smith, a bodyguard (see Toews, p. 43 n. 2), also accompanied Lincoln, but many reliable sources, including Neill and the foregoing *Tribune* and *American* articles, say only Forbes was with him.

168. *a one-car train: Philadelphia Inquirer,* February 6, 1865; *New York Times,* February 3, 1865; *New York Tribune,* February 3, 1865.

168. *"it struck them unfavorably":* Welles, vol. 2, p. 235; *New York Daily Tribune,* February 3, 1865; Nicolay, p. 65.

168. *"a snare and a peril": Richmond Sentinel,* February 2, 1865, reprinted in *New York Times,* February 7, 1865.

168. General Pegram and Hetty Cary: Harrison, p. 203; Henry Kyd Douglas, *I Rode with Stonewall* (Chapel Hill: University of North Carolina Press, 1940) ("Douglas, *Stonewall"*), pp. 325–26; Trudeau, pp. 309–10.

169. *It occurred to Seward belatedly:* Grant's Papers, vol. 13, p. 346.

169. Lincoln boards the USS *Thomas Collyer: New York Herald,* February 3, 1865, February 5, 1865; *New York Times,* February 3, 1865; *Philadelphia Inquirer,* February 6, 1865; Toews, p. 21; Cox, *Three Decades,* p. 333.

169. *the fastest ship on Chesapeake Bay: New York Herald,* February 5, 1865; Toews, p. 45 n. 31.

169. *resplendent with flags and pennants: New York Daily Tribune,* February 6, 1865.

169. *hours ahead of Lincoln: Daily Constitutional Union,* February 3, 1865.

169. *"the* M. Martin *is just coming alongside": New York Herald,* February 4, 1865.

169. *The tugboats: New York Herald,* February 5, 1865.

170. *Denied the freedom of movement: Richmond Examiner,* February 7, 1865, reprinted in *New York Times,* February 10, 1865.

170. *handed Major Eckert the letter: OR,* ser. 1, vol. 46, pt. 2, p. 512; Lincoln Papers, document 40621, Library of Congress.

170. *its closing line: Id.*

170. *Seward stayed put:* Welles Diary, vol. 2, p. 236.

170. *"I do not recognize them until he comes": OR,* ser. 1, v. 46, pt. 2, p. 352.

170. *three bottles of good whiskey:* Pierce, vol. 4, p. 205; Van Deusen, p. 383.

170. *and Seward had not yet seen them: OR,* ser. 1, v. 46, pt. 2, 352; *CW,* vol. 8, p. 283; Welles Diary, vol. 2, p. 236.

170. *"I ascertained that Major Eckert": CW,* vol. 8, p. 283.

170. *another equivocation that Lincoln had not seen: CW,* vol. 8, pp. 283–84.

171. *Word was sent to the* Martin: Kean, p. 195.

171. Eckert's wire to Stanton: *OR,* ser. 1, v. 46, pt. 2, p. 352.

171. *"Peacefully and fraternally": New York Herald,* February 5, 1865.

CHAPTER 18

The Peace Conference: Lincoln described the conference briefly and clinically in a report to the House of Representatives (*CW,* vol. 8, pp. 274–85). He recounted some anecdotes to friends, preserved at Carpenter, pp. 209–11 and Rice, p. 97. His impression that Seward implied that the meeting would be secret is in document 40622, Lincoln Papers, Library of Congress. Seward added some color in a February 7, 1865, dispatch to Charles Francis Adams, the ambassador to the Court of St. James's (*OR,* ser. 1, vol. 46, pt. 2, p. 471–73). Lincoln or Seward must have passed on to Charles Sumner the references to the conference in Pierce, vol. 4, p. 205. The Southerners left far more detailed accounts. Stephens's are in *CV,* vol. 2, pp. 599–618; in Avary, *Recollections,* pp. 137, 141, 264–65, 271, 280–81, and 373–75; and in *Augusta Chronicle and Sentinel, in New York Times, June 26, 1865.* Friends and colleagues of Stephens preserved some of his recollections. See *New York Times,* July 22, 1895; Johnson, "Peace Conference"; Rowland, vol. 10, pp. 20–21; Cleveland, pp. 197–200; and Johnston and Browne, pp. 484–85. Hunter recalled the conference in Hunter, "Peace Commission" and Hunter, "Reply." A letter from Hunter on the conference is in Lee, "Failure," p. 478. Campbell described it in *Reminiscences,* pp. 6–8 and 10–17; "Papers of John A. Campbell," 42 *Southern Historical Society Papers* (October 1917) ("Campbell Papers"), pp. 45–52; Campbell, "Hampton Roads Conference," *Southern Magazine,* p. 188; "The Hampton Roads Conference," 4 *Southern Historical Society Papers* (September 1917) ("Campbell, "Hampton Roads Conference, *Southern Historical Society*"), pp. 45–52; and Campbell, "Open Letters," pp. 951–53. Campbell's fresh recollections are in Kean, pp. 194–98 and 201–02. See also Connor, *Campbell,* pp. 165–71. The commissioners' report on the conference is in Crist, vol. 11, pp. 378–79 and Davis, *Rise and Fall,* vol. 2, pp. 619–20. Soon after the conference, North Carolina's Senator William A. Graham wrote about the Southerners' accounts of it (Graham, pp. 228–30, 232–37, and 246). Presumably after interviewing one or more of the commissioners, the *Richmond Examiner* ran a brief account of the conference, consistent with theirs, on February 7, 1865, reprinted in the *New York Times* on February 10, 1865. Details drawn from unpublished sources are in Burlingame, vol. 2, pp. 751–61. Sandburg's biography of Lincoln cites few sources, but Sandburg is said to have interviewed living witnesses and consulted written sources that do not survive. He reviews the conference in vol. 6, pp. 39–46. The foregoing accounts are remarkably consistent and are woven together in this chapter with little need to weigh one against another. The sequence of the conversation is also recoverable with reasonable accuracy if not with precision.

172. *a warm sun:* See Willcox, p. 605.

172. *on the vessel's upper deck:* Porter, *Grant,* p. 423.

172. The commissioners arrived first. See Stephens, *CV,* vol. 2, p. 599.

172. *the* River Queen's *saloon:* George P. A. Healy's carefully researched painting, *The Peacemakers,* on the cover of this book, portrays the *River Queen's* saloon when Lincoln, Grant, Sherman, and Admiral David Porter met there a few weeks after the peace conference (see chapter 24). See also Arnold, p. 423, and Harold Holzer and Mark E. Neely, *Mine Eyes Have Seen the Glory* (New York: Orion Books, 1993), p. 156. Photographs and descriptions of the *River Queen* and her furnishings are in Temple, *Lincoln's Travels.* See Wilson, p. 581.

172. Hawthorne's description: Wilson, pp. 462–67.

173. thirty pounds underweight: Winik, p. 204.

173. *"seamed with thought and trouble":* Joel Benton, ed., *Greeley on Lincoln, and Mr. Greeley's Letters* (New York: Baker & Taylor Co., 1893), p. 75.

173. *Campbell had met Lincoln:* Campbell, *Recollections of the Evacuation of Richmond* (Baltimore: John Murphy & Co., 1880) ("Campbell, *Recollections*"), p. 7; Saunders, p. 145.

173. *Lincoln's eye would brighten:* Hay, *At Lincoln's Side,* p. 135.

173. *The Southerners were gracious too:* Pierce, vol. 4, p. 205.

173. *"a rather tumbled up appearance":* Chesnut, p. 54.
174. *"The naturalness was like that of a child":* Peabody, "Elizabeth Peabody Visits Lincoln," p. 122.
174. *Campbell saw it too:* Connor, p. 190, quoting a letter from Campbell to Horace Greeley.
174. *"No one expects any result":* Gorgas, p. 167.
174. *"the perturbation in Washington":* Brooks, *Lincoln Observed,* pp. 161–62; Brooks, *Washington in Lincoln's Time,* p. 204.
174. *the Jacobins outbid each other: Id.,* pp. 225–26; *New York Daily Tribune,* February 3, 1865.
174. *Some thought it quite deliberate:* Brooks, *Washington in Lincoln's Time,* pp. 228.
175. *"vaguely dreadful, and dreadfully vague"; Forney often spoke for Lincoln:* Brooks, *Lincoln Observed,* p. 203; Brooks, *Washington in Lincoln's Time,* pp. 225–26.
175. *"We again advise our readers":* *New York Times,* February 4, 1865.
175. *The* Tribune *had "received some inklings":* *New York Daily Tribune,* February 3, 1865.
175. *the "rising storm of indignation":* *New York Herald,* February 3, 1865.
175. *so small an ear emerge from so much husk:* The accounts of Lincoln's remark vary slightly, but are all of the same ilk; e.g. Burlingame, vol. 2, pp. 755–56 and n. 137, citing Stephens himself, and Donald, p. 557.
176. *"a happy looking schoolboy":* Cleveland, p. 232.
178. *"was always singularly firm":* Stoddard, p. 150.
183. *one of Sherman's divisions was breaking through:* Grimsley and Simpson, p. 45.
184. *"as though he were engaged in conversation":* Dana, *Recollections,* p. 169.
186. *he never referred to himself as president:* Neill, p. 331; Brooks, *Lincoln Observed,* pp. 201–02.
186. *that would not be "so obnoxious as slavery":* Meade, p. 259.
186. *An unnamed Cabinet member would neither confirm nor deny it:* *New York Herald,* February 4, 1865.
187. *"a feverish anticipation": Id.*
187. *"such utter incredulity"; "a strong upward bound":* *Boston Daily Evening Transcript,* February 6, 1865, quoting *New York Commercial Advertiser.*
187. *Reverdy Johnson observed:* Johnson's remarks and his colleagues' replies are in the *Congressional Globe,* February 3, 1865, p. 586.
187. John Conness: *Biographical Directory.*
188. *"Not a great deal":* Campbell's report that Seward said ten states could kill the 13th amendment in a reunited Union (Campbell, *Reminiscences,* pp. 7-8) is corroborated. The day after the commissioners returned to Richmond, North Carolina Senator William Graham, an ally of Hunter and Campbell, had not yet spoken with them but had it "on good authority" that Lincoln and Seward said the seceded states could return "with slavery as it is," subject to ratification of the 13th amendment, which *"may* be made in future" (Graham, pp. 228-29; emphasis added). A week later, Graham said Lincoln told the commissioners "he could unsay nothing he had said" on slavery, the fate of which would stand on the amendment's ratification, which ten states could block. Graham also said leading Southerners were considering the prospect of blocking it (*Id.,* pp. 232 and 235).

191. *"Charles lost his head"*: There are minor variations in the reports of Lincoln's quip, which became well-known at the time. This is one of the pithiest, and may be the earliest to appear, in Stephens, *Augusta Chronicle and Sentinel,* reprinted *in New York Times, June 26, 1865.* It is modified here only to reflect the casual form of address noted in Stephens, *CV,* p. 613.

191. *"a wonderful power of expression"*: Stoddard, p. 149.

192. *"I'll tell you what I would do"*: Some historians question Stephens's claim that Lincoln suggested that Georgia ratify the Thirteenth Amendment conditioned on its gradual implementation (e.g., James M. McPherson, "Could the South Have Won?," *New York Review of Books* (June 13, 2002); William C. Harris, "The Hampton Roads Peace Conference: A Final Test of Lincoln's Presidential Leadership," *Journal of the Abraham Lincoln Association,* vol. 21 [2000], p. 51), but Stephens prided himself on his integrity (see Escott, p. 209), a trait to which Judge Cone could attest (see p. 64 *supra*), and there is no good reason to doubt his word. Lincoln's preference for a gradual emancipation was long-standing (e.g., Escott, pp. 34-36, 60, and 96-97; Donald, p. 362; Randall and Current, p. 301); he had good reason to be concerned about securing Southern votes for ratification (see Escott, pp. 138–39), through political bargaining, if necessary"; he had long put reunion ahead of emancipation as a priority (*id., passion*); and the advice Stephens attributes to him on the manner of Georgia rejoining the Union mirrors what he said two months later about Virginia (see chapters 25 through 27). See also Donald, pp. 559–60, postulating that Lincoln thought slavery was already dead, and tried to lead the commissioners to believe that a gradual abolition was possible, to encourage Southerners to abandon Davis.

193. *Seward tried to interrupt him:* See *Richmond Examiner,* February 7, 1865, reprinted in *New York Times,* February 10, 1865.

193. *"root hog, or die"*: Variations of this story too were published. Lincoln recounted this one only days after the conference, expressing some concern that it had leaked and created an impression of unseemly levity (Carpenter, pp. 209–11).

195. *A few days later, a friend saw it clearly:* Rice, p. 97.

197. *a habit in moments of intensity:* Welles Diary, vol. 2, p. 106; Hay Diary, p. 211.

197. *It was far from good enough:* Several friends of Stephens claimed that he told them that Lincoln said, "Let me write Union and abolition on the page and you may write what you please" (e.g., Johnson, "Peace Conference," p. 376). Others say Stephens denied this (Henry Watterson, *The Compromises of Life* [New York: Duffield and Col, 1906], p. 366; Carr, p. 3). Two decades after the fact, Grant wrote that Lincoln told him he had made it clear that if the commissioners would concede reunion and abolition, he was ready to negotiate, and "was almost willing to hand them a blank sheet of paper with his signature attached, for them to fill in the terms ..." (Grant, vol. 2, p. 422). But Grant did not say that Lincoln told the *commissioners* this, and no participant recorded it, memorable though it would have been. Julian Carr rightly thought there must have been a misunderstanding, with eight honest men saying Stephens told them it was said and eight insisting he denied it (*Id.,* pp. 25–26 and 33). Stephens probably told friends it was his *sense* that Lincoln would accept any terms that included reunion and abolition, and Grant's memoirs may have influenced their memories.

197. *Even before the war; Lincoln had supported:* Stahr, pp. 125-26; Escott, pp. 34-35, 55, 60, and 96-97.

199. *"We shall leave here on steamer* River Queen": *OR,* ser. 1, v. 46, pt. 2, p. 360.

199. *"The President directs me to say": Id.*

199. *The* River Queen *parted gently: Id.; Philadelphia Inquirer,* February 6, 1865; *New York Herald,* February 5, 1865.

199. *The faster* Thomas Collyer *followed: New York Herald,* February 5, 1865.

199. *"with gravity and without levity":* Campbell, *Reminiscences,* p. 5.

199. *"Keep the champagne! Return the Negro!":* Neill, p. 333; *New York Herald,* February 10, 1865.

CHAPTER 19

202. *The River Queen docked:* Toews, pp. 23 and 45 n. 25; *Philadelphia Inquirer,* February 6, 1865. See *OR,* ser. 1, v. 46, pt. 2, p. 360.

202. *Lincoln and Seward rebuffed a crowd of newspapermen:* Sandburg, vol. 6, pp. 46–47.

202. *The crew had spread the word: New York Times,* February 5, 1865.

202. *The B&O Railroad supplied a private car:* Toews, p. 23.

202. *fifty years' pay for a major:* Mark M. Boatner, *The Civil War Dictionary* (New York: D. McKay Co., 1959), p. 624.

202. *The attempted bribe:* Bates, pp. 340–42; Sandburg, vol. 6, p. 47.

202. *adorned with books and engravings:* Stahr, p. 265.

202–203. *All contrary rumors were false: Philadelphia Inquirer,* February 6, 1865.

203. *The stock market rose: New York Times,* February 6 and 7, 1865; *New York Daily Tribune,* February 6, 1865.

203. *As soon as he was free of Lincoln and Seward:* Flower, p. 258.

203. *A company of "colored cavalry": New York Times,* February 8, 1865.

203. William Sharp; Lieutenant Levy: W. B. Judkins, Memoir 1907, www.mindspring .com/~jcherepy/memoir/judkins.txt ("Judkins"), pp. 87–88.

203. *Thaddeus Stevens assured his fellow Jacobins: Congressional Globe,* February 4, 1865, p. 596.

203. *As Sunset Cox had promised:* Cox, *Three Decades,* pp. 335–36.

203. *in the same tent:* Randall and Current, pp. 337–38.

203. *so was Horace Greeley: New York Daily Tribune,* February 7, 1865; McPherson, p. 183.

203. *Ebon C. Ingersoll: New York Times,* February 5, 1865.

203. *Seward wrote home:* Seward, *Seward at Washington,* vol. 2, p. 261.

204. *He and Seward described their encounter:* Welles Diary, vol. 2, p. 236.

204. *"I have not brought back peace in a lump":* Burlingame, p. 759.

204. *Stanton's wire to Grant: OR,* ser. 1, v. 46, pt. 2, p. 365.

204. *Grant's reply to Stanton: Id.*

204. *Captured in the fall of Port Hudson:* Avary, *Recollections,* p. 141.

204. *Nothing good could come of this:* John Stephens's liberation is recounted by his descendant Robert Stephens in "An Incident of Friendship," 45 *Lincoln Herald* (June 1943) ("Robert Stephens"), pp. 18–21. See also Sandburg, vol. 6, p. 51.

205. Lincoln's wire to the commandant: *CW,* vol. 8, p. 259.

205. *a second father to John:* Their relationship is described in Schott, pp. 154, 175, 212–13, 447, and 468; Avary, *Recollections,* pp. 82–83; and Von Abele, pp. 156 and 314.

205. Beecher's letter to Lincoln: Lincoln Papers, Library of Congress; *CW,* p. 318 n. 1.

206. *commiserating with Grant:* OR, ser. 1, v. 46, pt. 2, p. 361; Stephens, *CV,* vol. 2, p. 619.

206. *He would approve a universal exchange: Id.;* Porter, *Grant,* p. 384.

206. *but could not secure his freedom:* Pryor, *Reminiscences,* p. 329; Sandburg, vol. 6, p. 130.

206. *The commissioners left City Point:* Grant's Papers, vol. 13, pp. 346–47.

206. *"prudent enough not to talk much about it":* Porter, *Grant,* p. 385.

206. *It was still in progress now:* New York Times, February 8, 1865.

206. *"an intense feeling of insubordination":* Crist, vol. 11, 386 n. 3.

206. *more than two hundred men would desert": Id.*

206. *to brief Jefferson Davis and Judah Benjamin:* Kean, p. 194; Stephens, *CV,* vol. 2, p. 621.

206. *"everybody was very much disappointed":* Stephens, *CV,* vol. 2, p. 619.

206. *"the suicidal folly"; Davis concurred, and accused Mr. Lincoln:* Mallory, vol. 2, p. 208.

207. *If Davis was right; He might be heard from again:* Stephens, *CV,* vol. 2, p. 621.

207. *"with the air of a sage":* Campbell, "Open Letters," p. 952; Campbell to Nathan Clifford, August 1, 1865, Johnson Papers, Library of Congress.

207. *"probably fallen into a trap":* Davis, "Peace Conference," p. 68.

208. *Stephens protested:* Stephens, *CV,* vol. 2, p. 622; Rowland, vol. 7, p. 61; Cleveland, p. 199.

208. *"entire change of their social fabric"; "more determined than ever":* Stephens, *CV,* vol. 2, pp. 622–23.

208. *"whether negotiations were possible":* Crist, vol. 11, p. 389.

208. *he was "bitterly hostile":* Mallory, vol. 2, pp. 208–09.

209. *"any dolt whose blunders":* Rowland, vol. 7, p. 65.

209. *The commissioners would have had to "conceal" them: Id.,* p. 61.

209. *a Yankee plan to "encourage treason": Id.,* vol. 9, p. 603.

209. *Judge Campbell unburdened himself:* Jones, vol. 2, p. 410.

209. *"a dead man galvanized": Id.,* vol. 2, p. 312.

209. *a reasonable arrangement to free the slaves:* Campbell, "Open Letters," p. 952.

209. *Hubbell and his friends awaited the newspaper eagerly:* Hubbell Diary, p. 68.

209. *"There is nothing left us but to fight it out":* David E. Johnston, *The Story of a Confederate Boy in the Civil War* (Portland, OR: Glass & Prudhomme Co., 1914), p. 302.

210. *"Most of us have fought our last battle":* Crist, vol. 11, p. 376.

210. *Richmond's Sunday morning was clear and cold:* Jones, vol. 2, p. 409.

210. *Judge Campbell composed the commissioners' report:* Campbell, *Reminiscences,* pp. 5–6.

210. *Hunter and Stephens endorsed it, and a messenger brought it to Davis: Id.;* Kean, pp. 197–98 and 202.

210. *just a stark recitation:* The report is in Davis, *Rise and Fall,* vol. 2, pp. 619–20, and in Pollard, p. 466.

211. *Davis was not satisfied:* Kean, p. 202.

211. *so as not to damage him politically: Augusta Chronicle and Sentinel, in New York Times,* June 26, 1865.

211. *He pressed them again to embellish their report:* Kean, p. 202.
211. *"their failure and the reasons for it":* Crist, vol. 11, 379 n. 3.
211. *Senator William Graham:* Graham, pp. 229 and 239.

CHAPTER 20

212. *Now he spent the Sabbath:* Nicolay and Hay, vol. 10, p. 133.
212. *Sometime that day:* Mark D. Katz, *Witness to an Era: The Life and Photographs of Alexander Gardner* (New York: Viking Press, 1991), pp. 111 and 128.
212. *Almost all of his photographs:* Braden, p. 105.
212. *invitations to his Cabinet to assemble:* Francis Fessenden, *Life and Public Service of William Pitt Fessenden*, 2 vols. (Boston: Houghton Mifflin, 1907) ("Fessenden"), vol. 2, p. 8.
212. *Seward did not attend:* Michael Burlingame, ed., *An Oral History of Abraham Lincoln: John G, Nicolay's Interviews and Essays* (Carbondale: Southern Illinois University Press, 1996) ("Nicolay"), p. 66.
212. *gaslight chandelier:* See Goodwin, plates 38 and 41.
212. *Lincoln's draft message and the Cabinet meeting:* Lincoln Papers, Library of Congress; *CW*, vol. 8, pp. 260–61; Nicolay and Hay, vol. 10, pp. 133–36; Nicolay, pp. 65–66; Welles Diary, vol. 2, p. 237; Fessenden, pp. 7–8; Rice, p. 98.
213. *he wrote a note to posterity: CW*, vol. 8, p. 261.
214. *Gideon Welles told his diary:* Welles Diary, vol. 2, p. 237.
214. *It had taken Stanton by surprise:* Thomas and Hyman, pp. 347–48.
214. *"and there I agree with him":* Pierce, vol. 4, p. 206.
214. *"Querulous and angular":* Welles Diary, vol. 2, pp. 239–40.
214. *Fessenden's exchange with Davis:* Quoted in Frank H. Alfriend, *The Life of Jefferson Davis* (Cincinnati: Caxton Publishing House, 1868), pp. 106–07.
214. *"It was evident":* Fessenden, pp. 7–8.
214. *Congress never heard:* Nicolay and Hay, vol. 10, p. 137.
215. *No one had broken the news to her:* Douglas, pp. 325–27.
215. *"among the first of those martyrs":* Pryor, *Reminiscences,* pp. 320 and 326.
215. *Lieutenant Stephens's encounter with Lincoln:* Robert Stephens, p. 20.
215. *According to Sunset Cox:* Cox, *Three Decades,* p. 334.
216. *He offered a resolution: Congressional Globe,* February 6, pp. 617–18.
216. *"furious in their opposition":* Cox, *Three Decades,* p. 335.
216. *Before he set sail:* Foote, *War of the Rebellion,* pp. 396–405.
216. *"He was on picket duty":* Judkins, p. 88.
216. *"compelled to retrace his steps":* Meade, p. 261.
216. *An accompanying message of his own:* Journal of the Congress, vol. 7, p. 545.
216. *It was moved in the Senate: New York Herald,* February 10, 1865.
217. *"quite within the decency": Richmond Enquirer,* February 6, 1865, reprinted in *New York Times,* February 10, 1865.
217. *"which disposed of" any question of peace: OR,* ser. 1, v. 46, pt. 2, p. 1208
217. *"no one could have been more chagrined":* Avary, *Recollections,* p. 375.
217. *The day was set aside:* Pollard, p. 469.

217. *Grant sent the news to Stanton:* OR, ser. 1, v. 46, pt. 2, p. 414.

217. *"what I believed to be impossible":* Johnston and Browne, p. 486; see Stephens to Linton Stephens, February 18 and 23, 1865, Manhattanville Library.

217. *The scene in the African Church:* Pollard, p. 469; Crist, vol. 11, pp. 382–83, *Richmond Dispatch,* February 7, 1865, reprinted in *Baltimore Sun,* February 11, 1865; and *Richmond Sentinel,* February 7, 1865, reprinted in *New York Times,* February 12, 1865; Rabun, pp. 292 and 319; Winik, p. 56.

218. *in an old gray suit:* Pollard, p. 471.

218. *William "Extra Billy" Smith:* John W. Bell, *Memoirs of Governor William Smith, of Virginia* (New York: The Moss Engraving Company, 1891), pp. 96 and 101.

218. *Extra Billy spoke first: Richmond Dispatch,* February 7, 1865, reprinted in *Baltimore Sun,* February 11, 1865; Pollard, pp. 471–72; Crist, vol. 11, pp. 382–88.

218. *Davis's speech:* The speech is described, quoted, and critiqued by Stephens in *CV,* vol. 2, pp. 624–25 and in Avary, *Recollections,* p. 183; and generally in *Richmond Enquirer,* February 8, 1865; *Richmond Dispatch,* February 7, 1865, reprinted in *Baltimore Sun,* February 11, 1865; Pollard, pp. 471–72; and Crist, vol. 11, pp. 382–88.

218. *Alec Stephens was there:* Avary, *Recollections,* p. 183; Johnson, "Peace Conference," p. 376; Schott, p. 448; Furgurson, p. 293; Rabun, p. 319; McElroy, p. 441.

219. *Repeated calls were made for the Vice President: Richmond Dispatch,* February 7, 1865, reprinted in *Baltimore Sun,* February 11, 1865.

220. *"a squalid, half-famished wretch":* Willcox, 605.

220. *Grant wired Washington:* OR, ser. 1, v. 46, pt. 2, p. 415.

CHAPTER 21

221. *Petroleum V. Nasby:* Welles Diary, vol. 2, p. 238.

221. *Thaddeus Stephens disagreed: Congressional Globe,* February 7, 1865, p. 645.

221. *"I hope you will burn all cotton":* OR, ser. 1, vol. 47, pt. 2, p. 342.

222. *"I hear of but few officers killed":* Meade, p. 261.

222. *"He told the boys to take this ring":* Bradds, p. 5.

222. *Lee lost over a thousand; The North lost more:* www.civilwar.org/battlefields/hatchers-run-history-articles/the-batttle-of-hatchers-run.

222. *"no favor in these parts":* Worthington Chauncey Ford, *A Cycle of Adams Letters 1861–1865* (Boston: Houghton Mifflin, 1920), pp. 252–53.

222. *Seward's message to Adams:* OR, ser. 1, vol. 46, pt. 2, p. 472; Escott, p. 271 n. 8.

222. A PEACE POLICY NOW TREASON: *New York Times,* February 7, 1865.

223. *"dream of a reunited country": Richmond Dispatch,* February 7, 1865, reprinted in *New York Times,* February 10, 1865.

223. *Snow had turned to rain:* Jones, vol. 2, pp. 411–12.

223. *Then he met with Judge Campbell:* Kean, p. 199.

223. *all was lost; he would stay a few weeks and go: Id.*

223. *"scramble is going on":* Jones, vol. 2, p. 412.

223. *"He has a ghostly appearance"; "with locked doors": Id.,* p. 413.

223. *Lincoln . . . called on Preston Blair:* Letter from Blair to Lincoln, February 8, 1865, Lincoln papers, Library of Congress.

223. *Lizzie knew how depressed her father was:* Elizabeth Blair Lee, p. 473.
223. *He would soon tell a New York Congressman: New York Daily Tribune,* February 6, 1865.
223. *Sumner introduced a resolution: Congressional Globe,* February 8, p. 657.
223. *they "drank thirstily":* Pierce, vol. 4, p. 205.
223–224. Lincoln's wire to Grant and Grant's reply: *OR,* ser. 1, vol. 46, pt. 2, pp. 473–74.
224. *a bright and frosty Thursday:* Jones, vol. 2, p. 415.
224. *began at high noon: Richmond Sentinel,* February 10, 1865, reprinted in *New York Times,* February 13, 1865.
224. *"perhaps he cannot decline":* Jones, vol. 2, p. 414.
224. *Campbell and Stephens did: Stephens* to Linton Stephens, February 18, 1865, *Manhattanville Library;* Connor, p. 171; Schott, p. 448.
224. *a stirring "La Marseillaise":* Winik, p. 56.
224. *"under the influence":* Hunter, "Reply," p. 306.
224. Hunter's speech: *Richmond Sentinel,* February 10, 1865, *New York Times,* February 13, 1865; and Crist, vol. 11, p. 380 n. 3.
224–225. Benjamin's speech: *Richmond Sentinel,* February 10, 1865, reprinted in *New York Times,* February 13, 1865; Jones, vol. 2, p. 415. Senator Graham said Benjamin's speech was "exceedingly indecorous and impolitic," beyond what the press reported (Graham, pp. 230-31 and 234).
225. *The Speaker of the Virginia House: Richmond Sentinel,* February 10, 1865, reprinted in *New York Times,* February 13, 1865.
225. *"but quietly abide"; "I therefore left on the 9th":* Stephens, *CV,* vol. 2, pp. 625–26; Cleveland, p. 200.
225. *Hunter was collecting statistics:* Jones, vol. 2, p. 416.
225. *"Thanks be to God":* Quoted in Pollard, p. 470.
225. *The Raleigh* Progress: Quoted in James Ford Rhodes, *History of the United States from the Compromise of 1850 to the Final Restoration of Home Rule in the South in 1877,* 4 vols. (New York: Macmillan, 1909–19) ("Rhodes"), p. 73 n. 5.
226. *"dull, helpless expectation":* Pollard, p. 473.
226. *the "worst" demanded peace: Id.,* p. 478.
226. *The idea was growing in the Southern mind: Id.,* p. 479.
226. *"There are ultras among us":* Welles Diary, vol. 2, p. 239.
226. Lincoln's report to the House: Lincoln Papers, Library of Congress (*literally cut and pasted); CW,* vol. 8, pp. 274–85. Noah Brooks describes its reading in *Lincoln Observed,* p. 163, and *Washington in Lincoln's Time,* pp. 229–32. The report is in the *Congressional Globe,* February 10, pp. 729–30. See *New York Times,* February 11, 1865.
227. *Washburne, Lincoln's friend and Grant's:* Hay Diary, p. 121; Simpson, *Grant,* p. 73.
227–228. Brooks, Washburne, and Stevens on the House floor: *Congressional Globe,* February 10, pp. 730–35.
229. *John went back to the White House; "Suppose you take this along":* Robert Stephens, p. 20.
229. Lincoln's note to Stephens: *CW,* vol. 8, p. 287.
230. *"I could hear his deep breathing":* Crook, "Lincoln As I Knew Him," p. 111.

CHAPTER 22

231. *a "considerate friend"; "I did not utterly abandon my duty":* Hunter, "Reply," pp. 306–07.

231. *"to save as much as possible from the wreck":* Lee, "Failure," p. 478.

231. The senators' visit with Davis: Hunter recounts the conversation in Hunter, "Reply," p. 307. He seems to have forgotten, twelve years after the fact, that Graham and Orr were with him, which Campbell confirms in Campbell, "Open Letters," p. 952. Davis tells his side of the story in Rowland, vol. 8, p. 124 . See Yearns, "Peace Movement," p. 18. See Wakelyn, pp. 334–35 for a profile of Graham and pp. 208–09 for one of Orr. On Orr, see also Welles Diary, vol. 2, pp. 358–59.

231. *"with such a well-bred grace":* Quoted in Yearns, *Confederate Congress,* pp. 221–22.

232. Robert Woodward Barnwell: Wakelyn, p. 88; Rable, p. 209; *Biographical Directory.*

232. *Davis summoned his Cabinet; Then he went alone to Senator Barnwell:* Rowland, vol. 8, p. 124.

232–233. Barnwell's conversation with Hunter: Hunter, "Reply," pp. 307–08.

233. *Hunter had the impression that Barnwell disagreed: Id.,* p. 307.

233. The senators' conversation with Campbell: Campbell, *Reminiscences,* p. 22; Campbell, "Open Letters," p. 952.

233. *"bruited all over Richmond"; "destined to learn":* Hunter, "Reply," p. 308.

233. *"Had Mr. Davis agreed":* Lee, "Failure," p. 477. See Rowland, vol. 8, p. 128.

234. Lee's conversation with Hunter: Hunter, "Reply," pp. 308–09. When Hunter's account of his meeting with Lee was published after the war, Davis refused to believe it, unlike his wife, who reminded him how he refused to believe in the final months that Lee thought the war was lost (Strode, pp. 469–70).

234. *He mentioned no duty of his own:* Nolan, *Lee Considered.* Nolan's revisionist assessment of the sainted Lee is eye-opening.

234. Hunter's conversation with Breckinridge: Hunter, "Reply," p. 309.

234. *"I cannot make you feel how large they were":* Campbell, "Open Letters," p. 950.

235. *a mortal political sin: Id.,* p. 951; Yearns, "Peace Movement," *passim;* Drew Gilpin Faust, *The Creation of Confederate Nationalism: Ideology and Identity in the Civil War South* (Baton Rouge: Louisiana State University Press, 1988), *passim;* Rable, pp. 271–73 and 280–81.

235. *"superstitious dread"; resulting in nothing at all:* Campbell, "Open Letters," p. 952.

235. Campbell's efforts to find leaders to negotiate peace: *Id.,* pp. 951–53; Campbell, "Papers," p. 69; Campbell, *Recollections,* p. 7–8; Campbell, *Reminiscences,* p. 42; Campbell, "Hampton Roads Conference," *Southern Magazine,* p. 188; Ambler, pp. 255–56.

235. *Davis, who repeated himself:* Campbell, "Open Letters," p. 952. See Davis, "Peace Conference," pp. 68–69.

235. *he dreaded being charged:* Mallory, vol. 2, p. 209.

235. *If the Senate had faced the truth: Id.*

235. *The idiosyncrasy of one man:* Campbell, "Open Letters," p. 952. South Carolina Senator James L. Orr put it more bluntly: "We have failed through the egotism the obstinacy and the imbecility of Jeff Davis" (Orr to Governor Pickens, April 29, 1865, Pickens and Dugas Family papers, Southern Historical Collection, the University of North Carolina at Chapel Hill).

236. *"with its usual malice"; "in the thickest of the fight"; "your Meade art gallery increased"*: Meade, p. 263.

236. *Lee called for "new resolution"*: OR, ser.1, vol. 46, pt. 2, pp. 1229–30.

236. *"I am afraid we were too faint"*: Pryor, *Reminiscences*, p. 329.

236. *"furloughing, detailing, and discharging"; "the sooner the better"*: Jones, vol. 2, p. 417.

236. *"immovable in his determination"*: Id., pp. 421–22.

236–237. Campbell's conversation with Kean: Kean, pp. 204–05. On the Northern conferees' disappointment that no Southern offer was made, see Graham, pp. 235-36 and 246.

237. *"the last days of the Confederacy"; "Mr. Hunter seems more depressed"*: Jones, vol. 2, p. 427.

237. *Sickness had slowed Alec Stephens:* Stephens to Linton Stephens, February 18 and 23, 1865, Manhattanville Library; *New York Times*, July 22, 1895; Johnston and Browne, p. 486.

237. *"He has been a weight for two years"*: Crist, vol. 11, p. 463.

238. *Stephens assembled his slaves:* Avary, *Recollections*, p. 144.

238. *In exchange for that sum; Then he taught him how to manage:* Id., pp. 144–45.

238. *Little Alec told friends at dinner:* Rowland, vol. 7, p. 61; vol. 10, pp. 20–21.

238. *Stephens told a fellow Georgian:* Id.

239. *Whom God would destroy:* Avary, *Recollections*, p. 145.

239. Senator Graham's letter: Graham, p. 252.

CHAPTER 23

240. *"I have nothing to report this morning of unusual interest"*: OR, ser. 1, vol. 46, pt. 2, p. 1254.

240. *a resolution declaring the unalterable determination:* John Goode, "The Confederate Congress," 4 *The Conservative Review* (September–December 1900) ("Goode"), p. 106.

240. *"still hankering after peace"*: Gorgas, p. 172.

240. Senator William Graham: For a profile of Graham, see Richard Current, ed., *Encyclopedia of the Confederacy* (New York: Simon & Schuster, 1993), pp. 705–08.

240. *Campbell replied in a letter:* The letter is in Campbell, "Papers," pp. 58–60, and in Campbell, *Reminiscences*, pp. 22–26. See Campbell, "Open Letters," p. 952; Campbell, *Reminiscences*, p. 68 n. 2; and Campbell, "Hampton Roads Conference," *Southern Magazine*, pp. 188–90.

241. *Graham shared Campbell's letter:* Id., p. 188.

241. *Campbell submitted a report to the Secretary of War:* The report is in OR, ser. 1, vol. 51, pt. 2, pp. 1064–67 and in Campbell, *Reminiscences*, pp. 26–31.

241. *"or even to veil its nudity"*: Id., p. 36.

241. *Paper money was trading at sixty to one:* See Akins, p. 105.

241–242. The Confederacy's desperate military condition: See Grimsley and Simpson, pp. 40–48.

242. *His son would soon be killed:* Nathaniel C. Hughes, *Bentonville: The Final Battle of Sherman and Johnston* (Chapel Hill: University of North Carolina Press, 1996), pp. 188–204.

243. *Campbell presented his report:* Campbell, *Reminiscences,* p. 31.

243. *"longer than we had reason to anticipate":* OR, ser. 1, vol. 46, part 2, pp. 1295–96; Campbell, *Reminiscences,* p. 34.

243. *The other reports were as grim:* "Resources of the Confederacy in February 1865," 2 *Southern Historical Society Papers* (July–December, 1876), pp. 56–128. See Campbell, *Reminiscences,* pp. 35–36; Campbell, "Open Letters," p. 952.

243. *"I was advised by Senator Graham":* Campbell, "Hampton Roads Conference," *Southern Magazine,* p. 188; Campbell, *Reminiscences,* pp. 37–38.

243. *a party that "knows not when it is beaten":* Id., pp. 36–37.

243. *The governor should be prepared:* Connor, p. 174.

243. *His own right arm was in a sling:* William Marvel, *Lee's Last Retreat: The Flight to Appomattox* (Chapel Hill: The University of North Carolina Press, 1980) ("Marvel"), p. 7.

243. *his cousin Julia Dent; Longstreet was one of three fellow officers:* Carol K. Bleser and Lesley J. Gordon, *Intimate Strategies of the Civil War: Military Commanders and Their Wives* (Oxford: Oxford University Press, 2001), p. 125.

243. *in contact only in battle:* James Longstreet, *From Manassas to Appomattox* (Philadelphia: Lippincott, 1896) ("Longstreet"), pp. 16–18.

243. *another friend of Longstreet's:* Smith, *Grant,* p. 391; McFeely, p. 209.

244. Ord's meeting with Longstreet: Longstreet, pp. 583–87 and 647–49; Grant's Papers, vol. 14, pp. 63–64.

244. *Then he wired his wife at Lynchburg:* Porter, *Grant,* p. 391.

244. *according to Porter, it was Longstreet's idea:* Id., pp. 391–92.

244. *Julia Grant stepped . . . into her husband's office:* See Julia Grant, p. 140–41.

245. *Longstreet and Lee were called to Richmond:* Longstreet, p. 584.

245. Correspondence between Ord and Grant: Grant's papers, vol. 14, pp. 63–64.

245. Ord's second meeting with Longstreet: *Id.;* Longstreet, p. 585.

245–246. Lee's note to Grant: OR, ser. 1, vol. 46, pt. 2, p. 824.

246. *he ordered a subordinate to tell Longstreet:* Id., p. 813.

246. Grant's wire to Stanton: *Id.,* p. 802.

246. *he spoke not a word and wrote a dispatch:* Nicolay and Hay, p. 158.

246. *An alternate account:* Carpenter, pp. 265–66, quoting *The Boston Commonwealth* newspaper.

246. *The President directs me to say:* OR, ser. 1, vol. 46, pt. 2, p. 802.

246–247. *"I will add that General Ord's conduct":* Id.

247. *"exact severe terms":* Welles Diary, vol. 2, p. 269.

247. *also known as Unconditional Surrender Grant:* See Dana, *Recollections,* p. 95.

247. *resented Lincoln's pardons of deserters:* Randall and Current, p. 350. Like others, Welles saw Lincoln's anguish for condemned prisoners as a weakness (Welles Diary, vol. 2, p. 207). See Stoddard, pp. 186–87.

247. *Stoneman never forgot the look:* Hay Diary, p. 306, n. 78.

247. *"You may say to General Longstreet":* OR, ser. 1, vol. 46, pt. 2, p. 830.

247. *"I have no authority":* OR, ser. 1, vol. 46, pt. 2, p. 825.

247. *"I can assure you that no act":* OR, ser. 1, vol. 46, pt. 2, p. 823–24.

248. *"the enemy had a purpose":* OR, ser. 1, vol. 46, pt. 2, p. 841.

248. *"and make our people desperate":* Kean, p. 203.

248. *[Lincoln] was bent on luring the South back in a reconciling mood before Congress could stop him:* See, e.g., Welles, "Lincoln and Johnson," p. 526.

248. *"The Senate, it is now said":* Gorgas, p. 174.

248. *Hill assembled an array:* Hill, p. 290.

249. *"Columbia is but dust and ashes":* Chesnut, p. 358.

249. Davis's conference with Lee: Davis, *Rise and Fall,* vol. 2, pp. 648–49.

249. *Lee had to change his plans; Davis approved the disaster-delaying plan: Id.,* p. 649.

249. *Sarah Pryor's husband:* Pryor, *Reminiscences,* pp. 39, 119; Sandburg, vol. 6, p. 130; John C. Waugh, *Surviving the Confederacy: Rebellion, Ruin, and Recovery; Roger and Sarah Pryor during the Civil War* (New York: Harcourt, 2002), p. 55; David J. Eicher, *The Longest Night: A Military History of the Civil War* (New York: Simon and Schuster, 2001), pp. 30–31.

250. John Yates Beall: Issac Markens, "President Lincoln and the Case of John Yates Beall," privately printed, 1911, available at www.archive.org/stream/presidentlincoln mark_djvu.txt.

250. Lincoln's meeting with Pryor and his friends: Pryor, *Reminiscences,* pp. 340–41.

250. *They tried me every way:* Sandburg, vol. 6, pp. 132–33.

CHAPTER 24

251. *William Cabell Rives:* Alexander Brown, *The Cabells and Their Kin* (Richmond: Garrett and Massie, 1939); *Biographical Directory of the United States Congress,* www.bioguide congress.gov; Escott, p. 149.

251. *"true policy required us to close the war":* Quoted in Ballard, p. 21.

251. *he had long supported Davis:* Foote, *Casket of Remembrances,* p. 304.

251. *had recently resigned, pleading age and ill health: Journal of the Congress,* p. 674.

251. Rives's resolution: In Campbell, *Reminiscences,* pp. 33–34, Campbell recounts his approach to Rives and reproduces the resolution Rives drafted.

251. *Davis would ignore it: Id.,* p. 33.

252. Davis's message to Congress: Reproduced in Campbell, *Reminiscences,* pp. 44–54.

252. *Davis gathered in his office; "He was a soldier"; Virginia stood ready:* Goode, p. 112.

252. *"the cup of humiliation":* Quoted in Rhodes, vol. 5, p. 81.

252. *Congress had abandoned its post:* Pollard, p. 457.

253. *a Senate committee lashed back:* The committee's report is in Campbell, *Reminiscences,* pp. 54–65.

253. *As late as 1957:* Yearns, "Peace Movement," p. 18.

253. *"an amalgam of malice and mediocrity":* Pollard, p. 162.

253. *"reconcile me to death"; postpone reading it:* Jones, vol. 2, p. 452.

253. *"in high disfavor":* Kean, p. 205.

253. *a captured blockade runner:* Temple, p. 27.

253. *"he is much worn down":* Welles Diary, vol. 2, p. 264.

253. *"He had leapt at the chance":* Randall and Current, p. 344.

253. *to shadow the commander in chief: CW,* vol. 8, pp. 372–73 n. 1.

254. *"he was almost willing to hand them a blank sheet of paper":* Grant, vol. 2, p. 422.

254. General Gordon's discussion with Lee: Gordon, pp. 386–93; Benjamin LaBree, ed., *Campfires of the Confederacy* (Louisville: Courier-Journal Job Printing Company, 1898), pp. 450–51.

254. *attack on Fort Stedman:* Foote, vol. 3, pp. 842–44.

254. *Hartranft and Gordon called a truce:* Bolton, p. 251.

254. *shattered legs and thighs:* Id., 255.

255. Douglas's exchange with Hartranft: Douglas, p. 329.

255. Lincoln, Grant, Sherman, and Porter on the *River Queen:* Sherman, vol. 2, pp. 324–31; Porter, *Incidents,* pp. 313–17; Grimsley and Simpson, p. 91; Randall and Current, p. 351; *New York Daily Tribune,* September 13, 1885.

255. *a conversation that never happened:* Julia Grant, pp. 137–38.

256. *"Mr. Davis gave me a pistol":* Varina Davis, vol. 2, p. 577.

256. *Davis had proclaimed that:* Quoted in *Richmond Examiner,* February 27, 1865, quoted in *New York Times,* March 2, 1865.

257. *"simply a measure of prudence"; the Frenchman could not tell:* Furgurson, p. 321.

257. *a frantic afternoon; smiled and waved:* Ballard, p. 45; Wise, p. 415.

257. *every senior Confederate official but one:* Dana, *Recollections,* pp. 265–66; Donald, p. 577; Randall and Current, p. 347.

257. *"heavy hearts and light luggage":* Welles Diary, vol. 2, p. 275.

257. *"renew my obligations":* Connor, p. 174.

257. *His son, two sons-in-law, and a nephew:* Campbell, *Recollections,* p. 4.

257. *"I could only await the ruin":* Quoted in Connor, *Campbell,* p. 174.

257. *"suspiciously like a dirty tablecloth":* Cadwalader, p. 310.

257. *"a forlorn body":* Pryor, *Reminiscences,* pp. 361–62.

257–258. The burning of Richmond: R. S. Ewell, "Evacuation of Richmond," 13 *Southern Historical Society Papers* (1885), pp. 247–52; Furgurson, pp. 331–36; Ballard, pp. 46–49.

258. *When the victors marched in; In the words of a Rebel officer:* Bill, p. 273–78; Furgurson, pp. 336–42.

258. *"could not be made to understand":* Phoebe Yates Pember and Irvin Wiley Bell, ed., *A Southern Woman's Story: Life in Confederate Richmond* (Columbia: University of South Carolina Press, 1959) ("Pember"), pp. ix and 79–82; Jones Diary, vol. 2, p. 470.

258. *"We have now entered upon a new phase":* Pollard, p. 510.

259. *"I walked around the burnt district":* Jones, vol. 2, p. 470.

259. General Weitzel's background: Godfrey Weitzel, *Richmond Occupied* (Richmond, VA: Richmond Civil War Centennial Committee, 1965) ("Weitzel"), p. 62; Henry A. Ford and Kate Ford, *History of Cincinnati, Ohio* (Cleveland: L. A. Williams & Co., 1881), pp. 137–38; www.Cincinnaticwrt.org.

259. *some 25,000 citizens of Richmond had no food:* Bill, p. 285.

259. *Weitzel ordered rations distributed:* Dana, *Recollections,* p. 266.

259. *Early that morning, Judge Campbell went over:* Campbell, *Recollections,* pp. 5–6.

259. Lincoln's visit to Richmond: *New York Herald,* April 9, 1865; Winik, pp. 118–20; Furgurson, pp. 341–44; Donald, pp. 576–77; Porter, *Incidents,* pp. 294–309; *New York Times,* April 8, 1865.

260. *"I'd let 'em up easy":* Weitzel, p. 56.
260. *Escorted by Admiral Porter:* Porter, *Incidents,* p. 302; Bill, p. 279.
260. *When Stanton learned:* Thomas and Hyman, p. 353; Flower, p. 270.
260. *Having heard of Weitzel's largesse:* Dana, *Recollections,* p. 266.
260. *Weitzel ordered rations distributed; "under what authority":* Weitzel, p. 57.
261. *An "acre of blood":* Quoted in Winik, p. 115.
261. *the Whig reopened:* Jones, vol. 2, p. 471; *New York Times,* April 8, 1865.
261. *"A staff officer came for me":* Campbell, *Recollections,* p. 6.
261. *Northern newspapermen noticed:* Myrta Lockett Avary, *Dixie After the War* (New York: Doubleday Page & Co., 1906) ("Avary, *Dixie*"), p. 36.
261. Campbell's meeting with Lincoln, Weitzel, and Shepley: *New York Herald,* April 9, 1865; Campbell, "Open Letters," p. 952; Campbell, *Recollections,* pp. 7–9; Campbell, *Reminiscences,* p. 39; and John A. Campbell, "Evacuation Echoes," 24 *Southern Historical Society Papers* (1896) ("Campbell, 'Evacuation Echoes'"), pp. 351–52; Connor, pp. 175–76, 188–90, and 195–96; Burlingame, vol. 2, p. 791; Saunders, pp. 179–80. Weitzel recalled the meeting briefly, years after the fact, in Weitzel, p. 56. For a fragment of Lincoln's account, see Ambler, pp. 255–56.
262. *a distinguished old Virginian:* Avary, *Dixie,* p. 35.
263. Julia Grant's visit to Richmond: Julia Grant, pp. 150–51.
263. *"not one of us who remained":* Eggleston, *Recollections,* p. 232.
263. *"Give them all the provisions they want":* Quoted in Sandburg, vol. 6, p. 181.
264. *he would always consider it the holiday:* Porter, *Incidents,* pp. 284 and 292.

CHAPTER 25

265. *It was warm in Richmond:* Jones, vol. 2, p. 471.
265. *Campbell tried to gather such men:* Campbell "Papers," p. 68.
265. A close friend of Campbell's: Saunders, p. 180.
265. *"an established member of the bar":* Id.
265. *"a little old lawyer":* Jones, vol. 2, p. 472.
265. *He was more than that:* Gustavus A. Myers, "Abraham Lincoln in Richmond," 41 *Virginia Historical Magazine* (October 1933) ("Myers"), p. 318.
266. *Campbell had hoped to bring to the President:* Campbell recounts his effort to recruit Virginians to meet Lincoln in "Open Letter," p. 952, and Campbell "Papers," p. 68.
266–267. Campbell's meeting with Lincoln on the *Malvern:* Campbell recalls the meeting, and presents the memorandum Lincoln handed him there, in Campbell, *Reminiscences,* pp. 39–42; Campbell, "Open Letters," pp. 952–53; Campbell, "Papers," pp. 63 and 68–70; Campbell, "Evacuation Echoes," p. 351–53; and Campbell, *Recollections,* pp. 11–13. See also Burlingame, vol. 2, pp. 792–93. Myers described the meeting within a few days of it (see Myers, pp. 319–22). Lincoln referred to the meeting in a message to Grant, at *CW,* vol. 8, p. 388. A biased rendition of Lincoln's account of the meeting, related years later by Governor Pierpont, is in Ambler, *Pierpont,* pp. 255–56. Weitzel gave a brief account of the meeting in *Richmond Occupied,* p. 56. Dana quoted Weitzel on the meeting contemporaneously in *OR,* ser. 1, vol. 46, pt. 3, p. 575. See also Avary, *Dixie,* pp. 37–38; Randall and Current, pp. 354–55; Saunders, p. 180; and Connor, pp. 177–91.

Some historians have questioned Campbell's claim that Lincoln spoke of empowering the legislature to restore Virginia to the Union as opposed to recalling her troops, but Myers's general recollections corroborate Campbell's specific ones: Lincoln said he was thinking of recalling the legislature to see whether "they desired to take *any* action on behalf of the States [*sic*] in view of the existing state of affairs." Myers, pp. 321–22 [emphasis added]. Recalling the legislature also comports with Lincoln's efforts to conciliate the South and promote a peaceful reunion (See Escott, *passim*).

266. Lincoln's memorandum of terms: *CW,* vol. 8, pp. 386–87; Library of Congress, Lincoln Papers.

266. *According to Duff Green:* Duff Green, p. 232.

269. *negligible support in the rest of the state:* For Lincoln, Pierpont's government had a "somewhat farcical" quality, having almost no support beyond the range of Union guns (*CW,* vol. 7, p. 487; Donald, pp. 577–79).

269. *North Carolina's legislature seemed ready to do the same:* Campbell, "Papers," p. 64.

270. *"I feel that this Diary is near its end":* Jones, vol. 2, p. 471.

270. Seward's accident and the sickroom: Welles Diary, vol. 2, p. 275; Carpenter, p. 290; Stahr, pp. 431–32; Van Deusen, p. 411.

270–271. Lincoln's message to Weitzel: *CW,* vol. 8, p. 389; Ambler, p. 256.

271. Campbell's meeting with Weitzel: Campbell's account is in Campbell, *Evacuation Echoes,* p. 352, and in Campbell, "Papers," p. 71. See also Connor, pp. 191–92.

271. *Then Campbell wrote a letter to an honor roll:* The letter is in Campbell, *Recollections,* pp. 23–25.

271. *Campbell read his draft; none of them objected: Id.,* pp. 14 and 23–25; Campbell, *Evacuation Echoes,* pp. 351–53; Connor, p. 194.

271. *Stanton told him to order Weitzel: Id.;* Flower, p. 269

272. *Campbell met with five Virginia legislators:* Dana, *Recollections,* p. 267; see Campbell, *Recollections,* p. 14; Randall and Current, pp. 355–56.

272. Campbell's letter to Weitzel: *CW,* vol. 8, p. 407 n. 1.

272. Lincoln's wire to Grant: *CW,* vol. 8, pp. 388–89.

272. Freedom of religion in Richmond: Dana, *Recollections,* pp. 270–71; Weitzel, p. 58; *CW,* vol. 8, p. 405; Thomas and Hyman, p. 354.

272. Wade's profane outburst: Burlingame, vol. 2, p. 794.

CHAPTER 26

274. *On Saturday morning:* Jones, vol. 2, p. 473.

274. *"thoroughly conscious that they were beaten":* Dana, *Recollections,* pp. 268–69.

274. *The Virginians read to the victors: Id.,* pp. 267–69.

274. *After Dana left, he was sitting in the lobby:* Dana, *Recollections,* p. 269.

274. *whose carpets had been ripped up:* Conolly, p. 80.

275. *Campbell later heard:* Campbell, *Recollections,* p. 14.

275. *faster than this legislature could think:* OR, ser. 1, vol. 46, pt. 3, p. 619.

275. *bright and beautiful Sunday:* Jones, vol. 2, p. 473.

275. *The story of Grant's compassion:* e.g., Porter, *Grant,* pp. 472–84; Winik, pp. 183–93.

275. *the president embraced it:* Randall and Current, pp. 351–52.

275. *Grant told Lee; Lee said little:* Porter, *Grant,* pp. 475–76.
276. *Unaware of the momentous event; went straight to the governor's home:* Stahr, p. 432–33; Van Deusen, p. 412; McFeely, p. 222.
276. *Stanton threw his arms around the President and ordered illuminations:* Thomas and Hyman, p. 353.
276. *At daybreak, the hollow boom of cannon:* Welles Diary, vol. 2, p. 278; McFeely, p. 222; Judith White McGuire, *Diary of a Southern Refugee during the War, by a Lady of Virginia* (New York: E. J. Hale & Son, 1867), p. 352.
276. *"God help us":* Quoted in Bill, p. 284.
276. *the president was effervescent:* Welles, *Lincoln and Johnson,* p. 523.
276. *"a great silence prevailed"; Judah Benjamin told a friend:* Ballard, p. 65.
276. *a leader "less resolute":* Davis, *Rise and Fall,* vol. 2, p. 658.
276. *He had turned and fought repeatedly:* Marvel, *passim;* Porter, *Grant,* p. 492; Badeau, vol. 3, p. 624.
277. Grant's horseback conversation with Lee: Grant, vol. 2, pp. 496–98; Porter, *Grant,* pp. 490–91; Dana, *Recollections,* pp. 271–72.
277. Pierpont's conversation with Lincoln: Ambler, pp. 255–57.
277. *"On to Mexico":* McFeely, p. 221.
277–278. *A festive breakfast; "Hush, Julia"; took the* Mary Martin *up the Potomac:* Julia Grant, p. 153; Porter, *Grant,* p. 493.
278. *On a misty, overcast day in Richmond:* Jones, vol. 2, p. 474.
278. *came together and issued an "Address":* Id., p. 478; Campbell, *Recollections,* pp. 14 and 25–27, including the message summoning the legislature, which is also presented in Jones, vol. 2, pp. 477–78. See Connor, pp. 180–94.
278. *The Cabinet met that day:* Welles Diary, vol. 2, p. 278; Welles, *Lincoln and Johnson,* p. 524.
278–279. Davis's meeting with Johnston and Beauregard: Joseph E. Johnson, *Narrative of Military Operations during the Civil War* (New York: D. Appleton and Co., 1874) ("Johnston"), pp. 398–400; Davis, *Rise and Fall,* vol. 2, pp. 679–81; Pollard, pp. 515–16; Ballard, pp. 81–84; and William B. Feis, "Jefferson Davis and the 'Guerilla Option'" ("Feis") in Grimsley and Simpson, pp. 118–19.
279. *"the war had now shrunk into narrow proportions":* Rise and Fall, vol. 2, p. 683.
279. *"smothered quarrels":* Mallory, vol. 2, pp. 205–06. See Pollard, pp. 296 and 382–84; Gabor S. Boritt, ed., *Jefferson Davis's Generals* (New York: Oxford University Press, 1999), pp. 3–27 and 46–65.
279. *"his piety held out the hope":* Varina Davis, vol. 2, p. 924.
280. *A crowd assembled on the White House lawn:* Welles, *Lincoln and Johnson,* p. 523; Brooks, *Lincoln Observed,* pp. 182–83.
280. *He honored his pledge:* Welles, *Lincoln and Johnson,* pp. 523–24; Keckley, p. 176–77. The speech can be found at *CW,* vol. 8, pp. 399–404.
281. *Standing in the crowd:* Bishop, p. 77; Goodwin, p. 728; http://law2.umkc.edu/faculty/projects/ftrials/lincolnconspiracy/booth.html.

CHAPTER 27

282. Lincoln's talk with Welles: Welles Diary, vol. 2, pp. 279–80; Welles, *Lincoln and Johnson,* p. 524.

283. Lincoln's telegrams to Weitzel: *CW,* vol. 8, pp. 405–06.

283. *Stanton worked on him for hours:* Thomas and Hyman, pp. 355–56; Flower, pp. 271–72.

283. Weitzel's telegram to Lincoln: *OR,* ser. 1, vol. 46, pt. 3, p. 724.

284. *Stanton was "full of feeling":* Flower, p. 272.

284. Lincoln's telegram to Weitzel: *CW,* vol. 8, pp. 406–08; *OR,* ser. 1, vol. 46, pt. 3, p. 725.

284. *Lincoln handed what he had written to the Secretary of War:* Campbell, *Reminiscences,* pp. 42–44.

284. *he had won his battle: Id.,* Connor, *Campbell,* pp. 182–84; Thomas and Hyman, pp. 354–56.

284. *"a man who never questioned his own authority":* Grant, vol. 2, p. 506.

284. *Hunter was back; He was ordered to leave:* Connor, p. 178.

284. *he and Campbell joined forces:* Campbell, *Recollections,* pp. 16–17; Bishop, pp. 200–01.

285. *every man was "making his separate treaty":* Campbell, "Open Letters," p. 952.

285. Campbell's communications with Ord: Campbell, *Reminiscences,* p. 41; Connor, pp. 186–87.

285. *Ord issued a public order: OR,* ser. 1, vol. 46, pt. 3, p. 735; Campbell Papers, p. 75; Jones, vol. 2, pp. 478–79; Campbell, *Recollections,* pp. 16–17.

285. The Cabinet meeting of April 14, 1865: Welles's Diary, vol. 2, pp. 280–83; Welles, *Lincoln and Johnson,* pp. 525–28. See Thomas and Hyman, p. 357.

286. Jacob Thompson: Williams, *Greeley,* p. 250; Burke Davis, *The Long Surrender* (New York: Random House, 1985) ("Davis, *Long Surrender*"), pp. 50–51.

287. Dana's conversation with Lincoln on Thompson: Dana tells the story in Dana, *Recollections,* pp. 273–74. After Lincoln spoke with Dana, Stanton pressed the point personally, and was rebuffed (Carpenter, pp. 282–83; Wilson, p. 587).

287–288. The Lincoln assassination: Bishop, *passim;* Winik, pp. 220–24; Donald, pp. 592–99; and Michael W. Kauffman, *American Brutus* (New York: Random House, 2004) ("Kauffman, *American Brutus*"), *passim.* Charlie Forbes gets special attention in Frederick Hatch, "Lincoln's Missing Guard," 106 *Lincoln Herald* (2005), pp. 106–117.

287. *"my friend Charles":* Forman, p. 150.

288. *The attack on Seward:* Stahr, pp. 435–37.

288. *"all was silent and sad":* Welles Diary, vol. 2, p. 290

288. *His wife had stayed:* Keckley, p. 188.

288. *Eliza Blair Lee would all but live in the White House for days:* Smith, *Francis Preston Blair,* p. 371.

288. *"who killed my father?":* Welles's Diary, vol. 2, p. 290. See Hay, *At Lincoln's Side,* p. 113.

288. *"President Johnson is not disposed to treat treason lightly":* Welles's Diary, vol. 2, p. 291.

289. *"a baker's dozen"; Johnson wanted to hang many more:* Smith, *Francis Preston Blair,* p. 385.

289. *Informed [Davis] of Lincoln's assassination:* Davis, *Rise and Fall,* vol. 2, p. 683; Foote, vol. 3, p. 998.

289. *He would not despair of the cause:* Rowland, vol. 7, p. 2.

289. *"personal malignity"; the embodiment of malignity:* Davis, *Rise and Fall,* vol. 2, p. 683.

289. *They liked each other immediately:* Fellman, pp. 238–40.

289. *"Then will I share with you the last cracker":* Id., p. 182.

289. *he granted Johnston breathtaking terms:* Id., pp. 239–40; Johnston, pp. 400–06; Foote, vol. 3, pp. 988–96.

290. *"the whole professed object of the war":* Stephens, *CV,* vol. 2, p. 635.

290. *The document Sherman signed; Sherman would later claim:* Sherman, vol. 2, pp. 324–31; Id., pp. 241–42; Randall and Current, pp. 352–53. See Donald, p. 682.

290. *Sherman produced a bottle:* Sherman, vol. 2, pp. 240–41.

290. *When the news arrived in Washington:* Id., pp. 245–47; Foote, vol. 3, pp. 994–95.

290. *When General Johnston was told:* Id., p. 996.

290. Breckinridge's communications with Johnston and Johnston's final surrender: *OR,* vol. 47, ser. 1, part 3, p. 835; *OR,* vol. 47, ser. 1, pt. 3, p. 836; Foote, vol. 3, p. 996; Feis, pp. 120–21.

290. *Only disconnected remnants:* Stephens, *CV,* vol. 2, pp. 628–29.

290. *Once the panic had passed:* Rowland, vol. 8, pp. 148, 158, and 189; Ballard, pp. 122–23; Davis, *Long Surrender,* pp. 117–18.

291. *"The calamity which has fallen upon us":* Gorgas, pp. 183–84.

291. *Davis would later say:* Davis, *Rise and Fall,* vol. 2, pp. 696–97.

291. *"designated by Arabic numerals":* Campbell, *Recollections,* p. 22.

EPILOGUE

293. *On May 10, 1865:* Ballard, pp. 141–43.

293. *He fought them physically:* Id., pp. 158–59. The shackles were removed after a few days (*Id.*).

293. *Preston Blair asked President Johnson to ease his treatment:* Lathrop, p. 642.

293. *"That would have been an excellent argument":* Charleston News and Courier, July 14, 1881.

293. *He was freed on a bond:* Lathrop, p. 644.

293. *"He had not changed his beliefs":* Varina Davis, vol. 2, p. 817.

293. Davis's post-imprisonment career: Cooper, pp. 585–89.

293. Davis's postwar exchange with Hunter on the Peace Commission: Davis, "Peace Commission;" Strode, p. 471; Hunter, "Reply."

294. *Davis still smarted:* Davis, "Peace Commission," p. 210; Davis, "Peace Conference," p. 68; Davis, *Rise and Fall,* vol. 2, pp. 617–18.

294. *"I could not with due self-respect":* Strode, pp. 526–27.

294. *An Episcopal minister:* Strode, pp. 481–83.

294. *"In the greatest effort of his life":* Varina Davis, vol. 2, pp. 923–25.

294. Varina Davis: Joan E. Cashin, *Varina Davis: First Lady of the Confederacy, Varina Davis's Civil War* (Cambridge, MA: Belknap Press of Harvard University Press, 2006, pp. 298–99); www.encyclopediavirginia.org/Davis_Varina_1826-1906.

295. Campbell's arrest, letter to Speed, release: Campbell, "Open Letters," pp. 952 and 954; Campbell, "Papers," pp. 66–74; Nicolay and Hay, vol. 10, p. 287; Connor, pp. 197–201, Saunders, pp. 187–89.

296. *returned to the Supreme Court; See* the Slaughterhouse Cases: 83 U.S. 36, 44 (1878).

296. *Judge Campbell had "hesitated as if about to speak":* Strode, pp. 471–72.

296. Hunter's arrest: *OR,* ser. 1, vol. 46, part 3, p. 1082, and *OR,* ser. 2, vol. 8, pp. 534–36.

296. *Campbell told Hunter:* Hunter, pp. 116–17.

296. Hunter's daughter died; he was charged with treason: Simms, p. 206.

296. *he wrote to a daughter from his cell:* Hunter, *Hunter,* pp. 123–24.

297. *Seward took Mrs. Hunter; He devoted himself to farming: Id.,* pp. 125–27.

297. *He is buried:* Rowland, vol. 7, p. 273.

297. *Treasurer of Virginia; defeated; his mill burned down; Collector of the Port of Tappahannock; they failed to raise the money:* Hunter, *Hunter,* pp. 125–26, 132–33, and 136; Simms, pp. 209–10 and 215–16.

297. *I almost wept over the letter:* Avary, *Recollections,* p. 141.

297. *On May 11, 1865, federal troops came for him:* Avary, *Id.,* pp. 99–102.

297. *"far from cordial"; empty pleasantries:* Avary, *Id.,* p. 114; Johnston and Browne, p. 487.

298. *General Custer: New York Times,* May 7, 1865.

298. *"My whole consciousness":* Avary, *Recollections,* p. 141.

298. *Frightened but well treated: Id.,* pp. 127–530, *passim;* Stephens, *CV,* vol. 2, pp. 660–61.

298. *he did not care to go to the expense:* Avary, *Recollections,* p. 220.

298. *with help from Grant and Seward:* Schott, p. 454.

298. *"a victim of the wreck":* Avary, *Recollections,* p. 241.

298. *Stephens led a reconciliation movement and was sent back to Congress:* Avary, *Recollections,* pp. 546 and 550. See Smith, *Grant,* p. 424.

298. *An immense cloak: Id.,* pp. 550–51.

298. *He served five postwar terms and spoke at the presentation: Id.,* p. 551; Hendrick, *Lincoln's War Cabinet,* p. 365. The painting of Lincoln and his Cabinet is on the cover of Goodwin and among the illustrations in Donald.

298. *stayed on as tenant farmers:* Cleveland, pp. 25 and 235–36; Von Abele, p. 268.

298. Letters to Stephens from his freed slaves: Stephens Papers, Library of Congress, microfilm reel 57.

299. *"excessive use of the pardoning power":* Avary, *Recollections,* p. 552.

299. John L. Stephens: Robert Stephens, pp. 20–21.

299. William Hatch: *Biographical Directory of the United States Congress,* www.bioguide congress.gov; Whitney H. Shepardson, *Agricultural Education in the United States* (New York: Macmillan, 1929).

299. Judah Benjamin: Davis, *Rise and Fall,* vol. 2, p. 694; Ballard, p. 154; Davis, *Long Surrender,* p. 274; J. P. Benjamin, *Treatise on the Law of Sale of Personal Property* (Boston: Houghton Mifflin, 1892).

300. Robert E. Lee: Emory, *Lee,* pp. 397 and 417; John D. Wright, *The Oxford Dictionary of Civil War Quotations* (Oxford: Oxford University Press, 2006), p. 215.

300. Sarah Pryor: Pryor, *Reminiscences,* pp. 394–96.

300. *desperately poor freed slaves:* Henry Latham, *Black and White, a Journal of a Three Months' Tour in the United States* (London: MacMillan and Co., 1867), p. 106.

301. Francis Preston Blair: Smith, *Blair Family,* vol. 2, p. 326; Smith, *Francis Preston Blair,* pp. 374–437.

301. *The attempt on his life; the procession and hearse:* Carpenter, *Inner Life,* pp. 291–92; Welles Diary, vol. 2, p. 293.

301. *welcomed a hundred Southern dignitaries:* Stahr, p. 449.

302. *typically served up with dessert:* Van Deusen, p. 492.

302. *to buy Alaska:* Dana, *Lincoln and His Cabinet,* p. 28; Van Deusen, pp. 537–49; Stahr, pp. 482–91.

302. *"the Secretary of State be compelled to live there":* Id., p. 490.

302. *to wide acclaim:* Id., pp. 530–41.

302. *"the only word of regret":* Hay, *At Lincoln's Side,* p. 129.

302. *"I sent Sheridan":* Grant, vol. 2, p. 546; see Phillip Sheridan, *Personal Memoirs of P. H. Sheridan,* 2 vols. (New York: C. L. Webster & Company, 1888), vol. 2, pp. 208–11; Smith, *Grant,* p. 415; Catton, *Grant,* pp. 489–90.

302. *a firing squad:* Van Deusen, p. 515.

302. *Orville Babcock was brought down:* Julia Grant, pp. 186 and 199 n. 16; Perret, pp. 441–42.

303. Julia Grant: Julia Grant, pp. 17–26; www.firstladies.org.

303. *Andrew Johnson was impeached:* Stahr, pp. 479–80, 495–97, and 507–15.

303. *knowing that Stanton was dying:* Flower, pp. 406–07; Thomas and Hyman, pp. 634–38.

303. *jumping three grades:* Temple, p. 18; Bates, p. 403.

303. *"imitated Stanton's arrogance":* Thomas and Hyman, p. 574.

304. *Stanton got Eckert a job at Western Union:* Bates, p. 408.

304. Horace Greeley: Mitchell Snay, *Horace Greeley and the Politics of Reform in Nineteenth-Century America* (Lanham, MD: Rowman & Littlefield Publishers, Inc., 2011), pp. 174–78.

304. *hemlock and strychnine:* Von Abele, p. 284.

304. Sherman: B. H. Liddell Hart, *Sherman: Soldier, Realist, American* (New York: Da Capo Press, 1993).

305. Thaddeus Stevens: See Brodie.

305. Sunset Cox: Davis Lindsey, *Sunset Cox, Irrepressive Democrat* (Detroit: Wave State University Press, 1959); *New York World,* October 2, 1872; *Cincinatti Enquirer,* May 7, 1883.

305. Robert Todd Lincoln: John S. Goff, *Robert Todd Lincoln: A Man in His Own Right* (Norman OK: University of Oklahoma Press, 1969), pp. 6, 260, and 262.

306. *distinction that "could not be made too conspicuous":* Mark Twain, Harriet Elinor Smith, ed., *Autobiography of Mark Twain* (Berkeley: University of California Press, 2010) vol. 1, p. 222.

306. John Hay's dream: Hay Diary, p. 369 n. 321.

Selected Bibliography

Primary Sources

BOOKS AND PAMPHLETS

Adams, Henry. *The Education of Henry Adams* (Boston: Houghton Mifflin, 1918).

Akin, Warren, Bell Irvin Wiley, ed. *Letters of Warren Akin* (Athens: University of Georgia Press, 1959).

Alexander, Porter. *Fighting for the Confederacy: The Personal Recollections of General Edward Porter Alexander* (Chapel Hill: University of North Carolina Press, 1989).

Allen, George H. *Forty-Six Months with the Fourth R.I. Volunteers in the War of 1861–1865* (Providence: J. A. & R. A. Reid, 1887).

Avary, Myrta Lockett. *Recollections of Alexander Stephens* (New York: Doubleday, Page & Company, 1910).

Badeau, Adam. *Military History of Ulysses S. Grant* (New York: D. Appleton and Co., 1885).

Bates, David Homer. *Lincoln in the Telegraph Office* (New York: Century Co., 1907).

Bigelow, John. *Retrospections of an Active Life*, 5 vols. (New York: Baker & Taylor, 1909–13).

Bolton, William J., Richard A. Sauers, ed. *The Civil War Journal of Colonel William J. Bolton, 51st Pennsylvania* (Conshohocken, PA: Combined Pub., 2000).

Brock, Sallie A. *Richmond During the War* (New York: G. W. Carleton & Co., 1867).

Brooks, Noah. *Washington in Lincoln's Time* (New York: The Century Co., 1895).

Brooks, Noah. Michael Burlingame, ed. *Lincoln Observed: Civil War Dispatches of Noah Brooks* (Baltimore: Johns Hopkins University Press, 1998).

Browning, Orville Hickman, Theodore C. Pease, and James G. Randall, eds. *The Diary of Orville Hickman Browning*, 2 vols. (Springfield: Illinois State Historical Library, 1925–1933).

Burlingame, Michael, ed. *An Oral History of Abraham Lincoln* (Carbondale: Southern Illinois University Press, 1996).

———. *At Lincoln's Side: John Hay's Civil War Correspondence and Selected Writings* (Carbondale: Southern Illinois University Press, 2000).

———. *Dispatches from Lincoln's White House: The Anonymous Civil War Journalism of Presidential Secretary William O. Stoddard* (Lincoln: University of Nebraska Press, 2002).

Cadwalader, Sylvanus. *Three Years with Grant* (New York: Alfred A. Knopf, 1955).

Campbell, John A. *Recollections of the Evacuation of Richmond* (Baltimore: John Murphy & Co., 1880).

———. *Reminiscences and Documents Relating to the Civil War during the Year 1865* (Baltimore: John Murphy & Co., 1877).

Carpenter, F. B. *The Inner Life of Abraham Lincoln* (Boston: Houghton Mifflin, 1894).

Chambrun, Charles Adolphe Pineton. *Impressions of Lincoln and the Civil War: A Foreigner's Account* (New York: Random House, 1952).

Chesnut, Mary. *A Diary from Dixie* (New York: D. Appleton and Company, 1905).

Cleveland, Henry. *Alexander Stephens, in Public and Private, with Letters and Speeches, before, during, and since the War* (Philadelphia: National Publishing Co., 1866).

Cox, Samuel Sullivan. *Eight Years in Congress, from 1857 to 1865* (New York: D. Appleton and Co., 1865).

———. *Three Decades of Federal Legislation, 1855 to 1885* (San Francisco: Occidental Publishing Co., 1885).

Crook, William H., Margarita Spalding Gerry, ed. *Through Five Administrations: Reminiscences of Colonel William H. Crook* (New York: Harper & Brothers, 1910).

Dana, Charles A. *The Life of Ulysses S. Grant* (Springfield, MA: Gurdon Bill & Company, 1868).

———. *Lincoln and His Cabinet* (New York: Souvenir of the Thirteenth Annual Lincoln Dinner of the Republican Club of New York, 1899).

———. *Recollections of the Civil War* (New York: D. Appleton and Company, 1898).

Davis, Jefferson. *The Rise and Fall of the Confederate Government*, 2 vols. (New York: D. Appleton and Co., 1881).

———, Lynda Lasswell Crist, ed. *The Papers of Jefferson Davis*, 12 vols. (Baton Rouge: Louisiana State University Press, 2003).

———, Dunbar Rowland, ed. *Jefferson Davis, Constitutionalist: His Letters, Papers and Speeches*, 10 vols. (Jackson: Mississippi Department of Archives and History, 1923).

———, Hudson Strode, ed. *The Private Letters of Jefferson Davis, 1823–1889* (New York: Harcourt, Brace & World, 1966).

Davis, Varina Howell. *Jefferson Davis, Ex-President of the Confederate States of America: A Memoir by His Wife*, 2 vols. (New York: Belford, 1890).

De Leon, T. C. *Four Years in the Rebel Capitals* (Mobile, AL: Gossip Print Co., 1892).

Douglas, Henry Kyd. *I Rode with Stonewall* (Chapel Hill: University of North Carolina Press, 1940).

Early, Jubal, Frank Vandiver, ed. *War Memoirs* (Bloomington: University of Indiana Press, 1960).

Eggleston, George C. *A Rebel's Recollections* (New York: Hurd and Houghton, 1870).

Executive Documents of the House of Representatives 1871–72, Special Report on the Customs-Tariff Legislation (Washington, DC: Government Printing Office, 1872).

Foote, Henry S. *War of the Rebellion* (New York: Harper & Bros., 1866).

———. *Casket of Reminiscences* (Washington, DC: Chronicle Publishing Company, 1874).

Gardner's Photographic Sketch Book of the War (Washington, DC: Philip & Solomons, 1865–66).

Garruth, Sumner, et al. *History of the Thirty-Sixth Regiment Massachusetts Volunteers* (Boston: Mills, Knight & Co., 1884).

Gilmore, James R. *Personal Recollections of Abraham Lincoln and the Civil War* (Boston: L. C. Page & Co., 1898).

Gordon, John B. *Reminiscences of the Civil War* (New York: Charles Scribner's Sons, 1905).

Gorgas, Josiah, Frank E. Vandiver, ed. *The Civil War Diary of General Josiah Gorgas* (Tuscaloosa: University of Alabama Press, 1947).

Gorgas, Josiah, Sarah Woolfolk Wiggins, ed. *The Journals of Josiah Gorgas, 1857–1878* (Tuscaloosa: University of Alabama Press, 1995).

Gould, Joseph. *The Story of the Forty-Eighth* (Philadelphia: Alfred M. Slocum Co., 1908).

Graham, William Alexander, J. G. de Roulhac, and Max R. Williams, eds. *The Papers of William Alexander Graham*, 8 vols., vol. 6 (Raleigh: State Department of Archives and History, 1976).

Grant, Julia Dent, John Y. Simon, ed. *The Personal Memoirs of Julia Dent Grant* (New York: Putnam, 1975).

Grant, Ulysses S. *Personal Memoirs of U. S. Grant*, 2 vols. (New York: C. L. Webster, 1885–1886).

——. John Y. Simon, ed. *The Papers of Ulysses S. Grant*, 32 vols. (New York: G. P. Putnam's Sons, 1975).

Greeley, Horace. *Recollections of a Busy Life: Reminiscences of American Politics and Politicians* (New York: H. B. Ford and Co., 1868).

——. Joel Benton, ed. *Greeley on Lincoln, and Mr. Greeley's Letters* (New York: The Baker & Taylor Co., 1893).

Green, Duff. *Facts and Suggestions, Biographical, Historical, Financial, and Political* (New York: C. S. Wescott & CC's Union Printing Office, 1866).

Harrison, Mrs. Burton. *Recollections Grave and Gay* (New York: Charles Scribner's Sons, 1911).

Hay, John, Michael Burlingame, ed. *At Lincoln's Side: John Hay's Civil War Correspondence and Selected Writings* (Carbondale: Southern Illinois University Press, 2000).

Hay, John, Michael Burlingame and John R. Turner Ettlinger, eds. *Inside Lincoln's White House: The Complete Civil War Diary of John Hay* (Carbondale: Southern Illinois University Press, 1997).

Hill, Benjamin Harvey, Jr. *Senator Benjamin H. Hill of Georgia, His Life, Speeches and Writings* (Atlanta: H. C. Hudgins, 1891).

History of Thirty-Fifth Regiment Massachusetts Volunteers (Boston: Mills, Knight & Co., 1884).

Hopkins, William P., and George B. Peck. *The Seventh Regiment Rhode Island Volunteers in the Civil War 1862–1865* (Providence: Snow & Farnham, 1903).

Houston, Henry C. *The Thirty-Second Maine Regiment of Infantry Volunteers: An Historical Sketch* (Portland, ME: Southworth Brothers, 1903).

Hunter, Martha T. *A Memoir of Robert M. T. Hunter* (Washington, DC: Neale Publishing Company, 1903).

Jarratt, Henry C. *A Guide to the Fortifications and Battlefields Around Petersburg* (Petersburg, VA: Daily Index Job Print, 1866).

Johnston, Joseph E. *Narrative of Military Operations during the Civil War* (New York: Appleton and Co., 1874).

Jones, John B. *A Rebel War Clerk's Diary of the Confederate States Capital*, 2 vols. (Philadelphia: Lippincott, 1866).

Journal of the Congress of the Confederate States of America, 1861–1865, 7 vols. (Washington, DC: Government Printing Office, 1904–05).

Judkins, W. B. *Memoir*, 1907 (www.mindspring.com/~jcherepy/memoir/judkins.txt).

Julian, George W. *Political Recollections* (Chicago: Jansen, McClurg & Co., 1884).

Kean, Robert Garlick Hill, Edward Younger, ed. *Inside the Confederate Government: The Diary of Robert Garlick Hill Kean* (New York: Oxford University Press, 1957).

Keckley, Elizabeth. *Behind the Scenes* (New York: G. W. Carleton & Co., 1868).

Lamon, Ward Hill, D. L. Teillard, ed. *Recollections of Abraham Lincoln, 1847–1865* (Washington, DC: The Editor, 1911).

Lee, Elizabeth Blair, Virginia J. Lass, ed. *Wartime Washington: The Civil War Letters of Elizabeth Blair Lee* (Urbana: University of Illinois Press, 1991).

Lee, Robert E. *Lee's Dispatches* (New York: G. P. Putnam's Sons, 1915).

——, Clifford Dowdey, ed. *The Wartime Papers of Robert E. Lee* (Boston: Little Brown, 1961).

Lincoln, Abraham, Roy B. Basler, ed. *Collected Works of Abraham Lincoln*, 9 vols. (New Brunswick, NJ: Rutgers University Press, 1953–1955).

Lincoln, Abraham, Don E. and Virginia Fehrenbacher, eds. *Recollected Words of Abraham Lincoln* (Stanford: Stanford University Press, 1996).

Longstreet, James. *From Mannassas to Appomattox* (Philadelphia: Lippincott, 1896).

Meade, George, George Gordon Meade, ed. *The Life and Letters of George Gordon Meade, Major-General of the United States Army*, 2 vols. (New York: Charles Scribner's Sons, 1913).

Neill, Edward D. *Glimpses of the Nation's Struggle* (St. Paul, MN: St. Paul Book and Stationery Company, 1888).

Nicolay, John G., and Michael Burlingame, ed. *With Lincoln in the White House: Letters, Memoranda, and Other Writings of John G. Nicolay, 1860–1865* (Carbondale: Southern Illinois University Press, 2000).

Nicolay, John G., and John Hay. *Abraham Lincoln: A History*, 10 vols. (New York: Century Company, 1917).

Official Records of the Union and Confederate Navies in the War of the Rebellion, 30 vols. (Washington, D.C., US Government Printing Office, 1894–1922).

Parker, Thomas H. *History of the 51st Regiment of P.V. and V.V.* (Philadelphia: King & Baird, 1869).

Pember, Phoebe Yates, Irvin Wiley Bell, ed. *A Southern Woman's Story: Life in Confederate Richmond* (Columbia: University of South Carolina Press, 1959).

Pierce, Edward L., ed. *Memoirs and Letters of Charles Sumner*, 4 vols. (Boston: Roberts Brothers, 1893).

Pollard, E. A. *Life of Jefferson Davis* (Philadelphia: National Publishing Company, 1869).

Poore, Benjamin Perley. *Perley's Reminiscences of Sixty Years in the National Metropolis*, 2 vols. (Philadelphia: Hubbard Brothers, 1886).

Porter, David Dixon. *Incidents and Anecdotes of the Civil War* (New York: D. Appleton and Co., 1885).

Porter, Horace. *Campaigning with Grant* (New York: The Century Co., 1897).

Pryor, Sara Agnes Rice. *My Day: Reminiscences of a Long Life* (New York: Macmillan, 1909).

——. *Reminiscences of Peace and War* (New York: Macmillan, 1905).

Rice, Allen Thorndike. *Reminiscences of Abraham Lincoln by Distinguished Men of His Time* (New York: North American Publishing Co., 1886).

Richardson, James D., ed. *A Compilation of Messages and Papers of the Confederacy, Including Diplomatic Correspondence 1861–1865*, 2 vols. (Nashville: United States Publishing Company, 1905).

Russell, William Howard. *My Diary: North and South* (London: Bradbury and Evans, 1863).

Seward, Frederick W. *Seward at Washington, as Senator and Secretary of State*, 2 vols. (New York: Derby and Miller, 1891).

Seward, William H. *Autobiography* (New York: Derby and Miller, 1891).

———, G. E. Baker, ed. *The Works of William Seward*, 5 vols. (Boston: Houghton Mifflin, 1884).

Sheridan, Phillip. *Personal Memoirs of P. H. Sheridan*, 2 vols. (New York: C. L. Webster & Company, 1888).

Sherman, William T. *Memoirs*, 2 vols. (New York: D. Appleton & Co., 1891).

Stephens, Alexander. *A Constitutional View of the Late War Between the States*, 2 vols. (Philadelphia: National Publishing Co., 1870).

Stoddard, William O., Michael Burlingame, ed. *Inside the White House in War Time: Memoirs and Reports of Lincoln's Secretary* (Lincoln: University of Nebraska Press, 2000).

Stone, DeWitt Boyd, ed. *Wandering to Glory: Confederate Veterans Remember Evans's Brigade* (Columbia: University of South Carolina Press, 2002).

The War of the Rebellion: A Compilation of the Official Records of the Union and Confederate Armies, 73 vols. (Washington, DC: US Government Printing Office, 1880–1901).

Tobie, Edward P. *History of the First Maine Cavalry* (Boston: Emery & Hughes, 1887).

Washburn, George H. *A Complete Military History and Record of the 108th Regiment New York Volunteers* (Rochester, NY: Press of E. R. Andrews, 1894).

Weitzel, Godfrey. *Richmond Occupied* (Richmond, VA: Richmond Civil War Centennial Committee, 1965).

Welles, Gideon. *Lincoln and Seward* (New York: Sheldon & Company, 1874).

———, Howard K. Beale, and Alan W. Brownsword, eds. *Diary of Gideon Welles, Secretary of the Navy Under Lincoln and Johnson*, 3 vols. (Boston and New York: Houghton Mifflin, 1911).

Willcox, Orlando B., Robert Garth Scott, ed. *Forgotten Valor: The Memoirs, Journals & Civil War Letters of Orlando B. Willcox* (Kent, OH: Kent State University Press, 1999).

Wise, John S. *The End of an Era* (Boston: Houghton Mifflin, 1899).

ARTICLES AND PUBLISHED LETTERS

Bradds, Hezekiah, "With the 60th Ohio around Petersburg," *The National Tribune* (April 8, 1926): 5.

Brooks, Noah, "Lincoln's Reelection," 49 *The Century Magazine* (April 1895): 865–70.

———, "Personal Reminiscences of Lincoln," 15 *Scribner's Monthly* (March 1878): 673–81.

Campbell, John A., "Slavery in the United States," 12 *Southern Quarterly Review* (July 1847): 91–134.

———, "Reply of Judge Campbell," *The Southern Magazine*, vol. VII, no. 2 (February 1874): 22–28.

———, "The Hampton Roads Conference, Letter of Judge Campbell," *The Southern Magazine*, vol. VIII, no. 5 (November 1874): 187–90.

———, "Evacuation Echoes," 24 *Southern Historical Society Papers* (1896): 351–53.

———, "Papers of John A. Campbell," 42 *Southern Historical Society Papers* (October 1917): 45–75.

———, "Open Letters: A View of the Confederacy from the Inside," 38 *The Century Magazine* (October 1889): 950–54.

———, *Transactions of the Southern Historical Society*, vol. 1, in *The Southern Magazine*, vol. 15 (January–December 1874): 187–94.

Conolly, Thomas, Nelson D. Lankford, ed., "The Diary of Thomas Conolly, M.P., Virginia, March–April 1865," 95 *The Virginia Magazine of History and Biography* (January 1987): 75–112.

Crook, William H., "Lincoln As I Knew Him," 114 *Harper's Magazine* (June 1907): 107–14 and 115 *Harper's Magazine* (June 1907): 41–48.

Davis, Jefferson, "Jefferson Davis: The Peace Commission," 4 *Southern Historical Society Papers* (November 1877): 208–14.

———, "Jefferson Davis, Letter Reply to Mr. Hunter," 5 *Southern Historical Society Papers* (May 1878): 222–27.

———, "The Peace Conference of 1865," 77 *The Century Magazine* (November 1908): 67–69.

Davis, Varina, "Christmas in the Confederate White House," *The New York World* (December 13, 1896).

Ewell, R. S., "Evacuation of Richmond," 13 *Southern Historical Society Papers* (1885): 247–52.

Gilmore, James R., "A Suppressed Chapter of History," 59 *Atlantic Monthly* (April 1887): 435–47.

———, "Our Visit to Richmond," 14 *Atlantic Monthly* (September 1864): 372–83.

———, "Our Last Day in Dixie," 14 *Atlantic Monthly* (December 1864): 715–26.

Goode, John, "The Confederate Congress," 4 *The Conservative Review* (September–December 1900): 97–112.

———, "The Hampton Roads Conference," 29 *Forum* (March 1900): 92–103.

Gorgas, Amelia Gayle, Sarah Woolfolk Wiggins, ed., "As I Saw It: One Woman's Account of the Fall of Richmond," 25 *Civil War Times Illustrated* (May 1986): 40–43.

Holden, C. W., "Horace Greeley," 3 *Holden's Dollar Magazine* (January 1849): 32–35.

Hunter, Robert M. T., "R. M. T. Hunter, The Peace Commission of 1865," 3 *Southern Historical Society Papers* (April 1877): 168–76.

———, "R. M. T. Hunter, The Peace Commission: A Reply," 4 *Southern Historical Society Papers* (December 1877): 303–18.

Johnson, Bradley T., "The Peace Conference," 27 *Southern Historical Society Papers* (January–December 1899): 374–77.

Lathrop, G. P., "The Bailing of Jefferson Davis," 33 *The Century Magazine* (February 1887): 636–40.

Lee, Fitzhugh, "Failure of the Hampton Roads Conference," 52 *The Century Magazine* (July 1896): 476–78.

Myers, Gustavus A., "Abraham Lincoln in Richmond," 41 *Virginia Historical Magazine* (October 1933): 318–22.

Nicolay, John, and John Hay, "Abraham Lincoln, A History: Blair's Mexican Project," 38 *Century Magazine* (October 1889): 838–44.

Peabody, Elizabeth, Arlin Turner, ed., "Elizabeth Peabody Visits Lincoln, February 1865," 48 *New England Quarterly* (March 1975): 119–24.

Scoville, James M., "Thaddeus Stevens," 61 *Lippincott's Magazine* (April 1898): 545–51.

Stephens, Robert, "An Incident of Friendship," 45 *Lincoln Herald* (June 1943): 18–21.

"The Truth of the Hampton Roads Conference," 24 *Confederate Veteran* (1916): 249–56.

Welles, Gideon, "Lincoln and Johnson: Their Plan of Reconstruction and the Resumption of National Authority," 13 *Galaxy* (April 1872): 521–33 and (May 1872): 663–74.

MANUSCRIPTS AND ORIGINAL DOCUMENTS

Blair Family Papers, Manuscript Division, Library of Congress, Washington, D.C. (microfilm).

Lincoln Manuscript Collection, Manuscript Division, Library of Congress, Washington, D.C. (microfilm).

Mallory, Stephen Russell, "Diary and Reminiscences of Stephen R. Mallory," 2 vols. (Typescript), Chapel Hill: University of North Carolina, 1941, vol. 2, 208–09.

Nicolay, John G., Manuscript Collection, Library of Congress, Washington, D.C.

Papers of Horace Greeley, Manuscript Collection, New York Public Library.

Stephens papers, Library of Congress, Manhattanville College of the Sacred Heart, Pennsylvania Historical Society.

Secondary Sources

BOOKS AND PAMPHLETS

Abele, Rudolph R. *Alexander H. Stephens: A Biography* (New York: Knopf, 1946).

Ambler, Charles H. *Francis H. Pierpont, Union War Governor of Virginia and Father of West Virginia* (Chapel Hill: University of North Carolina Press, 1937).

Applegate, Debby. *The Most Famous Man in America: The Biography of Henry Ward Beecher* (New York: Doubleday, 2006).

Ballard, Michael B. *A Long Shadow: Jefferson Davis and the Final Days of the Confederacy* (Jackson: University Press of Mississippi, 1986).

Beringer, Richard E., ed. *Why the South Lost the Civil War* (Athens: University of Georgia Press, 1986).

Bill, Alfred Hoyt. *The Beleaguered City: Richmond 1861–1865* (New York: Alfred A. Knopf, 1946).

Bishop, Jim. *The Day Lincoln Was Shot* (New York: Bantam, 1956).

Boatner, Mark M. *The Civil War Dictionary* (New York: D. McKay Co., 1959).

Bonds, Russell S. *War like the Thunderbolt: The Battle and Burning of Atlanta* (Yardley, PA: Westholme, 2009).

Boritt, Gabor S., ed. *Jefferson Davis's Generals* (New York: Oxford University Press, 1999).

Braden, Waldo W. *Abraham Lincoln, Public Speaker* (Baton Rouge: Louisiana State University Press, 1988).

Brands, H. W. *The Man Who Saved the Union: Ulysses S. Grant in War and Peace* (New York: Doubleday, 2012).

Brodie, Fawn. *Thaddeus Stevens* (New York: W. W. Norton & Co., 1959).

Burlingame, Michael. *Abraham Lincoln: A Life*, 2 vols. (Baltimore: Johns Hopkins University Press, 2008).

Carr, Julian S. *The Hampton Roads Conference* (Durham, NC: 1917).

Catton, Bruce. *Grant Takes Command* (Boston: Little, Brown, 1969).

Chadwick, Bruce. *1858: Abraham Lincoln, Jefferson Davis, Robert E. Lee, Ulysses S. Grant and the War They Failed to See* (Naperville, IL: Sourcebooks, 2008).

Connor, Henry G. *John Archibald Campbell* (Boston: Houghton Mifflin, 1920).

Cooper, William James, Jr. *Jefferson Davis, American* (New York: Alfred A. Knopf, 2000).

Current, Richard N. *The Lincoln Nobody Knows* (New York: Hill & Wang, 1963).

Davis, Burke. *The Long Surrender* (New York: Alfred A. Knopf, 2000).

Davis, William C. *Jefferson Davis: The Man and His Hour* (New York: HarperCollins, 1991).

Dirck, Brian R. *Lincoln & Davis: Imagining America, 1809–1865* (Lawrence: University Press of Kansas, 2001).

Donald, David H. *Lincoln* (New York: Simon & Schuster, 1995).

Escott, Paul D. *After Secession: Jefferson Davis and the Failure of Confederate Nationalism* (Baton Rouge: Louisiana State University Press, 1994).

———. *"What Shall We Do with the Negro?": Lincoln, White Racism, and Civil War America* (Charlottesville: University of Virginia Press, 2009).

Faust, Drew Gilpin. *The Creation of Confederate Nationalism: Ideology and Identity in the Civil War South* (Baton Rouge: Louisiana State University Press, 1988).

Fellman, Michael. *Citizen Sherman: A Life of William Tecumseh Sherman* (New York: Random House, 1995).

Fischer, John E. *Statesman of a Lost Cause: The Career of R. M. T. Hunter, 1854–1887*, in *Dictionary of American Biography* (New York: C. Scribner's Sons, 1943).

Flood, Charles B. *1864: Lincoln at the Gates of History* (New York: Simon & Schuster, 2009).

Flower, Frank A. *Edwin McMasters Stanton* (Akron, OH: Saalfield Publishing Company, 1905).

Foote, Shelby. *The Civil War: A Narrative*, 3 vols. (New York: Random House, 1958–1974), vol. 3, *Red River to Appomattox*.

Forman, Stephen M. *A Guide to Civil War Washington* (Washington, DC: Elliott & Clark Publishing, 1995).

Freehling, William W. *The South vs. The South: How Anti-Confederate Southerners Shaped the Course of the Civil War* (Oxford: Oxford University Press, 2001).

Freeman, Douglas S. *R. E. Lee: A Biography*, 4 vols. (New York: C. Scribner's Sons, 1934–35).

Furgurson, Ernest B. *Ashes of Glory: Richmond at War* (New York: Alfred A. Knopf, 1996).

Goldfield, David. *America Aflame: How the Civil War Created a Nation* (New York: Bloomsbury Press, 2011).

Goodwin, Doris Kearns. *Team of Rivals* (New York: Simon & Schuster, 2005).

Grimsley, Mark, and Brooks Simpson. *The Collapse of the Confederacy* (Lincoln: University of Nebraska Press, 2000).

Harris, William Charles. *Lincoln and the Restoration of the Union* (Lexington: University Press of Kentucky, 1997).

——. *Lincoln's Last Months* (Cambridge: Belknap Press of Harvard University Press, 2004).

Hendrick, Burton J. *Lincoln's War Cabinet* (Boston: Little, Brown, 1946).

——. *Statesmen of the Lost Cause: Jefferson Davis and His Cabinet* (Boston: Little, Brown, 1939).

Hess, Earl J. *In the Trenches at Petersburg: Field Fortifications & Confederate Defeat* (Charlotte: The University of North Carolina Press, 2009).

Johnson, John L. *The University Memorial* (Baltimore: Turnbull Brothers, 1871).

Johnston, Richard M., and William H. Browne. *Life of Alexander Stephens* (Philadelphia: Lippincott, 1884).

Kauffman, Michael W. *American Brutus* (New York: Random House, 2004).

Kimmel, Stanley Preston. *Mr. Davis's Richmond* (New York: Coward-McCann, 1958).

Kirkland, Edward C. *The Peacemakers of 1864* (New York: Macmillan, 1927).

Lindsey, Davis. *Sunset Cox: Irrepressible Democrat* (Detroit: Wayne State University Press, 1959).

Livermore, Thomas L. *Numbers and Losses in the Civil War in America, 1861–65* (Boston: Houghton Mifflin, 1900).

Marvel, William. *Lee's Last Retreat: The Flight to Appomattox* (Chapel Hill, NC: University of North Carolina Press, 2002).

McElroy, Robert. *Jefferson Davis: The Unreal and the Real*, 2 vols. (New York: Harper & Brothers, 1937).

McFeely, William S. *Grant: A Biography* (New York: Norton & Company, 1981).

McPherson, James M. "Lincoln and the Strategy of Unconditional Surrender," in Gabor S. Boritt, ed., *Lincoln, the War President: The Gettysburg Lectures* (New York: Oxford University Press, 1992).

——. "No Peace without Victory" in *This Mighty Scourge: Perspectives on the Civil War* (Oxford: Oxford University Press, 2007).

McWhitney, Grady. "Jefferson Davis and His Generals," in Grady McWhitney, *Southerners and Other Americans* (New York: Basic Books, 1973).

Miers, Earl S., ed. *Lincoln Day by Day: A Chronology* (Washington, DC: Lincoln Sesquicentennial Commission, 1960).

Nolan, Alan T. *Lee Considered: General Robert E. Lee and Civil War History* (Chapel Hill: University of North Carolina Press, 1991).

Page, Elwin L. *Lincoln on the River Queen* (Concord, NH: Published by order of the New Hampshire Legislature, 1943).

Parrish, William E. *Frank Blair: Lincoln's Conservative* (Columbia: University of Missouri Press, 1998).

Pearce, Haywood J. *Benjamin H. Hill: Secession and Reconstruction* (Chicago: The University of Chicago Press, 1940).

Perret, Geoffrey. *Lincoln's War* (New York: Random House, 2004).

———. *Ulysses S. Grant, Soldier and President* (New York: The Modern Library, 1999).

Rable, George C. *The Confederate Republic: A Revolution Against Politics* (Chapel Hill: University of North Carolina Press, 1994).

Randall, James G., and Richard Current. *Lincoln the President: Last Full Measure* (New York: Dodd, Mead, 1955).

Rhodes, James Ford. *History of the United States from the Compromise of 1850 to the Final Restoration of Home Rule in the South in 1877*, 4 vols. (New York: Macmillan, 1909–19).

Rice, Allen Thorndike, ed. *Reminiscences of Abraham Lincoln* (New York: American Publishing Co., 1886).

Sandburg, Carl. *Abraham Lincoln*, 6 vols., The Sangamon edition (New York: Charles Scribner's Sons, 1941).

Saunders, Robert, Jr. *John Archibald Campbell, Southern Moderate, 1811–1889* (Tuscaloosa: University of Alabama Press, 1999).

Schott, Thomas E. *Alexander H. Stephens of Georgia: A Biography* (Baton Rouge: Louisiana State University Press, 1987).

Sherman, William T. *Memoirs* (New York: D. Appleton and Co., 1886).

Simms, Henry H. *Life of Robert M. T. Hunter* (Richmond, VA: The William Byrd Press, 1935).

Simon, John Y. "Grant, Lincoln, and Unconditional Surrender," in Gabor S. Boritt, ed., *Lincoln's Generals* (New York: Oxford University Press, 1994).

Simpson, Brooks D. *Let Us Have Peace: Ulysses S. Grant and the Politics of War and Reconstruction, 1861–1868* (Chapel Hill: University of North Carolina Press, 1991).

———. *Ulysses S. Grant: Triumph Over Adversity, 1822–1865* (Boston: Houghton Mifflin Harcourt, 2000).

Smith, Elbert B. *Francis Preston Blair* (New York: Free Press/Macmillan, 1980).

Smith, Jean Edward. *Grant* (New York: Simon & Schuster, 2001).

Smith, William Ernst. *The Francis Preston Blair Family in Politics*, 2 vols. (New York: Macmillan, 1933).

Snay, Mitchell. *Horace Greeley and the Politics of Reform in Nineteenth-Century America* (Lanham, MD: Rowman & Littlefield, 2011).

Stahr, Walter. *Seward: Lincoln's Indispensable Man* (New York: Simon & Schuster, 2012).

Strode, Hudson. *Jefferson Davis, Tragic Hero: The Last Twenty Five Years, 1864–1889* (New York: Harcourt, Brace, 1964).

Taylor, John M. *William Henry Seward: Lincoln's Right Hand* (New York: HarperCollins, 1991).

Temple, Wayne C. *Lincoln's Travels on the* River Queen *during the Last Days of His Life* (Mahomet, IL: Mayhaven Publishing, 2007).

Thomas, Benjamin P., and Harold M. Hyman. *Stanton: The Life and Times of Lincoln's Secretary of War* (New York: Alfred A. Knopf, 1962).

Thomas, Emory. *Robert E. Lee* (New York: W. W. Norton & Company, 1995).

Toews, Rockford. *Lincoln in Annapolis, February 1865* (Annapolis: Maryland State Archives, 2009).

Trefousse, Hans. *The Radical Republicans: Lincoln's Vanguard for Racial Justice* (New York: Knopf, 1969).

Trudeau, Noah Andre. *The Last Citadel: Petersburg, Virginia, June 1864–April 1865* (Boston: Little, Brown, 1991).

Van Deusen, Glyndon G. *Horace Greeley, Nineteenth-Century Crusader* (Philadelphia: University of Pennsylvania Press, 1953).

———. *William Henry Seward* (New York: Oxford University Press, 1967).

Von Abele, Rudolph. *Alexander H. Stephens* (New York: Alfred A. Knopf, 1946).

Waddell, James D., ed. *Biographical Sketch of Linton Stephens* (Atlanta: Dodson & Scott, 1877).

Wakelyn, Jon L. *Biographical Directory of the Confederacy* (Westport, CT: Greenwood Press, 1977).

Walthall, Ernest Taylor. *Hidden Things Brought to Light*, reprint (Richmond, VA: Dietz Printing, 1908).

Watterson, Henry. *The Compromises of Life* (New York: Duffield and Co., 1906).

Waugh, John C. *Surviving the Confederacy: Rebellion, Ruin, and Recovery; Roger and Sarah Pryor during the Civil War* (New York: Harcourt, 2002).

Williams, Robert C. *Horace Greeley: Champion of American Freedom* (New York: New York University Press, 2006).

Wilson, Rufus Rockwell, ed. *Intimate Memories of Lincoln* (Elmira, NY: The Primavera Press, Inc., 1945).

Winik, Jay. *April 1865: The Month that Saved America* (New York: HarperCollins, 2001).

Yearns, Wilfred B. *The Confederate Congress* (Athens: University of Georgia Press, 1960).

ARTICLES

Brumgardt, John R., "The Confederate Career of Alexander H. Stephens: The Case Reopened," 27 *Civil War History* (March 1981): 64–81.

Harris, William C., "The Hampton Roads Peace Conference: A Final Test of Lincoln's Presidential Leadership," 21 *Journal of the Abraham Lincoln Association* (2000): 31–61.

Hatch, Frederick, "Lincoln's Missing Guard," 106 *Lincoln Herald* (Fall 2005): 106–17.

Johnson, Ludwell H., "Beverley Tucker's Canadian Mission, 1864–1865," 29 *The Journal of Southern History* (February 1963): 88–99.

———, "Lincoln's Solution to the Problem of Peace Terms, 1864–1865," 34 *The Journal of Southern History* (November 1968): 576–86.

McCormac, E. I., "Justice Campbell and the *Dred Scott* Decision," 19 *The Mississippi Valley Historical Review* (March 1933): 565–71.

McPherson, James M., "No Peace Without Victory, 1861–1865," 109 *The American Historical Review* (February 2004): 1–18.

Poore, Benjamin Perley, "Reminiscences of Washington," 56 *Atlantic Monthly* (December 1880): 53–66.

Rabun, James Z., "Alexander H. Stephens and Jefferson Davis," 58 *The American Historical Review* (January 1953): 290–321.

Sanders, Charles W., Jr., "Jefferson Davis and the Hampton Roads Peace Conference: 'To Secure Peace to the Two Countries,'" 63 *The Journal of Southern History* (November 1997): 803–26.

Turner, Justin T., "Two Words," 2 *Autograph Collectors' Journal* (April 1950): 3–7.

Westwood, Howard C., "Lincoln at the Hampton Roads Peace Conference," 81 *Lincoln Herald* (Winter 1979): 243–56.

———, "The Singing Wire Conspiracy," 19 *Civil War Times Illustrated* (December 1980): 30–35.

Yearns, Wilfred B., Jr., "The Peace Movement in the Confederate Congress," 41 *The Georgia Historical Society Quarterly* (March 1957): 1–18.

INTERNET

Beals, Thomas P., "In a Charge near Fort Hell: Petersburg, April 2, 1865," www.angelfire.com/ca4/forthell

http://bioguide.congress.gov/biosearch/biosearch.asp

http://freepages.genealogy.rootsweb.ancestry.com/~volker/history/civilwar/memoirs/60thmembradds.html

Scott Letter, www.dmna.ny.gov/historic/reghist/civil/artillery/.../27thIndBatCWN.htm

The Lincoln Log: A Daily Chronology of the Life of Abraham Lincoln, www.thelincolnlog.org

United States Military Railroad, www.nps.gov/pete/historyculture/united-states-military-railroad.htm

www.civilwar.org/battlefields/hatchers-run-history-articles/the-batttle-of-hatchers-run

www.civilwarreference.com

www.craterroad.com/fortphotos.html

www.craterroad.com/Christmas.html

INDEX